MW01516564

The Timing of Income Recognition in Tax Law and the Time Value of Money

Time itself creates advantages and disadvantages in the field of taxation. The timing of the recognition of income and expenses for tax purposes has two main implications: firstly, for the timing of the collection of tax, and secondly, for the question of quantification, i.e., how to ensure that the difference between the timing of the recognition of income or expenses, as opposed to the respective dates on which the amounts are actually received or paid, does not distort the determination of the amount of chargeable income.

The time component is a weapon in the confrontation between the opposing motivations of the taxpayers and the tax authorities. In any given fiscal year, taxpayers seek to present a minimal picture of their chargeable income, by "deferring" the recognition of income or "advancing" the recognition of expenses. As opposed to this, the tax authorities adopt the opposite strategy: maximizing taxable "profit" in any given year.

This book critically examines the various approaches that have been adopted in the tax systems in the UK, the US and Israel in relation to the timing of income recognition and expenses for tax purposes. It suggests an innovative tax model that identifies the advantages that arise to the taxpayer as a result of the differences between the timing of the recognition of income and expenses, and the timing of the receipt of the revenue or the payment of a liability, and taxes only that advantage.

Dr Moshe Shekel is the founder and senior partner of Shekel and Co. Law Associates, and a Lecturer at Tel Aviv University, Israel.

The Timing of Income Recognition in Tax Law and the Time Value of Money

Moshe Shekel

Routledge·Cavendish
Taylor & Francis Group
LONDON AND NEW YORK

First published 2009
by Routledge-Cavendish
2 Park Square, Milton Park, Abingdon, Oxon, OX14 4RN

Simultaneously published in the USA and Canada
by Routledge-Cavendish
270 Madison Avenue, New York, NY 10016

*Routledge-Cavendish is an imprint of the Taylor & Francis Group,
an informa business*

© 2009 Moshe Shekel

Typeset in Palatino by RefineCatch Limited, Bungay, Suffolk
Printed and bound in Great Britain by
CPI Antony Rowe, Chippenham, Wiltshire

All rights reserved. No part of this book may be reprinted
or reproduced or utilized in any form or by any electronic,
mechanical, or other means, now known or hereafter
invented, including photocopying and recording, or in any
information storage or retrieval system, without permission
in writing from the publishers.

British Library Cataloguing in Publication Data
A catalogue record for this book is available from the British Library

Library of Congress Cataloging-in-Publication Data
Shekel, Moshe.
 The timing of income recognition in tax law and the time value of
money : a comparative study and empirical study / Moshe Shekel.
  p. cm.
 1. Income tax—Law and legislation—Great Britain. 2. Income
tax—Law and legislation—United States. 3. Income tax—Law
and legislation—Israel. 4. Income tax—Accounting—Law and
legislation—Great Britain. 5. Income tax—Accounting—Law
and legislation—United States. 6. Income tax—Accounting—
Law and legislation—Israel. I. Title.
 K4464.S54 2009
 343.05′2—dc22   2008043875

ISBN 10: 0–415–47754–9 (hbk)
ISBN 10: 0–203–87967–8 (ebk)

ISBN 13: 978–0–415–47754–3 (hbk)
ISBN 13: 978–0–203–87967–2 (ebk)

Contents

5 Timing of recognition of income from deposits 87

Table of Cases

US Case Law

Israeli Case Law

Canadian Case Law

Table of Legislation

Israeli Legislation

Table of Secondary Legislation

UK Administrative Directives

US Administrative Directives

Israeli Administrative Directives

Abstract

This book presents a critical examination of the question of the timing of the recognition of income and liabilities for tax purposes.

In general, according to Generally Accepted Accounting Principles ("**GAAP**"), funds received by a person are regarded as "income" only if the funds have been "earned". On the one hand, under the "earning" condition, not all amounts recognized as income in a specific year are actually received in that same year. On the other hand, under the earning condition, not all amounts received by a person are regarded as income. For example, amounts received as a deposit by a person who is required to return them in the future or received as an advance against future sales or services are not considered to be "income" on the date of receipt. They will only be deemed "income" at a future date if the obligation to repay the deposit is cancelled or the advance is earned.

This comparative study of the tax systems of the UK, the US and Israel examines how these tax systems approach the question of timing the recognition of income for tax purposes. The analysis shows that the more a tax system considers itself free to deviate, for tax purposes, from GAAP, the more it tends to view unearned receivables (like deposits or advances) as "income" for tax purposes on the date of receipt, and defer the recognition of liabilities as expenses, placing emphasis on the theory of the time value of money. To the extent that a tax system regards itself bound by GAAP measuring and timing principles, it will tend to classify unearned receivables (like deposits or advances) as liabilities on the date of their receipt, deferring the timing of their recognition as income for tax purposes to a future date, while advancing the timing recognition of liabilities as expenses for tax purposes.

This study argues that, although following GAAP with regard to the timing recognition of income and liabilities for tax purposes may result in some untaxed economic advantages in contradiction of tax values, attempts to prevent such untaxed economic advantages by deviating from GAAP and transforming "liabilities" into "income" using tax accounting (created in *ad hoc* rulings of the courts) might violate other tax values.

The solution proposed in this study for all three tax systems reviewed is

xxxv

maximum uniformity with GAAP as to the classification and identification of receivables, and as regards the date of recognition of income and liabilities for tax purposes. However, if consistency with GAAP creates a time lag between the date of recognition of income or liabilities and the date of actual receipt or date of payment, and the possibility that taxes would be imposed only on the nominal value of income (and not on the real economic value of the income), then the creation of a solution that taxes the "benefits" caused by the passage of time is recommended. It will be submitted that tax values and the Proportionality Principle demand rejecting the existing solutions in the tax systems reviewed for the question of the timing of the recognition of income and liabilities, and adopting the proposed model as the solution for the taxation of the time "benefit" component included in unearned receivables or "unpaid liabilities", without deviating from GAAP. In this analysis the economic "benefit" that may accrue to the taxpayer in receiving an amount that is not yet recognized as "income" according to GAAP, or that may accrue to a taxpayer that deferred the performance of a liability that was recognized as an expense according to GAAP, is identified as the saving of alternative financing costs. It will be submitted that imposing taxation on that saving (as long as it exists) matches both the tax values that will be discussed in this study and the Proportionality Principle, since it ensures that the tax system will not relinquish the objective of taxing the economic advantages, nor adopt dubious measures of taxing "something" which cannot be regarded as "income".

In memory of my parents with undying sorrow

Acknowledgments

I would like to thank Professor A. Olowofoyeku, without whose constructive comments, experience and knowledge I would not have succeeded in writing and completing this study.

I would also like to thank my dearest friend Dr Samuel Harlap who, despite not being a "tax man", listened to me patiently and contributed his experience and knowledge. I am also grateful to Beatrice Michaeli, CPA (LLM, MBA) for her remarks relating to the accounting background, and to Benyamin Tovi, CPA (LLB) for his comments. A special word of thanks is due to my nephew, partner and colleague, Yaniv Shekel, Adv (LLM, Acct MBA).

1 Introduction

"Man will forever aim to achieve his goals by proper means only."*

Time itself creates advantages and disadvantages in the field of taxation. The perpetual confrontation between tax authorities and taxpayers creates opposing motivations: taxpayers strive to maximize tax advantages, whereas tax authorities endeavour to cancel such advantages. The time component (or timing) has become a weapon in such confrontations.

It is thus natural that taxpayers will seek to present a minimal picture of their taxable earnings in a given fiscal year, and this may be done, *inter alia*, by "deferring" the recognition of income or by "advancing" the recognition of deductions. For the same reason, it is natural that tax authorities adopt the opposite strategy: maximizing taxable earnings in any given year. Consequently, tax authorities will be inclined to advance the timing at which income is recognized for calculating taxable earnings, or to defer the timing at which the deductions that reduce earnings for tax purposes may be allowed.

This study focuses on the complex relationship between financial accounting and tax laws in all aspects relating to the timing of the recognition of income and expenses. Adopting, for tax purposes, the principles of financial accounting with regard to determining the timing of recognition of income and liabilities that lead to income and expenses being recognized without reference to the question of when the money was received or paid, can create both advantages and disadvantages for both taxpayer and the tax authority within the context of time. These advantages and disadvantages can be divided into two main issues:

The first is that of the timing of taxing the liable income or "profit" (hereinafter: "**the Collection Question**").

The second is that of the values or the terms by which income and liabilities will be measured in each fiscal year for calculating taxable income or "profit" (hereinafter: "**the Quantification Question**").

For example, with regard to the Collection Question, adopting the "accounting" realization principle which treats income as earned even if it has not yet been received by the taxpayer, requires that taxes be paid on as yet unreceived earnings, and thus compels the taxpayer to finance the tax from other sources.[1] The taxpayer's loss directly complements the state treasury's gain in collecting taxes on as yet unreceived income. Adopting the identical realization principle with regard to receivables (such as deposits[2] or advances[3]) so that amounts actually received by the taxpayer would be viewed as unearned would create a situation in which the taxpayer could avoid paying tax on funds actually in hand. In this case, in terms of cash flow, the taxpayer will benefit at the state treasury's expense.

Moreover, as mentioned above, the effect of the time value is not confined merely to the question of the date of the payment of the tax (i.e. the Collection Question). The time dimension also impacts upon the financial values that form the basis for calculating the income or expense (the Quantification Question).

The length of the period that has elapsed between the date of recognizing the income and the date it was actually received will result in a corresponding difference between the real value of that income and its nominal value. The same principle will apply to liabilities that the taxpayer is required to undertake in order to create his income in the same way that it applies to income. Determining the timing of the recognition of liability as an expense for purposes of assessing earnings according to financial accounting principles does not depend on the question of the time at which they are paid or performed. Adopting the principles of financial accounting with regard to the timing of the recognition of liabilities could also create advantages and disadvantages for the taxpayer and the tax authority, both in terms of the timing of tax collection as well as assessing the taxable income (or profits).

As regards the Collection Question, following the principles of financial accounting theory, and in given cases advancing the date of recognition of liability as an expense for tax purposes, even though it has not yet been paid or performed,[4] might result in reducing the tax burden in a specific year by using future liabilities. As regards the Quantification Question, the greater the period that has elapsed between the date of recognizing the liability as an expense and the date on which it was paid or performed in practice will correspondingly give rise to the difference between the real value of the amount of that expense and its nominal value.

This book examines the relevant aspects of the tax systems in the UK, the US and Israel (hereinafter: **"the tax systems reviewed"** or **"the tax systems"**). In these three countries, the Generally Accepted Accounting Principles (**"GAAP"**) applicable to the question of timing recognition of income and liabilities are commonly similar. In addition, some of the principles grounding these tax systems are similar. Nevertheless, each of these tax systems adopts different, and even conflicting, solutions to the timing recognition of income for tax purposes.

This book is divided into nine chapters, an overview of which is given below.

Chapter 1 provides a general introduction.

Chapter 2 elaborates the accounting background for the method by which GAAP relates to the timing of the recognition of "income". Moreover, it discusses how GAAP relates to the timing of the recognition of future expenses that are to be expended in order to create that "income". The subject of timing the recognition of income and deductions is an essential part of the question of measuring a taxpayer's profits and, in issues of measuring earnings, each of the tax systems must confront (at one level or another) the method of measuring earnings according to GAAP.

Chapter 3 presents a theoretical test of the tax values that are relevant to the timing recognition of income question that are common to all three tax systems.

Chapter 4 examines the methods by which the tax systems reviewed generally address the financial accounting and the accrual basis methods for measuring a taxpayer's profits (including questions of timing) for tax purposes. This chapter also examines the implementation of alternative reporting methods adopted by the tax systems reviewed for calculating and fixing the timing of recognition of income. This is coupled with an examination of the advantages and disadvantages of each method.

Chapter 5 critically examines the solutions offered by the tax systems for timing the recognition of income from deposits.

Chapter 6 critically examines the solutions offered by the tax systems for timing the recognition of income from advances.

Chapter 7 critically explores the solutions offered by the tax systems for timing the recognition of liabilities yet to be paid or performed.

Chapter 8 proposes alternative models to the solutions offered by the tax systems for timing the recognition of "income".

Finally, **Chapter 9** concludes the discussion by suggesting an alternative model based upon lessons learned from this comparative study.

2   Accounting background

The way in which tax systems address the timing of the recognition of income and the timing of the recognition of future deductions can be understood against the background of the theory of financial accounting, according to which a firm measures its earnings for its own purposes. As we will see below, regardless of whether the particular tax method has chosen to adopt GAAP in relation to the measuring of earnings (including the subject of the timing of their creation), or has chosen to deviate from GAAP for tax purposes, these principles were always in the background. From this it follows that in examining the solutions offered by the tax systems reviewed, it is important to provide a brief background of the underlying theory of GAAP in relation to the timing question.

In relating to Financial Accounting Theory or GAAP, it should be noted that two types of GAAP apply in the tax systems reviewed. In the US, for the purpose of financial reporting, the acceptable accounting principles are referred to as the US GAAP.[1] In the UK, as of 2005 the International Accounting Standards ("**IAS**")[2] were adopted as the binding, effective GAAP for purposes of financial reporting (hereinafter: "**IAS GAAP**" or "**IFRS**")[3] and in 2008, the IFRS was also adopted for financial reporting purposes in Israel.[4]

As a rule, the position of the current US-GAAP and the IFRS is that the date of recognition of income for calculating the "accounting" profit will be fixed on the date upon which a number of conditions are fulfilled.[5] Recently, as part of the process of globalization and the trend towards convergence of US GAAP and IFRS, the International Accounting Standards Board (IASB)[6] and the US Financial Accounting Standards Board (FASB)[7] embarked upon a joint project[8] to develop an alternative conceptual framework that is expected to change completely the current principles for revenue recognition.

2.1 The purpose of financial accounting and the concept of prudence

Financial accounting deals with the financial statements a business enterprise prepares and presents periodically in order to meet the information needs of a wide range of users including shareholders, potential investors, creditors and other relevant third parties.[9] The purpose of financial statements is to provide users with information about a firm's financial status and performance, and any changes therein[10] in order to enable them to make financial decisions.[11] The information regarding the firm's financial situation is presented in a manner that meets the "true and fair" criteria.[12] The concept of prudence is premised upon this aim, given the uncertainty that accounting practices must confront.[13] When a certain level of uncertainty exists, prudence must be exercised when preparing financial statements. According to the concept of prudence[14] (which can be regarded as a broad operating principle),[15] in cases of doubt or of possible errors in measuring income/expenses or assets/obligations, a degree of caution must be exercised, such that assets or income are not overstated and liabilities or expenses are not understated. In other words, in the absence of precise or realistic information, a more "pessimistic" picture is preferable to a more "optimistic" one.[16]

2.2 The distinction between income, revenue and gains

Over their economic life entities enter into various transactions and earn income. The term "income" is defined as "increases in economic benefits during the accounting period in the form of inflows or enhancements of assets or decreases of liabilities that result in increases in equity, other than those relating to contributions from equity participants".[17] As such, the term "income" includes both "revenue" and "gains". Revenues arise from the operating activities of the entity, and might be called sales, fees, interest, dividends, royalties, etc. Gains represent other items that meet the definition of income, but they may or may not arise from operating activities. For example, they may constitute capital gains on the disposal of assets or fair value gains.[18]

The distinction between "gains" and "revenues" allows the IFRS to focus on revenue recognition[19] and to avoid the recognition of items that are earned but not realized.[20]

2.3 Revenue recognition

2.3.1 The accrual basis

According to Financial Accounting, the mere receipt of money does not lead to recognition of revenue. According to a broad operating principle set by the IASB Framework, effects of transactions and other events are recognized when they occur (and not as cash or its equivalent is received) and they are recorded in the accounting records and reported in the financial statements of the periods to which they relate.[21] This principle is known as the accrual basis of the financial statements. Under this principle, the mere receipt of cash does not result in liabilities or deferred credit until it is realized and earned through the fulfillment of the required performance, without taking into account the time value of money.[22] It should be pointed out that GAAP posits the accrual basis as the only reporting method and rejects any other reporting method.[23]

2.3.2 *The realization principle and the earned requirement*

The operating cycle of an entity involves several stages: acquisition of raw materials, production of goods, sales of goods or services to customers, delivery and cash collection. Each stage adds economic value to the production, but the added economic value does not necessarily constitute revenue from an accounting point of view. Therefore, GAAP does not divide the revenue recognition process into economic-value-creating stages. The accepted accounting approach is to recognize income from a sales transaction at a specific point in time, as if the change in value of the output (in comparison to the input) has occurred entirely at one moment. Such a point in time is determined by the realization principle and the earned requirement.[24]

The basis of these principles is that the moment at which the seller has fulfilled his obligations towards the buyer is also the very moment at which his right to receive the entire yield is realized, and this is the moment at which the revenue may be recognized. The realization principle establishes that income is not recognized before the process of earning the income has been completed, or is complete in principle, and the exchange has been confirmed by means of the fulfillment of the buyer's obligation to pay for the goods or services provided.[25] According to this principle, income from the sale of goods is recognized when the main risks and rewards of the ownership of the goods have been transferred[26] and certain conditions with regard to this transfer of ownership have been met.[27] Furthermore, there is another condition for the realization principle to apply: the absence of material uncertainty with regard to the collection of the consideration.[28]

Sometimes, it is difficult to establish the moment at which revenue is earned. In order to estimate that moment, the critical event approach is used. It is based on the belief that the revenue is earned when the most critical decision is made, or when the most critical act is performed.[29] This critical event can occur at different stages: at the completion of production,[30] at the time of sale[31] or subsequent to delivery.[32]

Although according to IAS#18 the recognition criteria are applied separately to each transaction, sometimes it is necessary to apply the criteria to a combination of several transactions, or to segment a single transaction into identifiable components. In order to decide whether to do so, the economic substance of the transaction must be carefully examined. In cases when several transactions are linked in such a way that the commercial effect cannot be understood without referring to the combination of transactions as a whole, the recognition criteria should be applied to the combination of transactions.[33] Conversely, in certain cases a more complex contract may be separated into different identifiable elements with different moments of realization.[34]

GAAP distinguishes among revenues arising from three types of transaction: sale of goods, rendering of services and use of entity assets yielding interest, royalties and dividends.[35]

- Revenue from the sale of goods is recognized when the significant risks and rewards associated with the ownership of the goods sold to the client have been transferred,[36] and a few conditions with regard to this transfer of ownership have been met.[37] In cases where goods or services are exchanged for goods or services of a similar nature and value, no revenue is recognized.[38]
- Revenue from services, as opposed to the sale of goods, often has a continuous character spread over a period of time, which makes it difficult to determine when the rewards of ownership transfer to the buyer. In the case of a services transaction, the fulfillment of the same conditions as mentioned above is required for the recognition of income, but because of the special nature of continuous services, there are a number of accounting methods to determine the recognition of income and especially the timing thereof, such as: "the straight-line" method,[39] which is the most suitable method for the recognition of income from the provision of a continuous service in the absence of an indication of the expenditures of execution for significant stages of the project or other special circumstances resulting in different indications,[40] "the completed works" method, "the specific execution" method and "the rate of completion" method.

  IAS#18 adopts the "percentage of completion" method,[41] according to which revenue is spread over the relative completed parts of the project in comparison to the entire extent of the project, as the most suitable for income from services that extend beyond the term of one accounting period. Such relative parts are mostly determined according to the costs during the different stages in the project vis-à-vis the costs anticipated for the entire project.[42] Again, for the revenue to be recognized, certain conditions must be fulfilled.[43]
- Revenue arising from the use of entity assets yielding interest, royalties and dividends is recognized if the amount of revenue can be measured reliably and it is probable that the economic benefits will

flow to the entity.[44] As regards timing, revenues from dividends are recognized when the shareholder's right is established: revenue from royalties is recognized on an accrual basis according to the specific contract, and revenue from interest is recognized using the "effective interest method" set by IAS#39.[45]

2.3.3 Revenue recognition from real estate sale contracts

Contracts for the sale of property, plant and equipment are addressed under IAS#18,[46] which treats them as a sale of goods. Accordingly, the recognition criteria are built around whether the risks and rewards of ownership have been transferred to the buyer,[47] which usually occurs when the real estate is transferred to the customer.

Nevertheless, IAS#18 does not apply to long-term construction contracts, and those are specifically dealt with under IAS#11.[48] According to the latter, similar to service contracts, once the outcome of a construction contract can reliably be estimated, revenue should be recognized by reference to the stage of completion of the contract activity using the accretion approach, under which the revenue may be recognized during the process of production rather than at the end of the contract or when production is complete. The specific amount of revenue to be recognized is determined by the costs incurred in reaching the stage of completion.[49]

2.3.4 Future development of an alternative conceptual framework

The aforementioned realization principle in connection with the earned requirement is the basis for revenue recognition. In June 2002, within the framework of globalization and the trend towards the convergence of US GAAP and IFRS, IASB and FASB started a joint project to develop an alternative conceptual framework for revenue recognition and a general standard based on those concepts.

During 2007 and 2008, IASB and FASB discussed two models: the measurement model, which measures assets and liabilities at their fair value,[50] and the "customer consideration model", which utilizes an allocation of the amount of customer consideration. Both models focus on the asset or liability that will arise from the combination of the rights and obligations in a contract with a customer.[51] According to the new conceptual framework, on the date of a contract's inception, an asset or a liability is recognized in accordance with the method applied.[52] As the contract obligation is performed, the asset will increase or the liability will decrease. This increase in the contract asset or decrease in the contract liability that arises from satisfying the performance obligations is reported as revenue.[53] The final document describing the new conceptual framework is expected in 2011.

As can be seen from the above, although there are a few exceptions to the realization principle[54] that waive the earned requirement[55] (especially in cases where the earned requirement has nothing to do with the current value of the flow of resources that the item will produce in the future).[56] In most cases, "income" is recognized when it is earned according to the realization principle. The mere receipt of money does not represent "income" on the date of receipt if it is burdened with an obligation to deliver goods or render services in the future. Such receipts are treated as resulting in liabilities or deferred credits until they are earned through the fulfillment of the required performance.[57]

2.4 Expense recognition

A liability is a sort of "negative asset", representing an expected future sacrifice of economic enjoyment due to the firm's current obligations to transfer assets or provide services in the future to another entity, as a result of a past transaction or occurrence.[58]

The term "liability" is defined within the IASB Framework as follows:

> A liability is recognized in the balance sheet when it is probable that an outflow of resources embodying economic benefits will result from settlement of a present obligation and the amount at which the settlement will take place can be measured reliably . . .[59]

With regard to liabilities, one of the basic accounting principles is the matching principle.[60] According to this principle, in order to determine profit or loss from the activities in a defined period against each sum recognized as income, the expenses related with the generation of this income should be recognized at the very same time (in parallel).[61] Likewise, as the recognition of income is not dependent on the mere receipt of cash, the recognition of expenses is not dependent on their actual payment, and will be recognized as follows:

- Specific costs and expenses directly identifiable with revenues are chargeable against the income of the period in which the revenues are recognized.[62]
- General expenses[63] that are for particular periods of time are chargeable over such periods.[64]
- Other expenses incurred in the general conduct of the business are chargeable against the income of the period in which they are incurred, unless it is clearly evident that they are incurred for the benefit of future periods and there is a reasonable basis, both in terms of amount and of time, for allocating them to future periods, in which case they should be deferred and charged to such periods.[65]

In cases when the recognition of expenses is deferred to a future point in time, a liability is created, since it represents an expected future sacrifice of economic benefits due to the firm's current obligations to transfer assets or provide services in the future to another entity as a result of a past transaction or occurrence. In this regard, GAAP defines two specific terms: provisions and contingent liabilities.

2.4.1 Provisions

Provisions are defined as liabilities whose time of payment or amount is not certain. There are three cumulative conditions required for an obligation to be recognized as provision:[66] (a) the entity has a present obligation (legal or constructive) resulting from a past event; (b) it is probable (i.e. more likely than not)[67] that an outflow of economic resources will be required to settle the obligation; and (c) the amount of the liability can be estimated with sufficient certainty.[68] The amount to be recognized for the provision should be the best assessment of the expenses required to settle the liability as per the balance sheet date.[69] The assessment of the provision is based on: risks and uncertainties;[70] capitalization amounts;[71] future events such as changes in the law and technology;[72] reimbursements that will be taken into account when, and only when, the sum that will be received (to the extent the business will honor its liabilities) is virtually certain.[73]

A widely known example is the warranty provision where a manufacturer, at the time of sale, undertakes to repair or replace manufacturing defects within a certain period of time. Usually in such cases the revenue will be recognized,[74] but so will the economic outflow expected to occur (as a warranty provision). The value of the provision will be measured according to the present value of the costs to be incurred per item sold, according to the average expected date for this cost to be incurred.[75]

2.4.2 Contingent liabilities

Contingent liabilities might be:

- a present obligation that arises from past events, but that does not fulfill the required conditions to be recognized as a provision (i.e. the outflow of resources is not probable and/or the amount of the obligation cannot be measured with sufficient reliability); or
- a possible obligation that arises from past events and whose existence will be determined by the occurrence or non-occurrence of future events that is not within the control of the entity.[76] This uncertainty is only removed after the occurrence or non-occurrence of the future events. As long as those future events do not occur, a broad risk exists at a reasonable level that GAAP must express.[77]

2.4.3 *The difference between provisions and contingencies*

When dealing with provisions, even though the expense itself is expected, a level of uncertainty exists as regards the amounts.[78] However, in the case of a contingent liability, not only is the amount not determined absolutely, but the expense itself is not certain either.[79] The difference between the cases derives mainly from the fact that, with a provision, the event that created the obligation has already occurred, whereas in the case of contingent liability, the event creating the potential obligations has not yet occurred.[80] For accounting treatment, provisions are recognized as liabilities in the balance sheet, while contingent liabilities are not, even though IFRS requires that both provisions and contingent liabilities be disclosed in the notes to the financial statements.[81]

2.4.4 *The methods for measuring liabilities*

Modern financial accounting uses three methods for measuring liabilities and assets: the historical cost,[82] the fair value[83] and the present value[84] methods.[85] GAAP ordains the specific method to be used for each type of liability. GAAP acknowledges all methods for measuring liabilities as acceptable,[86] and in accordance with the circumstances of the case, refrains from stating a preference for one specific method over another. It validates all of the above methods, unless a specific standard exists proscribing the use of a specific method in a given case,[87] or provided that the present value method should not be used.[88] The most commonly used method is the historical cost, although in certain cases the fair value method and present value method are also used.

2.5 Advances and deposits

In this chapter "advance" will refer to a contractually due sum or part of it paid in advance before the receipt of the goods or services set by the contract and "deposit" will refer to an amount of money placed in an account to ensure future receipt of goods or services. While the deposit is returnable, the advance is non-returnable.

   In light of the aforementioned discussion, the proper presentation of client advances and deposits in the financial statements includes two questions: first, should they be recognized as income or as a liability; and second, if they are liabilities, what is the method for measuring the amount of the liability?

2.5.1 *GAAP treatment of deposits*

As stated, in this study the term "deposit" means a sum received from a customer that is intended to secure property belonging to the recipient or to secure the fulfillment of contractual obligations of the depositor, both being characterized by the fact that the deposit recipient is under an obligation to repay it to the depositor at a given time or upon the fulfillment of certain conditions. Due to non-compliance with the conditions of the earned requirement and the realization principle, deposits are not recognized as revenue at the moment of receipt, and GAAP classifies them as liabilities.[89] The recipient's increase of assets is balanced against two liabilities (to provide goods or services and to return the amount of the deposit, or part of it).

The classification of deposits as current liabilities[90] or long-term liabilities[91] is made according to the average period of time elapsing from the moment of receipt until the date of return to the client.[92] In respect of liability derived from a deposit, it seems that US GAAP chooses to present it mostly according to the historical cost method, even in cases of a "subsidized" deposit (e.g. in cases where the refund is made with no interest or with a low rate of interest). APB#21[93] adopts the PV method in relation to long-term "subsidized" liabilities. According to this method, the long-term subsidized liabilities and the gap between this value and the nominal amount of the liability (which is higher) must be represented as income. Nonetheless, according to APB#21, among a few other exceptions, deposits (including those that are on long-term subsidized conditions) should be presented as liabilities not according to the PV method, but rather according to the historical cost or current cost method.[94] It is clear that this choice is directed by the principle of prudence.[95]

At the basis of this choice lies the assumption that where deposits that do not have a defined moment of return are concerned,[96] each deposit should be measured individually as if it may be called in at any given moment. Clearly, an analysis of the individual deposit level will show that, on an expected time line, each deposit will be redeemable, and in light of this, the main substance of the formula for present value (that addresses the deposit's rate of return) will be found to be faulty. Moreover, the implementation of the PV method in relation to the presentation of the liabilities derived from deposits creates a situation where seeing the gap between the present value and the current value of the deposit as "income" is likely to infringe the matching principle. Indeed, if we are dealing with deposits, it is not always possible to pinpoint which expenditures are matched against the specific "income". Are the expenditures connected to the contract itself (that the deposit needs to secure), or are they connected to equipment that the deposit needs to secure, even though the equipment itself has not been sold to the client? Therefore, the implementation of the PV method in relation to deposits is clearly likely to create accounting dilemmas about how and which expenditures should be matched with the "income" resulting from the gap between present value and current value.[97] The production of "income" and the difficulty of attributing it to matching expenditures is sufficient reason (in addition to the "natural conservative choice") not to implement the PV method in relation to such deposits.

International GAAP treatment with regard to measuring deposits is a little bit different. The obligation to return the amount of the deposit is regarded as a financial liability ("financial instrument"), and is dealt with under IAS#39.[98] The IFRS accounting approach is to isolate the pure financial instrument from the remainder of the arrangement. Accordingly, on the receipt date, in addition to the "deferred revenue" displayed as a type of liability, a financial liability is recognized. This financial liability is measured at its fair value, estimated using different valuation techniques.[99] The difference between the amount received as deposit and the fair value of the financial liability will represent the amount to be reported as deferred revenue. The revenue will be recognized (and the deferred revenue liability will be decreased) the moment the conditions for revenue recognition are fulfilled. The following example may help to clarify the IFRS treatment of deposits:

Company A operates a home for the elderly. On 1 January 2008 a new customer is accepted and he places a deposit of $1,000,000. According to the contract, Company A will take care of the new customer and will provide him with different types of services, for which Company A will be entitled to 10 per cent of the amount placed as deposit annually. After the customer dies, the customer's heirs will be entitled to receive the remainder of the deposit. Since as of 1 January 2008 the revenue is neither earned nor realized, Company A cannot recognize the receipt of $1,000,000 as revenue. The increase in Company A's assets (cash received) of $1,000,000 will be balanced against two liabilities: financial liability to return part of the deposit and "deferred revenue" liability. Based on the expected time to provide services to the customer, Company A should estimate the amount to be returned to the customer's heirs. For example, if the expected service period is six years, Company A will need to return to the heirs the amount of $400,000 (= $1,000,000 − 6 × 10% × 1,000,000) in six years. The fair value of the expected amount to be returned will be calculated using the present value basis. For example, if the applicable discount rate is 3.5 per cent, the present value of the expected amount to be returned will be $325,400 (= $400,000/1.035). Subsequently, on 1 January 2008 Company A will record a financial liability of $325,400 and a "deferred revenue" liability of $674,600 (= $1,000,000 − $325,400). Company A will recognize in its financial statements the revenue from providing the services over the six-year period. In addition, it will recognize an annual interest expense

against increase in the financial liability, which finally, in year 6, will reach
the amount of $400,000 (hereinafter: **"the Deposit Example"**).

From this example it can be seen that according to the IFRS two components exist simultaneously – in addition to the "deferred revenue"
liability, a financial obligation is recognized and it is dealt with under a
different accounting standard.[100]

2.5.2 GAAP treatment of advances

As a result of non-compliance with the conditions of the earned requirement and the realization principle,[101] an advance received for sale or
future service is not recognized as revenue at the moment of the receipt.[102]
The recipient's increase of assets is balanced against a liability (to provide
goods or services) of matching size and, therefore, the receipt does not
constitute "income" or an increase of the recipient's wealth.[103] According
to GAAP, until the advance is earned, the receipt (being "Deferred
Revenue") is displayed as a type of liability,[104] measured on an historical
cost basis, i.e. the amount received as an advance. The revenue will be
recognized (and the deferred revenue liability will be decreased) the
moment the conditions for revenue recognition are fulfilled.[105]

This also relies on the fact that the entire amount of the advance payment is considered a (monetary) return in the event of the product or
services not being delivered.[106] Even at the moment an advance is considered to be earned, the amount presented as "deferred revenue" will be
regarded as "income" still subject to its being matched, according to the
matching principle, to the expected obligation to provide products or
services for which it was received.[107] This estimate of the amount of the
expenditure required and presented as a liability is generally based on an
assessment of expenditures known on the balance sheet date. In making
such an assessment, one should also take into account expected developments, such as re-organizations and price increases, and it is proper to
take the present value into account.[108] If it becomes clear later that the
expenditures, posted for the liability for the advance, are actually different
from what was expected, the difference should be matched in the year in
which the deviation came to light.[109] As stated, in case of deposits there
are two types of liabilities: (a) to provide goods and services; and (b) to
return the whole amount (or part) of the deposit. The obligation to provide goods and services is treated similarly to advances, i.e. until it is
earned, the receipt (being "deferred revenue") is displayed as a type of
liability.

The following examples may help to clarify the accounting approach to advances. On 1 January 2008 Company A signs a contract to deliver 300 computers it produces to Company B in two years. Company B pays $1,000,000 in advance. Since as of 1 January 2008 the revenue is neither earned nor realized, Company A cannot recognize the receipt of $1,000,000 as revenue. The increase in Company A's assets (cash received) of $1,000,000 will be balanced against a liability called "deferred revenue" of $1,000,000. On 1 January 2010, with the delivery of the computers and fulfilment of the revenue recognition requirements,[110] Company A will recognize revenue of $1,000,000 in its financial statements against the decrease in the "deferred revenue" liability (hereinafter: "**the Advance Example**").

The difference in the accounting treatment illustrated in the two examples (the Advance Example and the Deposit Example) stems from the fact that while in the Deposit Example two components exist simultaneously (i.e. the "deferred revenue" liability and the financial obligation),[111] in the Advance Example only the "deferred revenue" liability exists.

2.6 Accounting background – summary and comments

As explained in this chapter, the mere receipt of money does not lead to recognition of revenue. According to the accrual basis of the financial statements, the mere receipt of cash will result only in the recognition of liability or deferred credit, until it is realized and earned through the fulfillment of the required performance. At the first stage, liability is recorded and recognized according to the nominal value of the cash received. At the second stage, with the fulfillment of the required performance, the revenue is recognized according to the historical value of the liability recorded. In other words, financial accounting does not take into consideration the fact that the cash receipt and the performance take place at different points of time, and therefore it does not take into account the time value of money. From an economic point of view, this undoubtedly is a distortion, as the fair value of the goods or services to be provided in exchange for the cash paid in advance includes an interest component as well.[112] The longer the period of time until the goods or services are provided, the greater the economic distortion.

Likewise, as the recognition of income is not dependent on the mere receipt of cash, the recognition of expenses is not dependent on their actual payment. According to the matching principle, in order to determine profit or loss from the activities in a defined period against each sum recognized as income, the expenses related with the generation of the income are recognized at the same time (in parallel). Financial accounting does not take into consideration the fact that the cash payment of the expense and its recognition may take place at different points of time, and therefore it does not take into account the time value of money. Again, from an economic point of view this is a distortion and the longer the period of time between the two events – the cash payment and the expense recognition – the bigger the economic distortion.[113]

As previously noted, the purpose of the recent joint project between IASB and FASB is to develop an alternative conceptual framework for revenue recognition, which is expected to change the current principles completely. Hopefully, it will also address the above-mentioned distortion by setting a more economics-based measurement approach.

3 Tax values

We have seen that the main goal of GAAP is to provide precise information (to the extent that this is possible) to relevant parties concerning the
financial condition of the taxpayer.[1] We have also seen that in order to
achieve this goal GAAP is guided by a set of principles for quantifying
and measuring the results of business activity over a certain timespan.
The goal of tax laws is different, namely, to collect monies to provide
public goods.[2] However, it is accepted tax policy that it is not enough for
tax to be collected; the tax must be "just" or "fair".[3] In this context, it
seems that the aspiration to achieve "justice" ("fairness") in tax collection
is common to the UK,[4] the US[5] and the Israeli[6] tax systems. In light of this,
over and above the particular tax legislation existing in each country, we
will review below how these tax systems seek to uphold a number of
minimum requirements in order to achieve "fairness".[7]

3.1 General tax values

Among the minimum requirements in order to be considered "fair", the
tax systems reviewed include, *inter alia*, the following tax values.

3.1.1 *Principle of non-erosion of capital*

The UK[8] and the Israeli[9] tax laws adopt the "source system", whereby
only income arising from a certain defined source will be taken into
account for tax purposes. The US federal tax law is broader and imposes
tax on any addition to wealth.[10] However, what characterizes all of the
tax systems reviewed in this context is that the subject matter of the tax,
namely, "the raw material" on which they seek to impose tax, is not the
taxpayer's original capital, but only his earnings or the increase to that
capital as measured over a defined period of time.[11] The significance of
this principle is that tax is not imposed on wealth, but only on the addition
to wealth.[12]

3.1.2 Principle of equity

It would be difficult to apply a principle that is free from discrimination in tax laws. On the face of it, "simple equity" exists when the tax is imposed equally upon all. However, imposing an equal tax on everyone, without taking into account the unique circumstances of each individual, is itself inequitable. Accordingly, the principle of direct taxation equity is customarily examined in terms of horizontal as opposed to vertical equity.

The horizontal equity principle – is a tax system that strives to bring about a result whereby persons who are identical from the standpoint of their relevant variables will bear an identical tax burden. Under the UK tax system,[13] the US tax system[14] and the Israeli tax system,[15] efforts are made to avoid preference or discrimination in tax liabilities between two similar taxpayers who have earned the same profit (in real terms) from a transaction having similar characteristics.

The vertical equity principle – according to this principle, the difference between the various tax burdens matches the difference between the relevant variables of the different taxpayers. The UK tax system,[16] the US tax system[17] and the Israeli tax system[18] all seek to maintain a connection between the different tax burdens and the size of the income that is subject to tax.

3.1.3 Principle of neutrality

A tax system must strive towards achieving a situation of fiscal indifference in relation to an economic transaction made in one way and the same transaction made in another. The UK,[19] the US[20] and the Israeli[21] tax systems strive to eliminate tax considerations in the making of transactions, so that there should be no fiscal preference for a transaction being carried out one way as opposed to one that is carried out in another way.

3.1.4 Principle of certainty

Tax must only be collected in accordance with the law. The legality principle requires that a citizen know by what law his money is taken from him. A citizen plans his conduct in accordance with a given tax structure, and the citizen's legitimate expectations arising from a given tax structure must be respected. In order for the taxpayer to plan his financial activities properly, the tax system must provide him with maximum certainty regarding the tax that he will be required to pay. The UK tax system,[22] and the US tax system,[23] as well as the Israeli tax system,[24] emphasize this principle of certainty that requires that taxes be imposed only in accordance with clear legislation.[25]

3.1.5 Principle of efficiency

Tax must be collected in an efficient manner and achieve maximum collection. The greater the cost of tax collection, the less tax is left in the hands of the Treasury, and the greater the tax burden of taxpayers in order to meet the budget. The UK,[26] the US[27] and Israeli[28] tax systems address the principle of efficiency as a guiding value in determining tax laws. Within the scope of the efficiency principle, one can also include the principle that prevents unjust tax advantages or, in other words, unjust harm to the Treasury.

3.1.6 Principle of preventing unjust tax advantages

Since the question of what constitutes "tax advantages" and "tax disadvantages" is a relative one, the problem will always arise as to what the "advantage" or "disadvantage" is in relation to something else. The principle of efficiency requires that the tax system set boundaries beyond which a taxpayer's attempt to achieve tax advantages will be considered illegitimate. Beyond those boundaries, the tax system will prevent the taxpayer from achieving those advantages. The UK,[29] the US[30] and the Israeli[31] tax systems have used various legal tools (including the one known as "artificial transactions") to place "boundaries" beyond which it is possible to negate a tax advantage on the ground of its being "unjust".

3.2 The time value of money theory

Beyond the above-mentioned general tax values that have an impact on the issue of timing, the time value of money theory deals specifically with the timing question in tax law. This theory stipulates that the sum of money represented in certain nominal values at one point in time is not worth the same at another point in time. Payment in immediate values "is worth more" than the same payment made in the future at the same nominal values. The economic difference between two payments, one denominated in a principal sum designated for immediate payment, and the other nominally the same but designated for future payment, represents the capitalization (or discount interest).[32]

This theory and the tax value of preventing unjust tax advantages has led many writers to justify broadly rejecting the application of GAAP to all aspects of the timing of deducting expenses for tax purposes; and, even more so, to determine that the expression "income" for tax purposes should be imputed to a content different from that envisaged as its meaning according to GAAP. Halperin[33] raises the argument that in a long series of transactions, a disguised finance transaction is inherent (disguised loans) which creates an economic advantage that is taxable (e.g. in a case of advances the customer is the one who should be regarded as one who gives a loan with disguised interest to the supplier). Taxation may be imposed by means of three alternatives. The first imposes tax directly by taxing the recipient of the disguised interest in respect of such a "loan" (meaning taxing the customer). The second imposes tax indirectly, by disallowing expenses to the recipient of the disguised interest (in other words, disallowing expenses to the customer). The third – where no possibility exists of directly or indirectly taxing the customer who received the disguised interest – taxes the other party to the transaction (the supplier) by means of negating his right to allow the disguised interest expenses.

In principle, Halperin addresses loans without interest, or at interest lower than market prices, on which, on the face of it, it is possible to impose direct taxation (on the recipient of the "cheap" loan) on the difference between the low-rate interest and the market interest, or impose indirect taxation (on the party extending the cheap loan), by disallowing financing expenses due to the disguised interest. However, this in itself is not enough. As Halperin adds, in effect, in any sale or service transaction (hereinafter collectively: "**the base transaction**") the time difference between the supply of the service or the product sold and the making of the actual payment creates an ancillary financial transaction to the base transaction. Put differently, for tax purposes, any transaction in which a time lag exists between the supply date and the payment date (regardless of whether the payment preceded or is subsequent to the supply according to the base transaction), justifies treating the payments made in connection with that transaction as including consideration in respect of two transactions: one, the base transaction, and the other, a financial transaction (with disguised interest). In the opinion of Halperin,[34] Geier[35] and others,[36] for tax purposes, the value of preventing unjust tax advantages justifies deviating from any accounting principle that ignores the time value of money theory.[37]

3.3 Tax values relevant to the question of timing – summary and comments

As we have seen, the tax systems reviewed share various common values.[38] These tax values are of no concern to GAAP, which is totally indifferent to propositions like tax neutrality, preventing unjust tax advantages, and so on.[39] Those general tax values have an impact on the issue of timing. Whereas the taxpayer naturally hopes to defer the timing of the recognition of his income, while recognizing expenditure early, because deferring the recognition of income and bringing forward the recognition of expenditures translates into a deferral of tax payments, the tax authority naturally seeks to prevent the deferral of tax payments.[40]

Although GAAP, for its own reasons and principles, needs to address the timing of the recognition of income and expenses,[41] GAAP ignores these two conflicting motivations (of the taxpayer and of the tax authorities). This conflict becomes even more pronounced with regard to the timing of the recognition of deposits or advances as taxable income. It is not limited merely to the question of the timing of the tax payment, but also extends to the amount of the tax, and more precisely the measurement of the income on which tax will be imposed. Thus, as may be seen from our discussion above, adopting GAAP on the subject of the timing of the recognition of income while ignoring the effect of the time value of money, could lead to tax being imposed on an income that has been fixed in unrealistic terms.

Although, it is indeed possible to describe any transaction that deals with the time gap between the date of performing the liability and the date of making the payment as including a financing element, the conclusions of the abovementioned supporters of the time value of money theory are not free of criticism. Halperin is aware of the shortcomings of applying the theory by means of splitting each transaction into its "real" as opposed to its "financial" component. Since introducing mechanisms to determine "current value" is complex and requires considerable know-how, Halperin prefers the "simple" solution of deferring the recognition of expenses for tax purposes to a date as near as possible to that of the actual payment.[42] However, this logic would equally require deferring the recognition of income from the date it is recognized, according to the realization principle, to the date of the actual receipt of the money.

The logic of this theory of deferring the recognition of both income as well as liabilities to the date of actual payment brought Geier to favour the cash basis method for income tax purposes.[43] In my view, although the cash basis method certainly does not reflect an economic truth that is higher than GAAP,[44] Geier's view is preferable to Halperin's, in that it is consistent in its treatment of the recognition of income and expenses for tax purposes.

The economic parallel that Halperin's suggestion seeks to find between the timing of the expense in the hands of the payer and the timing of the recognition of the income in the hands of the recipient has nothing to do with the accounting matching principle, which refers to the correlation between the timing of recognizing income and allowing the expense that was used for the creation thereof, within the scope of the same taxpayer itself.[45] This approach could lead to distortions in respect of the recipient and the payer regarding the economic results of their respective businesses in the given year.[46]

Moreover, the idea of deferring the deduction of an expense to a future date (i.e. to the year in which the payment will actually be made) can create distortions in measuring taxable profits. The assumption is that an expense is created in a particular year according to GAAP, against which there was income that ran parallel to that expense. Who can say that the year in which the actual payment was made is the year in which there would be sufficient taxable income (and at the same tax rate by reason of which the expense was created from the outset) against which it would be possible to deduct the above expense?

4   Between GAAP and fiscal accounting

We have seen that GAAP and tax law have different goals.[1] We have also seen that in light of their different objectives, tax laws are governed by values that are related to the questions of timing and measuring, but which are totally unrelated to GAAP.[2] In light of these different goals and objectives, the question arises whether it is conceptually correct to determine that the purpose of tax laws justifies the use of different means to attain better the achievement of their objectives, including determining different tax accounting standards from those adopted by GAAP. Or perhaps it would be more correct to say that despite the apparently different objectives, GAAP should be regarded as comprehensive, and as complementary to tax law, and that in no event should the difference in objectives be regarded as justifying the creation of separate tax accounting.

4.1 The Dualistic Doctrine and the Singular Doctrine

Two main alternative concepts can be considered in relation to the question of adopting GAAP in order to resolve questions and make up deficiencies in tax laws: one concept will be called: "**the Dualistic Doctrine**", and the other which will be called: "**the Singular Doctrine**".

4.1.1 The Dualistic Doctrine

In *Thor*,[3] the US Supreme Court established the rule that the principal responsibility of financial accounting is to protect interested parties against misrepresentation. In contrast, the principal objective of tax accounting is to bring about the just collection of taxes, and the principal responsibility of the tax authorities is to protect the public coffers. In light of these different objectives, the court ruled that the guiding principle in GAAP is conservatism, and that this principle is inappropriate for tax accounting, where there is no room for "understatement" in all matters relating to determining income for tax purposes.

The financial accounting principles of conservatism, realization and matching[4] precipitated the main critique that has been raised by supporters of the Dualistic Doctrine, and the inapplicability of GAAP for calculating tax. Gunn argues that these principles on matters of timing have nothing to do with tax laws, which are aimed at safeguarding the interests of the "public coffers".[5] According to him, any presumptive matching between tax and GAAP would be unacceptable.[6]

Coplan believes that the conceptual perception of the term "income" for tax purposes must be distanced from the perception of that term for GAAP purposes. To his mind, the main question of interest to tax laws in the context of that term is the financial ability (from the standpoint of cash flow) of the taxpayer.[7] Silk also justifies the Dualistic Doctrine, and in her view a situation should be avoided where the standards of measuring and timing of GAAP will remove an item from the ambit of "taxable income".[8]

Johnson believes that while the principle of prudence, which guides GAAP, aims to reduce possible errors by way of minimizing assets and income, the rationale of tax is the reverse: to prevent the reduction or lowering of income.[9] In light of this, GAAP cannot be the "guiding light" for tax purposes.[10] Kleinrock, in addressing the prudence and matching principles,[11] states that the concerns and constraints which led to the development of these principles in GAAP are of no interest to tax laws.[12]

According to Geier, the transition to the cash basis method for tax purposes (in lieu of the accrual basis method) is the proper course.[13] Nevertheless, it is possible merely to match the taxpayer's accounting statements based on the accrual basis method, for tax purposes, by preventing the tax advantages created from the timing differences between recognizing income or expenditure according to GAAP on the one hand, and the timing of the receipt or actual payment, as appropriate, on the other.[14]

4.1.2 The Singular Doctrine

The Singular Doctrine may be suggested as the antithesis of the Dualistic Doctrine. The Singular Doctrine holds that, despite the diverse goals, "income" is "income" and what is proper for determining income for the purposes of investors, creditors, shareholders or other third parties is also appropriate for tax purposes (subject, naturally, to specific tax provisions that require otherwise). The Macdonald Martin Committee acknowledges that the taxpayer's motivation is to defer the timing of recognizing income, and that of the tax authorities is to advance tax collection. Still, this committee is hesitant to determine that these conflicting motivations constitute a real obstacle to the harmonization of GAAP with tax laws in all aspects of quantification and timing of income and expenses.[15]

The committee states that there is a conceptual problem in defining terms like "income" or "profits" for determining the tax basis and this is also the case in economic terms. The preferred solution, therefore, must be that despite the apparent differences in the motivations, tax laws will prevent an attempt to create their own definitions for those terms, and will leave the matter of measuring income and profits to be dealt with according to accounting standards.[16] The committee believes that relying on the standards of GAAP for tax purposes means relying on regulatory practices and standards, which confer a higher level of certainty and stability, and whose purpose sits well with the goal of tax laws, namely, *inter alia*, to prevent manipulations in the accounting results.[17]

Moreover, the committee takes the view that if in the past GAAP regarded itself as committed to the goal of measuring profits as a protective tool for safeguarding the taxpayer's capital, with the passage of time the goal of GAAP has come closer to what is the essential objective of tax laws as well, namely, the provision of maximum information on the economic performance of the taxpayer in its financial environment.[18] The committee believes that the advantages (and principally, convenience of operation) of consistency justify harmonizing and unifying GAAP and tax laws,[19] reducing to a minimum the cases in which tax accounting departs from GAAP.[20]

Dubroff, Chail and Norris believe that GAAP is to be regarded as reflecting scientific know-how that has been acquired by experts on the subject, and they argue that tax laws must resolve questions of timing and measurement by reference to GAAP.[21] Klein believes that the Dualistic Doctrine has brought about the creation of *ad hoc* case law giving rise to tax accounting that is separated from GAAP, and this has created non-economic results and contradictions in terms.[22]

4.1.3 *The practicable approaches*

The conceptual dilemma between the Singular Doctrine and the Dualistic Doctrine appears to produce three alternative positions in relation to the adoption of GAAP in order to resolve questions and make up deficiencies in the field of tax laws. These positions will be referred to as: "**the Consistent Approach**", "**the Separating Approach**" and "**the Consistent Selective Approach**".

The Consistent Approach. According to this approach (based on the Singular Doctrine), GAAP should "automatically" be embraced by the tax laws, and applied so long as there is no statutory provision to the contrary.

The Separating Approach. This approach (based on the Dualistic Doctrine) recognizes that GAAP and tax laws have different goals, and posits in light of this that tax laws are to be regarded as necessitating different accounting "solutions" that match tax values, and these are to be distinguished or separated from GAAP.

The Consistent Selective Approach. This approach seeks to have the best of all worlds, recognizing on the one hand the existence of different goals (like the Dualistic Doctrine), while on the other seeking to maximize the advantages of the Consistent Approach, mainly in the field of the operating convenience and savings that exist in two separate accounting systems. Put differently, this approach attempts to recognize these two polarized positions and find cases or conditions in which tax accounting follows GAAP, and cases or conditions where it does not (notwithstanding the absence of contradictory statutory provisions). The distinction between the cases is either according to the nature of the existing "deficiency" in the field of tax laws or according to the classification of the subject by reason of which an "accounting solution" is needed.

4.1.4 The practicable approaches – advantages and disadvantages

The main advantages of the Consistent Approach are the convenience and savings involved in keeping different accounting books, although most significant of all is the advantage of certainty and efficiency. That is to say, where GAAP provides a clear answer and there is no provision to the contrary in the tax regime, the taxpayer and the authorities may assume, to a large degree of certainty, how the taxpayer's tax accounting would be regarded.[23] Lack of certainty and efficiency, as well as lack of convenience to the taxpayer, are the main disadvantages of the Separating Approach and the Consistent Selective Approach. However, those who support the Dualistic Doctrine would probably argue that considerations of administrative convenience, in addition to the advantage of certainty, are outweighed by the need to collect "just tax", and that in light of the different goals of GAAP and tax laws, collection necessitates separation and independence between tax accounting and financial accounting.

The main difference between the Consistent Selective Approach and the Consistent Approach resides in the readiness of the former to deviate from the application of GAAP for tax purposes, not merely where an express contradictory provision exists, but also in cases where such application would compromise tax values. The main difference between this approach and the Separating Approach resides in the importance and weight attributed to GAAP, although according to that approach it is possible to deviate from those principles.

4.2 The reporting methods

Supporters of the Singular Doctrine and Consistent Approach seek to apply the principles of GAAP to tax accounting with regard to the quantification and timing of income (hereinafter referred to as "**the 'pure' accrual basis method**"), and still leave the possibility of determining quantification or other timing rules according to the law in relation to specific or defined income or a specific or defined transaction. As opposed to this, the supporters of the Dualistic Doctrine and the Consistent Selective Approach or Separating Approach do not limit themselves to the GAAP reporting method. That is to say, they do not limit themselves to the "pure" accrual basis method. The question therefore arises as to what are the alternative reporting methods for quantifying and determining the timing of income for tax purposes. These alternative methods are discussed in the tax systems reviewed below.

4.2.1 The accrual basis method

We saw that GAAP had adopted a series of principles and standards to determine the method of quantifying and timing "normal" income (meaning income other than that deriving from special transactions).[24] The first of these principles according to accrual basis method can be defined as the realization principle and the earned requirement (alongside the matching principle).[25] In a nutshell, the principles of this method can be described by saying that the timing of the recognition of income will be the date on which the taxpayer's right to receive arises, or his liabilities to pay expenses accrues, to the extent the income or the expense can be quantified at that particular point in time. That is to say, according to this method, the taxpayer does not need to wait to receive the revenues resulting from the income in order to recognize it. The income will be recognized in the fiscal year in which it is earned (according to the realization principle)[26] and the expense allowed as a deduction on the date on which it crystallizes, in parallel to the timing of recognizing the income.

Even if the tax system elects to adopt the GAAP position with regard to the timing of the recognition and quantification of income in "normal" transactions, and will determine express statutory provisions that obligate determining or quantifying otherwise than pursuant to the GAAP in relation to a particular transaction or certain income, we will continue to refer to that method as falling within the definition of the "pure" accrual basis method. In contrast, if the tax system adopts the timing of the recognition of "normal" income in the spirit of the principles laid down in GAAP, but adds conditions or qualifications regarding the timing of the recognition of income or expenses generally (as distinct from the transaction itself or the specific income), we will refer to this method as "**the 'mixed' accrual basis method**".

4.2.2 The cash basis method

Alongside the standards of GAAP, various accounting practices have evolved – mainly in relation to economic sectors or particular economic activities that are not supported by GAAP – that have not been accepted by GAAP as methods suitable for quantifying income or profit. One of these practices is the cash basis method. According to that method, all income generated by the taxpayer is deemed to be income liable to tax in the fiscal year in which it is received, regardless of whether it is received in cash or in its equivalent, whereas the expenses involved in producing the income are allowed for deduction in the fiscal year in which they are paid. That being so, when reporting according to the cash basis method, the timing of the creation of the profit on the income is unimportant since income is recognized independently of the question of the date on which the event of producing and crystallizing the income arose, being recognized only when the income is received.

If a tax system selects this method without any embellishments, qualifications or limits at the general level, then we will refer to this method as **"the 'pure' cash basis method"**. If the tax system elects to adopt this accounting practice for the timing of the recognition and quantification of income, but adopts statutory provisions that obligate determining timing or quantification otherwise than pursuant to this practice in relation to a particular transaction or certain income, we will still refer to that methodology as being included in the definition of the "pure" cash basis method. In contrast, if as a rule the tax system elects the timing of the recognition of "normal" income according to this practice, but adds conditions or general qualifications (as distinct from the transaction itself or the specific income) as regards the timing of the recognition of income or expenses, we will refer to this method as **"the 'mixed' cash basis method"**.

4.2.3 Hybrid methods

In a tax system where the controlling doctrine is the Dualistic Doctrine, coupled with the Consistent Selective Approach and the Separating Approach, there is nothing to prevent the invention or acceptance of accounting methods with regard to quantifying income and profits for tax purposes that are completely independent of GAAP. In such an environment, there is similarly nothing to stop the invention or acceptance of accounting methods that constitute a "patchwork" of principles and standards of quantification and calculation (including timing) that originate in GAAP, together with principles and standards that originate in other practices. Such a combination will be referred to by us as **"the hybrid methods"**.

4.2.4 The various methodologies and the Singular and Dualistic Doctrines

On the face of it, we would have expected that the more the tax system embraces the Singular Doctrine and the Consistent Approach the more likely that it will tend to determine timing and qualification rules of income for tax purposes in accordance with the "pure" accrual basis method, and accordingly adopt GAAP methodologies for handling special transactions.

As opposed to this, to the extent a tax system has been established in the spirit of the Dualistic Doctrine and Consistent Selective Approach or the Separating Approach, it will not regard itself as being limited to fixing the rules for timing and qualification of income for tax purposes according to the "pure" accrual basis method. A tax system guided by the spirit of the Dualistic Doctrine will not consider itself limited to GAAP or to any other practice that has not evolved in the world of tax accounting, or whose standards and principles were established for objectives inconsistent with tax law and tax values. Thus, a tax system that is established according to the Dualistic Doctrine will tend to adopt qualification and timing standards in the spirit of the "mixed" accrual basis method. Such a tax system will similarly not prevent a "patchwork" like the hybrid methods, provided their application accords with the purpose of tax law and tax values.

From this standpoint, the relationship between the Singular Doctrine or the Dualistic Doctrine and the cash basis method is interesting. On the one hand, it can be said that the tax system that adopts the cash basis method, either generally or in relation to specific cases, is one that has been established according to the Dualistic Doctrine, as it does not regard itself as being limited to GAAP in determining quantification and timing rules of income for tax purposes; while on the other hand, it can be said that a tax system that does adopt the cash basis method specifically emphasizes the Singular Doctrine to the extreme, that is, in the absence of any other provision tax accounting must not merely follow the standards of financial accounting (GAAP), but must also follow any other accounting practice that the taxpayer adopts for his own tax purposes, even if that practice does not accord with the standards of financial accounting. As we will see below, both of those conflicting approaches are manifest in the tax systems reviewed.

4.3 Between GAAP and fiscal accounting – UK tax law

In the UK tax law there is an awareness of the Dualistic Doctrine in its narrow meaning, i.e. awareness not specifically of the different goals of financial accounting and tax laws, but of the fact that there are matters or areas in tax law for which no assistance is provided by GAAP.[27] However, despite this awareness, it can be stated in general that the UK tax system follows the Singular Doctrine, and applies the Consistent Approach, both to subjects related to the timing of the recognition of income, as well as to all aspects of its quantification. Thus, it can be generally stated that as long as there is no contradictory statutory provision,[28] GAAP will be followed in the UK tax system, at least in relation to the overall question of timing and quantification.[29]

4.3.1 Legislation

Sections 226–227 of the Companies Act 1985,[30] and Schs 4–4A to that Act stipulate that accounting presentation must meet "true and fair view" criteria.[31] Section 256 of the Act contains a definition of the accounting standard required to meet those criteria.[32]

Section 836A of the Taxes Act 1988 (which currently constitutes s 50(4), Finance Act 2004) states that GAAP represents the accepted standards of accounting practice for tax purposes relating to UK companies that are required to provide a "true and fair view". The same applies to individuals, other bodies corporate that are not companies and companies other than UK companies.

Section 42 of the Finance Act 1998, which constitutes, in practical terms, a codification of the case law (which will be discussed below) provides that earnings for tax purposes will be computed on the basis of that accounting system "which gives a true and fair view". As an exception to this rule, s 42 of that Act states that the calculation of earnings for tax purposes will be effected subject to "any adjustment required or authorized by law". The expression "true and fair view", included in this provision, was changed in 2002 to "generally accepted accounting practice",[33] meaning the inclusion of GAAP practiced in the UK (the change in that wording not making in practical terms any material change to the provision).[34] Until 2005 the UK rule was that for the purposes of s 42, where a UK GAAP Standard (prescribed by the ASB) exists, it is to be followed, but where the ASB has prescribed no specific standard, the presentation of the transaction according to the International Accounting Standards (IAS) or the US GAAP Standards will comply with the requirement of "true and fair view".[35]

From 2005 onwards, s 42 FA 1998 has been changed, for income tax purposes, by s 25 of the Income Tax (Trading and Other Income) Act 2005 (**ITTOIA 2005**), and from that date onwards, according to the provisions of ss 50–54 and Sch 10 to the Finance Act 2004, and the provisions of ss 80–84 and Sch 4 to the Finance Act 2005, the International Accounting Standards (IAS) are also adopted for UK tax law purposes, with the intention of granting IAS-based standardization binding effect for tax purposes, in a manner equivalent to the standing granted to the UK GAAP.[36]

All of the foregoing indicates that the UK legislature has established strict formalization respecting the manner of preparing taxpayers' reports and the need to link them to GAAP (whether these principles derive from the UK GAAP or are taken from the IAS). In contrast to this strictness, the UK legislature prescribes, on the face of it, two "exceptions" where it is possible to reject the taxpayers' reports (insofar as they relate to quantification and timing of income and earnings). These "exceptions" will be called "the true and fair view criteria" and "subject to any adjustment by law deviation".

4.3.1.1 "True and fair view" criteria

The first "exception" provides that the earnings designated by GAAP to be used as a basis for tax purposes must meet the criteria of **"true and fair view"** (that, as stated, was replaced in 2002 with the terms "generally accepted accounting practice").[37] Those who support the Consistent Approach will no doubt say that this "exception" is not an exception at all, since in any event this expression is taken from GAAP itself which seeks to achieve this result.[38]

Thus, not only is this "exception" not an exception to the Singular Doctrine and the Consistent Approach, but it is that which fixed the status of the "pure" accrual basis method as one that most taxpayers prefer to use in reporting for tax purposes. While the US tax system uses, as we will show, an expression similar to "the true and fair view" as a powerful tool that enables the US tax authorities to deviate from reports that are based on GAAP,[39] the UK tax system interprets this expression in complete conformity with GAAP.

Historically, the **SSAP#2**[40] standard, which was later replaced by **FRS#18**,[41] regulated the four basic principles for accounting reporting. The purpose of the **SSAP#2** (published in November 1971) was to ensure proper disclosure of the explanations of the accounting policy adopted by the reporter in order to ensure true and fair view accounting reporting. For that purpose, the Standard supplied four basic reporting principles on which financial reporting should be based, namely: the going concern concept, according to which, from the operating standpoint, the business will continue to exist in the foreseeable future; the accruals concept, which we examined above;[42] the Consistent Approach, whereby accounting treatment is to be applied consistently in the various reporting periods; and the prudence concept, which we also examined above,[43] where we also stated that when there was a collision between the accruals principle and the principle of prudence (conservatism), the principle of prudence should be preferred.

Although Standard **FRS#18**, which replaced **SSAP#2**, adopted within it the "going concern concept" and "the accrual concept" in their entirety, it somewhat changed the two other principles, integrating within them four new criteria in light of which each accounting report will be tested. These four criteria are: relevance, reliability, comparability and understandability. The integration of objectives in financial reporting is made essential, according to the drafters of the Standard, because it is proper for financial information to be comparable with other reporting periods of the reporting entity, be free and clear of any material error, supply data that is relevant for use by readers of the reports in making decisions, and also be understandable to the reader who is equipped with reasonable knowledge of economic affairs. This specific and express reference to the criterion of "true and fair view" mentioned above, which is taken from

GAAP and which was subsequently replaced by an express reference to GAAP, testifies to the "pure" accrual basis method as the essential reporting methodology for tax purposes.

Although practitioners of certain free professions could previously use the cash basis method,[44] that method was inconsistent since some taxpayers placed the emphasis on the "pure" cash basis method, according to which they reported income or expenses when the monies were expended or actually received, compared with others who applied the hybrid method that integrated elements of the accrual basis, in that they reported their income when the tax invoices were issued, and not on the date on which the revenues were actually received.[45] However, this method was effectually cancelled with respect to those practitioners also, obligating them to report on the accrual basis method for tax purposes.[46]

4.3.1.2 "Subject to any adjustment by law" deviation

The other exception is "subject to any adjustment required or authorized by law". Here also, those who support the Consistent Approach will certainly have no difficulty in accepting this exception, to the extent that it relates to specific statutory provisions that require "specific accounting treatment" for tax purposes, which is inconsistent with GAAP. However, the term "authorized by law" (instead of "authorized by specific legislation") can be regarded as vague since it may "conceal" other methods that enable a deviation from GAAP. However, it seems that this exception by the UK legislature appears in only a limited number of provisions.[47]

4.3.2 The case law

Although support may be found in UK case law for the Consistent Approach, as well as for the Consistent Selective Approach, it appears that over time the Consistent Approach has become entrenched as the preferable and possibly exclusive approach in UK tax cases.

The Dualistic Doctrine was supported in the past in cases like *PE Consulting*[48] and *ECC Quarries*,[49] where it was held that although considerable weight is also to be attributed to testimony on accounting practice, the court is not limited in its findings and is not obliged to follow that practice for tax purposes. This Consistent Selective Approach was applied not merely to substantially legal questions (such as the distinction between capital and income), but also to matters of quantification and measuring, where the court reserved the right to disregard GAAP and apply principles of quantification (including timing), even where no express tax legislation exists contradicting the accounting practice on the concrete issue.[50] Moreover, the Dualistic Doctrine and the Separating Approach were also supported in *Southern Railway of Peru*.[51]

However, support can also be found in the past for the Singular

Doctrine and the Consistent Approach. In such cases as *Lothian Chemical*,[52] *Chancery Lane*[53] and *Odeon*,[54] it was held that the practice of financial accounting should be followed for tax purposes, unless tax legislation prescribed a provision to the contrary.

Moreover, prior to obligatory statutory provisions coming into effect that obligated reference to GAAP, and when the influence of the Dualistic Doctrine still resonated, the courts adopted the accrual basis method in the spirit of the GAAP in a long series of judgments, even if they did not consider themselves committed to the quantification and timing principles that had been created by GAAP. Case law provided, as a general principle, that income of a commercial nature would be recognized for tax purposes in the spirit of the realization principle on the day on which the taxpayer's right to receive it crystallized, even if the date on which it was actually received had been deferred to a later date.[55] Thus, for example, in the case of compensation received by a taxpayer four years after the date of the occurrence of the damage, the compensation was recognized during the reporting period in which the damage was caused, and not on the date on which the compensation was actually received.[56]

In another case it was held that commissions that were received by a taxpayer would be recognized as income on the date on which they were earned, and not on the date on which they were actually received.[57] In another case, payments that were received by an architect for future work were not included in the taxpayer's chargeable income in the fiscal year since they related to future periods.[58]

In more complex cases, where it was more difficult to determine the date of the recognition of the income, the courts stuck to the accrual basis. Thus, for example, in the *Cowen* case,[59] a taxpayer sold gift stamps to his customers to enable them to be distributed to their end-customers together with the products that they sold. The end-customers who received the stamps had the option of turning to the taxpayer and converting them into gifts. In that case, the taxpayer argued that he could not recognize the profit until the date on which the stamps were received back from the end-customers, as he did not know what his costs would be in respect of distributing the gifts. It was ruled, in accordance with the principles of the accrual basis, that the taxpayer must recognize a profit to the extent of the stamps that had been sold and were yet to be converted, less a provision that would reflect the amount of the stamps that would be redeemed.

In other cases, where it was difficult to determine the timing of when the income had been earned, it seems that the courts regarded the element of delivery as a fundamental without which the income did not crystallize, according to the accrual basis. Thus, for example, in the *Hall (JP)* case,[60] in which a company undertook to supply a customer with products on certain dates, but delivery of the products was delayed due to the outbreak of war, it was held that the profit would be recognized on the date of delivery of the products to the customer, and not on the date of the signature of the contract. In the *New Conveyor* case,[61] profit was recognized on the date of the delivery of the merchandise to the customer, in lieu of the date of the signature of the contract.

In *Gunn*,[62] a taxpayer sold two agricultural farms on condition that the crop on the farm would be sold to the customer at a certain value. According to the agreement between them, the crop was transferred to the buyer only after its value had been assessed during the reporting period following the sale of the farms. The question that arose related to the timing of the recognition of the income from the sale of the crops. The court in that case ruled that the income from the crop would be recognized on the reporting date on which the crop had been transferred and the cash in respect of it received, in lieu of the reporting period in which the contract had been signed.

However, although the case law clung to the principles of the accrual basis method, it did not disregard another important principle – the principle of prudence (conservatism) and this is also in the spirit of GAAP. Thus, for example, in a case in which by agreement the taxpayer was entitled to amounts computed pursuant to the results of his sales, the court ruled that the taxpayer could not recognize income from these amounts throughout the term of the agreement, and the amounts would be recognized as income only at the end of the contract since quantification of the income was not possible, and the profit was earned, in the opinion of the court, only on the date on which it was possible to verify the amount thereof.[63]

These cases show that in the past, prior to the legislation being altered to incorporate the "pure" accrual basis method (a creation of GAAP) as the reporting method favoured by tax law, and apart from a number of exceptional cases in which income was recognized for tax purposes on a cash basis,[64] and cases like those mentioned above that supported the Dualistic Doctrine, most of the cases in practice preferred the Consistent Approach and adopted the accrual basis method for tax purposes.

While the past reveals support for both the Dualistic Doctrine and the Singular Doctrine as well, it would appear that (since the 1980s) the Singular Doctrine and the Consistent Approach have prevailed, and the adoption of the "pure" accrual basis method for tax purposes is steady and uniform.

In *Llewedyn-Daries*,[65] it was held that while it is correct that "ultimately" it is the court that determines the relevant standards of financial accounting that are to be applied in measuring profit in a given case, nonetheless where there is no disagreement on how financial accounting treats the measuring of profit (and in such a case, the timing of its recognition) in a given case, and in the absence of a statutory provision to the contrary, the courts will adopt GAAP, for tax purposes.

It would appear that the leading case that finally settled the argument on the issue of whether GAAP should be followed on questions of timing and measuring for tax purposes was handed down in 1993, in *Threlfall*.[66] In that case, the question arose as to whether the accounting principles prescribed in SSAP#21 [67] (which does not even apply to unincorporated bodies like the taxpayer himself) should apply in measuring profits for tax purposes. The court ruled that GAAP is the only acceptable method of accounting for the measuring of profit for tax purposes,[68] and this is the preferred method as against a "judicial" finding of the profit.[69]

In *Britannia Airways*,[70] it was again held that GAAP is to be followed for measuring, mainly in relation to aspects of timing the recognition for tax purposes.[71]

In *Herbert Smith*,[72] the court was also prepared to determine that a provision for future losses expected, made in a particular fiscal year and which is not embedded in the matching principle but is required according to GAAP in accordance with the conservatism principle, will be binding for tax purposes.[73]

In *Tapemaze*,[74] the question arose, *inter alia*, whether tax accounting should only follow GAAP in cases of quantification and timing, as well as in the question of classification. The special commissioner expressly ruled that the issue of classifying the income was a question of law, and that tax accounting should not follow GAAP in this respect. The appeals court, relying on the Consistent Approach, ruled that tax is imposed on "profits", and in this context it is generally accepted that the quantification of "profits" (including timing) must be measured according to GAAP. With regard to the question of classification, the appeals court only addressed this question in passing, and this could be construed as acquiescence to the approach of the special commissioner. The appeals court finding that the advances discussed there should be classified as income from a business resulted from the fact that the underlying perception of GAAP is that the source of the profit was the original transactions due to which the income arose, and not the cash itself.[75] In such a case, the integration between the initial character of the advances at the time they were received (in the ordinary course of the taxpayer's business) and their becoming "income" with the company being released from its commitment towards "creditors" is what led to their classification as part of the business income.[76]

Whether this judgment is to be regarded as supporting the view that for tax purposes, GAAP should also be followed on questions of classification (or should be interpreted as supporting the view that the question of classifying income is a question of law and is not a derivative of GAAP), there is no doubt that on questions of quantification this judgment gave additional support to the rejection of the Dualistic Doctrine and adoption of the Singular Doctrine.

As we have seen, modern case law has embraced the Singular Doctrine, the Consistent Approach and the "pure" accrual basis method created by

GAAP, and these have been adopted into tax law as a matter of routine. This approach effectively makes the timing of the recognition of income a question of fact rather than of law. In other words, it seems that determining the timing of the recognition of income for tax purposes is now one of fact to be interpreted by accounting professionals, and the view of financial accounting is determinative for tax purposes.

4.3.3 Administrative directives

In a series of directives, the UK tax authorities (hereinafter "**HMRC**") instruct that in measuring (including determining the timing) profits the approach should be carried out in two phases: in the first phase, profits are to be measured according to GAAP, in the second, by adjusting those profits for tax purposes according to the specific statutory provisions that require deviation from financial accounting.[77] Moreover, in light of the *Britannia Airways* case,[78] HMRC has stated that the impact of GAAP on tax laws in the area of timing has been significantly expanded.[79]

It appears, however, that despite the considerable and unequivocal case law that adopts the Consistent Approach, HMRC finds it difficult to fully absorb the application of this approach in its directives, and lack of consistency may be found in the HMRC view regarding the adoption of that approach, or possibly its preference for the Consistent Selective Approach. In a number of directives, HMRC confirms, in accordance with the Consistent Approach, that as long as there is no other binding statutory provision the principles of financial accounting are those that should be used to determine "profit" for tax purposes.[80]

In the spirit of the Singular Doctrine and the Consistent Approach, the application of the "pure" accrual basis method for tax purposes has taken hold in a series of administrative Practice Notes on various topics. For example, in relation to deducting expenses on a financing lease, HMRC also provides that in cases where Accounting Standard SAAP#21 (which deals with leases) does not apply, the expenses on a financing lease may be deducted according to the principles of the accrual basis method, in like manner to the Standard itself.[81]

In reference to cancelling the possibility of using reporting on a cash basis method,[82] HMRC expressed its view that the enactment of s 42 of the Finance Act 1998 is no more than a widening of the application of the accrual basis method to additional taxpayers since, according to its view, it provided a "true and fair view" of the presentation of taxpayers' profits even before s 42 was enacted.[83] In its review of the rules of recognizing income as fashioned in the UK case law, HMRC sums up by arguing that, in its opinion, the case law that it presents in the Statement proves the courts' preference of the accrual basis method that recognizes income once it is earned.[84]

Nonetheless, a number of exceptions have been prescribed by HMRC to this rule. The main exception, for which support can be found in case law, is that the Consistent Approach will not apply to the classification of income (e.g. classification between "capital" and "income"), but will apply to questions of timing and quantification.[85] However, in addition to this basic rule, it seems that in the various directives HMRC seeks to minimize the application of the Consistent Approach in questions of quantification and timing, and broaden the HMRC stance not to allow quantification of the profit according to GAAP for tax purposes, even where there is no express statutory provision obligating a deviation from GAAP. Thus, for example:

In BIM35210, HMRC intermingles earlier case law (from the 1950s to the 1970s) with modern case law, concluding that auditors' testimony regarding the accounting practice should be treated as "informative but not determinative".

In BIM31003 and BIM42201 (where HMRC was willing to accept the idea, after the *Threlfall* case, that there is no tax principle overriding GAAP to the effect that revenue expenditure is allowable in the period in which it is incurred), HMRC states that the exception in s 42 of the Finance Act 1998 ("adjustment required or authorized by law") should be construed in a manner whereby the deviation from GAAP will be made not merely where an express statutory provision to the contrary exists, but also where a general and basic principle of the tax system is in question. Elsewhere, HMRC states that such a deviation will also be made where it is required by a judgment or necessitated by government policy.[86]

With respect to these statements it may be said that to the extent that these deviations are regulated by legislation (such as the prohibition to deduct fines and penal sums as an expense), this does not give rise to any difficulty from the Consistent Approach standpoint. However, to the extent that the intention is to allow a deviation from GAAP even in the absence of concrete legislation, and merely to rely on "general principles" of the tax system or government policy, this leaves the door wide open for not adopting the results of measuring profit according to GAAP, and for an attempt to introduce the Consistent Selective Approach through the back door.[87]

In BIM31019, HMRC states that a deviation may be made from accounting practice (even in the absence of contrary legislation) where financial accounting itself proposes an alternative for the accounting in a given case, and where the practice adopted by the taxpayer is itself unacceptable.

In BIM56420, HMRC emphasizes that the tax treatment must differ from the accounting treatment, without basing this statement on any explicit statutory provision to the contrary.[88] That statement can relate to either general principles of the tax system or even to the approach that in certain cases reliance on GAAP would be regarded as "avoidance schemes".

4.3.4 *Comments*

It seems that the academic commentary in the UK has adopted the Singular Doctrine and the Consistent Approach, almost without argument. In the CIOT Application,[89] the Institute points out that it was usual in the UK for statements drawn up according to recognized accounting practice to constitute the starting point for tax purposes, and the Institute's position is that the preparation of separate statements (one statement for the purposes of investors and others, and the other for tax purposes) should be avoided.[90] The CIOT goes on to state that the extent of the changes (adjustments) between the financial accounting statements and the income tax return must be minimal, and any deviation from the application of GAAP for tax purposes must be based on agreed and pre-known principles, and not on *ad hoc* decisions.[91]

The Macdonald-Martin Committee, which examined the conformity between accounting and tax profits, summarized its conclusions by recommending that there should be an aspiration towards harmonizing accounting profits and profits for tax purposes, and in light of this aspiration the existing fiscal laws should be reviewed and changed to accord with this trend.[92] Although the committee is aware of the fact that there are limitations to tax accounting following GAAP, nonetheless, in its view, a deviation from GAAP must be based on clear expectations and pre-known "game rules", and not on the basis of *ad hoc* decisions.[93]

The Macdonald-Martin Committee raises the argument (of HMRC) that the exception contained in s 42 of the Finance Act 1998 subordinates the use of GAAP also to the precedents laid down by the courts. In addressing this argument, the committee states that it is possible that this may mean that existing precedents will override the following of GAAP, although, in relation to new judgments, the committee determines that it is not the function of the courts to rule how profits ought to measured for tax purposes, and such power should be granted exclusively to the official institutions that oversee financial accounting.[94] Unfailing support for the Consistent Approach may also be seen in other comments.[95]

4.4 Between GAAP and fiscal accounting – US tax law

On the face of it, similar to the UK tax law, the rule in the US federal tax legislation preferred consistency with accounting practice, subject to exceptions enabling deviation from financial accounting. Nevertheless, these "exceptions" have been interpreted in the US very differently from the interpretations given to "similar" exceptions in the UK.

4.4.1 Legislation

The US federal legislator has exhibited considerable flexibility in relation to the accounting practice, according to which the taxpayer may file his tax returns, although the US federal tax authorities (hereinafter: **"IRS"**) have a sufficient measure of flexibility to deviate, for tax purposes, from the accounting method according to which the taxpayer prepares his returns. This may be clarified as follows.

4.4.1.1 Flexibility relating to reporting methods

Section 441[96] of the Internal Revenue Code (hereinafter: **"IRC"** or the "Code") establishes the rule that the tax year (whether it is a calendar year or fiscal year) will be set according to the accounting method by which the taxpayer keeps his books. Yet, on the issue of "the fiscal year", provisions have been set which enable IRS to deviate from the accounting method by which the taxpayer maintains his books.[97]

IRC§451[98] establishes the rule that any amount of income which has accrued to the taxpayer be included in the tax year in which it was received by the taxpayer, unless according to the accounting method by which he maintains his books, this sum is to be included in another reporting period. Although there are a number of exceptions to this rule,[99] on the issue of the timing of the recognition of income, the broad rule is that the accounting method by which the taxpayer keeps his books is that which will be operative for tax purposes.

IRC§446[100] provides that on the issue of timing the recognition of income, the taxpayer's accounting reporting method should be adopted as a general rule, unless no method of accounting has been regularly used by the taxpayer, or if the method used does not "clearly reflect income". The Regulations continue by determining that it is possible to use the cash basis method, accrual basis method or any other method that is, according to the provisions of this chapter, conditional on the directives and any combination of the above methods that is permitted according to the Regulations ("the hybrid method").[101]

However, this flexibility in reporting is not absolute, and in a number of statutory provisions the legislator has confined taxpayers of certain classes to a concrete reporting method. For example: IRC §448 limits assessees who are entitled to apply the cash basis as a reporting method for tax purposes. According to the restrictions provided in the section, subject to certain exceptions, *inter alia*, entities that are C-corporations, partnerships in which one of the partners is a C-corporation, and certain trusts cannot use the cash basis method unless their income turnover does not exceed $5 million. In addition, taxpayers that hold substantial inventory in their business cannot apply this method for tax purposes.[102]

According to IRC§447, a corporation that carries on trading or a business of farming as well as partnerships, one of whose partners is a corporation, must use the accrual basis method to report its income for tax purposes. Nonetheless, there are a number of exceptions to this rule, e.g. corporations such as S-corporations, whose business is in farming are not required to adopt the accrual basis method for tax purposes.[103] Another exception to this rule provides that corporations that meet the test of "gross receipts" are not required to report according to the accrual basis method for tax purposes.[104] In general, according to the "gross receipts" test, a corporation need not apply the accrual basis method with respect to fiscal years following the 1975 fiscal year, if they had no revenues that exceeded $1 million.[105] This flexibility on the one hand, and the restrictions mentioned on the other hand, seem to show that the tax legislator is of the opinion that the accrual basis method is preferable to the cash basis method from the point of view of adequacy of quantifying income, (including its timing). Otherwise there could be no explanation why mandatory provisions that require taxpayers having inventory, and "heavy" taxpayers, should specifically report according to this methodology. At the same time, this preference has not led the US legislator to deny completely the possibility of reporting using the cash basis method which it deems less reliable.

It can be said that while the UK legislator shows inflexibility with respect to the "pure" accrual basis method as a tool for determining the timing of the recognition of income, based on faith in the accrual basis method (created by GAAP), the US legislator shows apparent flexibility, and seemingly enables reporting by a number of methods. This, in my opinion, is not based on great faith in those systems, but is actually based on a lack of faith.

This lack of faith is expressed in two ways: first, the existence of the "safety valve" contained in IRC§446(b), which has also been interpreted in case law in the spirit of lack of faith; and second, the existence of a long series of statutory provisions that impose conditions and provide for exceptions and place limitations on those reporting methods that the legislator has *prima facie* adopted as legitimate for tax purposes. We will clarify this below.

4.4.1.2 The "safety regulator" – the exception of "clearly reflect income"

The expression "clearly reflect income" in IRC§446(b) has not been defined either by the Code or by the Regulations.[106] We thus see that the provision contained in IRC§446 is more flexible than its counterpart in the UK tax system, which mandates that returns will be made in accordance with GAAP.[107] This is because, subject to few exceptions, it allows "admission" to be made according to any reporting method that the taxpayer generally uses, whether it matches GAAP or not.[108] In those cases in which no reporting method has been dictated to the taxpayer, the US tax legislator has kept in reserve a single protective tool against multifarious types of reporting by the taxpayer, by means of an exception whereby IRS is entitled to deviate from the standards according to which the returns have been drawn up, if those standards do not "**clearly reflect income**". On the face of it, this exception appears to resemble that which appears in the UK tax system whereby the taxpayer's return according to accounting principles must meet the condition of "**true and fair view**".[109] But is this actually the case?

Set against these provisions, it would appear that a large number of the US cases treating of examining the actions of IRS can be understood only in light of the provisions of another statute, which does not stem specifically from the tax domain. Section 706(2)(A) of the Administrative Procedure Act (**APA**)[110] delineates and limits judicial review of the administrative agency's decisions to cases in which these decisions are not only erroneous, but also deemed to be an "abuse of discretion".[111]

As we will see, the US Supreme Court stated that the "abuse of discretion" standard greatly limits the power of the courts, and according to this view the reversal of an agency decision should be rare, and should only occur in the most extreme cases.[112]

4.4.1.3 *Statutory stipulations regarding the cash basis method*

Despite the fact that the cash basis has been *prima facie* recognized as the legitimate reporting method for tax purposes, the integration of a number of general statutory provisions (i.e. those relating to the reporting method generally, as distinct from a provision that relates to a specific transaction or specific income) has led to the result that this method has not been accepted as simply being the suitable reporting method for tax purposes.

We have already mentioned that, according to the "pure" cash basis method, all income that is earned by the taxpayer is deemed to be taxable in the fiscal year in which it is actually received or constructively received, whether in cash or in cash equivalent.[113] The expenses incurred in producing the income are allowed as a deduction in the fiscal year in which they were paid. This being the case, in reporting according to the cash basis method, the timing of the profit on the income is unimportant as the recognition of the income is made when the income revenues are actually received, independently of the question of the date of the occurrence of the event that generated and crystallized the income. However, legislation extended the concept of the receipt of the income for purposes of this method and included not merely revenues that were received in cash or cash equivalent, but also revenues that the taxpayer has the option or potential to receive. In other words, the legislator created a new source for recognizing income for persons who report on a cash basis, namely, constructive receipt. Regulation 1.451–2(a)[114] provides that for purposes of recognizing income of a party who reports on a cash basis, the following income will also be recognized even if it has not been received physically by the taxpayer:

- payments deriving from the income that have been credited to the taxpayer's account;
- payments deriving from the income that have been segregated and are designated for transfer to the taxpayer in the future;
- payments resulting from the income that have not been received by the taxpayer but to which he has access, so that he will be able to draw them on notice given to the party who holds the monies.

These Regulations, together with the cases that we will discuss below, which have adopted the Constructive Receipt Doctrine, have effectively rejected the use of the "pure" cash basis method and introduced considerations and principles taken from the accrual basis method to the cash basis method.[115]

4.4.1.4 Statutory stipulations regarding the accrual basis method

Despite the fact that the accrual basis has been recognized as being legitimate, the integration of a number of general statutory provisions (i.e. those that relate to the reporting method generally, as distinct from a provision that relates to a specific transaction or specific income) have led to the result that this method has not been accepted at face value as the appropriate reporting method for tax purposes. In other words, the "pure" accrual basis method (created by GAAP) has not been accepted as a reporting method that is sufficient for tax purposes, but is subject to changes, conditions and additions that changed it as a tool for quantifying (and timing) income and profit, and gave it a meaning for tax purposes that differs from the original meaning.

The nub of the changes can be summarized as follows: the realization principle that lies at the basis of the accrual basis method, established by GAAP as a condition for recognizing income,[116] has been replaced by the "all events test" (relating to timing recognition of income), and the matching principle that lies at the basis of the accrual basis method as a condition for recognizing a liability as an expense,[117] has been replaced by the requirements of the "all events test" and the "economic performance" test (relating to timing recognition of expense). The "all events test", as determined in legislation with respect to determining the timing of the recognition of income regarding taxpayers who report on the accrual basis method, is not substantially different from the realization principle laid down by GAAP.[118]

According to Treas Reg §1.446–1(a)(2), the "all events test" provides, *inter alia*, that income will be included in the taxpayer's report in the fiscal year upon fulfillment of the following two conditions: first, all the events that create the right to receive the income or to pay the expense have occurred; and second, quantification of the income or the liability can be reasonably determined.[119]

In a similar spirit to the realization principle, a further provision was also provided in IRC§448(d)(5) according to which in certain cases, where the taxpayer reports his income according to the accrual basis method, he will not be required to recognize his income that has been generated from providing services, if he believes, according to past experience, that this income will not be recoverable in the future.

However, if ultimately this income that has not accrued to the taxpayer according to the provisions of the section is recovered from the customer, it will be reported in the fiscal year in which they are recovered. It is further provided (similar to what is required according to the "pure" accrual basis method) in IRC§458(a) that subject to certain conditions, a taxpayer who reports his income according to the accrual basis method may, upon request, choose not to recognize his income that is imputed to the sale of magazines, books or records, to the extent they are returned to the taxpayer before the end of the merchandise return period. The maximum merchandise return period for magazines is two months and 15 days after the end of the fiscal year, and with respect to paperbacks and disks, four months and 15 days. Thus, for example, a distributor who markets records to his customers on the assurance that he agrees to take the merchandise back if they are unsuccessful in selling it, may choose not to accrue the income imputed to the sale of the records.

However, as we will see below, a provision such as IRC§458(a) is not the rule, but is to be regarded as an exception to the rule, as it deviates from the realization principle.[120] Moreover, the main point is that despite the apparent resemblance of the "all events test" to the realization principle with respect to the timing of the recognition of the income, the very giving of a "legal mantle" to a test that originated in accounting has opened a door for the development of case law that has completely deviated from the realization principle, as we will see below.[121] Moreover, as we saw above, the realization principle is only one side of the accrual basis method (as established by GAAP), and this accounting method cannot be described without the other, which deals with the recognition of the liability against income that will be recognized without the matching principle.[122] In this matter of the timing of the recognition of a liability, in which, *inter alia*, the criteria of the "all events test" and "economic performance" have been inserted within the framework of IRC§461, the US tax system has completely abandoned the original accounting method of the accrual basis and embarked on "an independent trail".[123] The linkage of these two components thus leads to the result that the accrual basis method that the US tax legislator has accepted as a legitimate system (and possibly, as we have stated, also one that is preferred in comparison to other reporting methods), is no longer the "pure" accrual basis method that GAAP created, but a kind of hybrid of rules and interpretation that jointly lead to the severing of the accrual basis method generated by GAAP from the accrual basis method for tax purposes.

4.4.1.5 *Statutory provisions regarding reporting of special transactions*

Over and above the statutory provisions that impose restrictions or make exceptions to applying the accrual basis method or cash basis method, the federal tax legislator has also been required to determine a number of provisions dealing with special accounting treatment in relation to defined transactions or defined income for tax purposes.

4.4.1.5.1 INSTALLMENT SALES

IRC§453 provides options both to taxpayers who report on a cash basis as well as those who report on an accrual basis (unless they have chosen not to report according to this system in their annual tax returns). The section provides for a special method for reporting for tax purposes in the case of installment sales. In general, sales where at least one of the installments is received after the expiration of the tax year in which the sale was made will be deemed to be an installment sale for purposes of the application IRC§453. According to the mechanism laid down in this section, on a sale of certain property, the capital gain that is created is recognized for tax purposes over the period of receipt of the revenues that are paid on account of the sale price. For that purpose, the section provides for a formula whereby "the gross profit percentage" that is obtained by dividing the profit from the sale by the amount of the consideration in respect of the sale is multiplied by the installments that are received by the taxpayer in the tax year, so that only the amount that is received from this multiplication process is recognized in that fiscal year. The assumption lying at the basis of this mechanism is that every receipt that is received by the taxpayer consists partly of the profit in respect of the sale of the property, and partly of payments that are on account of the cost of the property that was sold.

This mechanism, as stated, applies only with respect to those sales in which, at the least, one of the installments is received after the end of the fiscal year in which the sale was made, subject to certain exceptions. The application of the section to cases where the property falls within the definition is automatic, except for cases where (a) the taxpayer elects not to report according to this method, and (b) the sale is subject to another set of rules,[124] or (c) the sale has been made between related parties and the rules that relate to them apply.[125] According to the first option, taxpayers have the option not to report according to this method if they have reported their choice in the annual tax return.[126] This choice not to report according to the installments method can be revoked by IRS,[127] and will not be permitted in cases where one of the objects of that choice is to evade payment of tax.

In the *Roy* case,[128] it was held that in order for the transfer of the property from the seller to the buyer to be regarded as a sale for the purposes of the section, the fact that the title to the property did not pass in the initial stages of the sale, when the first installments were made, did not stop the sale from being treated as an installment sale according to the section. In this connection, it was held in *Wiseman*[129] that it is sufficient that: (a) the seller made a commitment according to the contract, (b) the buyer has undertaken to effect the installments, (c) the right of possession of the property has passed to the buyer, (d) the taxpayer regarded the transaction as an installment sale transaction, for the transaction to be reported according to the provisions of the section.

When dealing with long-term leasing contracts with an option to buy the property at the end of the contract term, the question arose whether or not the transaction could be regarded as an installment sale for the purpose of the application of the section. In the past, the answer given to this question in case law was that contracts such as these were lease contracts and not installment sale contracts.[130] However, it seems that newer case law takes the view that transactions should be classified according to their general economic substance, so that in cases where the economic substance of the transaction testifies to the fact that it is an installment-sale transaction and not a leasing contract, the transaction will be classified as a sale transaction for the purpose of the application of the section.[131]

For the purposes of the application of the section, a receivable is any receipt that is received in real terms or constructively.[132] A receivable can be in cash or other asset. Where the revenue is received other than in cash, the market value of the asset is what will be taken into account in applying the installment-sale method.[133] As explained above, recognition of the income on an installment sale is deferred until the date on which the revenues are actually received, so that on the date on which the revenues are received, that part of the receipt that is equal to multiplying the "gross profit ratio" (as defined below) by the amount of the revenue that was received in that fiscal year, will be recognized for tax purposes. However, in any event, the capital gain to the extent of the depreciation that was required in respect of that property is taxed in the year of the sale of the asset.

The "gross profit ratio" is computed as the gross profit in respect of selling the property divided by the amount of the sale price. The gross profit is computed as the sale price less the adjusted cost (plus depreciation that is required in respect of the asset) and the expenses of the sale. The total sale price is defined as the total sale price less debts (qualifying indebtedness) that relate to the asset,[134] and this is up to the amount of the cost of the asset sold. Where the debts relating to the asset exceed its cost, then the part that exceeds the cost of the asset will be recognized as income in the year of the sale of the asset. We will explain below the application of the method by way of illustration:

A taxpayer sells an asset whose amortized cost (after reducing depreciation expenses to the extent of $50) is $100, against a bill under which the buyer undertakes to pay $200 for the asset that has been sold. Payment of the bill will be made over a period of five years so that the buyer will make installments of $40 per year. The sale expenses relating to the sale are $20. The property is encumbered by a liability in the amount of $10, which is transferred to the buyer.

In order to apply the provisions of the section in this particular case, first the gross profit ratio must be found, as specified above. The numerator that we will use in finding the gross profit ratio is the gross profit that is received on the sale, i.e. $200 (the sale price) less $150 (the adjusted cost plus depreciation expenses) less $20 (expenses of the sale). The result obtained is thus $30.

For the purpose of calculating the denominator, we must deduct from the amount of the sale price the debts relating to the asset, which in our case are $200, which is the sale price less $10, which represents the liability attaching to the property. That is to say, the figure that is received in the equation is $190.

This being so, the ratio obtained is: 30/190 = 15.8 per cent.

That is, the income that will be recognized in the first year is the depreciation amounts that were formerly demanded in the sum of $50 only. In the second year, when the first installment will be made, the part of the payment that is received by multiplying the gross profit ratio (15.8 per cent in our case) by the annual payment ($40 in our case) will be reported for tax purposes. That is to say, the sum of $6.32 will be included as the chargeable income of the taxpayer.

In the event of an installment sale between closely related parties,[135] all of the future installments that are expected to be received by the seller will be deemed to have been received on the date of the sale. This means that the section is not applied in cases of a sale between related parties. The reason for this limitation may be the attempt to prevent artificial transactions that are aimed at obtaining expenses by way of depreciation by the buyer, and at the very same time, deferring the recognition of the income by the seller using the installment sale method.

4.4.1.5.2 RECOGNITION OF INCOME DERIVING FROM LONG-TERM CONTRACTS

The accrual basis method established by GAAP has, as we have seen, tackled long-term contracts (mainly for the supply of services) by means of methodologies such as "the percentage of completion method" in relation to long-term service agreements.[136] The tax legislator did not merely "make do" with referring to GAAP in this respect, but chose to determine its own statutory direction which, although influenced by the GAAP, is not a "pure" accrual basis method as it applied to long-term contracts.

IRC§460(a) lays down the rule that recognition of income from long-term contracts will be made pursuant to the percentage of completion method. In this connection, a long-term contract is defined in IRC§460(5)(1) as including any production contract, contract for the construction of buildings, installation or the building of property, that terminates other than in the fiscal year in which the contract was made. Fixing a special accounting method with respect to the timing of the recognition of income in the case of long-term contracts is justified on account of the great difficulty in predicting the profitability of the project that is being carried out within the scope of the contract. Thus, for example, the expenses that are involved in carrying out a long-term project vary throughout the period of the contract, and are difficult to estimate and foresee.[137]

In addition, contracts of this kind contain parameters that cannot be controlled by the taxpayer, such as: price changes of raw materials along the period of the contract; changes in costs arising from strikes, fines or delays in carrying out the work; and varying, unforeseen difficulties in carrying out the project under the contract. In general, calculation of the chargeable income according to this method is made in two stages: first, during the execution of the project, the taxpayer recognizes part of the income that relates to that year, except in certain cases, by the percentage of completion method, and in the second stage, on the date of the conclusion of the performance of the contract by using the "look back method", the calculation being carried out retroactively on the taxpayer's chargeable income at the time when all the data that could not have been assessed during the performance of the project become available. According to the result obtained the taxpayer supplements or takes the shortfall or surplus in his tax liability, with the addition of interest.

In addition to the percentage of completion method, as regards certain long-term contracts, the IRC permits the use of other income-recognition methods, including methods that combine, for example, the percentage of completion method with other accounting methods (including the cash basis method). According to the percentage of completion method, the taxpayer is required to include in his tax returns in each fiscal year that concludes after the fiscal year in which the contract was made, income in an amount equal to the aggregate sum of his expected income from the contract, multiplied by the cumulative completion rate of the contract at the end of the fiscal year (hereinafter: **"the supplementary amount"**), after having reduced the supplementary amount by the cumulative income amounts that were included in the preceding fiscal years.[138] In this connection, according to IRC§460(b)(1)(a), the completion percentage of the contract (except in certain cases) is computed as (1) the ratio between the aggregate accumulated expenses that are imputed to the contract, that have been caused in the fiscal year and in the preceding fiscal years, and (2) the aggregate expenses that the taxpayer expects to incur during the course of the performance of the contract. In order to determine the completion percentage according to the provisions of IRC§460(c)(1), all the direct expenses, including research and experimental expenses and the interest expenses relating directly to the taxpayer's activity in the scope of a long-term contract, are to be addressed, as well as the storage, handling and processing-related expenses that were incurred during the activities relating to the performance of the long-term contract. Indirect expenses, such as marketing, selling and advertising costs may be imputed to the various projects by specifically identifying the expenses or formulae that are based on charging of expenses for the various contracts on the basis of hours, direct labor costs or any other method that reasonably reflects the imputation of the various indirect costs among the different long-term contracts.[139] Costs that can be imputed according to the recognition method based on the completion rate are allowed for deducting in the fiscal year in which they were incurred. For this purpose, expenses are deemed to have been "incurred" in the fiscal year in which the "all events test" is fulfilled. Expenses that are imputable to a particular long-term contract that were expended before the project began will be deemed to be imputed to the contract, and are allowed for deduction in the fiscal year in which the contract was made.

According to the provisions of IRC§460(b)(5), taxpayers may recognize their income that results from long-term contracts by using the 10 per cent that substantially resembles the percentage of completion method. According to that method, a taxpayer is permitted not to recognize income in the performance of a long-term contract, and not bring into account any cost that is imputable to the long-term contract insofar as at the end of the fiscal year less than 10 per cent of the total estimated contract expenses have been incurred. In the first fiscal year in which the taxpayer exceeds the 10 per cent threshold, all the costs that were incurred as of the last date of that fiscal year will be brought into account in determining the completion percentage. This method (laid down in IRC§460(e)(5)) integrates the percentage of completion method and the normal accounting method that is generally applied by the taxpayer. According to the method, a certain part of the income deriving from the contract is recognized as such according to the percentage of completion method, while the balance is recognized for tax purposes according to the accounting method that is generally applied by the taxpayer (e.g. the accrual basis method that is based on the realization principle and the requirement of being earned, or the cash basis method).

According to the "look back method",[140] at the end of each long-term contract, a retroactive calculation is made of the taxpayer's chargeable income, whereby all the data that could not have been estimated during the performance of the project will now is available. Depending on the result obtained, the taxpayer either supplements or takes the shortfall or surplus of his tax liability, with the addition of interest. That is, the mechanism works by attempting to rectify the "errors" that were made at the time of calculating the taxpayer's liability during the period when he did not have information concerning the taxpayer's final income, and information respecting the expenses that would be needed to complete the labor were not available. At the end of the contract period, once all the costs incurred in performing the labor become known, and when certainty has been achieved regarding income from the contract, the taxpayer amends his relevant tax liability for the tax years during which income from the contract was reported. Thereafter, the taxpayer will receive or pay (depending on the direction of the deviations from the genuine tax liability) interest on his real tax saving or liability.

Application of this method is somewhat different in regard to certain entities that are deemed to be transparent for purposes of US law. Since the tax liability in the case of those entities is calculated not on the entity itself, but on the proprietors of the rights in the entity, every increase or decrease retroactively amending the chargeable income deriving from long-term contracts according to this method may vary the tax rates at which the proprietors of the rights in the entity are taxed. In order to avoid such a situation, IRS has provided a simplified method for applying the "look back method". According to this method, increases or decreases deriving from corrections that are made to income are carried out in regard to the entity and not the proprietors of the rights in the entity, according to the highest tax rates that apply to individuals or corporations.[141]

IRC§460 and the Regulations[142] enable taxpayers who comply with the conditions laid down therein, to report certain long-term projects according to the completed contract method.[143] According to this method, taxpayers may report their income in the fiscal year in which the labor under the contract is completed and received by the customer. The completion date and acceptance by the customer of the project is fixed according to all the facts and the circumstances that are relevant to the contract, including the agreements of the parties, the subject matter of the contract and the nature of the project. Like income, the direct expenses of the project and the indirect expenses that are identifiable with the specific project will be reported according to this method in the fiscal year in which the labor was completed,[144] and deducting them before the projects are completed is not possible. It is to be noted that the use of this method by taxpayers under the Regulations is subject to the method clearly reflecting the taxpayer's income.[145]

4.4.1.5.3 SHORT-TERM OBLIGATIONS ISSUED AT A DISCOUNT

According to IRC§454(a), in the case of a taxpayer who holds (a) an obligation bearing no interest and which is redeemable for fixed amounts increasing at stated intervals, or (b) holds a series E United States Savings Bond, if the increase stated in the redemption price of the bond is not recognized as income in the fiscal year in which the increase arose, according to the accounting method that the taxpayer applies, he may treat the same as income that was received in that fiscal year and thereby recognize the income in the fiscal year. Thus, even if the taxpayer reports his income from discounting according to the elected method only on the redemption date or sale date of the bond, he may report his income from discounting that resulted from the obligations of the types described above, according to the accrual basis method.

The provision contained in IRC§454(b), which also relates to taxpayers who report according to the accrual basis method, provides that in relation to income from discounting, a taxpayer who acquired an obligation issued at a discount for one year or more by the US Government will not recognize income from that discount until the date on which the obligation is repaid, sold or otherwise disposed of by the taxpayer.[146] That is to say, a taxpayer to whom the provisions of this section apply may defer payment of the tax in respect of his income from discounting to a later period at which the bond will be redeemed, compared with the timing of the recognition of that income according to GAAP. According to IRC§454(c), if the taxpayer holding such an obligation retains his investment in such a series after maturity, or exchanges his investment for another non-tradable obligation of the US Government, he will not be liable at that date to recognize his income from discounting that was not included in his returns in the preceding fiscal years. This income will be recognized for tax purposes only in the fiscal year in which the obligation is repaid or finally sold.[147]

4.4.1.6 Hybrid methods

As described above, IRC§446(a) also enables a taxpayer to report his income according to the hybrid method, which method is any possible combination of any of the permissible methods according to that section, subject however to the following conditions: that the hybrid method applied relates to income from trade or business; use of the method clearly reflects the taxpayer's income; and the taxpayer uses the method consistently.[148]

Thus, for example, a taxpayer may report his income from a trade or business according to the accrual basis method, and his expenses according to the cash basis method, subject to these expenses not being related to the trade or business that is being carried on by the taxpayer.[149]

Similar restrictions applying to taxpayers relating to the use of the cash basis method also apply where hybrid methods are used. For example, a C-corporation class taxpayer cannot apply a hybrid method for tax reports unless its income in the fiscal year does not exceed $5 million.

In addition to the hybrid methods, IRS is empowered to allow taxpayers to report their income according to a method that is not specifically authorized by the regulations, provided it has been consistently used throughout the period.[150] An example of such an irregular method is that of the Crop Basis of Accounting. According to this method, all crop planning, processing, harvesting and marketing costs are appropriated to a special account that is imputed to the crop, and are not permissible for deduction until all the revenues and payments in respect of that crop are reliably assessed, whereupon the income from the crop is recognized and deduction permitted of the expenses related to the crop. Another example is the "completed voyage method" that is occasionally applied in certain vessel businesses. According to this method, income and expenses related to the voyage are not recognized until the completion of the voyage of the vessel. After completion of the voyage, all the income and expenses are reported for tax purposes.[151] Another accounting method that has been permitted is the "retirement method of accounting", which is applied by automobile companies in certain cases whereby amortization costs are not appropriated until after the date on which the asset ceases to be usable.[152]

It should be noted that the hybrid methods or irregular methods are not always accepted by IRS, and in this context the lack of objection by IRS to the accounting method that has been applied by the taxpayer does not necessarily ensure that they have granted their consent to the method.[153] In order for the method to be deemed legitimate in their eyes, the method must be expressly approved by IRS.[154]

4.4.1.7 *Tax legislation as a tool for applying the Dualistic Doctrine*

We thus see that the "flexibility" of the US tax legislator in relation to the reporting method for tax purposes, which apparently originates from considerations of the taxpayer's convenience, did not emerge from faith in those reporting methods regardless of whether or not they originate in GAAP, but from lack of faith in the ability of the reporting methods that have developed outside the tax laws to provide an appropriate answer for quantifying income, including determining the timing thereof for tax purposes. From this standpoint it seems that the status of the accrual basis method is no better than that of other reporting practices.

The Dualistic Doctrine that guided the US tax legislator dictated that the application of the accrual basis method (like other reporting practices) would be subject to a series of conditions and restrictions that transformed it into a method that resembles the method developed for financial accounting in name, but whose content differs. Moreover, it seems that the essence of US tax accounting does not lie in the rule that enables flexibility in reporting, nor in the various conditions that relate to any particular method or transaction. Rather, ironically, the essence of this accounting method is an "exception" to that "safety valve" that is granted to IRS in IRC§446(b), which conditions each report of income on any method, provided the reporting meets the standard of "clearly reflecting income". As we shall see below, this expression that in substance resembles the term "true and fair view" that is to be found in UK tax accounting and in GAAP,[155] is what so distanced the tax system from the perception of GAAP.

4.4.2 *The case law*

In referring to the "rule" of IRC§446(a), the federal courts have held that the legislator's aspiration was to enable taxpayers to report according to the accounting method by which they kept their books.[156] In a few cases, the courts have also ruled that the particular accounting method preferred for tax purposes is not a question of law,[157] but rather a question of fact.[158]

Notwithstanding, it seems that this case law does not reflect the rule, and the courts' approach to the rule arising from IRC§446(a) leads to the following conclusion.

While, as we have seen, legislation has adopted both the cash basis and the accrual basis as reporting methods for tax purposes, it has also stipulated general conditions that cause the cash basis method and the accrual basis method (as they have been recognized for tax purposes) to deviate from the original methods that evolved from practice and GAAP. In the same spirit, the case law has intensified the degree of the deviation of those methods from their sources. Legislation and the various doctrines that have been developed in the case law with respect to the timing of the recognition of income for taxpayers who report on the cash or accrual bases has led to the result that, for tax purposes, these reporting methods have a meaning that differs from their original definition. If this were not enough, the cases in which the courts were required to interpret the expression "clearly reflect income" in IRC§446(b) created an unbridgeable gap between the reporting methods that had been created for other than tax purposes (including the "pure" accrual basis method) and US tax accounting in all aspects relating to the quantification and timing of the recognition of income, all set out below.

4.4.2.1 *Stipulations imposed on the cash basis method*

In certain cases, application of the "pure" cash basis method may provide taxpayers with a convenient springboard to plan their taxes by way of deferring them and bringing forward the income, and allow them to choose the most convenient timing for reporting their income. Attempts by the US courts and IRS to attack tax planning of this kind has led to the development of a number of tools aimed at confronting tax planning based on pure cash basis method, in the forefront of which is the Constructive Receipt Doctrine.[159]

The Constructive Receipt Doctrine, that has led to a deviation of the US tax system from the "pure" cash basis method, has evolved in the cases and the regulations as a means to prevent situations in which taxpayers *de facto* have full control over income payments to which they are entitled, but choose not to receive them in order to defer the recognition date of the income, thereby controlling the desired timing of the recognition of their income. Tax planning of this type can provide the taxpayer with a significant tax saving due to the time value of deferring income and advancing expenses. In addition, deferring income can also lead to a significant tax saving in periods when tax rates go down.

As a tool in the struggle against phenomena of this kind, and in order to prevent the diversion of income from one reporting period to another, the case law and the regulations have developed a number of conditions under which income revenues will be deemed to have been received by a taxpayer who reports for tax purposes on the cash basis, even if they have not effectively been received.

The purpose of this doctrine is to identify and seize income revenues already in the taxpayer's control and for which an economic right has already accrued, even though they have not actually been received by the taxpayer.[160]

However, so as not to go so far as to transform the cash basis method into one that resembles the accrual basis method (at least in relation to the timing of the recognition of income, as distinct from the timing of the recognition of the expense), a major exception has been added to the Constructive Receipt Doctrine. According to this exception, income will not be deemed to have been received by the taxpayer where material restrictions imposed on its actual receipt prevent taxpayers from exercising control over the economic right that has accrued to them.[161] Although there still remains some inconsistency in the case law, mainly in relation to the question of the taxpayer's power to dictate the timing of remitting payment by the customer. Of course, this power is subjective and, as the application of the doctrine widens to embrace income that has not yet been received, the method will lose its uniqueness and the income will be recognized on a cumulative basis on the date on which it was earned. It appears that the where the courts have expressed their awareness of this problem, they have accepted the position that the cases to which the doctrine should apply should not be extended, and they have attempted to set limits to its scope. For example, in the *Moran* case it can be seen that the court was cautious in its approach toward applying the doctrine to each and every case, and ruled that the doctrine is an artificial concept that must be applied in a limited manner.[162] However, later cases show that the courts have tended toward extending the boundaries of the doctrine.[163]

The Constructive Receipt Doctrine was fully applied to a case of salaries and income from the provision of services, but not, for example, in a case where an employee received a raise in salary that was only paid in the year following the tax year due to a policy regarding salary supervision. In that case, the raise was recognized only in the year in which it was actually paid.[164] Thus, the courts in that case regarded the policy of salary supervision as a material limitation on account of which constructive receipt by the employee did not arise. Likewise, the court did not apply the doctrine in the case of an employee who received pay for one tax year, in another tax year, due to delays that had been caused at his place of employment as a result of his transfer to a new department. The employee was not deemed to have constructively received his salary, due to the material restrictions that had been imposed over his eligibility to the salary, which were beyond his control.[165] In contrast, in cases of bonus points awarded to sales personnel by their employers, the points constituted income either on the date on which they received access to the points, or on the day they were actually paid, whichever was earlier.[166] In another case, payments that were given as advances in respect of services were recognized as income in the year in which they were actually received.[167]

A cheque received by a taxpayer reporting according to the cash basis method is generally deemed a liability for tax purposes, as the cheque is to be regarded as the equivalent of cash,[168] and the income is deemed received by the taxpayers when the cheque is delivered to the taxpayer or anyone on his behalf.[169] For example, a cheque delivered to a taxpayer after the bank's business hours on the last day of the tax year was included amongst the reportable income of the taxpayer for that tax year, despite the fact that it was not cashed and his account not credited.[170] However, in another case, a cheque sent to a taxpayer who was not at home to receive it and acknowledge its receipt, was not deemed income received by the taxpayer. In that case, the court ruled that the fact that the taxpayer was not at home amounted to a material limitation on receiving the income and, therefore, no constructive receipt arose. In another case, a taxpayer who, at the payer's request, agreed not to withdraw a cheque that he had received in the tax year, was regarded as having been subjected to a material limitation and, therefore, receipt of the cheque was not deemed to be revenue received in the tax year.[171] However, had the taxpayer been the party who was responsible for the limitation in cashing the cheque, then receipt of the cheque in such a case would have been deemed to have been income in the tax year.[172]

Dividends paid to a taxpayer who reports on the cash basis method are reported on the date when actually or constructively received. Dividends are deemed to be income when received, even if the taxpayer has demanded that the dividend be paid in a later tax year, since the taxpayer is deemed to have constructively received the dividend on the date on which he became entitled to it.[173] However, in the case of a dividend paid by a cheque sent on 31 December 1924, but received by the taxpayer on 2 January 1925, the dividend was recognized as income in the 1925 fiscal year.[174] Likewise, a dividend that was delivered by mail in the tax year following the year in which the dividend was distributed was deemed to be income only in the tax year in which it was received by the taxpayer, even though the taxpayer had the option of taking the cheque on an earlier date in the tax year.[175]

The operating mechanism of the cash basis method ensures that within the framework of the method, no balances should accrue to the taxpayer, such as income receivable, trade receivables and the like, that should properly be reported according to the accrual basis method, which recognizes income on the date on which it was earned, and does not wait until it is actually received. However, where the taxpayer's accounting method changes from the cash basis method to the accrual basis method, the taxpayer may have income that has already been earned but has not yet been received. In such cases, taxpayers must also include income to which they are entitled but have not yet received within the framework of their income in the tax year.[176]

We thus see that the case law has allowed taxpayers to recognize income for tax purposes on a "cash basis" that is not the "pure" cash basis method of bookkeeping. However, through the application of the Constructive Receipt Doctrine, the cash basis method has been adapted to incorporate elements that are completely foreign to it from the sphere of the accrual basis method.

4.4.2.2 *Stipulations imposed on the accrual basis method*

Pursuant to GAAP, and contrary to the cash basis method, the timing of the recognition of income is in most cases fixed according to the day on which it was earned, following the realization principle.[177] That is, it is fixed on the date on which the taxpayer's right to receive the income arose (subject to recoverability).[178] According to this accrual basis method, the question of cashflow is irrelevant for purposes of determining the timing of the recognition of income. The US tax system that determined that the accrual basis method is one of the legitimate methods for determining the recognition of income, could have *prima facie* "sufficed" with GAAP in this connection, but chose not to do so. Once the US legislator (as distinct, for example, from the UK legislator)[179] did not suffice with simply referring to GAAP, and replaced the realization principle and the earned requirement and other accounting principles by the "all events test" as a legal expression,[180] judicial tribunals are not required to determine the timing of the recognition of income or the timing of the recognition of a liability as an expense as these are matters of fact, based on the position of financial accounting.

The issue of determining the fulfilment of the conditions of this test is a question of law, for which the position of accounting experts is of no consequence. The courts have determined that the "all events test" for purposes of timing the recognition of income is a material and not technical, formal test.[181] With respect to the timing of the recognition of a liability as an expense, the "all events test" and other tests have been adopted within the provisions of IRC§461 in a manner that deviates dramatically from the matching principle.[182]

As regards the timing of the recognition of income for taxpayers who report on the accrual basis, on the face of it, the extent of deviation of the "all events test" from the realization principle established by GAAP, as expressed in case law, has been somewhat less. For example, in the spirit of the realization principle, the courts' approach to the effect of recoverability on the timing of the recognition of income has been that where there is material dependence[183] in connection with the receipt of certain income (similar to the realization principle), the amounts that relate to that income will be included upon the occurrence of the event on which the income depends,[184] and that the dependence (the contingency) can prevent the fulfillment of the all events test.

However, in this regard the courts have emphasized that not all contingencies that put the future receipt of the income in doubt are sufficient for the purpose of not recognizing income. It is not enough that there merely is a possibility that the income will not being received. The possibility must be genuine and material. For example, the apparent risk that one of the taxpayer's customers will not ultimately pay is not enough to refrain from recognizing income in the reporting year.[185] Likewise, a purely formal demand that must be fulfilled in order to perform a payment does not constitute true dependence, and does not prevent the accrual of the income.[186] In contrast, a dispute as to the taxpayer's right to the income constitutes material dependence, and recognition of the income will be deferred until the dispute will be settled. Similarly, in cases where there is a legal dispute regarding certain income, the income will not be recognized until a settlement is reached, or a final legal decision is made.[187]

One of the cornerstones of the realization principle is that income will only be recognized after it becomes clear to the taxpayer that the customer's debt to which the income relates is indeed recoverable.[188] This means that unless the taxpayer has the possibility of recovering the debt, the income cannot accrue. If this is so, then the question arises as to what degree of probability is required so as to enable the taxpayer not to recognize the income from the debt. While GAAP places emphasis on reasonable doubt in regard to the possibility of recovery as sufficient for not recognizing the income, the "all events test" (as interpreted in the case law) has not sufficed with reasonable doubt, but has demanded reasonable (but not absolute) certainty that the debt will not be recovered, in order not to recognize income according to the accrual basis method.[189] Likewise, when taxpayers are reasonably certain of their ability to recover the interest on account of their financial situation, the interest cannot be recognized.[190]

Nonetheless, if the probability of the debt not being repaid falls short of the required standard, the proper method of handling such a case is by accruing the income and making a provision for bad debts. Similarly, where the taxpayer's right to receive income from interest arises during the year, but after it arises it becomes clear that the interest income cannot be recovered, the proper handling of such a case is to register the income, and concurrently make a provision in respect of the principal of the loan and the interest, and not the non-recognition of the interest as income, from the very outset.[191]

However, over and above the question of recovery and the effect thereof on the timing of the recognition of the income, the deviation of the interpretation given by the courts to the "all events test" from the realization principle (that, as mentioned, constitutes a central element of the "pure" accrual basis method) was significant and was expressed, *inter alia*, in the development of doctrines such as the Claim of Right Doctrine,[192] the Open Transaction Doctrine,[193] the primary purpose test, the complete dominion test[194] and the tests that have been laid down with respect to recognizing advances.[195] These doctrines and tests have led to a major deviation of the "all events test" which was laid down as the touchstone for the timing of the recognition of income for tax purposes for taxpayers who report on the accrual basis from the realization principle that was established by GAAP.[196]

We thus see that the courts' interpretation of the general stipulations contained in the US tax legislation regarding the timing of the recognition of income for taxpayers reporting on the accrual basis method has further distanced the accrual basis method, as interpreted for tax purposes, from the original source of GAAP. It does, however, seem that this distance between the timing of the recognition of income according to GAAP (or according to other practices permissible for use for tax purposes) has led to an interpretation of the cases of the "unusual" provision contained in IRC§446(b). This is clarified below.

4.4.2.3 The "exception" of IRC§446(b)

In tandem with "the rule" of IRC§446(a), there is the "exception" thereto, contained in IRC§446(b), establishing the reservation whereby the accounting method according to which the statements have been made will not be blindly accepted for tax purposes but will be subject to the "clearly reflect income" condition. This "exception", so it seems, constitutes the very core of the tension between the rules of financial accounting and fiscal accounting in the US.[197] In attempting to breathe content into the expression "clearly reflect income", the case law has used a number of parameters, with a fairly high degree of consistency.

One of the main factors is the consistency between the return for tax purposes and GAAP,[198] although it has been held that this is not an exclusive condition.[199] Another factor is the matching between the bookkeeping method employed by the taxpayer and the particular branch in which he carries on business,[200] i.e. whether the bookkeeping method is unusual in comparison with that acceptable in the particular branch.[201] Another factor is the consistency in using the same method, from year to year.[202] Another factor that could be of influence is how IRS has related to the system used by the taxpayer in the past. The more IRS has expressed a positive opinion in relation to the method used by the taxpayer in the past, the greater the prospect of that method being accepted in the future.[203] Still another factor is whether IRS has been silent for a long period in regard to the system employed by the taxpayer. The greater the period during which IRS has not challenged that system, the greater the prospect of that system being accepted.[204]

At the same time, apart from these parameters, a review of the US case law covering the relationship between "the rule" contained in IRC§446(a) and "the exception" in IRC§446(b), incidental to a discussion of the comparison between GAAP and fiscal laws, leaves the reader bewildered given the many views and nuances surrounding the approach to be applied generally to the principles by which the quantification of income for tax purposes (including the timing thereof) will be determined. This may be explained as follows.

4.4.2.3.1 SUPPORT FOR THE SINGULAR DOCTRINE

On the face of it, what could be more suitable for meeting the condition of "clearly reflecting income" than GAAP, since, in a system that provides great flexibility generally to the standards according to which reports will be prepared, it is reasonable to assume that reports made according to GAAP will earn the description of "clearly reflecting income" (similar to the UK perception that inherently matches the expression of GAAP to "true and fair view").[205] Indeed, one can find support in US case law for the Consistent Approach in cases like *Caldwell*,[206] *Asphalt Products*,[207] *Osterloh*,[208] *Kentucky Chemical*[209] and *Fong*,[210] where it was held that if the taxpayer's reports meet the standards prescribed by financial accounting, then, on the face of it, the condition of "clearly reflecting income" will have been met. Support for the Singular Doctrine can be found both **"from the positive standpoint"** where the courts ruled on questions of quantifying or timing according to GAAP, as well as **"from the negative standpoint"** in which the courts ruled that reports filed otherwise than according to the accounting principles applicable to the specific taxpayer will not be deemed to have fulfilled the condition of "clearly reflecting income".

"From the positive standpoint" – in cases like *Electric Controls and Services Co.*,[211] *Franklin County Distilling*,[212] *Security Flour Mills*,[213] *Blaine, Mackay, Lee*,[214] *Hallmark Cards*,[215] *Collegiate Cap*,[216] *Key Homes*[217] and others[218] – the courts used GAAP tools (like the realization principle and the matching principle)[219] for fixing the timing recognition of income or expenses of taxpayers who reported on the accrual basis for tax purposes.

"From the negative standpoint" – in cases like *Caldwell*,[220] *Asphalt Products*,[221] *Franklin County*,[222] *Kahuku*,[223] *Koehring*,[224] *Resale Mobile*,[225] *Reading & Bates*,[226] *Key Homes*[227] and others[228] – "it was made clear" to taxpayers that tax returns which do not follow GAAP will not meet the condition required of "clearly reflecting income".

A review of these cases gives the impression that US case law interpreted the reservation of "clearly reflected income" according to GAAP (similar to the UK "reservation" of "true and fair view") and, by doing so, adopted the Singular Doctrine. *This, however, is not the case.*

As we will see below, the Dualistic Doctrine governs in the US tax system. According to this Doctrine, the various purposes of GAAP and of the tax laws require a result whereby it cannot be assumed that "income" determined by GAAP will necessarily be recognized for tax purposes. Therefore, not everything that constitutes "income" according to GAAP meets the condition of "clearly reflected income" for tax purposes. In a tax system that supports the Dualistic Doctrine, there is no room for the application of the Consistent Approach, and the cases cited above that positively support the Consistent Approach constitute an extremely small minority.

4.4.2.3.2 SUPPORT FOR THE DUALISTIC DOCTRINE

Although most case law determines that in order for the condition of "clearly reflected income" to pertain, the taxpayer's report must match the accounting principles that are applicable to him, the very measuring of the income and the earnings according to GAAP, is a primary condition, but does not, of itself, fulfill the condition of "clearly reflecting income". A review of the overall case law indicates two central intertwining themes

that characterize the ambivalent approach of the US tax system to financial accounting.

The first substantially extends the powers of IRS in all aspects
related to changing and adapting the accounting methods used by taxpayers for tax purposes, while limiting judicial review and providing
a broad interpretation to IRS's powers according to IRC§446(b) (hereinafter this will be referred to as the "**the broad interpretation of IRS
powers**").

The second translates the Dualistic Doctrine into a practical approach
according to which, given the gap between the different goals of financial
accounting and fiscal accounting, "accounting income", which is a creation of financial accounting, does not necessarily fall within the criteria
of "clearly reflected income". As a result of this approach, one can find *ad
hoc* judicial judgments creating "accounting rules" for tax purposes,
which are totally different from GAAP (hereinafter this will be referred to
as the "**adoption of the Consistent Selective Approach**").

4.4.2.3.3   THE BROAD INTERPRETATION OF IRS POWERS

The adoption of the Dualistic Doctrine on the one hand, and the extrane-
ous considerations lying at the basis of APA§706(2)(A) (mentioned above)
on the other, appear to have led to a broad interpretation of the powers of
IRS in relation to the changing and matching of the accounting
method generally used by the taxpayer for tax purposes, while limiting
judicial review and providing broad interpretative powers to IRS
according to IRC§446(b).[229] Thus, giving a broad interpretation to the
powers of IRS under IRC§446(b), the courts rule as follows: IRS has
broad discretion to determine whether the accounting maintained by the
taxpayer "clearly reflect income".[230] IRS may require taxpayers to
keep their books for tax purposes differently from the books they keep for
accounting purposes, provided that, according to IRS's position, the
different method will properly reflect their income.[231] IRS has the
power to require the necessary changes in order to make the taxpayer's
books reflect his income for tax purposes, despite the fact that they are
kept according to GAAP.[232] If the bookkeeping method adopted by the
taxpayer does not clearly reflect his income, then IRS has the power to
determine which method will indeed reflect the taxpayer's income.[233]
IRS is authorized to object to the accounting method adopted by the taxpayer even if it completely matches GAAP, as long as that method does
not faithfully reflect the taxpayer's income (in the authority's opinion).[234]
IRS is also empowered to oblige the taxpayer to adopt a method that
does not appear in the tax legislation or regulations.[235]

Moreover, IRS can raise objections not merely to the overall accounting method used by the taxpayer in keeping his books, but also to any
item or component that is included in the accounting method used by the

taxpayer, arguing that such item or specific component does not meet the condition of "clearly reflecting income", and providing that after the change requested, the income for tax purposes will be properly reflected.[236] It also has been held that the burden of proof in connection with IRS's decision according to IRC§446(b) falls on the taxpayer.[237] In this context, it has been held that the position of IRS, regarding change of the accounting method, enjoys the "presumption of correctness", and the taxpayer has to bear the burden of proving that IRS has erred.[238] Moreover, the courts have further stated in this context that the decision of IRS, according to IRC§446(b), will not be reversed unless it is clearly unlawful and a sheer mistake is insufficient.[239] That is to say, even an erroneous decision of IRS will not be reversed, as long as, according to the data available to IRS, it was lawful. In most cases, the court limited, of its own accord, the extent of its review of the tax authority to cases of "abuse of discretion",[240] and taxpayers are under a duty to show that IRS has abused its discretion in deciding that the method used by them in keeping their books does not meet the condition of "clearly reflecting income".[241]

Since IRC§446(b) confers upon IRS two powers, one to negate the method used by taxpayers, and the other to oblige them to employ another method, taxpayers may decide which of these two decisions they challenge, although they will have to bear the burden of proof in order to do this, and must show not merely that IRS has erred, but that their decision was illogical.[242] In the context of the burden of proof it has been held that the fact that the taxpayer "has proved" that his books were kept according to GAAP does not shift the burden onto IRS, and thus the burden remains on the shoulders of the taxpayer.[243] It also has been held that IRS may compel the taxpayer to maintain an accounting method for tax purposes retroactively as well, even if this is contrary to a previous decision that IRS itself made.[244] The courts have also held that the provision contained in IRC§448, which is binding in cases of taxpayers of certain kinds who keep their books (for tax purposes) based on the accrual basis, confers powers on IRS, according to IRC§446(b) and, this being so, IRS may oblige taxpayers who are required by IRC§448 to keep their books for tax purposes on the accrual basis, to keep their books for tax purposes on a "cash basis" if, in the opinion of IRS, this method complies with the condition of "clearly reflecting income".[245]

In the same vein, it has been held that by virtue of IRC§446(b), IRS may oblige taxpayers who, in accordance with their turnover (of less than $5 million), are exempt under IRC§448 from maintaining tax accounting on an accrual basis, nonetheless, to specifically maintain tax accounting on an accrual basis.[246] It has further been held that when a taxpayer is liquidated, IRS may compel the taxpayer to adopt an accounting method (for tax purposes) that will more properly reflect the taxpayer's income for tax purposes, even if that method differs from the method used over the years during which the business operated as a going concern.[247]

Thus, the courts have preferred a broad interpretation of the powers of IRS, either by the presumption of correctness, or by way of limiting the grounds for challenging those powers. Legal review on the exercise of the powers of IRS, according to IRC§446(b), has chosen to limit and restrict itself, and reflects an approach that posits that even if the taxpayer's reporting method properly reflects his income, that is not the question that will be examined. What will be examined is whether the decision of IRS that the reporting method fails to meet the test of "clearly reflected income" was made on a proper, lawful basis, and if so, IRS decision will be deemed valid.[248] In addition, in cases like *Catto*,[249] *Russell*,[250] *North American Coal*[251] and others,[252] the legal review of IRS decision has been limited by the view that IRS decision is deemed, in the main, to be final, unless it is found that it was unlawful or illogical. It seems that the limited scope of this intervention has enabled IRS to act, to a large degree, as it sees fit.[253]

4.4.2.3.4 ADOPTING THE CONSISTENT SELECTIVE APPROACH

Alongside the sweeping extension of IRS's powers mentioned above, stands the case law that for tax purposes creates an *ad hoc* tax accounting that totally ignores GAAP.[254] Many of these cases will be dealt with in chapters 5–7 below. It suffices simply to mention at this stage that in cases like *Brown*,[255] *London Butte Gold Mines*,[256] *South Date Farms*,[257] *Dixie Pine*,[258] *Security Flour*,[259] *DD Oil*,[260] *Capital Warehouse*,[261] *Consolidated Edison*,[262] *Prichard*,[263] *Hagen*,[264] *Lincoln Electric*,[265] *Burck*,[266] *GD*,[267] *Frank's Casing*[268] and *Cleveland Trencher*,[269] the courts have given a judicial "green light" for gross deviations from the principles of prudence, realization and matching. These rulings were based upon the view that the application of these accounting principles does not meet the condition of "clearly reflected income".[270]

4.4.2.4 The "divorce" of tax accounting from GAAP

The foregoing thus shows that both the case law interpretation of the terms and expressions that appear in the general stipulation sections in the legislation relating to the accrual basis method (mainly the "all events test") and the cash basis method (mainly the Constructive Receipt Doctrine), as well as the express statutory provisions regarding special transactions, and the interpretation given to the exception requiring reporting compliance with the "clearly reflect income" standard, have led to the result that the timing of the recognition of the income for tax purposes in the United States for taxpayers who report on the accrual basis is set on the basis of conditions and doctrines whose connection to the principles of the accrual basis (as established by GAAP) is, at most, random and inconsistent.

4.4.3 *Administrative directives*

Needless to say, in a very long line of directives, IRS "has taken upon itself" the powers and broad discretion generously granted to it by the case law.[271]

4.4.4 *Comments*

In US academic commentary, support may be found both for the Consistent Approach (that is based on the Singular Doctrine), as well as for the Separating Approach and the Consistent Selective Approach (both based on the Dualistic Doctrine). The main dispute among the various scholars turns on the question of the proper interpretation to be attributed to the expression "clearly reflected income" contained in IRC§446(b).

The most prominent example of academic commentary preferring the Singular Doctrine and the Consistent Approach appears to be that of Dubroff, Chail and Norris.[272] These scholars state that the original intention of Congress in the statutory provisions mentioned above was that the tax laws should follow GAAP as representing practices that reflect broad scientific know-how on the subjects of measurement that tax laws require.[273] According to their view, the intention of the legislature was that taxable income should be fixed according to these principles (subject to clear and defined exceptions – grounded in legislation).[274]

The time value of money theory has led a few scholars to support the Dualistic Doctrine and the Consistent Selective Approach, and to determine that the need to prevent tax advantages justifies broadly negating the application of the standards of financial accounting to all aspects of the timing of allowing expenses for tax purposes. Moreover, they take the view that, for tax purposes, the expression "income" should be given a meaning different from that accepted under the standards of financial accounting.

Thus, for example, Geier is of the opinion that the matching principle should not be used for determining "taxable income".[275] However, beyond this, any accounting principle that allows "advancing" the allowance date of an expense to a date earlier than that of the actual payment of the liability constitutes the antithesis of an even more important principle of tax law, namely the time value of money. It is more appropriate that this principle override that of matching.[276] To her mind, allowing an expense in the present due to a liability performable in the future erodes the tax value of preventing unjust tax advantage, i.e. preventing tax arbitrage.[277] Geier stated that the only "justification" for tax accounting relying on accepted accounting principles derives from the administrative desire to prevent the taxpayer from having to keep two accounting methods. However, since in any event, for tax purposes, the taxpayer is required to make various adjustments (e.g. in the amortization rates), there is no reason why adjustments should not be made between the accruing accounting method, according to which the taxpayer keeps his books, and the tax system in regard to the issue of the matching principle, as well. In any event, the argument of administrative convenience (which enables the taxpayer to report for tax purposes based on GAAP) cannot cause the erosion of tax values, and the value of anti-tax arbitrage is sufficiently important to prevent the taxpayer from deducting expenses in the current tax period, that will be payable in the future, even if those expenses are to be matched to income that has been reported in the current period according to the matching principle (except where the matter is insubstantial, or from the standpoint of the amount or the timing of the "advancing" of the expense).[278] As stated, according to Geier, the transition to the cash basis method for tax purposes (in lieu of the accrual basis method) is the proper course.[279] Nevertheless, it is possible merely to match the taxpayer's accounting statements based on the accrual basis method, for tax purposes, by preventing the tax advantages created from the timing differences between recognizing income or expenditure according to GAAP on the one hand, and the timing of the receipt or actual payment, as appropriate, on the other.[280]

According to Silk, it ought to be remembered that the value of consistency with GAAP is limited merely to the administrative advantage, and from this it follows that there is nothing to stop IRS from deviating from GAAP.[281]

Gunn does not discard the standards of financial accounting for tax purposes since they only have the value (albeit limited) of administrative convenience and effectiveness. According to him, the taxpayer should continue to be allowed to use his books for tax purposes (drawn up on the basis of GAAP) and, in that way, save the costs involved in maintaining two separate books of account (one for the firm's internal purposes according to GAAP, and the other for tax accounting). However, while maintaining that convenience, it ought to be remembered that its value is limited to the administrative advantage and from this it follows that there is nothing to stop IRS from deviating from accepted accounting principles. Based upon his examination of the statutory and judicial history, he deduced that tax accounting should not adapt itself to financial accounting principles.[282] Nevertheless, in the spirit of the Consistent Selective Approach, Gunn is prepared to confront not only rulings in which the case law has deviated from the perception of financial accounting, but also cases where the case law has followed accepted accounting principles, all on the basis of the criterion of whether, in the particular concrete circumstances, considerations of administrative convenience justified the deviation.[283]

Coplan is of the opinion that a "tax advantage" can be created when the taxpayer has the financial ability, from the cash-flow standpoint, in the context of "income" that has not yet been recognized as such according to GAAP. He does not object to the use of GAAP, up to the point at which the very use of GAAP creates such "tax advantages" for the taxpayer.[284]

According to Kleinrock, the advantage of GAAP for tax purposes is not limited merely to administrative convenience, but should be regarded as a threshold condition for complying with the requirement of "clearly reflected income", and should be viewed as an essential condition, and not merely a sufficient one.[285] Nevertheless, the significance of following GAAP for tax purposes is limited, and does not justify the creation of tax advantages from the standpoint of timing or quantification.[286]

Johnson, pushing the Dualistic Doctrine to its logical limits, favours the Separating Approach.[287] To his mind, in the past, income for tax purposes was defined in the framework of the Sixteenth Amendment to the Constitution, only as income "derived from capital from labor or from both combined".[288] However, this approach has been abandoned, and today the tax basis in the US includes every addition to wealth from whatever source, even if that "addition" has not been earned within the meaning of that expression according to GAAP.[289] Faithful to the Dualistic Doctrine, Johnson believes that accounting that is essentially applied on the basis of the principle of conservatism (prudence) (which requires following a minimalist approach in order to prevent optimism on the part of creditors and investors)[290] cannot serve as a "guiding light" for tax purposes where there is no room for minimizing income or profits.[291] According to him, both financial accounting and fiscal accounting are regulatory methods designed to operate against the interests of management to control its own self-reporting, in order to control and inspect management activity through financial reports that check the financial results of such activity for tax purposes.[292]

4.5 Between GAAP and fiscal accounting – Israeli tax law

In Israel, as in the UK[293] and in the US,[294] there is a series of specific statutory provisions in the Income Tax Ordinance (hereinafter: "**the Ordinance**" or "**ITO**")[295] that prescribe, in known and defined cases, accounting treatment for tax purposes that deviates from GAAP.[296] However, as distinct from the UK tax system, there are no clear statutory provisions that obligate following GAAP for tax purposes,[297] and by the same token there are no general provisions that enable a deviation from accounting principles or confer such a power on the Israeli tax authorities (hereinafter: "**ITA**"). For many years, the Singular Doctrine has reigned in all matters relating to timing and quantification.[298] Recently, however, it seems that this may no longer be the case.

4.5.1 Legislation

Unlike in the UK, no statutory provision exists that requires a tough "admission ticket" for tax purposes by means of requiring the filing of reports drawn in accordance with GAAP.[299] Unlike in the US, there is also no statutory provision.[300] This enables a flexible admission ticket specifying various possible reporting methods for tax purposes (some of which do not match GAAP).[301] In addition, the Israeli legislator has not drafted general statutory "exceptions" (as distinct from concrete provisions that relate to specific transactions) that determine when it is possible to deviate from financial accounting for tax purposes. In other words, exceptions such as "true and fair view" or "clearly reflected income" do not exist in Israeli tax legislation.

4.5.1.1 Flexibility relating to reporting methods

The ITO does not contain any general provision respecting the reporting method according to which taxpayers must file their returns. That is to say, on the face of it the ITO allows maximum flexibility in reporting for tax purposes, as in the absence of any other specific provision, taxpayers may report their income for tax purposes according to whatever method appears to them to be appropriate.

Notwithstanding this, some of the provisions contained in the ITO may be regarded as giving a legislative hint of that GAAP and the accrual basis method are starting points in reporting for tax purpose. Thus, for example, section 131(c) of the ITO, which adopts vague language, provides that a company's returns will be filed after being adjusted by the auditor, for tax purposes. It seems that while this provision of itself does not indicate the reporting method for tax purposes, it does hint at the Singular Doctrine and the Consistent Approach, as the section provides that "adjustments" are only to be made to the financial accounting reports that are obligatory under other provisions contained in the ITO.[302] In addition, the provisions of the Adjustments by Reason of Inflation Act[303] refer to reports of companies made according to GAAP for the purpose of making certain adjustments aimed at eliminating the inflationary effects in taxpayers' reports for tax purposes.[304] Although it is not possible to learn from this reference in and of itself, the manner of reporting for tax purposes, it can be seen as suggesting the Consistent Approach in the Israeli tax system.

Further evidence that the Israeli legislature regards GAAP as a starting point for reporting for tax purposes may be found in the tax reform bill regarding the adoption of IFRS Standards for tax reporting purposes.[305] The bill provides that in determining the chargeable income with respect to the 2007 and 2008 fiscal years, Accounting Standard No. 29, which the Israel Accounting Standards Board laid down as the directive regarding the making of financial reports by publicly traded companies according to the IFRS standards, will not apply.[306] It appears that had the legislature not assumed that reporting for tax purposes would be made in reliance on GAAP, then it would not have taken the trouble of preparing a bill in this regard.

In this regard, it should be noted that it is possible, *prima facie*, to view the bill as an expression of the deviation by the Israeli legislature from the Consistent Approach. However, the Explanatory Notes to the bill show that the legislative intent does not necessarily testify to a deviation from the new accounting principles, but is an attempt by the legislature to create a period of time during which the application of the rules will be tested. Thus, it does not necessarily express the deferral of the application of the new rules for tax purposes.

However, as we will see below, it does appear that the Consistent Approach of the Israeli tax system is a throwback from the past, and the upheavals that occurred in recent case law point to a new direction that deviates from the Consistent Approach.

4.5.1.2 *Statutory provisions regarding reporting of special transactions*

As distinct from US law, which comprises broad legislation regarding the reporting of special transactions, Israeli law is relatively slim on the subject, and suffices with surgical treatment in the form of provisions regarding the determination of the timing of the recognition of income in relation to certain classes of income and taxpayers.

4.5.1.2.1 RECOGNITION OF INCOME IN THE CASE OF CESSATION OF BUSINESS

With respect to persons reporting for tax purposes on the cash basis method, whose business has ceased, section 3(f) of the ITO provides that all the amounts in the hands of that taxpayer that have not been charged before the date of cessation will be regarded, due to the application of the cash basis method, as income in the fiscal year in which the income was received by the party entitled to those amounts, regardless of whether that person is a taxpayer himself or some other person. For the purposes of this section, cessation of a person's business also extends to a change in the taxpayer's activity, or his death. That is to say, the section sets and retains the cash basis method even after the taxpayer's activity has ceased. As a supplementary provision to this section, section 125A of the ITO provides that the tax rate that will apply to the taxpayer's income according to section 3(f) (that is received after death) will not exceed 40 per cent, in lieu of the marginal tax rates that could reach a tax rate of 47 per cent.[307]

4.5.1.2.2 RECOGNITION OF NON-RECURRING AND EXCEPTIONAL INCOME

Section 8 of the ITO regulates the timing of the recognition of income in the context of certain income for which the revenues are generally received on a certain date in a large non-recurring amount, where that income is generated over a number of reporting periods. The section enables the apportionment of that income over a number of reporting periods in order not to create a distortion with respect to the taxation of the income. Nonetheless, the purpose of the section is related to the progressive tax system customary in Israel, whereby the higher the taxpayer's income, the higher the tax rate imposed thereon. Thus, for example, were it not for the section, a taxpayer who worked over a number of reporting periods on developing a patent would be taxed on the income in respect of the sale of the patent in the fiscal year in which the amount was received.[308] As a result, the tax rate that would apply to him would be higher than that which would have applied had the income been reported over a number of reporting periods. The classes of income to which the section applies are, *inter alia*, income from the sale of a patent or design by the inventor, the sale of copyright by the author, salary differentials, vacation redemption monies and employee retirement benefits.

A provision similar to that described above, which this time relates to capital gains, may be found in section 91(e) of the ITO, whereby the tax on a capital gains in real terms will be computed as if the gain was produced in equal annual installments during a period not exceeding four fiscal years, or the period of the ownership of the asset (whichever is the shorter), and terminate in the tax year in which the gain arose. However, notwithstanding the similarity of the two sections, the provision contained in section 91(e) does not deal with the timing of the recognition of income, since apportioning the profit over a number of years is intended only for purposes of calculating the tax, but does not increase the income in those years. The entire gain is income in the year in which it was created.[309]

4.5.1.2.3 RECOGNITION OF CONTRACTORS' INCOME

Section 8A of the ITO provides for reporting methods for tax purposes regarding classes of taxpayers – a performing contractor and building contractor – who earn income from work where the execution period exceeds one year. In general, sections 8A(a) and 8A(b) provide for "work-in-progress" (which may also be called the supplementary rate method) for purposes of a performing contractor's reports who performs work following an order from customers, while section 8A(c) provides for the "completed works" method regarding a building contractor who builds at his own expense and assumes the risks and responsibility involved in the construction.

With regard to a "performing contractor": section 8A(a), which provides for the classes of work to which the provisions of the section apply, does not relate only to construction work, but applies to all classes of work where the execution period exceeds one year. This broad definition includes, in the main, work which by its very nature a single year report does not properly reflect the gain or the loss. Thus, this framework includes various forms of production, such as vessel and aircraft construction and the like. In any event, classes of work in which profit and loss can be determined with reasonable certainty in the scope of less than one year – except for construction work – will not be included within the ambit of this section. Section 8A(b) allows a taxpayer, within the framework of the "work-in-progress" method, to elect between two sub-methods for determining the pace of the progress of the work: the first is "the financial volumes" method, and the second is "the quantitative volume" method. According to these methods, the taxpayer will report his income in the fiscal year in which he completed at least 25 per cent of the "financial" or "the quantitative" volume of the work, according to the method that he has elected.

According to the financial reporting method, chargeable income in the fiscal year is computed according to the following formula:

Income reported until the year 0000

$$- \left\{ \begin{array}{c} \text{Assessment of profit} \\ \text{for the year} \end{array} \times \frac{\text{Total expenses until the year 0000}}{\text{Assessment of overall expenses}} \right\}$$

In the "financial volume" method, the only amount that is certain from the standpoint of the taxpayer is the amount of the expenses that have been invested in the project in the specific fiscal year and in the previous fiscal years, while the other two data – the total expenditure expected in the project and the amount of the estimated profit from the project in its entirety – are only based on assessments. The ratio of the progress of the work (or the progress in the financial volume of the work) in each year is fixed according to the ratio between the expenses that have been invested until that year and the estimate of the overall expenses. The percentage obtained is multiplied by the estimated profit, and the profit reported until that year is deducted from the result.

In the "quantitative volume" method, in each year the taxpayer will recognize part of the expected profit that is equal to the percentage of the completion of the project. The formula appears thus: estimated profit × the proportionate part performed in such year. That is, in such a case, the estimated overall profit will be multiplied by the ratable quantity that was performed as of such date, which will be calculated according to engineering data that will be fixed according to, and by, professionals who are expert in the field.

As regards losses of performing contractors, section 8A(b)(2) of the

ITO provides that a loss from continuing work will be available for setoff only after the taxpayer has completed at least 50 per cent of the quantitative or financial volume of the project.

With respect to a "building contractor": section 8A(c)(2)(a) of the ITO provides the "completed works" method according to which a building contractor reports his income as from the first tax year in which the building "is usable". In this connection, section 8A(c)(1) of the ITO provides that a building will be deemed "usable" if it is connected to the electricity grid, or the conditions for receiving a certificate of occupancy according to the Planning and Building Law 5725–1965 have been fulfilled. According to this method, in the first reporting year the taxpayer will report all the income that he had up to that year (including income in the tax year), and in the subsequent tax years, will report the income of the respective tax year. This means that all income received up to the tax year in which the building will be deemed to be usable will be regarded as income in advance that is not liable to tax until that date.

Thus, for example, if the taxpayer sells the entire building in a single tax year, he will report all the income and expenses that he had in that year. If, as opposed to this, the taxpayer sells the building in parts, then in the tax year in which the construction is completed and the building becomes usable he will report all the income that accrued in the preceding and the current tax years. Thereafter, each year he will report the income from the sales of each and every year. In the case of a sale in parts, the expenses will be computed according to the proportionate share of the expenses incurred on account of the part sold, the proportionate share being computed pursuant to the area that the part sold bears in relation to the entire area of the building. In any event, losses will not be permitted for set-off in the tax years preceding that in which the building becomes usable.

As we see, the deduction of direct costs in continuing works is inherently regulated by the recognition methods of income that have been fixed for two classes of contractors. However, these recognition methods show the need to arrange the deduction of administrative and general expenses and interest expenses, which, in most cases, cannot be specifically identified with the various working units. In order to solve this problem, specific provisions have been laid down in section 18D of the ITO, which permits administrative and general expenses and interest expenses for the working units that the contractor incurs or that accrue during performance, for land that is business inventory and for other income received in that tax year.

In general, the mechanism operates in a manner whereby the administrative and general expenses are appropriated against working units and land, for whose income the reporting date has yet to begin, and which are permitted on the recognition date of the income of the working units, in accordance with section 8A of the ITO, as described above. As regards administrative and general expenses, the section directs that for each working unit a proportionate share of those expenses will be appropriated, being the ratio between the total amount of the expenses expended by the taxpayer in the tax year for executing that working unit and the overall expenses that were incurred by him in that tax year for executing all the working units, with the addition of the other income that he had in the tax year. The balance of the administrative and general expenses that has not been appropriated to the working units according to this formula will thus be allowed for deduction on a current basis.

As regards the deduction of interest expenses, the section directs that a proportionate share of the interest expenses be appropriated to each working unit or to land in accordance with the ratio between the total accumulated expenses incurred by the taxpayer by the end of the tax year for making such working unit or for purchasing that land and the total sum of accumulated expenses that he incurred by the end of the tax year for executing all the working units and for purchasing all the land, with the addition of the amount of the other income that he had in the tax year. Here, also, in practice, the interest expenses that are not appropriated according to this formula to working units or land are permitted for deduction as a current expense.

4.5.1.2.4 RECOGNITION OF INCOME FROM RENTAL

Section 8B of the ITO makes provision regarding income arising from the sources specified in sections 2(6) and 2(7), since it will be included in the taxpayer's chargeable income in the tax year in which it was received, even if it is income in advance that relates to future periods. The income originating in section 2(6) is income from rent, royalties, key-money, premiums and other profits deriving from any residential property ("rental income"). Income under section 2(7) of the ITO is income that derives from any property other than residential property, land or industrial buildings (such as intangible assets) (hereinafter: "**royalty income**"). Thus, the section in practice provides for this income to be reported according to the cash basis by being recognized and reported for tax purposes as income in the year it is received, even if the taxpayer reports his remaining income according to the accrual basis method.[310] Although not expressly stated in the section, it is easy to see that the application of this provision to taxpayers who report according to the cash basis method is meaningless, since in any event such taxpayers report their income on the date it is received. With respect to the expenses incurred in the tax years following the tax year in which the above income will be recognized, the section provides that they will be permitted for deduction against income from any source in the tax year in which they were incurred, provided that if it was not possible to deduct the expense in the tax year following that in which they were incurred they will be permitted for deduction in the tax year in which the income was received and the assessment for that year will be regarded as having been amended accordingly. By means of this provision, the legislature seeks to solve problems that could arise due to advancing the recognition of income prior to the date of its receipt, since the expenses that will be incurred in the future were not allowed for deduction against the taxpayer's other income as they were not used to create it according to section 17 of the ITO, which makes the deduction of expenses conditional on their being used in the production of the income in the tax year.[311] It seems that this provision originated due to the difficulties that were encountered in regard to income from rent and royalties during periods of inflation, as taxpayers reporting according to the accrual basis method report income in its nominal amount while claiming expenses at their value in real terms.

4.5.1.2.5   RECOGNITION OF INCOME FROM PREMIUMS BY INSURANCE COMPANIES

According to section 49 of ITO, advances received by an insurance company (e.g. premiums in respect of insurance policies having an expiry date after the end of the fiscal year) are taxable in the year in which they are received. Coupled with "advancing" recognition of income for the insurance company as of the date on which the premium is received, the provision contained in the section enables the insurance company to deduct a reserve for risks as an expense for tax purposes according to the "accepted percentage adopted by the company in relation to its operations as a whole for such risks", on condition that the percentage is reasonable, and is in addition to the normal deductions to which it is entitled according to law.

4.5.1.2.6   RECOGNITION OF INCOME FROM EXCHANGE RATE DIFFERENTIALS

Section 8C of the ITO provides that a taxpayer's income from exchange rate differentials will be deemed income in the tax year in which it accrues, even where income is reported on a cash basis. It seems that this provision emerged from the *Central Printing* case,[312] in which the question arose regarding a taxpayer who reported according to the accrual basis method, as to the proper date for taxing exchange rate differentials inuring to the taxpayer for monies that he put on deposit. In this connection, the district court ruled that income deriving from exchange rate differentials on a deposit will not be recognized for tax purposes cumulatively, according to the accrual basis method, but only on the date on which the asset is realized. Before this ruling was reversed by the Supreme Court, the section was enacted to regulate the date of the taxation of exchange rate differentials in the hands of taxpayers generally, regardless of whether the differentials are reported for tax purposes or for accounting purposes.

4.5.1.2.7 RECOGNITION OF CAPITAL GAINS

In the case of capital gains, the Israeli legislature has determined special provisions regarding the timing of the recognition of a capital gain, as income in relation to both a capital gain deriving from the sale of real estate[313] as well as for any other capital gain.[314] According to these provisions, income from a capital gain will be imputed to the taxpayer according to the date of the agreement for the sale of the asset that resulted in the capital gain. This date does not depend upon the date on which the taxpayer's right to receive the income crystallizes (in the spirit of the accrual basis method), nor is it in any way related to the date on which the taxpayer actually receives the proceeds (in the spirit of the cash basis method).[315]

4.5.1.3 Silence on the part of the legislature

The foregoing thus shows that except for specific reference to a number of particular transactions or certain classes of income, Israeli law has refrained from laying down express provisions that favor any particular reporting method as against any other (except for an indirect reference to the accrual basis method with respect to companies), and has refrained from determining a binding standard for reporting (such as the "true and fair view" or "clearly reflect income"), and above all, it has not conferred any express power upon ITA to deviate from the reporting method that has been adopted by the taxpayer.

4.5.2 The case law

Although support may be found in Israeli case law for the Consistent Approach, as well as for the Consistent Selective Approach, it appears that in recent years the Consistent Selective Approach has become entrenched as the preferred approach. In the past, the accepted rule was that in the absence of a provision to the contrary in the tax legislation, GAAP should be followed for tax purposes. However, in using the expression "accepted accounting principles" for this purpose, the courts have not distinguished between GAAP (which is referred to by the courts as the accrual basis method) and the existing practice of reporting various classes of activities or sectors on a cash basis, although this practice (as mentioned above) does not in any way reflect the standards of financial accounting.

   In *Hashomrim*,[316] the question arose whether a taxpayer (whose business was providing printing services) that managed its books for financial purposes according to GAAP (i.e. on the accrual basis) was entitled to report its income for tax purposes based on the "cash basis", or whether it was required to report (for tax purposes) according to the accrual basis method, as ITA asserted. In light of the legislature's silence regarding the mandatory reporting method for tax purposes, and since the court's starting point was that GAAP recognizes both of the methods (i.e. both the accrual basis, and the cash basis methods), the Supreme Court ruled that the accounting practice that the taxpayer used in filing its returns were binding on ITA.[317]

The court also addressed the question of the timing of the recognition of income and held that in the absence of provisions in the ITO on the subject the accounting practice would apply for tax purposes.[318] Thus, this case can be interpreted as a quasi-adoption of an "extreme" Consistent Approach, in the sense that as long as there is no statutory provision to the contrary the reporting method used by the taxpayer according to any recognized accounting practice (not necessarily GAAP) will be the one that will be adopted. The above case is only one of many. In *Nakid*,[319] *Central Printing*,[320] *Israeli Shipyards*,[321] *Ginzburg*,[322] *Tambour*[323] and other cases,[324] the Israeli courts have repeatedly adopted the Consistent Approach. The extreme expression of the Consistent Approach in Israel can be found in *Dumbo*[325] and *Raznitzki*.[326] Both cases held that as long as there is no legislative provision to the contrary, the reporting practice used by the taxpayer for tax purposes will be adopted, even if that practice is not in accordance with GAAP, and even if the taxpayer used GAAP for financial purposes.[327] With respect to questions regarding the "classification" of income (as distinct from the question of measuring it), it seems that the controlling approach (as expressed, e.g. in *Bernstein*[328] and in *Yaacobi*,[329] and in the matter of *Pi Glilot*[330] and *Sharon*[331]) is that accountancy theory is to be regarded only as an aid and not as a source for making up a deficiency. The court will take note of it as an interpretive source, but nothing more.[332] Nonetheless, in recent years support for the Singular Doctrine and the Consistent Approach has eroded. The district court in the third *Amisragas* case[333] and the Supreme Court in the *Amisragas-Pazgas* case[334] (relying on the controlling approach in US case law discussed above) chose to abandon the Consistent Approach, and while adopting the Consistent Selective Approach, allowed a gross deviation from GAAP.[335]

4.5.3 Administrative directives

ITA has expressed its position that the tax returns of corporate bodies (as distinct from individuals) must be based on GAAP, unless those bodies are related to the services sector.[336] ITA also noted that both individuals and companies that carry on activity involving the holding of stock are bound to report on the basis of GAAP for tax purposes.[337] ITA issued instructions that a company that reports for its own purposes on an accrual basis (even if it is in the service sector), will not be allowed to report on a "cash basis" for tax purposes.[338] In all of those directives, no statement was made implying any intention on the part of ITA to allow taxpayers to deviate from the standards of GAAP on questions of quantification or timing.

4.5.4 *Comments*

It seems that the academic commentary in Israel has adopted the Singular Doctrine and the Consistent Approach almost without argument. According to Namdar,[339] Raphael and Mehulall,[340] Witkon and Neeman,[341] Strauss[342] and other scholars,[343] fiscal accounting, and in particular the question of the timing of income and expenses, must be based on GAAP, as long as this does not contradict other express provisions in the ITO.

4.6 Between GAAP and fiscal accounting – summary and comments

In reviewing how three tax systems address the relationship between financial accounting and the tax laws on subjects of measuring and timing, we have found diverse and opposing viewpoints.

The UK tax system favors strict conformity in the reporting method (according to GAAP), and severely limits HMRC from deviating from GAAP. By doing so, it seeks to ensure uniformity and certainty, although possibly at the price of eroding tax values in those cases where GAAP dictates solutions that do not necessarily coincide with the essential purpose of the tax laws. **The US tax system** exhibits flexibility in the reporting method, but grants IRS broad latitude to deviate from the principles of GAAP for the sake of maintaining tax values. The system thus seeks to ensure fiscal justice, for which it pays a price in terms of uniformity and certainty. **The Israeli tax system** allows maximum flexibility regarding the reporting method (in the absence of legislation to the contrary), although support may be found both for the Singular Doctrine as well as the Dualistic Doctrine. In this, the system seeks to secure liberalism and save reporting costs, although in doing so it may compromise fiscal justice, as well as uniformity and certainty.

We saw above that none of the various tax systems has created an independent, coherent method that is completely detached from either GAAP or accounting practices that have emerged outside the world of tax law, in order to determine separate, independent rules for quantifying and timing income for tax purposes. All of the tax systems reviewed took a reporting method based on GAAP (the accrual basis method) or another accounting practice (the cash basis method) as their starting point, and have based themselves on reporting methods that were created without any connection to the world of taxation.

The UK tax system currently favors adopting the "pure" accrual basis method for quantifying income and determining the timing thereof, subject to defined exceptions under which it is still possible to report according to the cash basis method. Adopting this method in the spirit of the Singular Doctrine and the Consistent Approach derives from the desire to harmonize financial accounting and tax accounting. It would appear that the desire for harmonization derives not merely from considerations of convenience, but emerges from a global perception that GAAP, generally, and the accrual basis method in particular, reflect an "economic truth" that should be preferred to any alternative reporting methods that may be employed for tax purposes.

The US tax system permits the adoption of the accrual basis method, the cash basis method, or hybrid methods. However, it does not adopt either the "pure" accrual basis method established by GAAP, or the "pure" cash basis method. In adopting these methods for purposes of quantifying income and determining the timing of income recognition, changes and adjustments have been introduced by legislation and case law. These changes make the accrual basis method and the cash basis method, as adopted for tax purposes, materially different from those very same methods as laid down by GAAP or the accounting practice by which they were created.

While the UK tax system favors the accrual basis method in recognition of the fact that this is the method most appropriate for tax purposes from the standpoint of the "economic truth", it would seem that the US tax system's choice of adopting a broad range of reporting methods was made for precisely the opposite reasons. The multiplicity of the IRC tax legislation sections that deal with the subjects of tax accounting, and the changes or general adjustments that have been made both in legislation and in the cases with respect to the accrual basis method and the cash basis method, merely testify to the US IRS's lack of basic faith in the reporting methods that have emerged outside of tax law. Although it might appear that the US tax system indeed favors the accrual basis method as against the cash basis method due to the mandatory provision that requires taxpayers of certain classes to report only by the accrual basis method, nonetheless, this preference is not sufficiently material to totally deny the possibility of reporting on the cash basis for some taxpayers and, in any event, even the preference for the accrual basis method is not for the "pure" accrual basis method as established by GAAP, but relates to the "mixed" accrual basis method that results from combining what has been developed by GAAP on the one hand, and the additions made thereto or detracted therefrom by legislation and judicial rulings.

We can thus say that while the UK tax system, in the spirit of the Singular Doctrine, has chosen the "pure" accrual basis method on the basis of an informed choice of income quantification and timing rules that it regards as preferable for tax purposes, the choice of the tax system in the US of a "mixed" accrual basis method and a "mixed" cash basis method has its source elsewhere. The choice of those methods was first and foremost made for considerations of administrative convenience, concurrently with the lack of basic faith in all of the reporting methods. Only against the background of this lack of faith can one explain many of the deviations from those authentic methods, and the manner in which they have been adopted for tax purposes, and only against the background of this lack of faith can we explain the very existence and widespread use of IRC§446(b), as examined above.

The Israeli tax system, like that of the US, does not impose the accrual basis method except in given, identified cases, and permits the use of the cash basis method for most taxpayers who perform services. Despite a number of expressions in case law and professional guidelines by ITA regarding the preference of the accrual basis method as against the cash basis method, these expressions have not been translated into any substantial conduct that would prevent or limit the use of the cash basis method.

As distinct from the US tax system, but like the UK tax system, until the IFRS was applied in Israel in 2008, the extent of the Israeli tax accounting deviations from the "pure" accrual basis method had been relatively few, and were limited to defined, identifiable transactions (such as service contracts, long-term construction projects, currency-linked transactions, and the like). However, recently, following the application of the IFRS in Israel, and the enactment of an express provision whereby IFRS will not apply for tax purposes (for a trial period) while reporting will be made according to the IS-GAAP prior to its being changed by the IFRS, the trend has changed. As of now, the accrual basis method is adopted for tax purposes in Israel, although not the "pure" accrual basis method, i.e. the position of the valid GAAP in Israel but the "mixed" accrual basis method, i.e. the reporting method according to the previous GAAP (prior to its having been changed by the GAAP that is based on the IFRS).

In contrast to the UK tax system, the extent of the Israeli tax accounting deviations from the cash basis method is limited, amid broad acceptance of that method. It seems that what lies behind the approach of the Israeli tax system to the proper reporting method of quantifying and timing income for tax purposes is not faith in the "economic truth" that is inherent in the "pure" accrual basis method, and certainly not the "economic truth" to be found in the cash basis method. The very acceptance of the two methods indicates the absence of an informed choice deriving from prior thought that is based on faith. In my view it can be said that what has guided the Israeli legislature in adopting the "pure" accrual basis method and the "pure" cash basis method is, first and foremost, considerations of convenience. However, as stated earlier, with the adoption of the IFRS for finance accounting purposes, and its non-adoption for tax accounting purposes (in close alliance to the accrual basis method established by the "old" Israeli GAAP), it can be said that these considerations of convenience no longer exist.

In my opinion, neither the Singular Doctrine nor the Dualistic Doctrine are immune from criticism, and by the same token it would also be proper to say that not one of the reporting methods for quantifying income and determining the timing thereof, as adopted by the tax systems reviewed, is immune from criticism. This criticism results in the main from the essential, proper relationship between the purpose of tax law, which maintains the preservation of tax values, on one hand, and determining the timing of the recognition of income as a means that is designed to accomplish this objective, on the other. This relationship must be examined (in the same way that any other examination of the relationship between the objective and the means is to be tackled) in accordance with the Proportionality Principle.

4.6.1 The effect of the Proportionality Principle

Determining the timing of the recognition of income (and expenses) for tax purposes is no more than a means to serve the purpose of tax law which is, as we have said, to collect fair tax, as well as tax values, which are a specification of the concept of "fairness" that is inherent in that objective. In testing the means for determining the timing of the recognition of income for tax purposes that is appropriate for serving tax values and the purpose of fairness, it is proper to test the relationship between them according to the Proportionality Principle.

According to this principle, it is not sufficient for the goal to be worthy, no less important (and possibly even more so) is that the means employed in order to achieve the goal be appropriate, inflicting no more harm than is necessary in order to achieve the goal.[344] There are three (cumulative) tests for measuring proportionality:[345]

First, the means will not be considered as meeting the Proportionality Principle if they do not serve the goal for which they are designed, i.e. the means must fit the purpose (**"the rational means test"**).[346]

Second, the means will not be regarded as meeting the Proportionality Principle if, despite the fact that they fit the purpose, other means can be found that achieve the same purpose but inflict lesser harm to other values (**"the less harmful means test"**).[347]

Third, the means will not be regarded as meeting the Proportionality Principle even though they are suitable for achieving the purpose and even if there are no other means that cause less damage to other values, where the damage that is caused to the other values by those means is so grievous that it justifies waiving the purpose itself (**"the relative means test"**).[348]

Applying the Proportionality Principle to all the above tests[349] for our purposes leads to the conclusion that a tax system must not attempt to achieve the proper purpose of the tax values (including preventing unjust tax advantages) by means that do not suit the purpose, or that would result in greater harm to other values.

As we noted above, determining the timing of the recognition of income for tax purposes necessarily comprises two issues: first, the question of the effect of the timing of recognition of income on the timing of collection of tax ("the Collection Question") and, second, the question of quantifying income for tax purposes according to the measure of the income on the date that it is recognized as such for tax purposes ("the Quantification Question").[350] The question of the timing of collection is not material for accomplishing the objective of collecting "fair" tax and achieving tax values (as long as just payment of the tax is ensured). But even if those objectives are achieved, the preference for advancing collection is problematic in light of other legitimate public purposes that are of no lesser value.[351] The quantification question goes to the very heart of the purpose of tax law and tax values. If as a result of time differences, income and profits for tax purposes will be quantified in a manner that results in tax not being imposed on profits in real terms, then the various tax values will be infringed and/or eroded, and the accomplishment of the objective of fair tax collection will not be achieved.

We shall thus examine the Singular Doctrine, the Dualistic Doctrine and the various reporting methods that have been applied in the tax systems reviewed in light of the Proportionality Principle.

4.6.2 Criticism of the Singular Doctrine

Supporters of this doctrine have emphasized considerations of convenience (mainly the saving of maintaining two separate account books), considerations of certainty (that have been mentioned above) and the consideration of the scientific knowledge that has been accumulated in GAAP.[352] As against the advantages of this doctrine, however, we cannot overlook the following disadvantages.

4.6.2.1 Limitations of GAAP

To say that financial accounting theory does not reflect economic integrity is an understatement. Accounting theory itself is aware of its own limitations. The IASB Framework states, *inter alia*, that financial reports, while they meet the common requirements of most users, are unable to supply all the information required to make economic decisions.[353] GAAP did not come about from an objective examination of the environmental economic conditions, but is based mainly on the tests of accounting practice.[354] Moreover, this theory leaves much to presentation of profits and losses, and cannot be "an exact science".[355] There are many examples where a certain form of presentation of an expense, or income, or "timing games" have transformed an economic loss into profit from out of nowhere, or the opposite.[356] Others emphasize with a certain irony the distinction between "generally accepted", which describes GAAP, and "generally acceptable".[357] GAAP itself allows a margin for different and varied improvisations.[358]

4.6.2.2 Possible erosion of tax values

If the intention of the Singular Doctrine is to attempt to apply GAAP for tax purposes in a "blind", strict and sweeping manner, it appears that doing so is problematic from the standpoint of the tax values that we addressed above,[359] since these tax values are of no concern to GAAP.[360] We have seen that the question of timing is fundamental in dealing with tax values like neutrality, efficiency and preventing unjust tax advantages. On the other hand, though it is not correct to say that GAAP completely disregards the time value of money;[361] nonetheless, we have already seen that on the issue of the timing of the recognition of income and liabilities, such disregard does exist.[362]

The "pure" accrual basis method, created by the GAAP, was designed to serve the purposes lying at the basis of the theory of financial accounting, and does so without imputing much meaning to the value of money on the axis of time, as the protection of investors and other third parties who are relevant will not be compromised even if the income and profitability of the firm will be presented in nominal values that are lower than the value in real terms of the money. This is not so when we are dealing with determining the timing of the recognition of income for tax purposes.

The tax system that unconditionally adopts the "pure" accrual basis method in fact waives collection of genuine tax in real terms, and thereby apparently uses means that do not serve the objective of "just" tax collection. In other words, such a tax system does not meet the first test of the Proportionality Principle that we mentioned above ("the rational means test"), namely the test according to which the means (and in our case the reporting method for tax purposes) serves the purpose for which it is intended (in our case the collection of "fair" tax and the preservation of tax values).

Thus, we see that the Singular Doctrine and the adoption of the "pure" accrual basis method for tax purposes are not free of criticism, mainly in relation to the concern over an erosion of tax values. However, as we will see below, the Dualistic Doctrine is also problematic and is not immune to criticism.

4.6.3 Criticism of the Dualistic Doctrine

The supporters of this doctrine have placed emphasis on the tax authorities' considerations of administrative convenience.[363] They have also sought to rely on legislative history[364] and on the various tax values that are inherent in this doctrine.[365] However, beyond the intrinsic operational inconvenience of two separate accounting systems,[366] two further considerations that raise grave doubt as to the logic of this doctrine need to be emphasized. The first I will call "the ethical consideration", and the second "the practical consideration".

4.6.3.1 *The ethical consideration*

It is indeed correct that the essential purpose of GAAP is not identical to the purpose of tax law.[367] This, however, is not enough to justify the deviation of tax accounting from GAAP. The question must be whether this difference in purpose justifies, by itself, the application of different rules to measuring profit (including the timing thereof). The investor, the creditor, as well as other relevant third parties (hereinafter collectively referred to as "**interested parties**") may all have different, varied object-ives, all of which may be legitimate. Nonetheless, despite the different objectives that interested parties have in the taxpayer's financial state-ments, each one is still "compelled to make do" with that financial infor-mation that is conveyed by means of financial statements drawn up in accordance with GAAP, and he is not entitled to separate accounting rules that better serve his objectives.

The proper question, therefore, is not whether tax laws have diffe-rent goals from those of accounting standards, but whether these different goals justify different accounting. It would appear that justifying different accounting for tax purposes depends, first and foremost, on what the precise nature of the interest that tax accounting (as opposed to GAAP) seeks to advance. If, according to the Dualistic Doctrine, tax accounting must "solve" the Collection Question[368] by promoting the interest of speedy collection by the Treasury (hereinafter "**the speedy collection interest**") then, this interest, as any similar interest of other interested parties, does not justify deviating from GAAP. This may be clarified as follows.

Since the *Thor* case,[369] the support expressed for the Dualistic Doctrine has served in most cases as a basis for preferring the interpretation that supports IRS.[370]

The argument regarding the existence of different goals, to the extent that it is intended to justify deviating from GAAP for tax purposes, appears more like an excuse intended to advance the "speedy collection interest". As conservatism does not serve the needs of other interested parties, the very fact that this feature does not serve the goal of tax collec-tion is not, in itself, sufficient. From this standpoint, it is difficult to see why the "speedy collection interest" transcends similar or opposing, but no less legitimate interests of other interested parties.

Preferring the "speedy collection interest" of the Treasury as grounds for creating tax accounting that is different from GAAP could lead to discrimination against other interested parties. Take, for example, the Dualistic Doctrine, whereby the Treasury takes its share of "profit" that has yet to be created. What happens if such profit does not materialize over time, and the taxpayer becomes insolvent? Generally, this advancing of tax would be regarded as a preference of the Treasury as a creditor. However, according to the Dualistic Doctrine, this problem is "resolved" by redefining "profit" for tax purposes. Is it proper that the "speedy collection interest" should create definitions of "profit" for tax purposes in a manner whereby another interested party will be precluded from obtaining its share in the indebtedness or profit, and will also be denied repayment following the preference of the Treasury as a creditor?

It is true that tax collection is an important public interest. However, by the same token, other public interests exist, such as that of development of proper trade relations, including payment of debts to creditors. It seems that even if one might say that public considerations override "the private pocket"[371] in the broader context, it is doubtful whether the "speedy collection interest" as grounds for deviating from GAAP indeed favour the "public pocket" (i.e. that same objective that this interest seeks to advance).

Even if an advantage results to the public pocket from not applying GAAP for tax purposes, this advantage does not necessarily exist in the long run. From the public consideration standpoint, applying the Dualistic Doctrine and deviating from GAAP merely in order to promote the "speedy collection interest" violates the tax value of certainty,[372] because of the lack of clarity concerning how to measure income for tax purposes. It also violates the tax value of efficiency,[373] because taxpayers would have to bear the costs of maintaining separate books (one for financial purposes and the other for tax purposes). Therefore, the tax values that the Dualistic Doctrine seeks to protect by creating separate tax accounting are undermined.

But most of all, it would seem that creating an advantage to the Treasury vis-à-vis not merely the taxpayer himself, but also against his creditors, employees, shareholders and other relevant third parties that have interests in the taxpayer's earnings, cannot be decided merely on the basis that GAAP and tax laws have different objectives. In other words, applying the Proportionality Principle (in all its tests, i.e. "the rational means test", "the less harmful means test" and "the relative means test") will show that the "speedy collection interest" (i.e. the interest of advancing tax payments) is not a worthy goal that justifies deviation from GAAP and by doing so paying the "price" of violating tax values (like certainty and efficiency), as well as other "prices" that the public pocket is required to pay.

4.6.3.2 The practical consideration

None of the tax systems reviewed that prefer the Dualistic Doctrine have succeeded in creating tax accounting as a regulated theory that constitutes a substitute for GAAP.[374]

It seems that even the ardent supporters of the Dualistic Doctrine and of the Separating Approach will not seek to adopt the "pure" cash basis method as a proper alternative for the accrual basis method.[375] The defects of this method are far too many to number and summarize in a work of this kind, but let us just say that this reporting method intermingles the means and the result. Both economic theory[376] and finance accounting[377] regardless of where the source lies, define "income" in terms of result, that is, an increase in property along the axis of time, or a reduction of liabilities along the axis of time. The cash basis method is totally unrelated to the result and focuses just on the means. Receiving money or paying money cannot of itself testify to the taxpayer's profits or his losses as the question immediately arises as to the purpose of receiving the money or for what reason is it being paid. Thus, for example, if the taxpayer has made a payment to purchase stock, his capital has not changed at all and the only thing that has happened is that one asset (cash) has been converted into another (stock) of equal value. The same applies to the receipt of cash in respect of inventory of equivalent value and of equivalent cost that has been sold.

Accrual accounting information more fully reflects the overall effects of managerial actions or efforts on future cash flows than cash flow realizations in any given period. As a result, accrual accounting information is more efficient than cash basis method information.[378] The cash basis method is very simple, but not as useful. It records cash transactions only and ignores everything else, like how much is owed to you for sales that have been made and not paid for, the unpaid vendors, and so on. With the cash basis method there are no accounts payable, no accounts receivable, and no inventory.[379] Since the cash basis method does not recognize receivables or payables, it is not an accurate method of measuring profit.[380] The cash basis method has been described more than once as the arbitrariness and evasiveness method of accounting,[381] and by using this method it is extremely difficult to determine the actual profit or loss, because cash basis accounting does not acknowledge money that is due or money that is owed.[382] Moreover, supporters of the Dualistic Doctrine will certainly not seek to adopt the "pure" cash basis method for tax purposes, as it so easily allows the planning of the timing of the recognition of income for tax purposes as a means of deferring acceptance of income or advancing the timing of the payment.

If supporters of the Dualistic Doctrine seek to rely specifically on the "mixed" cash basis method which has, by means of manipulations such as the Constructive Receipt Doctrine, attempted to downplay, to a certain extent, the tax advantages that can be derived from the cash basis method in all aspects relating to the timing of the recognition of income, we would note that this "patchwork" in the form of the "mixed" cash basis method cannot provide a real answer regarding the financial condition of the taxpayer and his income. It is no accident that the UK tax system has chosen to completely abolish the possibility of using the cash basis method, nor is it by chance that the US tax system (where it will be remembered the Dualistic Doctrine prevails) has greatly limited the possibility of using the cash basis method (which is also "mixed"), and is also aided by doctrines such as the "constructive receipt" and "safety valve" doctrines under IRC§446(b).

From the practical standpoint, therefore, with the absence of a real alternative, it seems that supporters of the Dualistic Doctrine are left with no more than alternatives such as the "mixed" accrual basis method and the various hybrid methods on which to rely. However, these methods, as their names imply, are an intermingling of rules and principles from the field of financial accounting and rules or principles that originate to some extent in the cases provided for by tax legislation. But in most cases, as we have seen, they have been created *ad hoc* by the courts, and in the exercise of the tax authorities' power in isolated cases for which they were relevant at the time.

In this way, tax accounting has been created by tribunals by means of *ad hoc* rulings.[383] In the absence of a clear and regulated system to measure income for tax purposes, the creation of tax accounting by means of *ad hoc* rulings not only violates the tax values mentioned above, but also results in harm to the administrative convenience of both the taxpayer and the tax authorities themselves.[384]

Hence, for both ethical and practical considerations, the Dualistic Doctrine does not stand up to scrutiny.

4.6.4 *The proper balance*

As we have seen, and as shall see below, the question of timing recognition of income for tax purposes can only be understood against the general background of the system's approach to the correlation between tax laws and accounting theory. In a tax system that is based on the Dualistic Doctrine (such as the US system) it is "easy" for the courts to find "solutions" to the question of timing recognition of income for tax purposes in a manner that deviates from GAAP. In a system that is based on the Singular Doctrine (such as that adopted in the UK), the fiscal solution in relation to timing recognition of income conforms to that of GAAP to the same receivables. Between these two opposing doctrines, a proper balance must be sought. That proper balance must aspire to embrace the strengths of the two opposing doctrines, and at the same time seek to neutralize their disadvantages. This balance must relate both to form and content.

4.6.4.1 *As to form (the means)*

It is submitted that the proper balance requires that acceptance of the Singular Doctrine will not allow reliance on GAAP in cases where such reliance violates the tax values mentioned above, including the value of preventing unjustified tax advantages. However, as distinct from the Dualistic Doctrine, deviation from GAAP must be made in the spirit of the Consistent Approach, namely only with clear and explicit legislation.[385] As we have seen, if, in order to safeguard tax values, deviation from GAAP will be allowed other than by means of legislation, then some of those tax values themselves, in whose name this deviation was requested from the very outset (including the values of "efficiency" and "certainty"), will be violated.[386]

4.6.4.2 *As to content (the Proportionality Principle)*

It is submitted that the very same "proper balance" dictates not merely the form (namely, by legislation), but must also dictate the content (of the legislation). As to that content, while we have not found any valid reason for justifying deviation from GAAP merely in order to solve the Collection Question by promoting the "speedy collection interest",[387] this is not the case where tax accounting seeks to advance the tax values to which GAAP is indifferent, including preventing unjust tax advantages.[388] As we have seen, in timing the recognition of income and expenses GAAP does not take into account the time value of money.[389] In order to uphold the tax value of preventing unjust tax advantages, tax law should not be indifferent to the economic distortion that could be generated if income and liabilities were measured in each annual year for calculating tax in nominal and unrealistic terms. Therefore, tax values demand a solution for the Quantification Question.[390] However, this in of itself is not enough. This content must not extend beyond the measure required to serve the tax values themselves. Put differently, the means should meet the Proportionality Principle (in all its tests, i.e. "the rational means test", "the less harmful means test" and "the relative means test").

Applying this principle for solving the Quantification Question will ensure that deviating from GAAP for tax purposes as a means for accomplishing the objective of preserving tax values (including preventing unjust tax advantages) is an alternative that should be used only where such means would not result in greater harm to other values, and only where it is not possible to find other means that achieve the same purpose while inflicting lesser harm.

As we have seen, and will see below, in dealing with timing of the recognition of income and expenses none of the tax systems reviewed has found a solution to prevent unjust tax advantages by reliance on GAAP that meets the Proportionality Principle (in all its tests). To our mind, such a solution to the Quantification Question does exist,[391] but prior to its presentation we will review the answers that have been given by the tax systems reviewed to the question of timing recognition of income in cases of unearned receivables (like deposits or advances), and to the question of timing recognition of liabilities as expenses for tax purposes.

5 Timing of recognition of income from deposits

A "deposit", in its ordinary, day-to-day meaning, is a sum received that must be repaid on a particular date or when certain conditions are fulfilled. In this sense, there is no difference between a "deposit" and any other loan. Loan monies will not be regarded as "income" in the borrower's hands, since the increase in his assets is correspondingly "balanced" by the increase in his liability. The "increase" in the recipient's economic wealth is zero, and the absence of increase in the recipient's economic wealth means that no income has been generated.[1]

As we have seen, GAAP states that a deposit – which constitutes the recipient's liability – is not "income", and for this purpose accounting generally makes no distinction between the conditions of the repayment of the deposit or the date of the repayment in the future.[2] Clearly, where there is no obligation to repay the principal, then according to GAAP we are not dealing with a "deposit" since the liability will not "balance" the property that was received. However, what would the situation be if, alongside the obligation to repay the deposit principal in full, the recipient enjoys an economic benefit from advantages inherent in the timing of the repayment, or in the terms of repayment (hereinafter "**the benefit component**").

How does the existence of a benefit of this kind, which does not negate the character of the deposit as a liability according to financial accounting, affect the tax situation?

5.1 The Loan Approach and the Income Approach

On this issue, the tax systems reviewed adopt one of two possible approaches, which will be called the "**Loan Approach**" and the "**Income Approach**".[3]

5.1.1 The Loan Approach

This approach posits (similar to GAAP) that as long as an obligation exists to repay the principal of the deposit, any benefit component accruing to the recipient should be disregarded, and the deposit should be seen as a liability (like any loan) which cannot be treated as income. Only if it transpires that the obligation to repay the principal has been cancelled, and the deposit principal has become the recipient's property, will this principal become the recipient's income.

5.1.2 *The Income Approach*

This approach adopts a completely opposite view. It seeks to classify a deposit as income, subject to certain conditions, despite the obligation to repay it. According to this view, any benefit accruing to a recipient of a deposit (either in relation to the deposit principal, or the timing of the repayment, or the conditions of the repayment) will constitute grounds for classifying the deposit as "income". In this approach, as well, the question arises as to the proper "timing" of viewing the deposit as income, whether on the date of its receipt or, possibly, on some other date that corresponds to the accrual of the benefit to the recipient.

On the face of it, we might have expected a correlation between those who favor the Singular Doctrine and those who support the Loan Approach, whereby any deposit that carries with it a duty to repay the principal (whatever the terms and dates of repayment may be), will be regarded as a loan that does not invoke tax consequences on the date of its receipt. We might also have expected those who favor the Dualistic Doctrine to rely on the various "tax values", and argue that a receivable should be classified as a "deposit" for tax purposes, according to tests independent of accounting. According to this approach, where a deposit creates an economic advantage for the recipient, the "tax values" would appear to justify classifying the receivable in a manner that would negate its character as a "loan" (i.e. the Income Approach) or, at the least, justify the imposition of tax on the benefit component.

5.2 Timing of recognition of deposits as "income" – UK tax law

In the spirit of the Singular Doctrine, the UK approach is that a deposit is perceived as a loan as long as the recipient is under a duty to repay the deposit principal. Regardless of what the repayment terms or the timing of the repayment may be, there is no statutory provision in the UK that charges deposit principal, or that provides that deposit principal is tax exempt or is to be treated as a loan.[4] It seems that this conclusion flows essentially from the "source system",[5] which taxes income only if it falls into one of the categories of the sources prescribed by legislation. There is no legislation that classifies an income source that relates to a deposit or loan principal as income[6] and it appears that the settled case law on this subject is unequivocal.

5.2.1 The case law

The case law, although scanty, deals with borderline cases in which, it appears, it was clear that an economic benefit was conferred upon the holder of the deposit. The rule that becomes clear from the case law is that the economic benefit linked to a deposit (with respect to both the terms of repayment and the timing of repayment) is "immune" from tax.

In *Messrs Tattersall*,[7] a partnership conducted public auctions of race-horses. In its activity, it acted on behalf of its clients, who sought to sell their horses, in the capacity of an agent. At no point did any of the horses pass into its ownership, and in any event, it did not hold its own stock. According to the agreement between the partnership and the client, the sums due to the client from the sale were to be sent to the client by mail, only after a written instruction from him was received. With the passage of time, substantial sums were accumulated in the partnership as unclaimed debts to clients. According to the terms of the partnership agreement, the partnership distributed those "client debts" amongst the partners (every six years). The partners assumed a liability that if a demand arose from a client to repay a debt, it would be divided amongst the partners, who would bear the cost according to their share in the partnership's profits on the date the distribution was made. This was done without the partnership previously recognizing those client debts as "income".

HMRC, which recognized that the debt towards the client was not income at the time the sale proceeds were received, sought to treat the sums as income on the date on which those "debts" were distributed among the partners. However, the court ruled that a liability towards the client that is subject to the duty of repayment is the client's property, and the very distribution of this debt amount among the partners bore no legal significance with respect to the existence of such a debt towards the client. The debt remained a debt toward the client, and would not be regarded as income for tax purposes, even if the debt amount had been distributed to the partners, so long as those partners assumed the aforementioned liability.

In *Jay's Jewellers*,[8] it was held that deposits are not "income" on the date they are received, nor throughout the entire period that they are held by the recipient (whatever the repayment terms thereof may be). They become income only at the stage and on the date at which the recipient's obligation to repay expires.

In *Prices Tailors*,[9] the court ruled that "deposits" (which were in substance advances in respect of a future sale) that had been received at the time orders were placed (to purchase tailor-made suits), and which were not returned to customers, should be regarded as income on the date on which they were received, despite the fact that these deposits entitled the customer to a refund upon demand, and could be applied as payment for another suit when needed. The court drew an interesting distinction between this case and the *Messrs Tattersall* case, stating that in that case the deposits were, in effect, the customers' property and not the property of the taxpayer, while in the present case, the deposits were the taxpayer's property, despite the fact that a duty to repay or credit attached to them. Therefore, the court ruled that the judgment in *Messrs Tattersall* could not be applied to the facts of the present case, as the ownership of the money had already passed to the taxpayer at the moment the deposit was made, and the liability to repay the same was not absolute. This was sufficient in order to reject deferral of the timing of the recognition of the deposits as income.

As we will see below, this case was effectively overruled later.[10] It should also be emphasized that even if this case law had remained in effect (in relation to deposits that had not been returned to the payers), this judgment would be of no consequence for the question of the timing of the recognition of income from a deposit (which is meant to be repaid to the payer as distinct from the circumstances in the *Prices Tailors* case).

In *Anise*,[11] advertising companies occasionally received overpayments from customers (e.g. following the non-cancellation of standing orders), and in some cases, these overpayments were not returned to the customers. Until 1993, the sums were recorded to the credit of the customers, under "creditors", for six years. Thereafter, the sums were transferred to the profit and loss account, as exceptional income. In 1993, the companies decided to reduce the period during which they would treat the sums as a debt to customers to two years, so that "debts" that accrued during the five years preceding that date were transferred as income to the profit and loss statement. HMRC sought to regard these sums as business income when transferred to the profit and loss statement.

The special commissioner, who adjudicated the case, relying on the *Messrs Tattersall* case, ruled that these overpayments should not be regarded as part of the advertising companies' income from the business. In other words, that they had no source. In distinguishing this matter from the *Jay's Jewellers* case mentioned above, the special commissioner stated that, in that case, the receipt of the deposits was an integral part of the taxpayer's business, but this was not the situation here.

5.2.2 Administrative directives

HMRC itself rejected any reliance on the *Prices Tailors* case,[12] which is the only case from which a tax result can be inferred for a "deposit", and is different from what is required according to GAAP, and adopted under the Loan Approach.[13]

In addition to this, there are directives that relate to specific transactions that also adopt the approach that a deposit is to be treated like a loan in all respects, and not as "income", without discussing the question of the timing of the repayment of the deposit or the applicable terms of interest.[14]

5.3 Timing of recognition of deposits as "income" – US tax law

As we have said, in the UK the "source system" applies to all aspects of the definition of "income" for tax purposes. This leads to the result that only economic wealth from the specific sources enumerated in legislation will be taxable. In contrast, the US approach has adopted a broader interpretation, and the Supreme Court has repeatedly taken a broad view of the definition of "income" according to IRC§61(a), which includes income from any source within the ambit of that expression.[15]

However, for US tax purposes, not every financial benefit will be deemed "income" for the purpose of the Code. At least two minimum conditions must obtain: first, that something will be added to the taxpayer's economic wealth,[16] and second, that a "realization" event will occur, i.e. that such addition to wealth has been realized by the taxpayer.[17]

In the US, as in the UK, there is no statutory tax "exemption" for "income" from deposit principal. Similarly, there is no statutory provision that grants a tax exemption to the principal of a loan. The rule is that when the taxpayer receives money or another asset that he has an obligation to repay, the taxpayer has not been "enriched" from the transaction, and he has obtained no "income" within the meaning of that term contained in IRC§61(a).[18]

Following the *al-Halkim* case,[19] the US legislature recognized that in economic reality there are no "free" loans, and prescribed a general statutory directive, in IRC§7872, that interest-free loans are to be treated as "income" for tax purposes to the extent of the benefit arising from the non-liability for interest.[20] However, current taxation of "disguised interest" does not, of itself, help us with regard to the questions of when a deposit will be considered a liability, when it will be recognized as income and what is the impact of accounting on this distinction. The case law on these questions is as follows.

5.3.1 The case law

In the US, the rule that loans do not fall within the definition of "income" is considered so self-evident that there is little case law on this point.[21] Nonetheless, court rulings have been sought on more than one occasion on the question whether a specific transaction should be classified as a loan.[22] The need for the courts to address this question first arose in cases where IRS sought to exercise its power under IRC§446(b), not to recognize deposits (that have been recognized as such according to financial accounting) as "deposits" for tax purposes. It appears that two main questions have arisen in the case law, one – the question of timing, and the second – the question of classification.

The first question – that of timing – deals with the issue of when a receivable that has been *ab initio* classified as a "deposit" will lose that classification and be reclassified as "income"[23] (hereinafter: "**the Timing Question of Income from a Deposit**"). As we will see below, it would appear that there is no dispute in US federal tax law, and the case law on the question is clear.

The second question – that of classification (that substantively precedes the question of timing) – deals with the issue of whether a receivable that has been termed by the taxpayer a "deposit" is indeed a deposit, or should perhaps be classified as income (or, more precisely, as an "advance" on account of income) (hereinafter: "**the Deposit Classification Question**"). In a tax system that is prepared to apply the classification tests of GAAP, it would seem that the question should not arise. However, the US tax system was not willing to adopt the Consistent Approach in regard to measuring (and, even more so, on questions of classification). And so the question arises as to the test or tests that should be employed in determining whether a particular receivable is, indeed, a "deposit".

We will address these two questions below.

5.3.1.1 *The timing question of income from a deposit*

The question of how long a receivable that has been classified as a "deposit" will retain that status, and at what stage it will become "income" (if at all), was determined in *Boston Consol.*[24] This case concerned deposits paid by customers to a gas company as collateral to ensure payment of their monthly gas bills (as distinct from collateral against loss or damage to the taxpayer company's equipment).[25] These deposits, which were meant to remain as collateral until the end of the term of the agreement between the company and its customers, were classified as a liability (even according to IRS itself). However, a question arose regarding deposits that customers had not reclaimed upon the termination of the service agreement. A similar question arose in relation to overpayments made by customers who had terminated their engagement with the company without demanding repayment. These unclaimed deposits and overpayments were transferred as "income" (in accounting terms) to the company's profit and loss statements. However, for tax purposes, the company continued to treat them as "a liability". The appeals court ruled that in order for amounts that had been recognized as deposits and overpayments (of customers) "to change their stripes" and be deemed as income, two conditions must be fulfilled.

First, the customers themselves terminated their engagement with the company, and did not claim repayment of their deposits even after some time had elapsed from the termination of their engagement with the company, i.e. the prospect that the company would be required to repay those "deposits" was very slight.

Second, the company included the unclaimed deposits as income in its profit and loss statements, thereby making them available for any use by the company, including for the purpose of distributing dividends to its shareholders.[26]

Conclusions in a similar vein may also be found in *Langwell*[27] and *Warren Service*.[28] In these cases, it was held that a deposit (to secure the fulfillment of a tenant's liabilities toward the landlord) that was classified from the outset, as such, would become the landlord's "income" in the year in which the landlord was released from the liability to repay the deposit to the tenant.

On the timing question of income from a deposit, we can therefore conclude that when the recipient of a deposit has not been asked to repay it when it comes due, and recognizes it as "income" for accounting purposes, the deposit cannot escape the tax net and will be deemed to be "income" for tax purposes.[29]

The answer given by US tax case law to the question of when deposits become income is consistent, in part, with UK case law,[30] and also matches the reply given by UK tax law to the same question (to the extent it is inferred from the UK tax directives).[31] However, it does not necessarily correspond to all the UK case law which, as stated, indicates that "at the end of the day" it may be possible that some unreturned "deposits" will escape the tax net.[32]

However, the question of the timing is not sufficient. The second question that we raised, which is effectively the preliminary question, is when will a receivable that has been described by the taxpayer as a "deposit", and which according to accountancy is indeed a "deposit", be classified as such (that is, as a liability) for tax purposes? On this question of classification, the US case law has provided neither a "simple", nor a uniform, answer.

5.3.1.2 The deposit classification question – former case law

As we shall see, according to the case law in the US, advances received by a taxpayer in respect of income that he will be entitled to receive in the future will be taxable on the dates on which they are received.[33] Against this background, the question arose how to classify a receivable described as a "deposit" that was given to secure the performance of contractual obligations, such as to make payments or retain property of a party to an agreement. Will such advanced payments be classified as a "liability" or possibly as an "advance" of taxable income from the date they are received? The reply to this question has been inconsistent, confusing and devoid of any economic sense.

In *Warren*,[34] it was held, in the spirit of financial accounting, that a deposit made at the beginning of the term of a tenancy by a tenant as security for the tenant's obligations relating to the tenancy, without the landlord having a right to the deposit amount or a claim to its ownership, will not be deemed to be "income" for tax purposes in the hands of the landlord in the year in which the deposit was made, unless an event has occurred that entitles the landlord to convert the deposit or any part thereof to his property. In such a case the deposit, or that part of it that has become the landlord's property, will be deemed to be taxable only in the year in which the landlord acquired ownership of the deposit or a part thereof. This approach, which classifies the customer's deposit as a "liability" as long as the taxpayer sees himself bound by it (hereinafter: **"the accounting test"**), and which also characterizes the initial classification made for customer deposits in *Boston Consol*,[35] was quickly replaced by completely different tests.

In *Clinton Hotel*,[36] at the commencement of the lease of a hotel, the tenant paid the landlord, under the heading "Deposit", an amount equal to the annual rent. The conditions of the agreement stated that this sum had been paid on account of the last year of the lease under the lease contract (that is, the tenth year of the lease term). The agreement provided that this sum had been paid to secure both the payments of the current rent, as well as to secure any damage that might be incurred by the landlord as a result of a breach of the lease.[37] The taxpayer – the landlord, reporting on an accrual basis – treated the sum that he received as a liability, and did not include the sum mentioned in the scope of his income in the year in which it was received (or in any other year). The court of first instance ruled in favor of IRS, holding that this "deposit" was an advance in respect of rent for the tenth year and should be taxed on the date it was received. However, this ruling was overturned by the appeals court, which found that the purpose of the deposit was not an advance payment of rent, but was intended to secure the payment of the rent and for securing the premises. In those circumstances, the court held that "the deposit" indeed served that purpose. The court therefore was not satisfied with the accounting test, and examined the purpose for which the deposit had been given (hereinafter: **"the purpose test"**).

In *Lyon*,[38] in which the factual circumstances were similar to those discussed in *Clinton Hotel*, the court examined the general provisions of the tenancy agreement in order to "address the parties' intention". In applying this test (hereinafter: **"the subjective intention test"**), the court reached the conclusion that it was the intention of the parties to offset the deposit amount against the balance of the rent, and that being so, and relying on the Claim of Right Doctrine,[39] ruled that the amount was an advance on account of the future rent, and despite the purpose that it would be used as collateral for performance of the tenant's liabilities, it should not be treated as a "deposit", but as rent taxable at the time it was received. The subjective intention test was also applied in *Williams*,[40] in order to determine that an amount described as a "loan", and which was equal to payments for 10 years for a tree-felling concession (out of 66 years to which the concession agreement related), and which was to have been refunded by the grantor of the concession by means of offsetting the annual concession payments, effectively constituted an advance on account of the annual concession fees, and should have been regarded as taxable on the date it was received.[41] The court ruled that the "loan" in those circumstances was devoid of the characteristics of a loan, since no fixed repayment dates had been set, no collateral had been given, and the link between it and the concession agreement was unseverable, in a manner whereby the one could not exist without the other.[42] The same test was also adopted in *Adams*.[43]

In *Astor Holding*,[44] the factual circumstances were almost identical to those discussed in the *Clinton Hotel* case, but here the court did not apply the purpose test but ruled that the deposit should be regarded as an advance on account of the rent, and taxable on the date it was received, in light of the fact that the item received bore no interest and the landlord had used and dealt with the same "in the manner of owners", i.e. had control and use of the deposit monies.[45] Thus, the court here needed to apply two new tests, the first, "**the interest test**" (and, more precisely, the criterion of absence of interest), and the second, "**the control and use test**").

The control and use test was applied yet again in *Heininger*,[46] *Hogle*,[47] *Blum*,[48] *James*,[49] *Estate of Holzwarth*,[50] the *First Sec. Bank*[51] and other former case law.[52]

In *Hirsch Improvement*,[53] the court was again required to address the question of whether an amount of money received by the landlord as a "deposit" to secure the tenant's obligations constituted rent paid in advance. The court, basing its decision on the language of the tenancy agreement, ruled that the prospect of a financial refund of the deposit was so slight that in practice it should be regarded as having been paid on account of the rent, and from this it followed that it should be taxed on the date it was received.[54] That is to say that the purpose test, the subjective intention test, the control and use test, nor any other tests were applied, but rather "**the prospect of refund test**", such test not being deduced either statistically or retrospectively, but rather according to the wording of the agreement from the very outset.

A combination of the control and use test, the interest test and the subjective intention test was adopted in *Van Wagoner*.[55] Relying on those tests the court determined that deposits that had been given to a partnership that managed an insurance agency to secure the payment of insurance premiums, in effect constituted advances in respect of insurance premiums intended to be paid for future services, and as advances should be taxable on the date they were received.[56] The combination of those tests was also used in the *Fairchild* case.[57]

In *Re Point Loma*,[58] the control and use test was abandoned, and instead the court chose to address only the question of the intent of the parties (i.e. the subjective intention test). In that case, it was held that a tenant's deposit to secure the performance of obligations under a lease should not be regarded as "income" if the landlord had undertaken to refund that deposit in its entirety at the end of the lease agreement (assuming that the tenant had performed his obligations under the agreement). The court was even prepared to accept the position that there was no difference between repaying a deposit in cash and allowing the tenant to use the same deposit in order to renew the lease for a further term, or to use it in order to purchase the premises. The fact that the landlord had the benefit of the deposit monies did not influence the court's decision.[59]

The control and use test was similarly abandoned in *Arlen*.[60] In that case, a music publisher granted a composer an interest-free loan in the sum of $50,000 for renewal of a royalty contract. The loan was to be repaid at a rate of $5,000 a year (not necessarily against royalties). The court held that this would indeed be regarded as a loan and not as an advance against royalties (despite the fact that the songwriter had control and use of the loan monies, and notwithstanding the fact that the loan had been repaid by way of a setoff against royalties). The court was satisfied that the loan served a valid business purpose, and that the agreement provided for repayment of the loan even if it were not possible to repay it by way of a setoff.

The foregoing indicates that what characterized the case law that preceded the *City Gas*[60a] case is that receivables were classified as a "deposit" or advance on account of income by applying various diverse legal tests that were not necessarily compatible. Tests like the prospect of refund test, the purpose test, the control and use test, the interest test and the subjective intention test led to complete chaos in the way the courts generally addressed the classification (or non-classification) of receivables as deposits.

Eid[61] is of the opinion that the common characteristic of all these cases is that where the court believes that the item received will never add to the recipient's wealth (even if the recipient held the same forever as a substitute for property damage incurred by him, and for the security of which the amount was received), that amount will be regarded as a non-taxable deposit. In contrast, an item received that, at a certain point of time, will add to the taxpayer's wealth (as it does not "equate" the expected property damage) will be regarded as an advance taxable on the date it was received. Two main tests have been used by the courts in classifying a deposit as non-taxable or as an advance taxable on the date it was received: the first, the purpose test, and the second, the control and use test. According to this system, the remaining tests mentioned above are no more than aids.

Burke and Friel,[62] emphasizing the control and use test, regard the remaining tests as secondary. However, I believe that despite the attempt of those scholars to find some sort of logic or "guideline" in this legal chaos, in certain cases, even according to the purpose test, it was appropriate to classify the item received as a "deposit" (in most cases according to the subjective intention test or the control and use test), although it was ultimately classified as a taxable advance[63] when the court "sensed" that "ultimately" the item received would constitute payment for a service or property.[64] In other cases, however, despite the purpose of the item received for use as security for future payments in respect of a service or property, and despite the control and use by the recipient of the deposit monies, the items received were classified as "a deposit".[65]

5.3.1.3 The deposit classification question – the City Gas case

The *City Gas* case[66] could have presented a golden opportunity for the court to regulate comprehensively the question of when pre-payment can be regarded as a "deposit", and when it should be regarded as an advance. It seems that the US Court of Appeals, Eleventh Circuit, indeed attempted to determine a single, exhaustive test, while addressing the remaining tests that had previously been proposed. In that case, the appellant, a natural gas supplier, took deposits from its customers to secure the customers' current payments to the company, and to be returned (subject to a setoff in respect of debts) at the end of a customer's contract with the company. Out of all the various tests that had previously been proposed, the court chose the purpose test as the sole criterion for determining whether an amount received by a taxpayer constitutes a non-taxable deposit on receipt, or an advance that, according to the "trilogy",[67] is liable to tax upon being received.[68]

According to the court, the purpose test should be construed in a manner whereby the purpose of the amount received was to secure the proprietary interest of the recipient – the receivable being treated in the same way as a non-taxable deposit. If, however, the purpose of the item received is, on the face of it, to secure future payments for a service or property that will be supplied in the future, the received item constitutes pre-payment (since repayment will be by way of offsetting future debts), and is an advance chargeable to tax upon receipt.[69] The court further held that it would be unrealistic to expect that any amount received and called a "deposit" would clearly match one of the two categories that have been presented above, according to the purpose test. The court stated that situations could certainly arise in which the purpose of the deposit was two-fold, i.e. to secure future payments, having the character of income, and to secure contractual liabilities, which do not constitute income (e.g. looking after leased premises). In this respect, the court went one step further by determining "**the primary purpose test**". That is to say, if it transpires in a specific case that, according to the purpose test, a payment meets both purposes at the same time, then a further test is to be applied, namely the primary purpose test.[70]

Thus, according to the overall surrounding circumstances of the case, what must be tested is the prime purpose. If it is found that the prime purpose is securing payments constituting, of themselves, "income" (e.g. rent), then the payment constitutes income. If the primary purpose of the deposit is to secure an item that does not have the character of income (e.g. securing the entirety of the leased premises), then it does not fall within the category of "income".[71]

In applying this test to the circumstances of the case, the court ruled that since the prime purpose of the deposit was to secure ongoing payments having the character of income, it should be regarded as a taxable advance on the date it was received.[72]

5.3.1.4 *The deposit classification question – the* IPL *case*

In *IPL*,[73] the factual circumstances were similar to those discussed in the *City Gas* case. This case was brought before the Court of Appeals, Seventh Circuit a few years after the *City Gas* case. IRS sought to apply the *City Gas* rule, according to which a deposit primarily intended to secure the payment of taxable ongoing liabilities constitutes a taxable advance, while a deposit given in order to secure the soundness of equipment does not constitute taxable income. However, since in the circumstances of the case the deposits were given for mixed purposes, the court ruled that the deposits should not be regarded as income since the primary purpose was to serve as security. The court further ruled (contrary to the *City Gas* case) that an item received should be regarded as a non-taxable deposit so long as it served as security, even if it served to secure the performance of payments having the character of "income" and not merely to secure "non-income" property and items.[74]

The Supreme Court was called to rule upon the conflicting decisions of the appeals courts in the *City Gas* case and in the *IPL* case.[75] However, while both Courts of Appeal used the primary purpose test (arriving at contradictory results), this was not the road taken by the Supreme Court, which completely abandoned the primary purpose test, and did not even examine the primary purpose of the deposit. The Supreme Court in effect set aside all the tests that had previously been proposed and instead preferred to focus on the complete dominion over the deposit test (hereinafter "**the complete dominion test**"). Put simply, it can be said that, according to this test, the more the item received resembles the principal of a loan, the more it will be regarded as a "deposit" that is not a taxable "advance". The only relevant test according to the court is whether the receiver of the deposit was guaranteed that it could continue to keep the money.

In adopting this test, the Supreme Court negated not only the primary purpose test, but also rejected or abandoned the tests that had previously been adopted. The court negated the control and use test stating that the control of the monies and the ability to use the same freely did not create a presumption that the deposit in question was taxable.[76] In addition, the court ruled that the fact that the taxpayer "profited" from using the items received did not, of itself, transform them into taxable advances (as distinct from deposits), since, from this standpoint, ordinary loans that a firm may receive may be used, and such use does not make the principal of the loans taxable.[77] Moreover, the Supreme Court also rejected the interest test by stating that the issue of interest on the deposit should have no validity with respect to determining whether the item was a "deposit" or an advance, since it in no way assisted the complete dominion test.[78]

According to the court, the differences between a non-taxable deposit and an advance is that while the party who gives a deposit retains the right to demand the repayment of his money upon fulfillment of all the terms of the agreement, the party who pays an advance for a service or future sale effectively waives his right to receive the money back if indeed the recipient fulfills the obligations for which the advance was given. The very fact that, by paying his bills, the customer (the payer of the deposit) could have prevented a situation where the company would take the deposit as "income" and the fact that he had not undertaken to continue his engagement with it, were the factors that gave rise to the company (the recipient of the deposit) not having complete dominion over the item received.[79] Just as a borrower does not enjoy complete dominion over the principal of the loan that he receives and must eventually pay it, so *IPL* did not have complete dominion over the deposits, nor was there any certainty that it would be able to continue to hold the money. Although the purpose of the amounts received was to secure payment of taxable bills, and *IPL* also used them for its own purposes, the very fact of its commitment to eventually repay the deposits by means of a cash refund (and the absence of its ability to determine that "the refund" would be by means of supplying services or products), and its dependence on the wish of the customer who was entitled to terminate the receipt of the services from the company and thereby receive the deposit back, was sufficient in order to classify those amounts received as "non-income" deposits.[80] Moreover, the fact also that most of the customers who paid a deposit chose to use it to pay their electricity bills did not help IRS. The Supreme Court held that such autonomous choice by customers regarding the method of repaying the deposit (by means of offsetting their electricity bills rather than by cash refund) did not change the deposits into income *ab initio*, and such setoff transactions should be regarded as separate from the original deposit transaction.[81]

5.3.1.5 *The deposit classification question – later cases*

The *IPL* case currently serves as a touchstone for other cases in which US courts have been asked to address the question of classifying receivables in the hands of taxpayers (with respect to the recognition date of the income for tax purposes). In those cases, the courts were asked to determine whether the sum in question was a deposit that was substantially similar to a loan that must be repaid to the customer – in which case it would not be income – or income controlled by the taxpayer.

In the *Oak Industries* case,[82] handed down shortly after the decision of the Supreme Court in *IPL*, the company (hereinafter: "**NST**") supplied broadcasting services to its customers by means of satellite dishes. In addition to the monthly subscription fees, NST charged its customers a deposit of $25 to secure the decoders that it supplied to its customers. According to the contract, either party could terminate the engagement at any time by written notice. The company did not undertake to pay linked interest on the repaid deposit on the termination date of the engagement, and the customer undertook to pay all his liabilities to the company, and return the decoder in good condition. The company reserved the right to offset the customer's debt on the date of terminating the engagement against the deposit, including offsetting expenses that were required to repair the decoder if it was returned in defective condition. If the decoder were not returned, the company was entitled to receive $350 from the customer to cover its cost, in addition to the deposit that it held. The company further did not undertake to keep the deposits in a trust account, and used the monies to finance its business activity. It was further found that NST, in practice, offset on average between 60 and 70 per cent of the deposit monies against customers' debts on the termination date of the engagement.

Following the *IPL* ruling, the court was asked to address the NST affair in light of the complete dominion test. The court analyzed the application of the doctrine to the case before it and concluded that NST had no guarantee that it would retain the deposit, and not refund it to the customer at the end of the engagement, particularly since the setoff would only be made if the customer would fail to comply with his undertaking towards NST. Therefore, repayment depended solely on the customer, and not on NST.[83]

In light of the *IPL* ruling, the court held that the fact that NST had used the monies for its own benefit was of no significance from the standpoint of the complete dominion over those deposits. The situation could be compared to that where a borrower used the deposit monies for his own purposes until the date on which the loan was due to be repaid.[84] It was further held that the key to the test is whether NST was obligated to repay the deposit at the end of the engagement.

The court did not address the absence of the obligation for interest as an advantage justifying regarding the deposit as "income",[85] and added that, in any event, the use that would be made of such a deposit would create income that was liable to tax.[86] The court imputed no importance to the fact that the deposits were used to offset current debts at the date of the termination of the engagement, as this argument matched the principal object test that was replaced by the complete dominion test that considers the offsetting of current debts against the balance of the deposits of no consequence. The court noted that, in practice, the customer (who was likened to a lender) had the option of choosing whether to take back the entire balance of the deposit in cash, or alternatively take the refund in the form of service from the borrower (the company).[87] In light of the foregoing, the court concluded that the case before it resembled the *IPL* case, ruling that: "NST did not have any guarantee that it could keep the deposits because the subscriber controlled whether his deposit would be refunded. Lacking such a guarantee, NST did not have sufficient rights in the deposits for the deposits to be taxable income upon receipt."[88]

In the *Houston Industries* case,[89] the company in question was an energy corporation that supplied electricity to its customers. Following regulatory changes in calculating electricity bills, the company was required to repay its customers for sums that had been overcharged, with the addition of interest. The company petitioned to view these over-recoveries not as income, but as a loan that should not be included in its chargeable income, and to view the undertaking to repay overrecoveries, together with interest, as a liability, in respect of which it was entitled to reduce its chargeable income. The balance of the anticipated refunds was not included in its chargeable income. IRS sought to tax those balances, arguing that the monies served as sources to finance the company's activity, and the company had no undertaking of any substance to repay them.

The tax court accepted the company's argument that the monies should not be regarded as income according to IRC§61(a), since the company was required by regulation to repay the monies and, therefore, did not have complete dominion over them, even though it was a financing source for the company's business for the interim period. Based on the *IPL* case, the appeals court upheld the ruling of the lower court, repeatedly emphasizing that the key to the issue was whether the taxpayer had some guarantee that he would be allowed to keep the money.[90] In the spirit of the *IPL* ruling, the appeals court regarded the over-recoveries as an undertaking that the taxpayer was obligated to repay by virtue of its administrative responsibility. Therefore, despite the use that it was making of the money during the interim period, according to the complete dominion test, these over-recoveries were not to be regarded as part of the taxpayer's income.[91]

The *Florida Progress* case[92] also concerned a company that supplied electricity. The customers' liability for the use of electricity was computed according to the inputs that the company paid to the state authorities. The company effectively charged the customers according to an assessment of the inputs that was anticipated in respect of the use that was actually made, as the accounting with the state was made retroactively, after the customers had been debited. As a result of the calculation method, differences were registered with the company to the credit of its customers, and it was that which IRS sought to classify as part of its income on the date received. The taxpayer argued that these surplus amounts were not to be regarded as income on the date received, but as a quasi-loan that had to be repaid to the lender (the consumer) immediately on demand. Therefore, the company effectively had no right to retain the monies for itself, and was subject to the consumer's decision. The court was asked to distinguish between the Claim of Right Doctrine (which we will discuss below)[93] and the complete dominion test which, as stated, is a test of the question of whether the receipt should be classified as a deposit.

The court made it clear that the Claim of Right Doctrine arose where an asset or cash was received by the taxpayer, and was treated by him as belonging to and held by him, without any undertaking to repay. In contrast, this doctrine does not apply where the cash or the property received is subject to a substantive restriction on its use, or where an undertaking exists to repay it. In such a case, the amount received will not be regarded as income. IRS attempted to argue that the *IPL* ruling was only limited to deposits and did not apply to an undertaking originating in an overrecovery, but the court rejected the argument, ruling that "Florida Power does not have complete dominion over the overrecoveries and is not required to recognize them as income when received".[94] This case extended the application of the test laid down in the *IPL* case that where the mechanism and timing of the refund to the customers is fixed by a third party (e.g. by the state authorities), the company holding those monies does not have complete dominion over them.

In the *Karns* case,[95] an appeal was filed against a decision of the tax court that had found that monies received by a grocery store ("**the Store**") from its supplier constituted part of its income and not a loan, as claimed by the Store. In that case, the Store was in need of $1.5 million to expand its business, and for that purpose the company contracted with its supplier and it was agreed that the supplier would transfer $1.5 million to the Store, to be repaid in six annual installments. The main point, however, was that the agreement between the parties prescribed, *inter alia*, that if the Store would make a certain minimum annual purchase, the supplier would waive its right to the annual installment that was due to in respect of the loan.[96]

Once the Store exceeded the minimum purchase that entitled it not to pay the annual installment on the loan, it registered that repayment amount (that had not in fact been repaid) as a reduction of the cost of the sale in the year in which it was scheduled to repay it. That is to say, it registered the amounts that it was scheduled to repay to the supplier as a "quantity rebate" on the repayment date. IRS argued that the Store ought to have included the entire amount that was received ($1.5 million) in its income on the actual date on which the loan was received, since control of whether to repay or not to repay was vested in the Store. According to IRS, the Store was the party that determined the amount of the merchandise to be ordered from the supplier and from this it followed that it had complete control at the date on which the loan was received.

The appeals court accepted IRS's position that the amount that the Store had already received should be included on the date of receiving the loan. The court referred to the *IPL* ruling that had distinguished between classifying a receipt as a liability or income, noting that the analogy between the cases was not an easy one as the transactions and the circumstances were different. The court further noted that if the parties had defined the amount that was received as a prepaid discount, the analogy would have been much clearer. However, the court ultimately succeeded in applying part of the rule that had been laid down in *IPL*, finding that in this case the taxpayer has complete dominion over the money.[97] The court referred to the loan agreement and the quantity rebate as a single package and, adopting the test that had been established in the *IPL* case, ruled that the control that the Store had over receiving the "rebate" by virtue of the agreement with the supplier was enough to determine that the amount already constituted income chargeable to tax on the date on which the loan was received.

In contrast, in *Westpac Pacific Food*,[98] where the circumstances were similar, it was found as a matter of fact that, in the same circumstances, the loan agreement and the taking of a quantity rebate could not be regarded as a single package. Against the background of that factual determination, the court concluded that the "loan amount" ought not to be taxed on the date on which it was received, and the recipient should only be taxed on the date on which "he became enriched" as a result of cancelling the duty to repay the loan. That is to say, in each case the courts examined the wording of the contract and reached a different factual conclusion in relation to the link between the loan and the future purchases that would be made from the lender. In other words, where not repaying the loan depended completely on the quantity purchased, which was in the borrower's control, the loan monies would already be treated as income on the date they were received. However, where not repaying the loan did not completely depend on the borrower's activities, then the income would be attributed to him only on the day on which his undertaking to repay it was cancelled.

In the *American Valmar* case,[99] a securities investment company supplied brokerage services to its customers and opened a bank account for each of its customers in which the customers' monies were deposited to enable the company to effect securities purchases on their behalf. Concurrently with the purchase of the securities, the company invested the cash in bonds and deposits that earned interest income which was retained by the company itself. Out of the profits from the company's securities activity, it would buy further securities, or repay the customer some of the profits on demand. In addition to the interest profit from the bond and deposit investments, the company charged its customers a percentage based upon its performance. IRS sought to tax the company at the time the monies that were intended for investment were received from its customers, in light of the fact that those monies were used by the company to generate its business profits (the interest from the bonds). The tax court accepted IRS's position and the company brought an appeal against that decision. The appeals court overturned the decision of the lower court, holding that the issue should not be examined in relation to the profits that were generated by the company from those deposits. Rather, the applicable test laid down in *IPL* required that the ability to control those deposits that had been received from its customers be examined. The court found that the company was committed to use those deposits in accordance with the customer's wishes, and therefore there was no justification in taxing the entire balance of the deposit at the time it was received, even if the company earned profits from those deposits.[100]

Thus, in that case, the court also rejected the economic benefit test (or the interest test), and applied the test laid down in *IPL*, namely the complete dominion test.

However, the decision of the Supreme Court in the *IPL* case did not put an end to the various tests by determining a single test for classifying deposits.

In *Iowa Southern Utilities*,[101] it was held, relying on the control and use test, that over-receipts paid by consumers, which were used by the taxpayer to finance construction and infrastructure costs, and which were meant to be repaid without interest to customers over a period that would not exceed 30 years, did not constitute a liability, but income. In *Wood*,[102] it was held that payments received by a taxpayer from the sale of marijuana, and which were in his control should be regarded as his taxable "income" despite the fact that, by law, all fruits from such an unlawful sale belong to the government, and according to the court, the very control and use of the monies received before they were supposed to pass to the government was sufficient to regard them as the recipient's taxable income.

In contrast to these cases, other later cases criticized the control and use test as a criterion for classifying a received item subject to the duty of repayment as income.[103] In addition, it is difficult to reconcile this test with the *City Gas* and *IPL* cases which indicated that, according to this test, every loan could be classified as "income". It is also difficult to reconcile those cases with other cases that dealt with an agency or trustee relationship in which it was held that the control and use made by an agent or trustee of monies belonging to a third party do not make them the owners of the income.[104]

Relying on the subjective intention test, it was held in *Lehew*[105] that an advance in respect of future commissions which the parties intended be regarded as a loan, and which were subject to an absolute and unconditional liability of the recipient to repay, would not be regarded as income, but as a loan, and be appropriated to the recipient's income only on the date of the earning of the commissions and offsetting them against the above "loan". Thus, neither the primary purpose test (which ought to have imputed such a loan to future payment having the character of "income"), nor the control and use test were applied. In *Firetag*,[106] the opposite of the control and use test was used in ruling that the absence of the taxpayer's ability to make use of the money at the time it was received would not preclude the conclusion of its being income which should be taxed at the time it was received.

The *Dana Distributors*,[107] *Colonial Wholesale Beverage*,[108] *Wilson*[109] and *Fred Nesbit Distributing*[110] cases dealt with deposits that were received by distributors of merchandise packed in bottles and containers. The distributors were required to return the deposits to the customers when the bottles or containers were returned. In all of these cases it was held that these deposits constituted part of the product price for both the contents and the packaging, and should be regarded as income, despite the fact that according to the test established in the *IPL* case (the complete dominion test) the customer had the power to require the distributor to return the deposit by returning the bottle or the container.[111]

In *Highland Farms*,[112] the control and use test was once again abandoned, in addition to the interest test and the purpose test, and recourse was made to the complete dominion test. The case concerned payment of a deposit to the owners of a protected tenancy building, where part of the deposit was to be used to offset against future rent, and the balance was to be applied as security for the performance of the tenant's obligations, and was to have been refunded to the tenant or his successors after he vacated the property or died. The court determined that the deposit should be divided into two parts.[113]

Thus, if it was thought that the Supreme Court's decisions in the *City Gas* and *IPL* cases sealed the fate of the multiple classification tests and laid down a single substantive test, later case law quashed that belief, and tax accounting being the creation of the courts was left confused and devoid of any consistency or certainty.

5.3.2 *Administrative directives*

In a series of administrative decisions, IRS recognized that deposits should not be taxed on the date of their receipt, and attempted to find the distinguishing line between deposits and taxable advances on the basis of tests from outside the world of financial accounting.

Rev. Rul. 68–19[114] relates to the question of timing by determining, *inter alia*, that the entire deposit will be regarded as income when a landlord is released from his duty to repay a security deposit in exchange for his consent to the early cancellation of a lease.[115] This, however, also implies the reverse, i.e. as long as no event has occurred entitling the landlord not to repay the deposit, it will not be deemed as income.

Rev. Rul. 72–519[116] addresses both the question of the timing as well as the question of classification. This Rule determines that although advances are taxable at the time they are received, or on the date on which the services or products to which the advances relate are supplied (whichever is the earlier); nonetheless, deposits received as collateral will only become liable to tax on the date on which they are used. In other words, the Rule adopts the control and use test on the question of classification.[117] However, in referring to payments made by a retailer to a fuel company in the form of "deposits" that are meant to be repaid to the retailer in cash or against a setoff of his debts, the Rule determines that the control and use test "does not transform" a deposit into an advance, provided it is intended to secure a "non-income" item in accordance with the purpose test.

Rev. Rul. 75–152[118] prescribes that a deposit will not be classified as a liability where the customer is required by the deposit agreement to purchase products or services from the supplier in a particular quantity or at a fixed price, or where the customer is not entitled to a cash refund or to cancel the purchases.

5.3.3 Comments

Dubroff, relying on the *City Gas* rule, describes the primary purpose test as the principal test on which an item received will be classified as a non-taxable deposit or as an advance on account of taxable income on the date it is received.[119] However, distinguishing the wish of the *City Gas* case to use the primary purpose test as the exclusive test, Dubroff believes that this test is nothing more than a criterion in using the subjective intention test. In addition, he states that coupled with this test, assistance should be drawn from three ancillary tests: first, the interests test (i.e. the interest rate that the holder of the deposit is required to pay within the scope of repaying the deposit); second, the control and use test; and third, the prospect of refund test. In his view, the primary purpose test, coupled with the ancillary tests, will give an indication of the subjective intention of the parties, which will determine the classification of the deposit. Dubroff does not deal with the question of what would happen when, in the same set of circumstances, this test leans in one direction, while another test would point in an opposite direction.

In addressing timing, Bittker and Lokken, rely on the *Boston Consol* case[120] and determine that, where a deposit exists, this deposit will not be recognized as income for tax purposes as long as the debtor's liability has not ended.[121] Nevertheless, the classification tests can advance the date on which the liability will be regarded as having expired.[122] In dealing with the classification question, Bittker and Lokken state that although the *IPL* ruling rejected the control and use test, this test might be useful in applying the complete dominion test as some sort of consideration as to how the taxpayer himself regards the item that he receives.[123]

Eid believes that the Supreme Court acted rightly in cancelling the primary purpose test in the *IPL* case, since this test was difficult to apply in cases of deposits that were intended to secure different purposes when the parties themselves did not regard one purpose as more important than the other.[124] At the same time, the complete dominion test, proposed in the *IPL* case, should also not be accepted as exclusive. This test places emphasis on two elements: first, the deposit being subject to an express liability to be repaid (in cash), and second, that customers, not having undertaken to purchase services or products from the taxpayer in the future, had the right to terminate the agreement and demand a cash refund of the deposit. In Eid's opinion, this two-element test attributes greater weight to the form as opposed to the economic substance. It is also not an effective "filter", and is not able to block tax planning based on the use of the instrument of deposits.[125] According to Eid, the complete dominion test should be limited to circumstances that are similar to those discussed in the *IPL* case.[126] In other circumstances in which the obligation to repay does not apply by virtue of law (but by agreement only), the complete dominion test should not be used, and certainly not as an exclusive test. It is appropriate to reapply the tests that were abandoned in the *City Gas* and *IPL* cases, and particularly the parties' subjective intention test, which may be deduced from the overall circumstances surrounding the transaction.[127]

Eid criticizes the *IPL* case for the very creation of the possibility of such a "tax saving" (by means of fixing a test that does not sufficiently filter). Looking from the opposite perspective, Klein does not oppose "tax saving" that is created in relation to the deposit, but is of the opinion that the same logic should also be used to cover advances.[128] The court in the *IPL* case found two justifications for distinguishing between a deposit (that is not taxable) and an advance that is taxable on the date of its receipt. The first justification, according to the court, is that a deposit which meets the complete dominion test resembles a loan, while in contrast, in the case of an advance, even where there is a possibility of its being returned to the payer, this is so remote as to allow it to be ignored.[129] The second justification found by the court is that, in the case of an advance, the recipient may use the money in order to create sources of income for himself and keep at least some of the costs if the other party to the agreement commits a breach. This does not exist in relation to a deposit, in which the entire principal debt is subject to the obligation to repay depending solely on the wish of the customer.[130] Klein criticizes these distinctions by saying that currently, in the main, according to the complete dominion test, in the case of a deposit, as well as in the case of an advance, the recipient can control and use of the monies received. More importantly, even if the prospect of returning the advance is low, there is no economic reason for the difference between the tax consequences of a deposit, to which the duty to repay money applies, and the tax consequence of an advance, for which the main obligation is to supply either a product or a service, with a secondary obligation to return the money where such product or service is not supplied. The court, while being aware of the profit that could be generated by the recipient of the loan as a result of using the principal of the deposit, nevertheless did not impute any importance to that profit with regard to the finding that it was a deposit, and the same logic must also apply in relation to an advance. Here, too, according to Klein, the very fact of its being liable to repayment is sufficient in order to justify referring to it as a liability that does not constitute income so long as it has not been earned. According to Klein, the court in the *IPL* case missed the opportunity of cancelling the senseless distinction between a deposit and an advance, and ought to have regarded both of them as a liability as long as the duty to repay the deposit or the amount of the advance had not lapsed.[131]

Geier similarly challenges the *IPL* case, but from precisely the opposite direction to that of Klein.[132] While in Klein's opinion the logic of the Loan Approach should be extended to advances according to the *IPL* test, according to Geier, in light of the time value of money theory, the Income Approach applying to advances should be extended to deposits, and certainly to those of the type discussed in the *IPL* case, in which the interest added to the amount to be repaid is significantly lower compared to the "market interest", and the current value of the repayment amount (taking into account the interest rate and the deposit period) is significantly lower than the nominal amount of the deposit.[133] In such circumstances, Geir believes that the court should determine that the entire deposit principal is to be treated as "income", while the duty to repay is nothing more than a contingent liability that should not be recognized as an expense.[134] Geir considers that the Loan Approach should be limited only to cases in which it is clear that the amounts received will be repaid in cash, and the refund will be in real values, and should certainly not be extended to cases in which the refund will be by way of future liabilities for providing services or sales.[135]

5.4 Timing of recognition of deposits as "income" – Israeli tax law

There is no specific statutory provision in Israel that provides that a deposit principal is tax-exempt or is to be treated as a loan. However, it appears that in Israel, as in the UK, this conclusion is necessitated by the very "source method"[136] which taxes income only if it falls within one of the sources prescribed by legislation, there being no source of "income" that classifies the principal of a deposit or a loan as income. In the past, in Israel as in the UK, following the Consistent Approach, the basic rule was that a deposit was perceived as a loan as long as the recipient was under a duty to repay the deposit principal, whatever the terms of the repayment were, and whatever the timing of the repayment.[137] But in recent years, under the influence of US case law, both ITA and the courts have raised doubts concerning the accounting perspective that classifies any deposit that is subject to a duty of repayment as non-income, and have started to propose other tests.

5.4.1 *The case law*

Up until 2001, Israeli case law was unequivocal and consistent in its view that a deposit received by a company from its customers, and which it must repay, will not be regarded as "income" (until such obligation has lapsed), and will be classified as a liability for tax purposes. This interpretation holds, even if: the taxpayer has control and use of the item received; he has used the deposit for its own commercial purposes; the purpose of the deposit is to secure the performance of contractual liabilities having the nature of either "income" or "non-income"; the interest paid on the deposit is significantly lower than market interest; there has been no separation between the deposit monies and the remaining sources that are available to him; and even when the average time span of the deposits exceeds 30 years; and even when statistically the repayment rate of the deposits is extremely low. In all such cases, the deposit will be classified as liability and not as "income" as long as the recipient is under a duty to repay the deposit principal.

The *First Amisragas* case[138] discussed the question of the deduction of financing expenses relating to the re-evaluation of deposits received by a gas company from its customers. The court had no doubt that the deposits themselves (for which the gas company had sought to deduct the financing expenses) did not constitute income, despite the fact that most of the "US tests" mentioned above had not been fulfilled. The court examined the matter from the viewpoint of GAAP, and regarded the item as a liability in all respects, regardless of the use of the deposit monies and whatever the repayment terms of the deposits might have been.

In a similar vein, it was also held in the *Second Amisragas* case[139] and in *Pazgas*[140] that deposits should be regarded as a liability, and not classified for tax purposes differently than the classification according to GAAP.[141] However, things changed in the *Third Amisragas* case[142] and the *Amisragas-Pazgas* case.[143]

In the *Third Amisragas* case, the district court ruled that US tax law should be applied to this issue[144] and determined, relying on the Claim of Right Doctrine,[145] that a deposit may be classified as "income" for tax purposes, according to the control and use test, the prospect of refund test and the primary purpose test.[146] In reliance on the Claim of Right Doctrine, and the three classification tests mentioned above, the court ruled that the advances that were being discussed in that case, while being subject to the duty of (cash) repayment, and regarded as a "deposit" by GAAP, should be classified as "income" for tax purposes on the date of their receipt, in light of the control and use test, and the prospect of refund test (a statistical test), and because the primary purpose was to secure "income" items. This ruling was approved by the Supreme Court in the *Amisragas-Pazgas* case, which adopted the Income Approach, at least in cases where the repayment rate of the deposits is statistically extremely low.

5.4.2 Administrative directives

In the Income Tax Codex,[147] ITA, *prima facie*, recognizes the rule that a deposit does not constitute income in the hands of its recipient, although it asserts that not every cash receipt that is due to be repaid and that is classified as a deposit according to financial accounting will be deemed to be a liability for tax purposes. In relying on the Claim of Right Doctrine,[148] ITA determines that the principal test whether a deposit is classified as a liability or as income is the control and use test. However, the distinction made by ITA is, at best, quite unclear, and at worst, leaves a very large gap. On the one hand, it stipulates that where the recipient of a deposit uses or has the benefit of the deposit this will completely negate the character of the item received as a deposit.[149] On the other hand, other sections in that Codex indicate that ITA had in mind a situation where the principal of the item received would still be regarded as a deposit, even though the recipient uses the deposit and has the benefit of it. It is difficult to reconcile these two approaches.[150]

5.4.3 Comments

In Israel, no academic commentary exists relating to the question of the taxation of deposits in general, or to the question of what tests should be applied to classify an item received as "a deposit", in particular, except for one recent article by the author.[151] The article challenges the attempt to rely on US rules in Israel, whatever the test or tests laid down therein. These rules, it is argued, should only be understood in light of IRC§446(b) and the broad interpretation given to the powers of IRS there-under.[152] As stated above, in Israel no statutory provision like IRC§446(b) exists, and reclassification of "liability" into "income" contrary to GAAP without statutory power to do so, is "a prodigal son" in the Israeli tax system.

5.5 Timing of recognition of "income" from deposits – summary and comments

The UK tax system, unlike the US tax system, made no attempt to suggest "classification" tools for classifying a receivable as a "deposit" or as "income" differently from GAAP. By following GAAP, the UK tax system

adopts the Loan Approach, i.e. the deposit is a liability that does not constitute income as long as the recipient is bound to repay it to the payer,
whatever the future repayment date or repayment terms may be. There
is no reference to the economic benefits inherent in the deposit by its very
holding and use, or to the conditions or timing of its repayment. The
latter, on the face of it, does not affect the question of the recognition of
the deposit or any part thereof, as income.

In the US tax system, ample support exists for the two extreme
approaches, i.e. both the Loan Approach and the Income Approach, by
means of using classification instruments that have been independently
created by tax accounting. The classification, or so it seems, will not necessarily depend on the nature of the item received, but will primarily
depend on the character of the judge sitting in judgment or, in other
words, on the test that he seeks to apply in the particular case. Thus, for
example, in relation to the same deposit, one can get a totally different
classification result by applying the subjective intention test, the interest
test, the prospect of refund test, the primary purpose test, the complete
dominion test or the control and use test.[153] The tax accounting that has
been created by the courts, *ad hoc*, on the subject of the classification of
deposits has been such that when one test or another "points" in the
direction of the item received as being a "deposit", the court that has
supported that test disregards any component of a benefit inherent
therein and rules that the entire amount received is to be regarded as a
deposit. As opposed to this, when the test "points in the direction of
interpreting the item as 'income'", the entire item received is classified as
income that is liable to tax on the date of receipt, without the court taking
the trouble to split the benefit component from that component that ought
properly have been treated as a liability, and which is no different from
any other loan.

In the Israel tax system, as in the US, authorities may be found that
support the two extreme approaches, i.e. both the Loan Approach and
the Income Approach, employing classification methods independently
created by tax accounting.

None of the tax systems reviewed adopted any intermediate approach
between the extremes of the Loan Approach, on the one hand, and the
Income Approach on the other.

It is submitted that both the Loan Approach and the Income Approach
should be rejected for the following reasons.

5.5.1 Criticism of the Loan Approach

The main advantage of the Loan Approach is the fact that it follows
GAAP. In this way, all the defects that characterize the Dualistic Doctrine
mentioned above are avoided.[154] The main disadvantage of the Loan
Approach lies in the fact that regarding a deposit as a liability that is not

subject to tax, whatever the period in question may be, and whatever the repayment terms may be (including the interest rate applicable to the repayment), erodes fundamental tax values. This approach harms the horizontal equity principle, the neutrality principle, the efficiency principle and, most of all, leads to the creation of unjust tax advantages. A brief look at the UK case law mentioned above[155] (in cases of the type discussed in *Messrs Tattersall*[156] or *Anise*[157]) is sufficient to point out the problematic aspects of the Loan Approach. How can tax values be reconciled with the fact that, under the Loan Approach, a taxpayer will not be required to pay tax on deposits that he may hold for many years (even decades), from which he may enjoy benefits, and which he can repay (if at all) on favorable financing terms?

5.5.2 Criticism of the Income Approach

The main advantage of the Income Approach is its attempt to prevent unjust tax advantages under the "protective shell" of GAAP. The disadvantage of the Income Approach pertains to the method, the result, and to the erosion of the Proportionality Principle.

With regard to the method:
    In the absence of legislation regulating separate tax accounting rules, the courts have been required to deal with the unjust tax advantages that are created by the Loan Approach without tools appropriate to the task. This situation has led to the creation of a series of legal tests designed to distinguish between a deposit that constitutes "income" on the date of its receipt according to the Income Approach, and a deposit that does not constitute "income" according to that approach.
    As we have seen,[158] these tests can create chaos in which the deposit itself can be regarded as "a liability" (if, for example, the complete dominion test will be adopted) or as "income" on the date of its receipt (if, for example, the control and use test is applied to it). Use of the different and conflicting tests laid down by US case law, including the principal objective test, the subjective intention test, the prospect of refund test, the interest test and the like, lead to the erosion of tax values such as certainty and efficiency.[159]

With regard to the result:
    The classification tests developed by the case law to determine when a deposit will be regarded as income have been applied to the total amount of the deposit without taking into account the fact that, over time, this capital may (in whole or in part) revert to the depositor. The Income Approach becomes absurd to the extreme in those cases where classifying the deposit as income is made on the basis of an uneconomic test according to which tax is imposed on the total capital of the deposit. Thus, for

example, according to the control and use test that reappears time and again in US case law, the recipient of a deposit (like the recipient of a loan) may be regarded as receiving "income" to the full extent of a deposit or a loan, without being able to deduct the liability involved in returning it, even if he derives no benefit from it, or his benefit is limited, merely because he has used the deposit/loan monies.[160]

The erosion of the Proportionality Principle:

In light of the above, there can be no better example of a system that has "lost its sense of proportion". The essential purpose of preventing unjust tax advantages employs the means of the Income Approach that are repugnant to the Proportionality Principle. Although the Income Approach serves the interest mentioned, and satisfies the rational means test,[161] it does not fulfill the two other sub-tests of the Proportionality Principle, namely, the less harmful means test and the relative means test,[162] since the Income Approach infringes tax values that are no less important than eliminating unjust tax advantages.

On the one hand, taxing a receivable that does not constitute addition to wealth (all or in part) infringes the tax value of non-erosion of capital.[163] On the other hand, in our opinion (as we will see below),[164] there are other means to prevent unjust tax advantages without violating this tax value. Therefore, the Income Approach does not satisfy the less harmful means test that is part of the Proportionality Principle.

The purpose of preventing unjust tax advantages does not justify means that create (at least in the intermediate stage) tax liability that is contrary to the principle of non-erosion of capital when less harmful means are available to serve this objective. Furthermore, even if no other means existed (of the type that we will propose below), the imposition of tax on what is in no way an addition to wealth is sufficiently weighty to preclude the use of the Income Approach (according to the relative means test), even at the price of relinquishing the goal of preventing unjust tax advantages, since the harm outweighs the benefit in achieving that goal.

In light of the foregoing, it is submitted that both the Income Approach and the Loan Approach should be rejected, and another possible model should be examined.

6 Timing of recognition of income from advances

An advance can be described as an item received by a person in exchange for his obligation to supply a service or a product, or to provide capital on a date later than the date on which such item is received.[1] As has been clarified above, GAAP does not regard the very receipt of an item in respect of a service or sale that has yet to be implemented as "income" on the date of its receipt. In effect, it addresses such an item as a liability that resembles deposit in substance.[2] According to GAAP, an advance becomes income only on the date it was earned, and until the occurrence of that event the date of recognizing the advance as income is deferred. In the following discussion we will concentrate on the timing of the recognition (for tax purposes) of income from advances received by taxpayers in respect of a future service or sale.

6.1 The Deferral Approach and the Advance Approach

On this issue, we will see below that the tax systems reviewed adopt one of two possible approaches, which will be called: "**the Deferral Approach**" and "**the Advance Approach**".[3]

6.1.1 The Deferral Approach

This approach posits that GAAP should be followed, and determines that income from advances should be recognized not on the date on which they are actually received, but on the date on which they are regarded as "income", upon having been earned (within the GAAP meaning of that term).

6.1.2 The Advance Approach

This approach seeks to make a separation between GAAP and tax values, and tries to recognize advances as early as possible for tax purposes.

On the face of it, we would expect a correlation between those who favor the Dualistic Doctrine and its application by means of the

Separating Approach or the Consistent Selective Approach, which attribute weight to "tax values", and those who support the position that advances are to be taxed as early as possible (the Advance Approach). By the same token we would expect a correlation between those who favor the Singular Doctrine and those who favor deferring the recognition of income from advances until the date on which they have been earned according to the standards of financial accounting (the Deferral Approach).

6.2 Timing of recognition of income from advances – UK tax law

The UK tax system does not include a specific provision that relates to the date of recognition of income from advances. As we have seen above, the legislation dictates linkage to GAAP in all aspects of measuring a taxpayer's income and profits for tax purposes[4] and, in its wake, the case law has also applied the Consistent Approach.[5] Based on the Singular Doctrine, the UK tax system adopted the Deferral Approach which determines that the timing of recognition of advances as income for tax purposes will adhere to the timing prescribed by GAAP.

6.2.1 *The case law*

An examination of the UK cases shows that the courts have recognized that the date on which tax is chargeable is the same as that on which the taxpayer's revenues are deemed to be income according to the "proper trading rules", or for our purposes, according to GAAP. Thus, the Deferral Approach, which treats income as having been earned on the date on which the income is regarded to have been earned according to GAAP, is applied in the UK.

In *Sun Insurance*,[6] the House of Lords ruled that an insurance company was entitled to establish a reserve to the extent of 40 per cent of the premiums it received. It relied, *inter alia*, on the accounting realization principle in determining that income is only earned after the services in respect thereof have been provided, and it is therefore appropriate to spread the income over the policy period.

In *John Cronk*,[7] a building contractor built houses for sale to purchasers of limited means who could only make small down payments and who obtained the balance of the purchase price from a building society. The buyers paid the builder according to schedule that also took into account the extent of the purchaser's debt to the building society. In certain cases, the amount of the advance paid by the purchasers exceeded the amount that the building societies were required to pay according to the pace of the building progress. In order to secure the sale, the builder deposited that part of the purchasers' advances that exceeded the amount he was entitled to receive, according to the pace of construction (hereinafter: "**the Surplus Amounts**") as a deposit in those building societies. The deposit was "released" to the builder on the date on which the purchaser would have reduced the mortgage debt to the amount originally agreed upon with the building society. As long as the deposits had not been released, the building societies paid the contractor interest on account of the deposits. In calculating his taxable profit, the contractor deducted from his taxable income the surplus amounts that he had deposited with the building societies in the fiscal year, and added to his income the amount that had been released to him by the building societies from the deposits he had made in respect of the surplus amounts that he had previously received.

HMRC sought to tax the surplus amounts on the date of completion of the sale (without regard for the fact that they had been deposited by him with the building societies). HMRC argued that if on a later date it would transpire that the purchaser had not complied with the mortgage agreement with the building societies, then the builder could set off the loss from the transaction for which the income had been recognized on completion of the sale. The House of Lords rejected HMRC's argument, ruling that those surplus amounts should be included in the builder's income from the date of completion of the sale, not in their current values, but in their value as a sum that took into account the risk that they would ultimately not be paid by the building societies (in the event of the purchaser failing to meet his commitments under the mortgage agreement with the building societies). Although if it was not possible to make such a valuation of the risk, the timing of the recognition of the income from those surplus sums should be deferred until the date on which the deposits would be released to the builder by the building societies.[8]

In the *Brookfield (Harold)* case,[9] it was made clear in the context of similar facts, that if the building societies agreed to release all or any of the deposits, and they were "at the builder's call", then those deposits would be included in the builder's income in their full value on the date of the conclusion of the building. HMRC has indicated that this ruling is exceptional to the rule whereby income would be recognized for tax purposes on the date it is earned, adding that, in exceptional cases, a doubt regarding the completion of the transaction will lead to the deferral of the recognition of the income, despite the fulfillment of the principle of realization.[10] Nonetheless, as we have already mentioned above, this rule is not to be regarded as an exception in the spectrum of GAAP, since, according to GAAP, income will not be recognized even though the fundamentals of the principle of realization exist where there is a material doubt as to the ability to collect.[11] What makes this case special for our discussion is the willingness of the House of Lords to consider a possible connection between the timing of the recognition of income and the amount that will be regarded as income, where the amount that will be recognized is meant to bring into account the risk component relating to future non-payment.

As opposed to the above-mentioned support for the Deferral Approach, support for adopting the Advance Approach may be found in *Lincolnshire Sugar*[12] and *Prices-Tailors*.[13]

In *Lincolnshire Sugar*, the taxpayer received grants under a contract that had been made according to a special statute that stipulated, *inter alia*, that the grants were subject to a duty to repay if market prices rose. The court held that despite the fact that, in the relevant year, it was not yet known with absolute certainty if the grants would remain with the taxpayer, they should be regarded as taxable in the fiscal year in which they were received.

In *Prices-Tailors*, the taxpayer engaged, *inter alia*, in custom tailoring. The customer would pay part of the price as an advance to be repaid if he was dissatisfied with the suit. The court ruled that the advance was taxable in the year in which it was received, despite the fact that the taxpayer might be asked to refund it. As will be clarified below, these cases were subsequently overruled.

The *Try* case[14] dealt with compensation received by a company that engaged in building and development under to the Ribbon Development Act. The question before the court concerned the timing on which the compensation should be recognized as income. According to the court, it was incorrect and misleading to include any amount in the taxpayer's taxable income for which the conditions of its being earned had yet to be fulfilled and, accordingly, its existence as "income" only fell within the scope of an assessment.[15]

The *Gardner, Mountain* case[16] addressed the proper method for calculating the profit of an insurance underwriter. The Houses of Lords ruled, *inter alia*, that the timing of the recognition of income for tax purposes, and the quantification of the "profit" for tax purposes, should be set according to GAAP. Thus, the timing of the recognition of income for tax purposes is a derivative of the date on which accounting theory regards the income as having been earned. When dealing with advances, the House of Lords ruled that these will not be recognized as income on the date of their receipt, but only on the date on which, according to GAAP, the income is to be regarded as having been earned.[17] According to the rulings of the House of Lords, income is to be recognized for tax purposes only when earned. The timing on which it will be deemed to have been earned does not necessarily fall in the year in which it was received, nor in the year in which the taxpayer has a contractual right to receive it, but according to GAAP, it falls on the date on which the services in respect thereof are provided.

A similar ruling was made in *Sturge*,[18] where the court reiterated the holding in the *Gardner Mountain* case, adding that advances are not earned for tax purposes, i.e. they do not constitute taxable income as long as the services undertaken to be provided by the company had not been completed in respect of the amounts so received.

In *Weeks*,[19] the timing of the recognition of the income was raised yet again. That case dealt with the income of architects from contracts for an ongoing service in connection with building projects whereby, according to an accounting standard in force,[20] the income received from the project was spread over a long term according to the performance stages of the service provided, regardless of the actual receipt of the payments. This led to the result that most of the amounts were received in the early stages of the project, but were posted as income for tax purposes at a later time (according to the performance stages), while most of the expenses being claimed over the project period related to payments that were only paid in the later stages. Throughout that period, the advances were recorded as liabilities under "payables". HMRC argued that spreading the income (despite the fact that most of the receipts were taken at the early stages of the project) while recognizing expenses and matching them to that income (despite the fact that they were actually paid only at the later stages of the project) created disproportion. The court rejected HMRC's argument that the taxpayer should include all the payments that it was entitled to receive in its income for tax purposes, and instead accepted the taxpayer's position that the recognition of the income must be set according to GAAP. The court concurred with the judgment in *Odeon*,[21] which totally rejected the claim that determining profit for tax purposes is different from determining profit according to GAAP. In the spirit of the Consistent Approach, the court adopted the principle that the timing of the recognition of income from an advance for tax purposes would be in accordance with GAAP. In light of this, it ruled that the taxpayer's receipts did not constitute profit on the day they were received, and should be recognized as income over the period of performance of the project's stages, applying the matching principle that required imputing the expenses in respect thereof, even if they had not yet been actually paid.

In practice, the determination in the *Weeks* case led to the deferral of the recognition of income until the later stages of each project, and not on the spread of the income on a straight line. In the same case, the court expressly rejected the Crown's attempt to rely on the *Lincolnshire Sugar*[22] and *Prices-Tailors*[23] precedents. It determined not only that those two cases had not adduced any evidence regarding the accounting principles that had been applied, but that there were special and exceptional circumstances in both those cases, which should only be applied to their special facts, and that no general principle should be deduced therefrom.[24]

In *Tapemaze*,[25] a company engaging in long-term car leasing would receive advances from its customers for one year in advance. The company did not recognize income from advances on the date they were received. Rather, in the year in which the advances were received they were recorded as liabilities according to GAAP, and the payers of the advances (the vehicle hirers) were entered as "payables". The recognition of those advances was spread over the year in a manner whereby a proportionate share of the advances was posted to the year following that in which they were received, matching the recognition of the income to the relevant expenses. However, during the tax year ending on 31 July 1994, the company sold its entire activity to a third party. In the scope of the sale transaction, the un-discharged balance of the advances passed into the company's ownership, and the company requested that this balance be regarded as exceptional income relating to the capital transaction of the sale of its activity. HMRC regarded the income from the balance of the advances remaining with the company according to the sale agreement as part of the company's normal business income from vehicle rental that had been created during the year ending on 31 July 1994, within the meaning of that term in s 18(1)(a)(ii) of the Income and Corporation Taxes Act 1988.

Both the special commissioners and the appeals court that dealt with the question of the classification of the income from the un-discharged balance of the advances passing to the company's ownership, accepted that had it not been for the sale transaction that transferred the un-discharged balance of the advances to the company's ownership, these advances would have fallen into the pure definition of a liability at the end of the tax year in which they had been received, as required by GAAP according to which income from an advance should not be recognized on the date of its receipt but only on the date earned.[26] Even more so, HMRC accepted the rule that the recognition of income from advances should be spread for tax purposes over the period in respect of which the advances were received, and that they should be recognized as income in the ensuing year, as stipulated in GAAP.[27] However, in the particular circumstances of the case, where the business was completely sold and the company released from its obligation to provide services against the advances, HMRC asserted that, in practice, those "advances" had already been earned in the year in which the company had been released from its obligation, and they should therefore be classified as "business income".

The appeals court reached the conclusion that the advances in the tax year in question should be classified as "business income", relying on the argument that releasing the company from its obligations to customers could not create a separate source of income. Rather, this "release" should be regarded as integrated with the fact that those liabilities had been created during the normal course of business of the taxpayer, and the character of the income resulting from the release from those commitments ought to be classified accordingly.[28] For our purposes, the overall result is less important than the principle established, namely, the broad acceptance of GAAP for tax purposes, both on the part of the taxpayer as well as on the part of HMRC, and also on the part of the court, at least in all matters relating to the timing of the recognition of the income from advances.

It can thus be said that, in general, the case law in the UK adopts the

Deferral Approach whereby advances should be recognized as income for tax purposes not on the date they are received, but according to a timing corresponding to its recognition for purposes of financial accounting.

6.2.2 Administrative directives

Long lists of directives in various areas appear to indicate that HMRC has adopted the Deferral Approach.[29]

6.2.3 Comments

The Macdonald-Martin Committee,[30] which, as mentioned, recommended, as a rule, the adoption of the Consistent Approach,[31] was commissioned to distinguish between the question of the timing of the recognition of income from an advance, and the question of when payment in advance could cause a transaction to be classified as being of a capital nature, with all that that entails, both with respect to the issue of the tax rate on the capitalization profits, as well as with respect to the timing of the payment of the tax in respect of the transaction. The committee examined, *inter alia*, the judgment in the *John Lewis* case,[32] which addressed this issue, and which held that an advance paid by a third party for the acquisition of the right to receive rent for a number of years in advance, constituted a transaction of a capital nature. According to the committee, the court did not impute appropriate weight to GAAP. The committee recommended amending the legislation to ensure that the overall tax consequence obtained as a result of taxing a receipt in advance (receivable in the present value of the rent at the time it was paid) and taxing the return obtained thereon over the terms of the lease in respect of which it was received, should be the same as the tax result that would have ensued had the landlord ("the seller of the right") continued to receive the rent in its full value throughout the term of the lease, and to pay the applicable tax to the full amount of the rent.[33] The committee stated that taxing the advance receipt (even if classified as capital income) should bear in mind the accounting treatment relating to that advance, which, for our purposes, mainly means addressing the fact that, in doing so, the income would be spread throughout the term of the lease.

6.3 Timing of recognition of income from advances – US tax law

The Dualistic Doctrine that governs the US tax system[34] has necessarily led to the creation of tax accounting, which purports to base itself on tax values different from those applied by financial accounting theory.[35] This tax accounting has chosen, among other things, to eliminate the possibility of the creation of untaxed economic advantages inherent in advances paid on account of "income" that has not yet been earned, by providing a drastic solution of adopting the Advance Approach, while disregarding GAAP. This drastic solution, as we will see below, has on the face of it "solved" the problem of the untaxed advantages of those who receive advances, but has also created a host of other problems.

6.3.1 Legislation

As distinct from the UK tax legislation that sufficed with a general reference to GAAP, the US federal tax legislation has attempted to determine specific statutory provisions for the timing of the recognition of advances as income for tax purposes. This may be clarified as follows.

As we will see below, until 1954, by virtue of IRC§446(b),[36] the courts ruled, on more than one occasion, that advances received by a taxpayer should be taxed on the date of their receipt, even if the income in question has yet to be earned. These cases have effectively obligated taxpayers who keep their books according to the accrual basis method, based on GAAP, to keep two sets of books: one for purposes of their business, and the other for tax purposes. This gave rise to the US federal tax legislator coming to their aid by enacting, in 1954, IRC§452,[37] IRC§68A and IRC§462,[38] according to which taxpayers who keep their books on the accrual basis are allowed not to recognize income from advances for tax purposes on the date of their receipt, and the recognition of income will be deferred until the date on which it is to be regarded as earned according to GAAP. However, one year later, these provisions were repealed,[39] following pressure by the US Treasury, which argued that such a deferral was causing heavy losses to the Treasury.[40]

In 1957, Regulation 1.446–1(c)(1) was promulgated, determining that an accrual basis method taxpayer must include an item of income in gross income "for the taxable year when all the events have occurred which fix the right to receive such income and the amount thereof can be determined with reasonable accuracy".[41]

On the face of it, this Regulation cancels the ramifications of repealing IRC§452, since, despite the repeal of the statutory reference to GAAP, Regulation 1.446–1(c)(1) sought to determine the timing of the recognition of income covered by the "all events test", which is similar in substance to the test provided by GAAP itself.[42] In any event, for a taxpayer who reports on the accrual basis method it negates the timing of receiving the money as an event which, of itself, creates the date on which income would be recognized.[43] Moreover, like GAAP, the "all events test" contained in this Regulation has been interpreted as negating the recognition of income for which a material doubt exists regarding the ability to collect it.[44] However, as we will see below, adopting the "all events test" as a determining test for fixing the timing of the recognition of income has not been construed in case law as necessitating the conclusion that advances will not be recognized as "income" at the time they are received, at least with respect to a taxpayer who reports on the accrual basis.

A number of specific statutory provisions (which replaced the general provisions that were enacted in 1954 and were repealed in 1955) made it possible to impose a spread in relation to certain types of income. In IRC§455, a right was granted to distributors to spread recognition of the income for tax purposes in respect of an advance that they had received for subscriber fees for selling and supplying newspapers, magazines or other periodicals throughout the entire period in respect of which the subscription fees had been received, and for which there was a liability of the recipient taxpayer to supply the newspapers, magazines and periodicals. In IRC§456 (enacted following the "trilogy" that will be discussed below), the possibility of spreading income from advances received by various types of companies and organizations was fixed. Thus, ironically, as we will see below, the main case law on the basis of which the Advance Approach was adopted in the US, and which was made in relation to membership fees in organizations, was cancelled by legislation with respect to those cases for which it was made, but continued to apply to all the other cases.

A further concession (compared with the case law) was made within the scope of Treasury Regulation 1.451–5.[45] As we will see below, the Advance Approach that was adopted in US case law was applied both to advances for the provision of services, as well as to advances relating to the sale of goods. Regulation 1.451–5, that was promulgated in response to the above case law provided, *inter alia*, that a taxpayer reporting on a accrual basis may include advances that he received in respect of goods at the time they were actually received (in the spirit of the case law set out below), or at the time the advances are deemed to be earned for purposes of its financial statements, this being subject, for example, to the fulfillment of a number of conditions.[46] Other similar Regulations exist that are intended to facilitate matters (compared with the case law that will be discussed below), and allow taxpayers who report on the accrual basis to recognize advances received in connection with certain transactions as income other than on the date on which they are actually received.[47]

As we will see below, two central items of legislation have influenced the courts to adopt the Advance Approach: the provision contained in IRC§446(b) with respect to the powers of IRS, by virtue of its very existence; and IRC§452, which was (originally) intended to allow the spread of income pursuant to GAAP to persons reporting on the accrual basis by virtue of its very cancellation.

6.3.2 *The case law*

The case law treating of the timing of the recognition of income from advances payable in respect of a future sale or future service can be divided into three periods: the early case law (in which we find support both for the Deferral Approach and the Advance Approach); the "trilogy" (that adopted the Advance Approach); and the later case law.

6.3.2.1 The Claim of Right Doctrine

In *North American Oil*,[48] legal proceedings were conducted between the appellant and the US government in relation to the question which of the two parties was the beneficial owner of the rights to income deriving from an oilfield. To secure the right alleged by the US government, a receiver was appointed in 1916 over the oilfield whose operation was in dispute, including supervision of the operations conducted there and the disposal of the resultant profits. Following a district court decree of 1917,[49] the income generated by the oilfield in 1916, and held by the receiver, was transferred to the appellant. IRS believed that the appellant was required to report the monies it received from the receiver in 1917, as part of its taxable income for 1916 (by way of amending the return).

The Supreme Court rejected the position of IRS, and ruled that the monies that were received in 1917 were not part of the company's taxable income in 1916, because at no time during that year did the company have the right to demand that the receiver pay over the money, and it was uncertain who would be declared entitled to the profits. The Supreme Court also rejected the taxpayer's argument that it had earned the income for tax purposes only in 1922 (when the government's appeal was denied, and the decree became final). The court declared that the income was liable to tax in 1917, being the year in which the company first became entitled to it and effectively received it. The court developed the Claim of Right Doctrine by ruling that monies received by a taxpayer will be taxed in the year they are received, even if a doubt exists as to his entitlement to receive them, and even if he is later required to repay them.[50] This is subject to three conditions: the money being received; absolute control of the money; a claim of right to the money ("**the Claim of Right Doctrine**").[51] Although adopting these three conditions, as they stand, could lead to a loan becoming taxable income, the doctrine does not deal with the classification of the money received as being income or not.[52]

In this spirit, one can understand the logic of the judgments in such cases as *American Tel*,[53] *Patel*,[54] *Roberts*[55] and others[56] that share the view that a preliminary condition for the application of the doctrine is the classification of the item that is tested as being "income".[57] Moreover, it should be stated that contrary to later case law which developed in the US (and in Israel as well), an examination of the *North American Oil* precedent and the conditions prescribed therein does not support the view that an amount that has actually been received (even if it has the character of "income") will be liable to tax at the time it is received merely because it was received.[58] It should be remembered that the determination that the income was to be imputed to the taxpayer in 1917 was based not merely on the fact of the monies actually having been received. It was also (and mainly) based on the fact that the taxpayer had the right to receive them (which right only became clearly unequivocal later), and not on the fact that another party denied the existence of this right in order to prevent or defer recognition of that income.

Lister,[59] Malman,[60] Dubroff[61] and others[62] emphasized that another condition for the application of the Claim of Right Doctrine (apart from the condition that the receipt constitutes "income") is that the receipt constitutes income that has already been earned by the taxpayer. Where the receipt might be income, but the income has yet to be earned (e.g. in the case of an advance), the doctrine does not apply.

With the development of the complete dominion test by the Supreme Court in the *IPL* case,[63] the question arose regarding the interplay between that doctrine and the Claim of Right Doctrine. On the face of it, these two doctrines deal with totally different circumstances. The complete dominion test deals with the question of classifying, when a deposit will be deemed to be income, and when it will be deemed to be a liability. In contrast, the Claim of Right Doctrine does not concern itself with classifying a receipt as income or not, but with the question of determining the timing of the recognition of the income that has been recognized as such. Nonetheless, the borderline between these two doctrines remains vague, especially after the complete dominion test was extended beyond the "classic" cases of deposits, and applied to other liabilities of taxpayers towards customers (including those resulting from the collection of overrecoveries).[64]

In *Florida Progress*,[65] the court had to distinguish between these two doctrines after the tax authorities argued that the complete dominion test should not be applied to overrecoveries that customers had been charged, because according to them, the test only applied to deposits and therefore, the Claim of Right Doctrine should be applied in the particular case. The court ruled otherwise, after it concluded that the case in question effectively dealt with a liability, and the taxpayer had no control with respect to the origin of the overrecoveries that it had charged customers, and which were subject to an obligation of repayment.

In the *Inductotherm Industries* case,[66] an American parent company signed an agreement in 1989, through its subsidiary, to sell three machines that Iraq represented would be used to manufacture prosthetics for war veterans (it later came to light that Iraq actually intended to use them in its nuclear weapons program). On the date on which the machines were ready for export to Iraq, the Iraq army invaded Kuwait. On 2 August 1990, the US President issued an executive order blocking the export of all property intended for Iraq without receiving approval (hereinafter: "**the Order**"). Subsequently, the government refused to grant approval to sell the machines to the Iraqis.

Given the Order, the company requested to sell the machines to other customers in order to mitigate its losses. From our standpoint, the ensuing sale of the first machine is relevant as it was sold in 1991 to the Mitsubishi Company despite the restriction under the Order that determined that the machines should not be transferred outside of the US without the government's approval. The company did not include the income from the sale of that machine in the tax return for 1991, reasoning that it did not have unfettered commercial discretion over the sale of the products, and it was compelled to sell them elsewhere. Therefore, the revenues should not be recorded as income for tax purposes as the company had no real commercial rights to fix the profit from the sale of the machine. Conversely, the tax authorities sought to tax that sale in 1991 as the company itself had used the machine as its own in selling it despite the government restrictions.

The issue was discussed in the court of appeals after the local New Jersey court had accepted the government's position. In order to test the company's claim, the appeals court referred to the origin of the doctrine that had evolved in the *North American Oil* case, noting that monies that had been received by the taxpayer would be deemed to be income according to the doctrine if the following two conditions were fulfilled: first, the monies were received by the taxpayer under a claim of right; second, on the date that the monies were received, there were no restrictions on the property that the taxpayer had sold, and from which the proceeds were received.

The court ruled that the company itself had admitted that receipt of the monies from the sale of the machine was by virtue of its right to receive the monies from the purchaser, and therefore the first condition was met with respect to those monies. With respect to the second condition, the court ruled that in light of the fact that the company had sold the machine without any restriction in 1991, the income should have been recognized in that year, despite the government order, since the company had not effectively addressed that restriction.[67] The court went on to refer to judgments that related to different circumstances in which the courts had been required to determine whether to apply the doctrine, referring, for example, to the *IPL* case.

Another example given by the appeals court was the *Houston Industries* case[68] that held that monies received from end-customers to finance costs would not be regarded as income on the date of their receipt as ultimately they would be repaid to the customers. The court indicated that, in the case in question, the State had not invoked the provisions of the Order with respect to the monies that became due from Mitsubishi, and therefore the effective control over the monies that were received from the sale of the machine was retained by the company. In light of the existence of both conditions required to fulfill the right in the property sold, it was held that the company was liable to tax in respect of the sale of that machine as of the date on which the monies were actually received.

The Claim of Right Doctrine has also been applied according to its intended purposes in cases like *Penn,*[69] *Hanna,*[70] *Dominion Resources*[71] and others,[72] where the courts held, *inter alia*, that if the three conditions obtain, then even if in a later tax year it becomes evident that the recipient's claim to the money has failed, in whole or in part, this will not detract from the recipient's duty to pay tax in respect of that money in the year it was received (so long as the above three conditions obtain).[73] However, as we will see below, this doctrine seems to have been extended to areas for which it was not originally intended (including the area of unearned advances).

6.3.2.2 Other early case law (prior to the trilogy)

In *Brown,*[74] commissions were received by a company that acted as a general insurance agent, and these were calculated as a percentage of the premiums that the policy holders paid. In light of the decision not to allow provision for the repayment of the commissions that it would have to make upon cancellation of policies as a deduction for tax purposes,[75] the taxpayer argued that he should be allowed to spread his income from those commissions over the insurance period for which they had been received. In response to this argument, the court responded that it had not been proved that those commissions constituted, in whole or in part, consideration for a service that was supposed to be granted in the future.[76] It can be argued that by specifically making a substantive reference to the argument of spreading the court did not, in principle, negate the Deferral Approach, but preferred it over the Advance Approach, although making it subject to the production of proof that the services to which the advance related had yet to be granted, and the income would be earned only in the future.[77]

Both the *North American Oil* case and the *Brown* case dealt with receipts that, by their nature, were received and also earned. Therefore, it was not possible to consider the receipts advances that had been received in respect of a future service or sale. Prior to the trilogy, the case law that addressed the question of advances that had yet to be earned in substance was effectively divided into two opposing approaches: the Deferral Approach and the Advance Approach, as we shall explain below.

Support for adopting the Advance Approach in the case law that preceded the trilogy may be found, *inter alia*, in the following paragraphs.

In the *Automobile Underwriters* case,[78] the taxpayer solicited applications for automobile insurance on behalf of applicants. These applicants paid him a one-year or three-year membership fee for his services on their behalf. The taxpayer claimed that he should report as income only those fees earned by him during the years that he provided services. The court rejected this argument, stating that cash received "ripened into gross income" by reason of its receipt. The same result was reached in

Bradstreet,[79] *Northern Illinois College,*[80] *South Tacoma Motor*[81] and other cases.[82]

In the field of real estate, it has been held in *PR.R.,*[83] *Gates,*[84] *Renwick,*[85] *Lyon,*[86] *Clinton Hotel*[87] and other cases[88] that payments of rent in advance by a tenant to a landlord (for a future term), where the landlord is not limited in his ability to use the advance, will not spread over the term of the lease in respect of which the payments were received, but will be regarded as income in the year in which they were received. As we saw above,[89] the presentation of an amount received in advance as a "deposit" designed to secure payment of future rent, and which might be refunded to the tenant, did not prevent its classification as an advance on account of income, according to various tests. More importantly for our case, it led to the finding that the "advance" in respect of future rent should be regarded as income for tax purposes in the year in which it was received.[90]

In this spirit, it was also held, in *Heininger,*[91] *Northern Illinois College,*[92] *South Tacoma Motor,*[93] *Andrews,*[94] *Schaefer*[95] and other cases[96] that the possibility of advances being refunded in the future does not alter their recognition as "income" in the year in which they are received.

This early case law that supported the Advance Approach was not been limited only to advance income for future rent, or to advances on account of other passive income, but also applied to advances on account of income of a business character that had yet to be earned. Thus, for example, the *Streight Radio* case[97] concerned a company that sold services for TV sets, and that reported on the accrual basis. The court held that, for tax purposes, it was not entitled to spread warranty payments that it had received in a particular year in respect of services that it would also provide in the following year. In *London Butte,*[98] it was ruled that income of a taxpayer reporting on a accrual basis for tax purposes would be recognized in the fiscal year in which he became entitled thereto (i.e. he earned it), or in the year in which he actually received it, whichever is earlier. That is to say, for tax purposes the taxpayer who reports on an accrual basis the date of actual receipt of an item may create income even if the right to receive it has yet to accrue to the taxpayer.[99]

However, alongside these cases, which upheld the Advance Approach, there were also a few pre-trilogy cases that upheld precisely the opposite approach, namely, the Deferral Approach.

Thus, for example, in *Beacon Publishing,*[100] the court rejected the argument of IRS that subscription fees received in advance by a newspaper distributor for subscription periods of up to five years, should, according to the Claim of Right Doctrine, be taxed in the year in which they were received. The court affirmed the taxpayer's view that the income from the subscription fees should be recognized for tax purposes over the period during which the services would be supplied. The court went on to rule that the Claim of Right Doctrine is silent regarding the timing recognition of income that has yet to be earned.[101]

6.3.2.3 The trilogy

The Supreme Court addressed the issue of advances in *Michigan*.[102] An accrual basis taxpayer received membership dues for one year in advance. In return, the taxpayer rendered various services, such as emergency road service and the furnishing of maps and travel information. For GAAP as well as tax purposes, the dues were credited to a liability account entitled "unearned membership dues" and the taxpayer recognized the advances as income during the period of providing the services according to the "straight-line" method.[103] The court concluded that the allocation of the membership dues in monthly amounts is purely artificial and bears no relation to the services that the petitioner may in fact be called upon to render to the member.[104] Relying on *North American Oil*, the court determined that the taxpayer received its dues under a claim of right, and had unrestricted use of these funds. Accordingly, it determined that all the dues had to be reported in the year of receipt. The court emphasized the differences between this case, where the future services were to be performed only upon a member's demand and not on fixed dates, and *Beacon Publishing*,[105] in which the future services were to be performed on fixed dates, and the court did not seem to indicate that the taxpayers accounting method was "purely artificial".

Two years later, In *Bressner*,[106] the taxpayer received advances on contracts to service television sets over a 12-month period. The taxpayers allocated 25 per cent of the service contract price to installation costs, and deferred the balance evenly over the life of the contract. The appeals court reviewed the Claim of Right Cases[107] and concluded that they were not a departure from, but rather an insistence upon, sound accrual accounting for earned income, and neither case dealt with unearned receipts.[108] The court further concluded that *Michigan* had not rejected a realistic deferral of income, but that the taxpayer's deferral in *Michigan* was not realistic. Here, however, the court found that the taxpayer's method was not artificial. The court stated that the taxpayer had proved that it was subjected to a reasonably uniform demand for services, and it could and did anticipate the expenses incident to the performance, which alone would entitle it to regard the sum received as earned for tax purposes across the life of the contract.[109]

The decisions in *Michigan* and *Bressner* raised the question of what evidence a taxpayer needed to present in order to prove that his method of deferral "clearly reflected income". It was this question that the Supreme Court addressed in the second case of the trilogy, *AAA*.[110] The facts of *AAA* are similar to those of *Michigan*. The national Automobile Association reported as gross income that portion of total prepaid annual membership dues that corresponded to the number of membership months covered by those dues during the taxable year. The balance was deferred to the following year as unearned income reflecting estimated future service expenses to members.[111] The court, by a five to four majority, upheld the rejection of the taxpayer's accounting system, even though it did not dispute that that system was in accordance with GAAP. The court stated that this case was identical to *Michigan* in that the services were subject to the customers' demand and would not be given on fixed dates. Relying on *Michigan*, the majority characterized the taxpayer's method of accounting by the average cost per customer as "artificial".[112] The majority considered the determination to fall within the wide discretion and authority of IRS under IRC§446(b), and corroborated this rejection of GAAP for tax purposes.[113] The court interpreted repeal of IRC§452[114] as a "congressional recognition of complications inherent in the problem and its seriousness to the general revenue".[115]

This decision implicitly overruled *Bressner*. The minority opinion in this case stated that the result reached by the majority – that a taxpayer (reporting on a accrual basis) must include in his taxable income advances that he received in respect of a service that he has not yet supplied, in the year of receipt – effectively means compelling the taxpayer to make hybrid accounting in the form of a "cash basis for dues and an accrual basis for all other items".[116]

In *Schlude*,[117] the last of the Supreme Court trilogy, an accrual basis taxpayer operated a dance studio and received a non-refundable payment in advance from students for non-cancellable contracts, for lessons ranging from five to 1,200 hours. The lessons would not take place on a fixed schedule, but would be arranged individually between the student and taxpayer. The taxpayer accounted for the receipts by setting up a deferred income account each time a contract was signed. At the end of each tax year, the taxpayer calculated the number of hours taught, and multiplied this by its hourly rate. This sum was deducted from the deferred income account and reported as gross income. Furthermore, if no lessons had been given with regard to a particular contract for over a year, the taxpayer would cancel that contract, reduce the deferred income account by the amount still remaining on the contract and report this as gross income. IRS required the taxpayer to report all of the advances in the year they were received. The court upheld IRS's ruling, finding this case to be entirely similar to *AAA*. Here, the lessons were not provided on fixed dates after the tax year, but on dates to be arranged by the student and his instructor. At the end of each tax year, the taxpayer could not know whether none, some or all of the remaining lessons would be rendered.[118]

6.3.2.4 *Post trilogy cases*

Congress relieved auto clubs of the burden of the decisions in *Michigan* and *AAA* by enacting IRC§456,[119] but this relief was narrower in scope than the holding of the trilogy, and since the trilogy decisions in the early 1960s, there have been only two significant cases allowing deferral of income:

Artnell[120] and *Boise Cascade*.[121] In both cases, the court interpreted the trilogy as disallowing a deferral of income where the time and extent of the services to be performed were uncertain, but not rejecting a deferral system employed in cases where there is certainty in the timing of future services to be provided.[122] A few lower court decisions have followed *Artnell* in situations where the time for the performance of the future services has been fixed[123] or where the advances were refundable in cash.[124] However, these exceptions to the general rule that deferral accounting for advances do not meet the requirements of IRC§446(b) constitute a small minority.[125]

Despite *Artnell* and *Boise Cascade*, most of the cases since the trilogy have determined that income may not be deferred and taxpayers must recognize advances as income when received, even though this would mismatch expenses and revenues in contravention of GAAP. This can be explained as follows.

With respect to the sale of goods, although, in cases like *Veenstra*[126] and *Consolidated Hammer*,[127] the US courts have addressed advances in respect of a future sale differently from those for a future service, after the trilogy the case law adopted the concept that the trilogy also applied to the sale of goods and not merely to the provision of services.[128] In *Fifth and York*,[129] *Boeing*,[130] *McAllister*[131] and *Hagen*,[132] it was held that advances received by a taxpayer reporting on the accrual basis in connection with the sale of goods (that had yet to be supplied) will be regarded for tax purposes as "income" in the year in which they were actually received, and the date of the recognition thereof for tax purposes would not be deferred until the date on which merchandise would be supplied.[133]

With respect to rent and user fees, the case law after the trilogy continued (even more vigorously) the approach that preceded the trilogy. Thus, for example, in *New England Tank*,[134] it was held that payment received in advance as user fees for five years use of facilities should be included in the taxpayer's income for tax purposes at the time they were received, despite the accrual basis method used by the taxpayer. In *Adshead*,[135] it was held that an advance for an unlimited use of property would be included in the owner's income in the year of its receipt, despite the fact that the owner's right to receive the money was spread over a period of 10 years.

As for interest, in *Franklin Life*[136] it was held that interest received in advance for loans according to policies pursuant to a binding agreement, where the receiving company would not be limited with respect to the use of the money, should be liable to tax in the year in which it was received.

With respect to insurance commissions, it was held in *George Blood*[137] that advances received by an insurance agency, and that were entered in its books as a liability in view of their being subject to the duty of repayment in cases where the insurance contract was cancelled, should be liable for tax on the date of receipt. In this case, the court distinguished a cash refund (which might then be regarded by it as a "loan") and a refund by means of a setoff against future advances that the insurance agency would be entitled to receive. The court did not regard such a refund by way of setoff as a financial liability sufficient to defer the timing of the recognition of those advances to a future date on which the duty to refund would expire.[138] According to the court, this duty to repay was no more than a contingent liability, which, not only did not allow deferring the timing of the recognition of income, but also (as will be set out below)[139] could not be deducted as such.[140] A similar ruling was made in relation to advances received by an insurance agent (which were subject to the duty to repay). In *Prichard*,[141] the taxpayer had an unlimited right to use the monies of the advance that he had received. The court ruled that an advance for burial services received by a taxpayer reporting on the accrual basis in respect of services that would be granted in the future, should be included in the taxpayer's income for tax purposes in the year in which it was actually received, despite the fact that the service had yet to be supplied, and despite the fact that the taxpayer was exposed to making a refund in respect of that advance (on the payer's demand).

With respect to warranty fees for user and repair services, in *RCA*[142] the taxpayer serviced television sets upon the customers' demand, for contractual periods of three to twenty-four months, in exchange for prepayment of a lump sum. The accrual basis taxpayer included in income the cost of selling and processing each contract, plus a profit. The balance of the revenues to be derived from each contract, i.e. the portion to be earned through future performance, was deferred. Each month, a percentage of the deferred amount was included in income based on the taxpayer's estimate of how much had been earned through performance. The estimate was based on past experience, and included such factors as seasonal variation and the number of working days in each month.[143] IRS rejected the income deferral, and required the taxpayer to report service contract revenues upon receipt. The taxpayer appealed, and was successful in the tax court, which understood the trilogy to proscribe only those methods of deferring income that are not based on demonstrably accurate projections of future expenses required to earn the income. IRS appealed, and the circuit court reversed the judgment. In so doing, the court seemed to squarely reject any deferral that was based on customer demand, even if that demand was forecast with statistical accuracy. It read the policy considerations underlying the trilogy as rejecting any deferral of income in case of advances in respect of services to be performed in the future upon demand, because it is impossible for the taxpayer to know, at the outset of the contract term, the amount of service that his customer will ultimately require, and, consequently, it is impossible for the taxpayer to predict with certainty the amount of net income (i.e. the amount of the excess of revenues over expenses of performance, that he will ultimately earn from the contract). It concluded that this uncertainty was tolerable for purposes of GAAP, but not for tax accounting, which can allow for no uncertainty in the vital collection of governmental revenues.[144]

In *Chesapeake*,[145] the court disallowed the taxpayer's deferral of loan commitment fees, finding that all the events that fixed the taxpayer's right to the fee had occurred at the time of receipt.[146] The court added that even if some of the post commitment services are assumed to be provided to the borrower, the taxpayer did not provide the factual basis for this.[147] In *Johnson*[148] and *Bob Wondries*,[149] it was held that payment received by a vehicle seller for a multi-year warranty service would be regarded as part of his income in the year in which the amount was received, and spreading this sum over the period for which the warranty was granted did not meet the condition of "clearly reflected income" contained in IRC§446(b). According to that ruling, in addition to advancing the income to the date of receiving the actual amount, the taxpayer was precluded from deducting any provision to cover his liability to provide a warranty, and was only entitled to deduct as an expense payment that he had actually paid to a third party for performing the warranty services.[150]

With respect to agricultural products, in *Philmon*[151] it was held that advances received by a nursery from the sale of citrus trees that had yet to be supplied, would be included in its income for tax purposes in the year they were received, despite the fact that the merchandise had yet to be supplied, and despite the fact that the seller was under a duty to repay the same (in cash) if something occurred that prevented the merchandise from being supplied.

Most of the case law mentioned above, and cases like *Park Chester*,[152] *Popular Library*[153] and *Farrar*[154] where the Advance Approach was adopted, emphasized the "economic advantage" arising to the taxpayer from his very ability to make use of the advance monies.[155] In *American Valmar*,[156] it was held that where the taxpayer is precluded from making use of the advance monies, they should not be regarded as income on the date they were received. In *Houston Industries*,[157] and in *Florida Progress*,[158] it was held that where the customer retains the power to determine that monies he had deposited to cover fuel costs would be returned the sums would not be regarded as income.[159] At the same time, in cases like *Stendig*,[160] *Firetag*[161] and *Iowa Southern Utilities*,[162] the Advance Approach was adopted although the taxpayer did not have the "economic advantage" of being able to use the advance monies, and he had to maintain the amount in a separate account in order to secure the performance of a service in the future, or to secure repayment to the customer.

6.3.3 Administrative directives

Alongside the directives that clarify the meaning of the Advance Approach, as adopted in US case law,[163] IRS has made a substantial effort to assist taxpayers who keep their books according to GAAP to bring closer, to a certain extent, the timing of the recognition of their income from advances according to accounting theory, and the timing of the recognition of their income for tax purposes:

In Rev. Proc. 71–21,[164] IRS provided for a limited exception and permitted accrual basis taxpayers to defer income received in one tax year for services to be performed by the end of the following tax year. Taxpayers who, pursuant to an oral or written agreement, receive payment in one tax year where the agreement provides that all the services will be performed by the end of the following tax year, may include such payment in gross income as earned through the performance of services.[165] If any portion of the services is to be performed by the taxpayer after the following tax year, this deferral option is not available.[166]

Although this directive did not include a restriction with respect to the class and volume of the services to which it applies, case law has found it appropriate to limit the scope of its application. In *Barnett Banks*[167] and *Signet Banking*,[168] the very same question arose as to whether annual membership fees received by the issuer of credit cards could be spread over the twelve months of the tax year in which they were received (commencing in the year in which they were received and terminating in the ensuing year), by virtue of this directive. While, in the *Barnett Banks* case, the court approved the spread after being satisfied that the payment was for future services, the duration of whose performance did not exceed one year,[169] in the *Signet Banking* case (which was given on exactly the same day) it was held that Rev. Proc. 71–21 did not apply to membership fees received by the credit company, and that these fees should be included in income on the date they were actually received.[170]

In the *American Express* case,[171] the appeals court ruled that this directive is not applicable to annual membership fees paid by credit card holders. According to the court, the membership fees were mainly paid for "credit", and although the term "services" was not defined in the above directive, the court asserted that this term should be construed as not including "credit".[172] Later on, in Rev. Rul. 2004–52,[173] IRS stated that annual fees for credit cards are not treated as interest, and should be included as income for tax purposes on the day of receipt, even in cases of refund liability.

Rev. Rul. 78–212[174] allows, on certain conditions, spreading the recognition of income in certain cases of the sale of goods, mainly coupons and similar documents that were given to an identified public or potential group of consumers for free, and may be converted unconditionally and without "any further payment" into cash, merchandise or other assets.[175]

Rev. Proc. 92–98[176] and Rev. Proc. 97–38[177] relate to transactions in which a seller of products offers his customers (for additional payment) a multi-annual service and warranty contract in connection with the product sold. As we saw, the case law adopted the Advance Approach in relation to payments paid by a customer in advance for a multi-annual warranty, and the position that against this income, which is liable to tax in the year in which it was received, it is not possible to deduct as an expense the future liability involved in providing warranty services.[178] In certain defined cases, these directives allow the sellers of vehicles and other consumer products, who keep their books on an accrual basis, and who receive payments in advance for a multi-annual warranty, to spread for up to a period of six years the recognition of income in respect of those warranty services accompanying the sale throughout the life of the warranty liability.[179] This spread is conditional on adding to the taxpayer's income an amount that reflects the difference between the amount paid in advance, to which the spread applies, and the present value of the future payments that he is supposed to pay in respect of purchasing the warranty.[180]

These directives (like others mentioned above), which are designed, in the defined field in which they operate, to limit the difference created between the Advance Approach and GAAP,[181] have been interpreted narrowly. Thus, in *Bob Wondries*,[182] for example, the court accepted IRS's position that the spread of the income according to this directive must begin from the beginning of the year in which the advance was received, while the calculation of the current value of the future payments to the insurer must not be made from the beginning of the year in which the advance was received, but from the specific date on which the insurance period began. Here also, it is not the final (technical) result that is relevant for our discussion, but rather the underlying approach of the court.

While the court rejected the taxpayers' argument relying on GAAP (namely the matching principle), it replied that, in practical terms, the alternative that was available to the taxpayers was not to adopt these directives. In such a case, their situation would have certainly worsened, since they would have had to recognize the full amount of the advance as income in the year in which it was received. However, once they had chosen to act according to the directives, they had no choice but to do so along with all their attendant conditions and reservations, whatever the "difference" might be between them and GAAP.[183]

In Rev. Proc. 2004–34,[184] the cases in which the "concession" was granted were greatly extended. This directive provides that the taxpayer who receives advances for the provision of services or assets to which the directive applies,[185] may spread the recognition of the income from those advances on the following conditions: the spread is permitted according to the accounting practice by which the taxpayer keeps his books, the taxpayer recognizes that income which has yet to be earned not later than the year following the year in which it was received, even if it is still not regarded as having been earned in the ensuing year.[186] Although the directive is limited, both from the standpoint of the period of the spread (until the end of the ensuing year),[187] as well as from the standpoint of the volume of the transactions to which it applies,[188] it is significantly wider than that which preceded it. While Rev. Proc. 71–21 precluded the possibility of allowing a spread where the income was supposed to be earned beyond the range of the year of receiving the advance payment and the ensuing year, this directive does not preclude the very making of the spread in cases where the services, or the goods sold to which it applies, will be delivered beyond the range of that time frame, provided that the spread will, at most, continue until the end of the year following that in which it was received.

With respect to taxpayers who receive advances that can be imputed in part to transactions to which the aforementioned directive applies, and part of them cannot, Rev. Proc. 2004–34, contrary to the narrower approach of Rev. Proc. 71–21 (which precluded any reliance on the directive for the purpose of making the spread) provides that, with respect to that part of the advance that is paid for a transaction to which the directive does not apply, that part will be included in any event as income in the year in which it was received (regardless of whether or not it is liable to the duty of repayment).[189] With respect to the spreading itself, it has been stated that this may be made either on a statistical basis (if suitable data exists) or on a "straight line" basis along the period of the agreement, assuming that the agreement contains fixed conditions or other accounting methods that meet the condition of "clearly reflecting income".[190]

We thus see that the administrative directives have, to a certain degree, eased the results of the application of the Advance Approach, and reduced the difference created between the timing of the recognition of income for purposes of GAAP, and the timing of the recognition of the income for tax purposes. However, this is true only to a limited extent, both from the standpoint of the volume of the transactions to which IRS would be prepared to allow a certain spread, as well as to the spread that is of concern to us here. In the main, the spread of the recognition of income for tax purposes is short-term. It would appear that IRS has assumed that the "loss of tax" in permitting such a spread will be lower, and in those circumstances preferred the considerations of convenience by, apparently, keeping to the accounting financial statements.[191] Case law on its part, read these directives narrowly, and has given an advantage to IRS in its general interpretation, so that there is doubt as to whether it is possible to regard them as any real amendment to the accounting injustice that was created following the trilogy.

6.3.4 Comments

For over fifty years criticism has been leveled at the application of the Advance Approach, while support has been expressed for the Deferral Approach. However, it seems that while, in the past, the criticism was only one-way, in recent years we find support for the Advance Approach in the academic commentary. This will be explained below.

Before the trilogy, during the 1940s and 1950s, AICPA[192] and scholars like Lasser and Peloubet,[193] May,[194] Heffner,[195] Rothaus,[196] Jacobs,[197] Emery,[198] Shapiro[199] and Behren[200] argued that immediate taxation (i.e. adopting the Advance Approach) is a "strange" interpretation of the law and almost entirely devoid of any technical accounting knowledge.

After the trilogy, during the 1960s scholars like Kramer,[201] Behren[202] and Aland[203] were arguing that the Supreme Court trilogy is a misunderstanding of tax law and a misapplication of accounting concepts. During the 1970s, Nolan argued that taxing unearned receipts, which are not even destined to be "income", is unconstitutional within the meaning of the sixteenth amendment.[204] Weary argued that IRS should stop harassing taxpayers by applying cash basis concepts to accrual taxpayers.[205] But in the same year that Nolan published his article, Silk was the first to support the Advance Approach by stating: "if an item of income has been received, it becomes subject to tax because the taxpayer has the funds to pay the tax."[206]

During the 1980s and the beginning of the 1990s, scholars like Stewart and Woods,[207] Scarborough,[208] Dodge,[209] Stanger, Vander Kam and Polifka,[210] Raby[211] and Sheppard[212] criticized the trilogy and supported the Deferral Approach, advocating alignment of GAAP and tax concepts of income. Nevertheless, in the same period, other opinions supporting the Advance Approach were voiced.

Malman said that the court in *AAA* failed to distinguish between fixed and variable liabilities.[213] The taxpayer will incur significant fixed expenses, such as salaries and rent, as long as it anticipates that it will be required to perform its contractual obligations, and holds itself in readiness to do so. She also criticized *Schlude* and the rest of the trilogy for distorting income, if the result of these cases is to require that income be taxed on receipt, regardless of when earned.[214] Malman suggested limiting the Deferral Approach and permitting the spread of income if the circumstances indicate that performance is reasonably certain.[215] The perception of J.M.B. is similar.[216] J.M.B. states that it was not the Claim of Right Doctrine that led to the adoption of the Advance Approach, but the court's concern of the lack of treatment of the performance dates of the future services, and the spread on a straight line throughout the period. In J.M.B.'s opinion, the main consideration behind the trilogy was administrative convenience, which was behind the broad powers that were granted to IRS under IRC§446(b). These considerations derive from the fact that uncertainty in relation to the performance dates of future services, statistical values and the like would cause IRS difficulties in determining a genuine assessment, and it is those assessments that count.[217]

Coplan does not explicitly deal with Malman's analytic proposal, but would presumably be antagonistic to it.[218] He set forth a framework to allow IRS to disallow a taxpayer's use of accrual basis method accounting if it had been manipulated in order to distort income. According to Coplan, the major weakness of GAAP is its failure to account for the time value of money and therefore IRS should disallow a taxpayer's use of GAAP if it had been manipulated in order to distort income.[219]

Lister said that adopting the Advance Approach overall (and the trilogy in particular) was based on removing the tests that were set in the *North American Oil* case from their context, and a mistaken understanding of the Claim of Right Doctrine.[220]

Both Bittker[221] and Dubroff[222] examine the history of the case law that adopted the Advance Approach and show that while, at first, the cases relied on the Claim of Right Doctrine in adopting the Advance Approach (and this was also the spirit of the first judgment in the trilogy),[223] nonetheless, in the two other cases in the trilogy,[224] and also in the cases which arose subsequently, the court expressly avoided relying on the Claim of Right Doctrine and the Advance Approach was adopted not on the basis of that doctrine but on the fact of the repeal of sections 452 and 462 of the Code, in particular relying on the interpretation of the court of the expression "clearly reflects income" contained in IRC§446(b).[225] Dubroff, faithful to the Singular Doctrine, criticizes the adoption of the Advance Approach in that it deviates from the realization principle and taxes receipts that have yet to be earned.[226] Lister, by comparison, adopts the view of Malman, and distinguishes between a case where there is a liability not only to perform services or sell in the future, but where there is certainty with respect to the dates of their performance, in which case the spread is to be permitted until such dates, and a case in which there is no such certainty and the Advance Approach is then justified.[227]

Halperin states (justifiably) that there are no "free" loans.[228] While GAAP, in applying the realization principle, by virtue of which the timing of the recognition of income from advances is deferred, regards the entire amount received as relating to the same component of the goods or the services.[229] Halperin believes that the amount of the advances is to be regarded as including disguised interest, beyond the price of the product or the service, which is meant to be commensurate with the current value of the payment compared with the date of the supply in the future. Although Halperin says that it is more correct to tax the customer who pays an advance than the recipient thereof, since he is the one who has the economic benefit of a reduction in the price to the extent of the interest that must be paid on the credit component that he granted the supplier, he still supports the Advance Approach.[230] The significance of shifting the tax burden for the interest (that is saved) from the recipient of the advance to the payer will lead to the result that the Advance Approach will not be applied in relation to the recipient of the advance. Rather, the income of the recipient of the advance should be taxed in practice at the end of the period (not even according to the Deferral Approach according to GAAP), while in comparison the payer of the advance is the one who will be taxable on the disguised interest as, had he not paid the advance, it can be assumed that he would have paid it at the end of the period, together with interest that would have been taxable (assuming that the payer is liable to tax and the payment cannot be deducted as an expense by him).[231]

Kleinrock set out the perception of the term "income" according to accounting theory and according to the perception of this term in the tax laws (in relation to the timing of the recognition thereof), as well as the economic perception of the term "income" according to the Haig-Simons model.[232] The economic model of "income" does not match the Advance Approach, but at the same time it does not match GAAP on the question of timing either.

Gunn says that without any clear and absolute preference to either approach, under tax neutrality value and macro-economic tests, the only consideration that must determine in choosing between the Advance Approach and the Deferral Approach is the consideration of administrative convenience.[233] However, contrary to Malman and J.M.B., who for reasons of administrative convenience justify the application of the Advance Approach in order to save IRS the need to make evaluations and calculations relating to the performance of the liabilities in the future, according to Gunn's view, it is precisely the considerations of convenience that justify adopting the Deferral Approach. This is not because GAAP has discovered some sort of general truth with respect to the method of measuring income, but only on grounds of the "convenience" that derives from the essential saving of maintaining separate systems of bookkeeping.[234]

Schuldiner attacked the Advance Approach by stating that a look at a transaction overall, both from the standpoint of the recipient, as well as that of the payer, will lead to the result that adopting this conception will bring about over-taxing transactions which contain advances and improper intervention of tax laws in the manner of conducting business.[235] While Gunn relates to the macro-economic question, as one that does not provide any clear and absolute preference to either approach, Schuldiner addresses the macro-economic question as one that provides a clear advantage to adopting the Deferral Approach. According to him, in paying an advance in respect of a future service, the customer cannot generally deduct the advance as an expense on the date it is paid, and the timing of the recognition of the deduction thereof will be deferred to the date of the supply of the service or asset. He may even be required to capitalize it (as a capital investment), since it is paid in order to grant a customer a continuing advantage (beyond the fiscal year in which it was paid), indicating that from a customer's standpoint the amount that has been paid (and which has not been permitted to be deducted at the time it was paid) was paid out of monies that the customer earned and had already paid tax on. On this assumption, Schuldiner states if the payer has an advance amount that will not be recognized as an expense at the time it is paid, while the recipient according to the Advance Approach is required to pay tax on it on the date it was received, the practical result will be "a tax advantage" to the Treasury, which violates tax neutrality and essentially creates a tax disadvantage for making transactions by means of advances.[236]

Klein opposes adopting the Advance Approach, relying on the argument that there is no economic difference between an advance and any other liability, regardless of whether it is a liability to provide a service or goods, or a liability to repay money within the scope of a loan or deposit.[237] According to him, sacrificing GAAP in order to reduce the administrative cost involved in auditing the tax returns by IRS, and saving the need to make evaluations and assessments of future liabilities, is not equal to the price of creating inconsistency between the accounting measurement of income and measuring it for tax purposes, and does not equal the creation of inconsistency between the fiscal handling relating to advances and the fiscal handling of other liabilities, such as deposits or loans.[238] In this context, states Klein, the rulings of the trilogy relating to advances as against the fiscal cases relating to deposits, originate in a distinction between form and not of substance. The very fact of a person receiving money has no relevance for the measuring of his income, and if indeed receiving the money had such significance, it would be inapt to distinguish between "advance" and a "loan" and a "deposit". A "deposit", a "loan" and an "advance" all involve the expenditure of resources in the future by the firm, and, against that background, there is no economic sense for the distinction made between deposits that are not liable to tax on the date they are received, and advances which are liable to tax on the date they are received.[239] Proper tax handling of an advance obligates that the financing component involved in the advance will be separated from its remaining parts.[240]

It is true that it can be argued that in loans (as well as deposits) the element of the liability is clearer (to repay the principal and the interest), whereas in advances it can be said that some uncertainty exists with respect to the liability to "repay" the advance, in the form of providing services or a sale, and that such uncertainty requires evaluation. But it should not be deduced from this that such uncertainty justifies transforming every advance into "income". Although it is possible that an alternative can be suggested for enabling a taxpayer to deduct against the "income" (from the advance) the current value of the expected expenses for providing the service or the sale,[241] nonetheless, as indicated by the trilogy, even this possibility has not been afforded. Economically, states Klein, an advance does not enrich the recipient, and where it is clear that based on a contract to sell a service or sale in the future the seller may receive a loan from the bank (to be repaid on the date the proceeds are received following the performance of the contractual obligations) and this will be deemed to be income in his hands, there is no logic in imposing tax on the advance at the time it is received.[242] It is true that the agreement of itself creates the potential for economic wealth, but no one has yet proposed imposing tax following an agreement merely because of the current value of his expected income. If this is so, Klein asks, does the fact that a person receives an advance by virtue of such an agreement of itself cause a liability for tax before he has earned the advance?[243]

Klein responds to this question in the negative, and raises three arguments: first, receiving an advance can be likened in substance to any other liability that the recipient assumes. The basic weakness of the Advance Approach lies in the fact that in relatively simple tax planning the advances that are liable to tax can be changed into a "deposit" that is not liable to tax. Second, imposing tax on an advance on the date it is received (as distinct from not imposing tax on deposits and loans) causes preference of one activity as against another, but harms the value of tax neutrality, without, in effect, there being any economic difference between them. And third, this rule, which disregards economic reality, could create an incentive to the taxpayer to effect uneconomic activities (such as canceling advances and taking deposits or loans instead, on less favorable conditions from the taxpayer's standpoint), whereas, if advances were handled equally in the same way as deposits, the effect of this kind of waste would be prevented.[244]

To his mind, the majority ruling in the trilogy did not in any way deal with the problem posed by this kind of waste,[245] nor did the majority deal with the problems raised by the minority view that held that adopting the Advance Approach would cause distortion of "income" for tax purposes, *inter alia*, following the non-fulfillment of the principal of matching. The majority view that the accounting system that was used by the taxpayer was "artificial" disregards the fact that accounting systems must be aided by evaluations. In practice, adds Klein, the cause of "artificiality" and of deviating from economic reality is actually the tax authorities, who concentrated on receiving the money in cash.[246] In addressing the scholars who believe that considerations of administrative convenience justify adopting the Advance Approach, at least in those cases where uncertainty exists with respect to the manner and timing of performing the future liabilities, Klein suggests, with irony, that according to such logic – why wait at all to tax the advance? In any event, it is neutral and devoid of any relevancy from the economic standpoint, so why wait when it is possible to charge the taxpayer while he is still making the agreement, and possibly even earlier, when he becomes aware of the economic potential of his future income.[247]

According to him, in order to avoid the absurdity created in US law between advances on the one hand, and loans and deposits on the other, one of the three following alternatives should be followed: (1) cancel the

Advance Approach and adopt the Deferral Approach; (2) impose tax in advance on deposits and loans (at least on those transactions where the interest is lower than the market interest) so that the Advance Approach would apply not only to advances, but to deposits and loans as well, and, in this way, the neutrality of tax would not be harmed, and the principal of vertical equity would not be infringed;[248] (3) allow the recipient of the advance to deduct the full amount of the future liabilities required to attain the income as an expense in calculating the tax in the year in which the advance was received.[249]

Johnson supports the Advance Approach not only in cases of uncertainty in relation to the manner and dates of performing liabilities in the future (as Malman and J.M.B., for example, also believe), but also in cases in which there is certainty relating to the manner and dates of performing the liabilities in the future.[250] In his view, the Deferral Approach, which includes the condition that income will be earned for the purpose of the recognition thereof as such, is erroneous and not legitimate, and constitutes "bad economics", "bad accountancy" and "bad tax law".[251]

He explains that adopting the Deferral Approach is "bad economics" since this approach does not match modern economic theories relating to investments, as in terms of "current value", deferring the recognition of income gives a distorted picture of the real monetary value that the recipient has as a result of the advance. Adopting the Deferral Approach will present the recipient in an inferior position compared to his real economic position, having regard to the fact that the recipient enjoys the full amount of the nominal value of the advance. The Deferral Approach will lead, therefore, to a result whereby the income that will be attributed to the recipient for tax purposes will only be equal to the nominal value of the advance sum. According to him, traditional accounting has disregarded the time value of money principle by reason of the matching principle, according to which income and expenses that have been used to create income are simultaneously reported. This creates an inherent difference between the timing of the recognition of income and expenses and the timing of receivables or the actual making of payments. But this difference has led to a disregard of the fact that there is financial value to the effect of time itself, to the extent it relates to actual payments or actual receipts.

Johnson states that GAAP, which regards an advance that has yet to be earned as an item received, similar in substance to a loan, to the extent it holds that against this increase on the assets side there is a corresponding increase on the liability side, does not match economic reality, for two reasons: first, although the recipient of the advance has to supply a product or service in the future, such liability does not offset at least the profit component inherent in the advance. If the liability to provide a service or sale of an asset were to equal the consideration received in respect thereof, then a firm would never have any profit from providing services or from a sale (even if this income has been earned);[252] second, even the possibility that, in the absence of the supply of the service or product, the recipient will be required to repay the advance in the future does not justify (offset) the amount of the advance, since the amount of the repayment must be measured in current values, taking into account both the timing of the repayment as well as the very prospect that the repayment will indeed be made. If both of these are taken into account, it is doubtful that it will be appropriate to give this amount any real financial significance in canceling (offsetting) the income component in the advance.[253]

Johnson (like Klein and similar to Halperin) also states that an advance has a fundamental element of credit, and contains disguised interest as there are no "free" loans. According to him, the interest inherent in the advance is not expressed in a discount on the product component or the future service, but reflects the full return that can be obtained on the entire principal of the advance, from the date on which it is granted until the date on which the service or product is supplied. The current value of this benefit is equal to the full amount of the nominal sum of the advance.[254]

According to Johnson, adopting the Deferral Approach is also "bad accountancy", since in recent years changes have been made in GAAP relating to the adoption of the present value method in a number of fields, although GAAP still disregards the time value of money in most cases.[255] The fact that the taxpayer has received an advance can have considerable effect for purposes of determining the taxpayer's value (based on the present method of the expected income flow in the future), and it is certainly inappropriate to disregard this for the reason that it has yet to be earned.[256]

Furthermore, adds Johnson, the Deferral Approach is also "bad tax law" since in tax law there is no requirement of earning the income in order to recognize it (for tax purposes).[257] In light of that position, Johnson believes that the full amount of the advance must be included in the recipient's income at the time it is received.[258] The fact that liabilities that are not yet known with certainty may arise does not justify, in itself, regarding the total amount of the advance as income that has yet to be earned.[259]

In addressing Halperin's theory, which shifts the tax burden inherent in the advance onto the payer of the advance and not the party receiving it, Johnson states that the main problem in this theory is that it also starts from the assumption that an advance is identical in substance to a loan, while Johnson believes that in any case one should not equate the situation of a borrower to that of the party who has received an advance.[260] According to him, even if there is some sort of justification for shifting the tax burden in connection with the advance onto the paying customer, such justification does not have to release the recipient of the advance from the tax burden, on the date it is received.[261]

Geier states that GAAP does not constitute values for tax purposes, and certainly does not justify ignoring tax values (including the time value of money).[262] While for GAAP there is no significance to the timing of the actual receipt of cash flows resulting from income, for tax purposes, she states the concept of "income" will be distorted if a difference arises in the timing between the date of actual receipt and the date of its recognition as income.[263] In the event of a deviation between tax values and GAAP, the tax value should always be preferred, unless deviating from tax values is so minor that allowing it would not detract from considerations of administrative convenience[264] by preventing the tax advantages or the tax disadvantages that are created from the timing differences between the recognition of income or an expense according to financial accounting theory, and the timing of the item received or the actual payment, as appropriate. These tax advantages will be prevented, *inter alia*, by means of adopting the Advance Approach in relation to income from advances, while expenses that have been or will be used for creating that income will not be recognized under the matching principle, but only on the date of their actual payment. Alternatively, along with recognizing income from advances on the date they are received, expenses will be permitted for deduction only in the present value that takes into account the timing of the payment thereof in the future, rather than in their full (nominal) value.[265]

6.4 Timing of recognition of income from advances – Israeli tax law

Israeli legislation does not include a general provision for the timing of the recognition of income from advances, nor is there any provision (such as that found in the UK legislation) referring to GAAP, from which principles may be learned regarding the timing of the recognition of income. However, Israeli legislation does have two provisions that adopt the Advance Approach in the case of two specific transactions: advances in respect of rental[266] and advances in respect of insurance premiums.[267] In these cases, it is provided that the timing of the recognition of the advances as income will be the date on which they are received (whatever the reporting method applicable to the taxpayer may be).[268] Against the background of these two specific provisions, it would be reasonable to expect that the Deferral Approach would be adopted for other types of transaction. However, this is not the position adopted by case law. Case law has actually rejected the Deferral Approach and adopted the Advance Approach for other categories of advances.

6.4.1 The case law

In *Yatziv*,[269] in which the question of the timing of the recognition of income from advances was raised incidentally, the court preferred to leave this question open, and did not determine whether the US case law adoption of the Advance Approach should be followed in Israel.

In the *First Amisragas* case[270] and in the *Aharon* case,[271] the court discussed the timing recognition of income from amounts that were termed "advances", that were received by gas companies from new customers, and which would be returned to those consumers when they terminated their agreements. In both cases, the district court ruled that these payments fall within the definition of taxable income in the year in which they are received. The court based its ruling on the fact that the payments were not "advances" in the normal sense, but were aimed at compensating the gas companies in respect of the financing expenses that they bear for gas supplied to central distributing systems, that is not paid for until after actual consumption.

While these judgments can be explained as not expressly adopting the Advance Approach, since each stated that the item in dispute does not relate to an advance in respect of a future service or sale, the *Third Amisragas* case,[272] and the *Amisragas-Pazgas* case,[273] expressly adopted the Advance Approach (at least in cases of gas companies). Adopting the Advance Approach in US case law can only be understood against the background of the interpretation given in the US to IRS's powers according to IRC§446(b), and the repeal of the provisions contained in sections 452 and 462 of the Code. Nevertheless, in Israel, where ITA has no similar power, the courts relied upon US case law in adopting the same approach. In doing so, the courts did not address why the Israeli legislature found it necessary to enact statutory provisions that specifically apply the Advance Approach to two transactions (rental and insurance premiums) if this approach applies in other cases as well.[274]

6.4.2 Administrative directives

On the one hand, following the judgment in the *Aharon* case, ITA issued a directive under which it adopted the Advance Approach relying, *inter alia*, on the Claim of Right Doctrine.[275] On the other hand, in practice, in most cases (not related to gas companies) ITA does not reject using the spread method for advances received by taxpayers who keep their books according to GAAP and report on an accrual basis method.

6.4.3 Comments

Raphael supports adopting the Deferral Approach as part of the conception of following GAAP.[276] In contrast, Rosenberg[277] is of the opinion that advances should be regarded as income for tax purposes on the date they are received (even if they have yet to be earned).[278]

6.5 Timing of recognition of income from advances – summary and comments

The UK tax system, which is the most consistent and coherent among those that have been examined, treats advances according to the Consistent Approach pursuant to GAAP, and determines, according to the Deferral Approach, that so long as these have yet to be earned, they should not be included in income. By doing so, it correlates advances to deposits. The US tax system, not being committed to GAAP, has zigzagged in relation to deposits, and has adopted different and conflicting tests with respect to the question of whether they are to be regarded as a liability or as income. However, it is much more unequivocal in relation to advances, and determines that they are to be taxed in the year in which they are received, disregarding the obligation to repay them, whether according to law or agreement.[279]

It seems that one main factor and three secondary factors led the US case law, in the trilogy and in the cases following it, to adopt the Advance Approach. The main factor was based on the broad interpretation given by the courts to the powers of IRS according to IRC§446(b), coupled with a willingness to deviate from GAAP (including deviation from the realization principle) in the spirit of the Dualistic Doctrine.[280] To this major factor were added secondary considerations, like inappropriate interpretation of the Claim of Right Doctrine,[281] the "gut feeling" of the courts that the essential ability of the taxpayer to make use of the advance monies is that which creates an economic advantage justifying the imposition of tax and, ultimately, that IRS's considerations of convenience (which take preference over those of the taxpayer) justify, on the face of it, the imposition of tax on the date on which there is an "encounter with the cash", without IRS being compelled to become involved in complex calculations involving the spread of income.[282] The same "gut feeling" brought the Israeli case law to the same conclusion and to the adoption of the Advance Approach (as in the US tax system), despite the fact that the Israeli legislature did not grant ITA any power similar to the one granted to IRS in accordance with IRC§446(b).

None of the tax systems reviewed found room for any alternative approach between the Deferral Approach on the one hand, and the Advance Approach on the other.

It is submitted that both the Deferral Approach and the Advance Approach should be rejected, for the following reasons.

6.5.1 *Criticism of the Deferral Approach*

The main advantage of the Deferral Approach is that it follows GAAP, and thus avoids all the defects that characterize the Dualistic Doctrine, as mentioned above.[283] This conception, coupled with the Loan Approach, creates a uniform, coherent overall picture that "sends out a message" of stability and certainty.

The main disadvantage of the Deferral Approach is that regarding an advance as a liability that is not subject to tax on the date of its receipt, regardless of the period in question, and of the terms of the transaction for which the advance was received, erodes basic tax values, including the tax neutrality principle, the horizontal equity principle, the efficiency principle and failure to prevent unjust tax advantages.

Violating the tax neutrality principle – the Deferral Approach that is applied under GAAP leads to the result that tax will be imposed at a future date on the present value of the advance, instead of on its future value. Thus, the Deferral Approach intrinsically contains the potential for imposing different taxation on precisely the same transaction and in respect of the same consideration in real terms, merely by reason of the time difference between the date on which the money is received and the date on which it is earned.

Violating the horizontal equity principle – the Deferral Approach has the intrinsic potential of imposing tax in a sum that in real terms is different for two identical taxpayers who have earned, in the same transaction itself, identical profit in real terms, although the nominal terms of the consideration were different (due to the time difference).

Violating the efficiency principle and failure to prevent unjust tax advantages – where the use of the Deferral Approach leads to overall taxation at a rate that is lower than that imposed on income from transactions of the same type in which the advance is received, the efficiency value will be harmed and unjust tax advantages will be created. This potential exists in the Deferral Approach not because of the very deferral of the tax payment (since the question of the timing of the payment of the tax in real terms is not necessarily part of the efficiency principle),[284] but due to the possibility that the income (in nominal terms) on which the tax arising from the advance is calculated will not reflect the real value on the day on which that calculation is made for purposes of payment of the tax.

6.5.2 *Criticism of the Advance Approach*

The main advantage of the Advance Approach is its attempt to prevent unjust tax advantages under "the protective shell" of GAAP. The disadvantages of the Advance Approach are as follows.

Absence of consistency in defining the meaning of the transaction – in substance the Advance Approach is predicated on the present value of the advance being regarded as reflecting its future value on the date that it is recognized as income according to GAAP. Therefore, according to that conception, imposition of tax at the time of receipt of the advance on the full amount of the nominal value reflects the proper economic tax, as if it had been imposed on the future value of the advance on the date on which it was earned. In other words, according to this view, the advance is to be regarded as a loan that matures together with "the market interest" on the date on which income is earned. Consequently, two transactions are created as far as the recipient of the advance and the payer thereof are concerned: first, the base transaction (i.e. the sale transaction or the services);[285] second, a financing transaction in which the advance creates interest income for the payer at the end of the period, and on that date he pays the principal of the advance plus the interest that has (theoretically) accrued in the hands of the recipient of the advance.[286]

Therefore, a consistent application of the Advance Approach would necessitate taxing the payer of the advance on the "theoretical" interest component (to the extent of the difference between the present value, as opposed to the future value, of the advance),[287] and in parallel, allow the recipient of the advance (the taxpayer) to deduct such financing expenses in calculating his income from the base transaction. The Advance Approach is not consistent with the abovementioned theory of the two transactions, since this conception not only refrains from taxing the payer (of the advance), but actually imposes tax on the recipient on account of the additional interest income instead of allowing him to deduct this difference.

Calculating the tax on the theoretical interest – according to the Advance Approach, the advance recipient's economic income is always the future value amount of the advance in the year in which it was earned, and in any event, this value is always equal to the present value thereof in the year of receipt (which is also its amount in nominal terms).[288] The result of this conception is that taxing the recipient on the advance will not target his "genuine" economic profits resulting from receipt of the advance, but his profits as they might have been, had the advance amounts been invested in an interest-bearing deposit at "market interest".

Violating the tax value of "non-erosion of capital" – as we will see below, in the tax systems reviewed that have adopted the Advance Approach (i.e. in the US and Israel), no parallel mechanism is created (that resembles the accounting matching principle) whereby the timing will also be advanced for the recognition of all or any of the liabilities that have been taken for the transaction at the time the advance was received.[289] In the absence of such a mechanism, the Advance Approach creates a result whereby, in the year in which the advance is received, tax is imposed on the full advance turnover irrespective of the question of what constitutes the "profit" on which the taxpayer should be taxed.

This is mainly seen in the US, where, alongside adopting the Advance Approach, both the legislature and the courts "have endeavored" to prevent taxpayers from enjoying the benefits of economic advantages in relation to the timing of the recognition of liabilities as an expense. However, in its effort to do so, the US tax system has deferred the timing of the deduction of the liabilities for making a sale or for providing services in respect of which the advance was received, as an expense for tax purposes, "almost" until the date of the actual payment thereof.[290] This time difference creates a distortion in the calculation of the tax, and provides the Treasury with the option of benefiting from the use of the cash flow that accrues to it as a result of the early collection of the tax calculated on the turnover.[291] Moreover, this time gap might ultimately lead to a result whereby collection of the tax, while incidentally violating the principle of non-erosion of capital,[292] would harm other interested parties of the taxpayer, both from the intrinsic dilution (in the immediate term) of the taxpayer's resources (as distinct from tax on addition to wealth), which could violate the taxpayer's stability, and from the very preference that IRS enjoys as against other creditors.[293]

Violating other tax values – the Advance Approach originated, as we have seen, in the attempt made by the Dualistic Doctrine to protect tax values against violation by means of the use of GAAP.[294] However, it appears that it is actually the Advance Approach itself that violates tax values in the name of that which it seeks to protect. Thus, applying the Advance Approach (together with negating the option of deducting the liabilities related to that advance as an expense on the date on which it is received)[295] leads to payment of tax in advance in respect of the full advance turnover. Economically, it is easily possible to "transform" almost every advance into a loan, and as long as it is not possible to tax the principal of the loan, to bring about the undesirable result whereby transactions that are substantially identical appear to be taxed differently.[296] The same applies to the use of the device of a deposit as a substitute for an advance.[297] There is no economic advantage in determining the tax results of a transaction according to the nature of its financing and the nature of the repayment of the principal that has been granted as a loan.[298] Therefore, the value of tax neutrality could be violated in the implementation of the Deferral Approach by creating a tax advantage in the case of advancing payments as opposed to a case of making payments in the same real terms on a later date. Nevertheless, the same tax value itself could be violated in the implementation of the Advance Approach by creating a tax disadvantage in a case where an advance is received in contrast to one where a loan is received that will be repaid to the lender (in its future value) on the date on which the income is earned.[299]

Erosion of the Proportionality Principle – the Advance Approach, (like the Income Approach in relation to deposits), is an example of "loss of proportion". According to the tests that we proposed above,[300] the Advance Approach fulfills the first test of the Proportionality Principle ("the rational means test"), since this approach is a rational means that serves the objective of preventing unjust tax advantages which it is intended to serve.

However, the Advance Approach fails two other tests of the Proportionality Principle, namely the "less harmful means test" and the "relative means test". The failure of the Advance Approach to meet the second test of the Proportionality Principle ("the less harmful means test") results from the fact that, as we will see below, it is possible to achieve the same objective by alternative means, whose harm to other values is somewhat less.[301] The Advance Approach also does not meet the third test of the Proportionality Principle ("relative means test"), since the result of the implementation of this approach (in combination with deferring the recognition of the deduction of the liabilities that were undertaken) involves imposing tax on the full amount of the advance (including the liability component). This result of imposing tax on an amount received is totally unconnected with the addition to wealth and harms the non-erosion of capital value to an extent that justifies negating the use of this approach even at the price of relinquishing the objective of preventing unjust tax advantages.

In light of the above, it is submitted that neither the Advance Approach nor the Deferral Approach provides a proper response to the question of the timing of the recognition of income from advances, for tax purposes, and therefore the possibility of implementing another model should be examined.

7 Timing of the deduction of future expenses

The subject of the timing of the recognition of income is not "motionless in space". When measuring profit during a defined period, the respective timing of the recognition of the income and that of the liabilities that are required for producing it cannot be divorced from one another, regardless of whether the liability is financial or relates to the supply of goods or services.[1]

Not every liability is deductible for tax purposes. The various tax systems have prescribed different substantive conditions for deducting an expense in calculating taxable income.[2] Moreover, even if the liability is deductible for tax purposes, on the subject of timing there are specific statutory provisions that provide restrictions for certain liabilities which create a correlation between the timing of the recognition of the expense and that of the actual payment.[3]

This study does not examine the substantive criteria for deducting an expense, but only the question of the timing of the recognition of the expense, and this only where no specific statutory provision exists that lays down in a given case the defined timing for deducting a liability which has not yet been paid (hereinafter: "**future expenses**").

In confronting the question of the timing of the deduction of a liability for tax purposes, tax laws must address two elements.

The first is the risk that, ultimately, the liability for which the deduction is requested may not fully, or may only partially, materialize (hereinafter: "**the risk element**").

The second concerns the value at which to deduct a liability that will be performed on a future date, where it is clear that the longer the period between the time of the deduction and the date of its performance the greater the difference between the future nominal value of the liability and its present value (hereinafter: "**the time-difference element**").

7.1 The certainty level question and the time gap question

Assuming that no statutory provisions exist that prohibit the deduction of a future expense in a given case, and assuming that no statutory provisions define the timing for deduction in a given case, how should the timing of the recognition of future expenses be determined for tax purposes? This question is raised on two levels.

The first is the question of the risk element, which concerns determining the level of certainty required in regard to the future performance of the liability in the year in which the taxpayer seeks to deduct the liability as an expense (hereinafter: "**the certainty level question**").

The second is that of the time-difference element, which concerns what the amount of the deduction should be in light of the timing of the expected payment in the future (hereinafter: "**the time gap question**").

While the first question relates in the main to the relationship between GAAP and tax laws, the second question relates to the time value of money theory.

7.1.1 *The certainty level question*

On the question of the level of certainty required as a condition for deducting a future expense, the tax systems reviewed adopt one of three approaches, which will be called: the "**Absolute Certainty Degree**", the "**High Certainty Degree**" and the "**Accounting Certainty Degree**".

The **Absolute Certainty Degree** means that only liabilities that have crystallized before the end of the specific year ("the current year") will be eligible for deduction as an expense. In these cases, certainty must relate to the very existence of the liability as well as its amount, and also to the timing of its payment. Where this degree of certainty is required, there is no possibility of deducting a liability that is uncertain,[4] even where the uncertainty relates only to the timing of the performance or amount of the liability.[5]

The **High Certainty Degree** means that liabilities that have crystallized before the end of the current year will be deductible, even if there is an element of uncertainty relating to the amount or the timing of the performance, provided that the amount of the liabilities or the day of payment can be proven by means of objective evidence, and not by means of evaluations or calculations.

The **Accounting Certainty Degree** means that the liability that has to be deducted according to GAAP in calculating the "financial profits" (provided the liability is deductible under the substantive criteria of the law) should be deductible for tax purposes at the same time. The main difference between being satisfied with this degree of certainty and the requirement of high certainty relates to "provision". In the absence of certainty relating to the amount of the liability or the timing of perform-ance, the High Certainty Degree requires objective evidence, while this level of certainty will permit the amount of the provision to be deducted as an expense, even if it is based only on evaluations and calculations unsupported by objective evidence.[6]

7.1.2 *The time gap question*

In addition to the question of the level of certainty required as a condition for deducting a liability as an expense, another question should be raised regarding the relationship between the timing of the deduction, and the date of payment. On this subject, the tax systems adopt one of three approaches, which will be called the "**Full and Immediate Deduction Approach**", the "**Deferred Deduction Date Approach**" and the "**Partial Deduction Approach**".

The Full and Immediate Deduction Approach holds that if the required level of certainty for deducting a liability as an expense exists, the full amount of the liability ought to be recognized as an expense on that date.

The Deferred Deduction Date Approach, which is the opposite of the first, asserts that even if the required certainty exists in relation to the future performance of the liability, deduction of the liability should be deferred in order to bring as close as possible to the actual performance date, in order to obviate the tax advantages that would ensue from "advancing" the deduction.

The Partial Deduction Approach would not allow the deduction of the full amount of the liability, but would take different factors into account, including the prospect of the performance of the liability, as well as the expected timing of the actual payment, and would allow the deduction of only a portion of the liability amount in the current year. The precise portion would take the probability of future payment into account, as well as the formula that calculates the present value of the future payment.

7.1.3 *Compatibility to the timing recognition of income*

In cases in which the income has already been earned, the question of matching this income to the liabilities undertaken for producing it is of great importance. This question becomes even more important when dealing with receivables (like deposits or advances), which have not yet been earned, because such receivables, by their very nature, are interconnected with future expenses.

We might have expected that those who support the Singular Doctrine with respect to the relationship between GAAP and tax law, and who support the Loan Approach (in relation to deposits) or the Deferral Approach (in relation to advances), would certainly seek to bring tax laws to "adopt" the Accounting Certainty Degree and the Full and Immediate

Deduction Approach, to the extent that it applies to liabilities.[7] Moreover, based on the matching principle,[8] it is probable that the supporters of the Singular Doctrine would also support deferring the day of deduction of liabilities which were undertaken in order to achieve an income from deposit or advance, until the date of the recognition of that income.[9] In contrast, we would have expected that even if the Deferral Approach were accepted, those who support the Dualistic Doctrine[10] would not necessarily accept the Accounting Certainty Degree and the Full and Immediate Deduction Approach. To their way of thinking, just as the various tax values justify "advancing" the timing of the recognition of income in respect of advances that have yet to be earned, the advantage deriving from "advancing" the timing of the recognition of future expenses that have yet to be actually paid should similarly be rejected. They will therefore prefer the Absolute or High Certainty Degree, accompanied by the Deferred Deduction Date Approach or the Partial Deduction Approach.

If the Income Approach is accepted (in relation to deposits), or the Advance Approach (in relation to advances), then applying one of the above-mentioned requirements of certainty in fixing the timing of deduction of future expenses might lead to the result that tax will be imposed on the full amount of the deposit or the advance in the year in which it had been received (and not on the profit inherent therein).[11]

7.2 Timing of deduction of future expenses – UK tax law

As stated, our question deals with the timing of deducting a liability as an expense based on the assumption that the liability itself is indeed deductible according to statute,[12] and on the assumption that no specific statutory provision exists with respect to the timing of the deduction.[13] In relation to this question, UK tax system "has made do" with a reference to GAAP[14] for measuring purposes, and has not statutorily fixed general conditions for the timing of the deduction of future expenses.[15] In light of the general reference to GAAP, the legislation has also not fixed a method for measuring the amount of expenses deductible in the future for tax purposes.[16] Where no such specific statutory provision exists, it seems that the UK tax system, relying on the Singular Doctrine, adopts the Accounting Certainty Degree,[17] in order to determine the timing of the recognition of a liability as an expense. Furthermore, consistent with the Singular Doctrine, this system adopts the Full and Immediate Deduction Approach,[18] except in the case of provisions which, according to accounting theory itself, are to be fixed in an amount that takes account of the timing component and the risk factor.

7.2.1 The case law

The UK case law in relation to the deduction of future expenses for tax purposes will be divided into two: the case law that deals mainly with the question of the degree of certainty required in relation to the existence of a liability as a condition for its deduction for tax purposes, and case law that deals with the time gap question.

7.2.1.1 The required degree of certainty

In UK case law we find a borderline dividing the territory of liabilities into two: liabilities that have not been permitted for deduction in the current year for not meeting the required conditions of certainty, and liabilities that meet the conditions and are allowed for deduction in the current year.

In *Southern Railway of Peru*,[19] the company sought to deduct provisions that it had made for statutory liabilities that it was required to bear for the dismissal of its employees at the termination of their employment. The provisions were calculated as a comprehensive sum that it would be required to pay if all its employees were dismissed at the end of the current year (i.e. on the basis of the most "catastrophic" case), without making any reduction. The House of Lords (per Lord Radcliffe) asked two questions in respect of such provisions: "The first is – Have I adequately stated my profits for the year if I do not include some figure in respect of these obligations? The second is – Do the circumstances of the case, which include the techniques of established accounting practice, make it possible to supply a figure reliable enough for the purpose?"[20] With respect to this last question, the learned judge rejected the evidence concerning accounting practice by stating that it was not sufficient in order to show that the provision reflected the need to give a correct picture of the company's profits.[21] However, despite the taxpayer's non-compliance with the required conditions in the specific circumstances of that case, since that case the rule has been that a provision for a liability that has yet to become absolute will be deductible if, according to accounting theory, such a provision should be taken into account in calculating the profit/loss in that year, and if GAAP provides for making a sufficiently reasonable assessment.[22]

In *Britannia Airways*,[23] the company operated charter aircraft, some owned and some operated under charter agreements. According to statute, it was not possible to operate aviation lines without a permit. As a condition for granting such a permit, the aircraft engines were required to undergo a general overhaul after every 17,000 hours of operation. The company sought to deduct a provision for such maintenance.[24] HMRC refused to allow the provision as a deduction for tax purposes. The court affirmed the special commissioners' decision by ruling that there was nothing by law to prevent the deduction for tax purposes of a provision that reflected the "true and fair view" of the firm's condition, and which had been made according to accepted accounting principles.[25]

In the *Jenners* case,[26] the directors of the company made a feasibility test with respect to the repair and renovation of the company's shop. At the end of the fiscal year in which the check was made, the company sought to deduct a provision that it had made in respect of such renovations as an expense, although the company had yet to enter into an agreement with a contractor. Thus, the work creating the liability had not yet been carried out and, in any event, the obligation to pay for the work had not yet crystallized.[27] The company's appeal to the special commissioners was allowed with the ruling that inclusion of this provision in calculating the company's profits complied with accounting principles. It should be noted in that case that the company had a pre-existing commitment to maintain the premises, by virtue of the lease between the company and the landlord. Therefore, it could be said that there was an existing liability (not vis-à-vis the contractor but towards the landlord) and, this being so, upon making the evaluation of the amount required for making the repairs all the required conditions had been fulfilled in order to allow the provision for deduction according to GAAP.[28]

In *Herbert Smith*,[29] a lawyers' partnership requested to deduct for tax purposes a provision that it had made in respect of a liability to pay rent for a property that it had leased and vacated, although it was clear that it would not use the property for purposes of its business. The provision was calculated as if the partnership would be compelled to pay the full rent on the property it vacated, without making any reduction on account of the possibility that this rent might be reduced in the event of the property being leased to others. In addition, no reduction had been made for the time component until the making of payment. The court allowed a full deduction of the provision. According to the court, there was no directive or general principle in tax law that prevented the deduction of amounts that had been taken into account in calculating the profit/loss according to GAAP, even if the reason for their inclusion in this calculation resulted from the prudence principle and not from the matching principle. In addressing the previous case law, which had found that a future loss should not be deducted as an expense,[30] the court stated that deducting a provision for future expected expenses should not be regarded as "the evaluation of losses" in the fiscal years in the future, but a condition required for assessing the profits in the current year.[31]

In the same vein, in cases like *Lion Brewery*,[32] *Sun Insurance*,[33] *Titaghur Jute Factory*[34] and *Lo*,[35] the court allowed the deduction of provisions in relation to liabilities that had been created in the past and whose existence was certain, although there was uncertainty relating to the amount or timing of their performance.

In contrast to these examples, the courts have refused to allow the deduction of provisions for pending debts in two types of case.

The first type is where the provision relates to a liability that is not substantively available for deduction because it is a liability of a capital nature, or its essential deduction is prohibited by statutory provision, or where the law dictates the timing of the deduction of the liability in respect of which the provision is made.[36] Regarding this exception, it is clear that where it is not possible by law to deduct the liability itself when it becomes certain and absolute, a provision in respect of that liability may not be deducted before it has become certain and absolute.[37]

The second type of case disallowed deduction of provisions that have been made before certainty arises with respect to the essential existence of the liability itself. That is to say, in the year in which the deduction is claimed uncertainty applies not only with respect to the amount of the liability or the timing of its performance but also to the actual existence of the liability itself.[38] Thus, e.g. in *Navel Colliery*[39] and in *Merchant*,[40] provisions relating to reconditioning works that had yet to be carried out were interpreted as contingencies and not allowed.[41] In *Monthly Salaries*,[42] provisions in respect to future collection operations for debts that had been incurred in previous years were not allowed. In *H Ford*,[43] *Spencer (James)*[44] and *Niddrie & Benhar*,[45] provisions relating to demands or claims in dispute were not allowed. In *Worsley Brewery*,[46] provisions in respect of wage demands made by service-suppliers that had been made in later years, but which related to work that had been carried out in previous years were disallowed. In *Albion Rovers*,[47] provisions in respect of a wage liability to players where the obligation to pay according to the agreement only crystallized in the future (after the end of the current year) were not allowed. These provisions were interpreted by the court as an attempt "to advance" the timing of deducting the expense. In *Collins*,[48] *Young*,[49] *Whimster*[50] and *Barrie*,[51] provisions that the court interpreted as having been intended to "advance" the recognition of the expected assessed losses in the future that were not necessarily reflected in an existing commitment in the present were not allowed.[52] However, it is possible that following the *Herbert Smith* case, the result in relation to some of the above cases would today be otherwise.

7.2.1.2 The time gap question

From cases like *Paisley*,[53] *London Cemetery*,[54] *Vallambrosa*,[55] *Duple Motor*[56] and *Threlfall*,[57] it seems that UK case law has embraced GAAP for tax law not only in respect of the level of required certainty, but has also adopted the Full and Immediate Deduction Approach. That is to say, identical to GAAP, the performance timing of the liability "has no role to play" in determining the timing of the deduction and its amount.[58] In this context, it should be noted that it appears that the cases that sought to follow GAAP and "sever themselves" from the actual date of payment, did not always display awareness of the distinction that GAAP itself makes.

According to GAAP, whereby general future expenses will be reduced in calculating the profit/loss on the date they crystallize (regardless of the date of their payment in the future), specific future expenses (that can be imputed specifically to certain income) will not be deducted in calculating the accounting profit/loss on the date they crystallize, but their deduction will be deferred by virtue of the matching principle to the date on which this certain income will be recognized (irrespective of the date of the payment).[59] Nevertheless, due to unawareness of this distinction, some cases have established a "quasi-legal rule" to the effect that, in any event, the timing of the recognition of the future expenses will be the date on which they crystallize (as distinct from their date of payment).[60] For our purposes, the absence of this distinction is immaterial, as long as the case law has the insight to separate the timing of crystallization of the liability as operating for tax purposes from the date of the future performance.[61]

7.2.2 *Administrative directives*

On the question of the required level of certainty – HMRC has also adopted the position that the existence of the Accounting Certainty Degree is sufficient as a condition for the timing of the date of the recognition of a liability as an expense. In this vein, HMRC has determined that provisions for covering contingent debts will be deductible for tax purposes subject to the existence of four conditions:[62] first, the provision relates to a liability that, by substantive law, may be deducted; second, the provision is required according to GAAP; third, the provision does not deviate from any legal rule that applies on the date on which the deduction is requested; and fourth, that sufficient tools exist to estimate the amount of the provision with reasonable probability.[63]

On the question of time gap between the date of the deduction and the date of expected payment – HMRC's position has also been accepted in the spirit of the Consistent Approach. In other words, where GAAP directs the Full and Immediate Deduction Approach, this will also be the accepted position for tax purposes. Where GAAP directs that the time component ought to be taken into account (as is the case, for example, in relation to provisions), the amount of the deduction will be correspondingly fixed. Where GAAP defers the timing of recognition of a liability to a date subsequent to the date on which it crystallizes (mainly where this deferral is required by the matching principle), the timing of the recognition of the expense for tax purposes will correspondingly be deferred, irrespective of the timing of the making of the payments.[64]

7.2.3 *Comments*

It seems that the academic commentary has followed the results of the cases, and states that provisions relating to a liability that is substantively available for deduction will be deductible, subject to the fulfillment of the conditions laid down by GAAP.[65] It also seems that the academic commentary has accepted the idea of allowing future expenses to be deducted at their current value for tax purposes, whatever the future payment date might be.[66]

7.3 Timing of deduction of future expenses – US tax law

US federal legislation (like that of the UK and Israel) provides for a series of substantive conditions for deducting a liability as an expense for tax purposes.[67] In certain cases, it also provides the timing on which liabilities may be deducted for tax purposes.[68] However, as we have mentioned, our question relates to the timing of the recognition of a liability as an expense, assuming that the liability itself may be deducted by statute, and assuming further, that with respect to the timing of the deduction thereof, no specific statutory provision provides otherwise. With respect to this question, the Dualistic Doctrine and the various tax values underlying the development of the Income Approach (alongside the Loan Approach) in relation to deposits, and the Advance Approach in relation to advances, have also led to the adoption of strict standards with respect to the timing of the deduction of future expenses for tax purposes.

7.3.1 Legislation

As mentioned above, similar to the UK and the Israeli tax legislation,[69] US tax legislation has determined some provisions relating to the timing of the recognition of an expense in specific defined cases.[70] Nevertheless, US federal tax legislation has also expressly determined general conditions regarding the timing of the recognition of expenses for tax purposes. These conditions apply, as a rule, to all taxpayers, whatever their reporting system may be, and regardless of the type of liabilities that may be in question.

IRC§461(a)[71] establishes the rule that the timing of the deduction of an expense, which, by law, is available for deduction as such, will only fall in the fiscal year that is the "correct" year in which it may be deducted according to the accounting system in which the taxpayer keeps his books.[72] However, the legislature, true to its previous practice, imposed conditions and set exceptions to this rule. Over and above specific exceptions,[73] the legislation has been extended to impose diverse conditions on the timing of the recognition of expenses, as follows.

Alongside the "rule" contained in IRC§461(a), the "exception" contained in IRC§446(b) enables IRS not to recognize the timing of the recognition of a liability as an expense for tax purposes where this timing fails to fulfill the condition of "clearly reflect income".[74]

In addition, the "rule" contained in IRC§461(a) has been limited to the determination contained in Treas Reg §1.461–1(a)2, which states that in affixing the timing of the recognition of a liability as an expense for tax purposes, the "all events test" condition should be met.[75]

However, the legislature, not satisfied merely with the condition contained in IRC§446(b), and the condition of Treas Reg §1.461–1(a)(2), added, in the 84 Reform,[76] a further condition in regard to the timing of the recognition of an expense for tax purposes, namely "economic performance".[77]

According to the "economic performance" condition, the timing of the recognition of a liability as an expense for tax purposes will be deferred with regard to four types of liability:

First, in regard to a liability with respect to the acquisition of services or assets by the taxpayer, the deduction timing will be deferred until the actual date of supply of the services or assets (or be used for the assets in connection with which the liability was created), and the mere existence of the liability will be insufficient.[78]

Second, for a liability to a customer to supply services or assets in the future (generally being liabilities on account of which the taxpayer receives advances), the deduction timing will be deferred until the date on which the taxpayer will indeed supply those services or assets.[79]

Third, for a liability to make payments relating to claims for damages or employee relations, the deduction timing will be deferred until the date of the actual making of the payment.[80]

The fourth type, deals with "other liabilities", for which the Regulations determine a specific timing.[81] Such Regulations were enacted with respect to financing liabilities, and determined that the deduction timing will be deferred until the actual date of making the payments. Other Regulations were enacted with respect to liabilities undertaken for future rent and payments for the acquisition of equipment, determining that the OID method will be adopted, according to which the liability will be accounted in the present value of the liability amount.[82] Other Regulations provide that if a taxpayer is liable to pay a tax, economic performance occurs as the tax is paid to the governmental authority that imposed it.[83]

Treas Reg §1.461–5(b)(1) provides a recurring item exception to the general rule of economic performance. Under the recurring item exception, a liability is treated as incurred for a taxable year if: (a) at the end of the taxable year, all events have occurred that establish the fact of the liability, and the amount can be determined with reasonable accuracy; (b) economic performance occurs on or before the earlier of (i) the date that the taxpayer files a return (including extensions) for the taxable year, or (ii) the 15th day of the ninth calendar month after the close of the taxable year; (c) the liability is recurring in nature; and (d) either the amount of the liability is not material, or accrual of the liability in the taxable year results in better matching of the liability against the income to which it relates than would result from accrual of the liability in the taxable year in which economic performance occurs.[84]

Thus, the "rule" contained in IRC§461(a) is subject to compliance with three further conditions regarding the timing:

- the first is that in the year in which the taxpayer requests deduction of the liability as an expense ("the current year"), the "all events test" condition will pertain; and
- the second is that deduction of the liability as an expense on that date will meet the "clearly reflect income" condition; and
- the third is that in relation to various liabilities (as prescribed in IRC§461(h)), the "economic performance" condition applies.

7.3.2 The case law

US case law will be divided into two: the case law that deals mainly with the question of the degree of certainty required in relation to the existence of a liability as a condition for its deduction for tax purposes, and the case law that deals with the time gap between the date of the deduction and the date of actual performance.

7.3.2.1 The required degree of certainty

Contrary to the UK system of "making do" with the Accounting Certainty Degree for determining the date of allowing the deduction of a liability,[85] US case law has disregarded GAAP in determining the required degree of certainty as a condition for deducting a liability as an expense. The broad interpretation given by the US courts to the powers of IRS under paragraph 446(b) in defining the term "clearly reflect income", and the narrow interpretation given to the "all events test", have resulted in rejecting the Accounting Certainty Degree,[86] and demanding a higher degree of certainty as a condition for deducting a liability on a specific date.[87]

7.3.2.1.1 REJECTION OF THE ACCOUNTING CERTAINTY DEGREE

In *Bauer*,[88] it was held that an expense would not be allowed even if a legal commitment existed to pay it, and that the timing of its recognition for tax purposes would not be earlier than the year in which the conditions of the "all events test" make the expense an absolute and fixed sum.

In *Brown*,[89] commissions received by a general insurance agent were subject to a partial duty of repayment to the insured, where the insured cancelled the policies. Following GAAP, the company made a provision in respect of part of the commissions that it had received, calculating the expected rate of repayment for cancelled policies based upon an evaluation of its five years' previous experience.[90] The court held that no deduction of an uncertain liability should be allowed in a tax year, even if it is highly probable that it would be realized in the future. The court refused to allow the deduction of the provision, ruling that the event that created the taxpayer's commitment to return the commissions it had taken (i.e. cancellation of specific policies in the ensuing year) had yet to occur in the current year (in which the provision for deduction had been claimed). The event occurred in a later year, upon the effective cancellation of the policies, and only in that (later) year was the taxpayer entitled to deduct an expense in respect of the return of the commissions.

In *Dixie Pine*,[91] it was held that according to the "all events test", laid down in the *Brown* case, it is not possible to deduct a liability that was created in the past, so long as the amount of the liability is not clear and certain. It was therefore held that provisions made according to GAAP could not be deducted as an expense even if there were a high degree of probability that the taxpayer would be required to pay it in the future.[92]

In some cases (like in *Harold*,[93] *Ohio River Collieries*,[94] *Pacific Grape*,[95] *Schuessler*,[96] *Beacon*,[97] *Jefferson*,[98] *Bituminous*[99]), provisions were allowed for deduction although based upon estimates or assessments relating to the liabilities.

Nevertheless, these cases were exceptions. It seems that, since the *Brown* case, US case law has not allowed deducting of provision for future expenses based upon estimates or assessments relating to the liability. According to US case law, the Accounting Certainty Degree is insufficient, even if the liability was created in the past there was a high degree of probability that the taxpayer would be required to fulfill it in the future, and the taxpayer was required according to GAAP to deduct this provision in calculating the profit. As long as the liability amount was not clear and fixed, and relied on evaluations or assessments of the extent of the liability, this would be sufficient to disallow the deduction of the expense on the date on which the provision was made. Thus, in cases like *Harrison*,[100] *Vang*,[101] *Quality Roofing*,[102] *American Code*,[103] *Old Dominion*,[104] *Southeastern Express*,[105] *Strother*,[106] *Acacia Park*,[107] *Security Flour Mills*,[108] *Stevenson*,[109] *Bell Electric*,[110] *Peoples Bank*,[111] *All-Steel*,[112] *Continental Illinois*,[113] *Fox*,[114] *Diversified Fashions*,[115] *Exxon*[116] and many others,[117] it was held that the deduction of a provision would be denied, at least until the date on which the amount of the liability for which the deduction was sought was fixed, and would not be dependent on evaluations or assessments.

7.3.2.1.2 THE DISTINCTION BETWEEN CASH LIABILITIES AND OTHER LIABILITIES

The reluctance to be aided by calculations and evaluations has led to a distinction between those cases in which the liability was for the making of a cash payment (where there was no problem to supply objective evidence regarding the extent of the liability) (**"the cash payment liability"**), and cases where the liability was to provide future services, where the amount involved necessarily relied on evaluations or calculations ("**the service provision liability**"). While, usually, a cash payment liability has been allowed for deduction, whatever the payment date in the future,[118] it was held in *Villa Franca*,[119] *White & Prentis*,[120] *Harris*,[121] *Bell Electric* [122] and other cases[123] that the service provision liability was not allowed for deduction, even if the date on which it will be made in the future was far closer than the performance date of the payment liability. While GAAP does not distinguish between these two types of liabilities, the cases have chosen to address a service provision liability, under the heading of "contingent liabilities", even where absolute certainty exists with respect to the liability itself, and the uncertainty relates only to the amount of the liability.[124]

7.3.2.1.3 ADOPTING THE HIGH OR THE ABSOLUTE CERTAINTY DEGREE

From our discussion until now, we have learned that US case law has not allowed a provision that meets the Accounting Certainty Degree as a deductible expense. The question then arises as to what is the required degree of certainty for deducting a liability as an expense.

In *Brooklyn Radio*,[125] *American Hotels* [126] and *Joseph*,[127] the court accepted the approach that it was not possible to allow a liability as a deduction unless not only was the liability certain and absolute, but its amount had also become final and absolute in the fiscal year in which the expense had been claimed.

In *Baltimore*,[128] *Stiver*,[129] *Rhodes*,[130] *Shoolman* [131] and *Bickerstaff*,[132] the court allowed a liability to be deducted in the current year if the events that transformed the liability into absolute and certain already existed. However, it was not required that the amount of the liability be a clear and absolute sum, as long as the sum could be fixed with "reasonable certainty".

In the *Crescent Wharf* case,[133] the appeals court interpreted the "all events test" as requiring certainty and absoluteness in relation to the intrinsic existence of the liability in the present year, although it would be sufficient for the liability amount to be fixed with "reasonable accuracy".

In addressing the precedents in *Milwaukee & Suburban Transport Corp*,[134] *AAA* [135] and the *Consolidated Edison* cases,[136] the appeals court stated that despite the certainty of the existence of the liability in the present year, its deduction as an expense was disallowed not because of the absence of absoluteness with respect to its amount, but because the amount of the liability itself was in dispute, or the subject of legal proceedings,[137] or was speculative.[138] The main innovation of this judgment was the very willingness of the appeals court to allow the deduction of the provision as an expense, despite the fact that the liability amount itself was neither absolute nor certain. In this regard, the court directed that assistance be gleaned from opinions of experts that would fix the expected indemnity amount according to the State legislation.[139]

It would appear that in 1986 this willingness was overruled by two Supreme Court decisions.

In *Hughes*,[140] a provision was made by a casino owner for an additional win accumulating over an unknown number of years. IRS believed that the casino owner was only entitled to deduct the liability to pay the accrued win amount as an expense at the date when a person actually won it (i.e. on an unknown future date), since only on this future date would the liability meet the conditions of "fixed and certain", "unconditional" and "absolute", as required under the "all events test".[141] This position of IRS, which was affirmed by the appeals court a number of years earlier in a similar matter,[142] was rejected by the Supreme Court. The court ruled that the Nevada Gaming Commission Regulations made the taxpayer's liability fixed and certain, and the fact that the identity of the future recipient who would win the prize was not yet known, and that the time of the payment was similarly unknown, made no difference regarding the timing of the recognition of the liability as an expense. The court ruled (in the spirit of the matching principle) that the commitment to pay the accrued win was inseparably connected to income in the current year from those machines in respect of which the liability arose, and therefore it was correct to allow the deduction of that provision in that year.[143] However, in the very same year in which the Supreme Court handed down its decision in the *Hughes* case, the same court appears to have done an about face.

In *General Dynamics Corp ("GD")*,[144] a company served as "self-insurer" in relation to its employees' medical insurance plan. According to this insurance plan, the insured employees were entitled to make claims for participation in their medical costs. After examination of the claim forms and approval of the medical coverage, the taxpayer (like an insurance company) would confirm the amount of its participation in covering the employee's medical costs. The taxpayer did not ask to deduct provisions in respect of its assessment of covering its expected future payments regarding insurance cases that had yet to occur, and in respect of which it would have to pay amounts that it had collected from its insured employees. This was not even discussed.[145] The company sought to deduct as an expense the provision that it had made in respect of its liability to pay the indemnity amounts on account of cases that had already occurred during the fiscal year, but for which the insured employees had yet to submit claim forms, and with respect to these cases only. Notwithstanding the expectation that, following the *Hughes* case, the taxpayer would also succeed on the question of the timing of allowing the expense,[146] the result was actually the reverse. The majority opinion relied, *inter alia*, on an empirical test, according to which a certain shortfall existed in previous years between the indemnity amounts that the company had actually paid, and what it ought to have paid had all its employees who received medical services actually claimed a refund.[147]

This shortfall justified, according to the majority view, the conclusion that the provision that had been made was not available for deduction, since the liability had not crystallized to an absolute and certain liability at the end of the year for which the expense was claimed.[148] Based on prior case law,[149] the majority view was that whatever the measure of probability might be concerning the expected realization of future expenses, the performance of the liability crystallized through a number of stages, and that liability would be available for deduction only after the date on which "the last stage in the chain" of the events whose performance created the liability, was completed.[150] The fact that the insured parties received medical services, entitling them to receive indemnity amounts from the company, was merely one link in the chain creating the company's liability. The non-submission of the claim forms by those insured parties constituted the last and missing link needed to transform the company's liability into a certain and absolute debt.[151] The minority view believed that even if it recognized the gap between the goals of financial accounting and the tax laws, the majority view had completely delegitimized the legislature's willingness to allow taxpayers to keep their accounts for tax purposes according to GAAP, on the accrual basis method.[152]

Despite the fact that the majority opinion attempted to distinguish between this case and the ruling in the *Hughes* case by stating that in *Hughes* the possibility of the jackpot not being paid appeared to be remote and speculative, whereas in this case there was a more reasonable possibility that the liability would not be realized, it seems that the situation was in fact precisely the opposite. It is possible that there would not be a winner of the accumulated jackpot over many years, whereas it was reasonable to assume in relation to the indemnity monies to which the insured were contractually entitled, that the timing of their payment would be a short time after deduction. Moreover, according to the logic of the majority view, it was possible to deny the allowance of many certain expenses based on liabilities to suppliers, since it was additionally possible that they might not submit a bill at the end of the performance of their services. Is it conceivable that such a possibility would prevent the expense from being allowed?[153]

Furthermore, this rule reflects a regression from the basic principle that had also been recognized in the *Hughes* case that a liability could be recognized as an expense despite the existence of the possibility that ultimately it would not be paid. Beyond anything else, this rule constituted a further distancing from GAAP, and a total regression from the matching principles. The judgment in the *GD* case reversed (in my understanding) the ruling of the court of appeals in the *Crescent Wharf* case,[154] and limited (although it did not overrule) the ruling of the Supreme Court in *Hughes*.[155] Nevertheless, it seems that the *GD* ruling is that which had the greatest impact upon fixing the demand of certainty in US case law from the latter part of the 1980s onwards. Thus, e.g., in *Challenge Publications*,[156]

Dana Distributors,[157] *Arkla*[158] and *Cleveland Trencher,*[159] relying on *GD*, deduction of provisions was disallowed on the ground that at the time the provision had been recorded, "the last event in the chain of events" creating the taxpayer's liability had yet to occur.

An exception to this trend can be found in the *Gold Coast Hotel Casino* case.[160] In this case, in light of the rule in *GD*, the court of appeals was required to address the question of when the last link in the chain of events creating the liability occurred.[161] Did this last link in the chain occur at the time the club member accumulated sufficient points entitling him to a prize (as asserted by the taxpayer) or possibly when the club member demanded conversion of the points that he had accumulated, into prizes (as argued by IRS). The appeals court ruled that this case had to be distinguished from the circumstances that had arisen in the *GD* case. In the latter case it was held that the last link in the chain of events creating the liability was fulfilled on the date of the filing of the claim forms, following the involvement of a third party (namely the supplier of the medical services). The court ruled that this case more closely resembled the circumstances of the *Hughes* case, where the very existence of the liability was independent of any third party.[162] Thus, the court of appeals ruled that reaching the stage at which the liability became absolute and final did not depend on the making of a demand by the club member to convert the points into prizes. The last link in the chain creating the liability had already been fulfilled at the stage at which the member accumulated sufficient points to entitle him to a prize.[163]

This test has created an inherent distinction between the timing of the recognition of income and the timing of the recognition of those liabilities that were used for obtaining income.[164]

7.3.2.2 *The time gap question*

Indeed, the higher the degree of certainty required for deducting a liability as an expense on a given date, the more probable it is that the time gap between the date of the deduction and that of the expected payment will be shortened. However, there are still cases, most of them relating to cash payment liabilities,[165] where a time gap exists between the date on which the required degree of certainty obtains and the date of the expected payment. In relation to the time gap question, we mentioned that there are three possible approaches, which we called the Full and Immediate Deduction Approach, the Deferred Deduction Date Approach and the Partial Deduction Approach.[166]

Perusal of US case law shows that support may be found for each of these approaches.

7.3.2.2.1   SUPPORT FOR THE FULL AND IMMEDIATE DEDUCTION APPROACH

The Full and Immediate Deduction Approach was adopted in most cases relating to cash payment liabilities (which by nature have a certain and absolute amount). Even where the expected payment date of the cash payment liability was remote from the date of the requested deduction, the liability was permitted for immediate deduction at its full value.

In cases like *Anderson*,[167] *Laurens Steel*,[168] *Franklin County*,[169] *Cyclops*,[170] *Inland Steel*,[171] *Washington Post*[172] and *Reynolds Metals*,[173] with respect to liabilities to make financial payments (i.e. the cash payment liability), it was ruled that deduction thereof may be made immediately (in the current year) in the full value (i.e. its nominal value) even where the timing of the payment and the identity of the recipient are unknown. The Full and Immediate Deduction Approach was also accepted in *Cooper*,[174] *Crescent Wharf*,[175] *Hughes*[176] and *Gold Coast*,[177] where the liability amount necessarily involved relying on evaluations, and therefore could not be defined as relating to the "cash payment liability".[178] In these cases, not only did the court find it appropriate to prefer a less strict interpretative approach regarding the degree of certainty required as a condition for deducting in a given year, but additionally allowed the deduction in the full amount of the liability, despite the fact that the timing of the expected payment in the future was unknown.

It seems that the Full and Immediate Deduction Approach was strictly applied in the *Burnham* case.[179] In this instance the taxpayer undertook, under a compromise agreement that had been made during a legal proceeding regarding a patent, to pay the plaintiff $1,250 per month throughout the entire life of the plaintiff (with a minimum period of at least four years). The taxpayer estimated that the plaintiff would live for another 16 years, and claimed an immediate deduction of his expected expenses by virtue of the agreement, in the sum of $240,000.[180] The court examined the existence of the "all events test" conditions, and allowed deduction of the full amount of the liability, ruling that the liability was certain and absolute, and the possibility that the plaintiff would not live through the entire period (16 years) was not an event that made the debt uncertain or not absolute.

7.3.2.2.2   SUPPORT FOR THE DEFERRED DEDUCTION DATE APPROACH

Within the scope of the 84 Reform, IRC§461(h) was added, establishing the "economic performance" test.[181] However, the case law hardly needed to apply this section in order to achieve the same result of deferring the timing of the recognition of expense, due mainly to the strict, narrow interpretation applied to the "all events test" in *GD*,[182] and the cases that followed it.[183]

The interpretation of the "all events test",[184] as requiring the existence of the "last of the chain of events" that creates the liability, was not the only means used to achieve the result of deferring the timing of the recognition of expense. The "clearly reflect income" test[185] was also employed to achieve that result. This was the case in *Mooney Aircraft*.[186] That case dealt with a manufacturer of light aircraft that, at the time of the sale of an aircraft, gave the customer a voucher called a "mooney bond" which entitled the purchaser to $1,000, to be received in the event of the plane going out of service (which was expected to occur some 20 years or more after the sale). As required by the matching principle, the company sought to deduct this liability (of $1,000) in the year of the sale of the aircraft, against its income from the sale. IRS raised two arguments against allowing the expense. The first was that deducting the liability in the year of the sale of the plane was too early since the expense did not meet the "all events test". The court rejected this argument, ruling that the future retirement of the plane from service, which was the only condition set for the customer's entitlement to receive the money, was an event that was expected to occur with certainty and this, consequently, created an absolute commitment that met the "all events test". Nevertheless, the court agreed that the liability is not deductible in the year of the sale of the plane, relying on the "clearly reflect income" test. The court held that in light of the broad power that IRC§446(b) conferred upon IRS to act for tax purposes according to a different accounting system or part thereof, he had the power to disallow the deduction as an expense at such an early stage before the company was required to actually pay it.[187]

A different conception of the giving of a warranty in similar circumstances may be found in *Hodge*.[188] In that case, an airplane distributor, like the manufacturer in the *Mooney Aircraft* case, was in the practice of giving buyers a certificate conferring the right to collect $3,000 in the event of the aircraft becoming permanently unusable. However, in an examination produced to the court, it was found that during a period of 12 years, the distributor had never been asked to meet this liability (except in cases of destruction of the aircraft as a result of an air or ground accident). In those circumstances, it was held that the taxpayer could not deduct this liability as an expense in the year of the sale of the aircraft, not by reason of IRS's powers according to IRC§446(b), but due to the absence of compliance with the required degree of certainty according to the "all events test".

7.3.2.2.3 SUPPORT FOR THE PARTIAL DEDUCTION APPROACH

Alongside the Full and Immediate Deduction Approach and alongside the Deferred Deduction Date Approach, we noted that, conceptually, there is an additional interpretation that considers it correct to allow immediate deduction of future expenses, while asserting that the amount deducted should be a derivative of the present value of the liability, capitalized from the date on which the future payment is expected, until the date of actual deduction. This interpretative option is mainly relevant where a substantial time gap exists between the date of the crystallization of the liability and the date of the expected actual future payment, as in cases of the type discussed in *Burnham*, *Mooney Aircraft* and *Hodge*, in which a determination was made on the question of the relationship between the timing of the deduction of the liability and that of the expected payment, pursuant to the Full and Immediate Deduction Approach or the opposite Deferred Deduction Date Approach.

The Partial Deduction Approach won support in only one case in US tax case law. In *Ford Motor Corp*,[189] the circumstances were substantially similar to those which were discussed in the *Burnham* case,[190] but the result was clearly different. In that case, the taxpayer reached a settlement in regard to several injury claims that had been brought due to safety defects in vehicles that it had manufactured. The taxpayer undertook to pay the plaintiffs the sum of $24,477,699 over the course of many years. In one case, the period of the compensation extended to 58 years. In order to make these payments, Ford acquired a one-time insurance policy at a premium of $4,424,587 to cover all the costs of the settlement agreements, the premium amount effectively covering the full amount of the future payments under the settlements. For financial statements, Ford only reduced the calculation of the profit by the amount of the premium. However, for tax purposes, it sought to deduct the full nominal amount in the same year that the company had undertaken to pay the plaintiffs under the settlement agreement. Ford claimed that it was entitled to deduct the full amount of the liability towards the plaintiffs as an expense, without taking into account the time factor, since the liability was certain and absolute, as was its amount, thereby meeting the case law criteria for the "all events test". In contrast to the other cases reviewed above (and particularly contrary to *Hughes* and *GD*), the court recognized the fact that the main problem was not the required degree of certainty as a condition for determining the timing of the deduction of the liability as an expense, but the time component. Put differently, the gap between the timing of the deduction of the liability and the date of its actual payment could create tax arbitrage. The court ruled that it was within IRS's power, and within the framework of "clearly reflected income", to allow deduction only of the premium amount that reflected the present value of the taxpayer's future expenses under the settlement arrangements, and not the full amount of the liability that would be paid throughout dozens of years in the future.[191]

It must be emphasized that in that case the court did not reject reliance on the matching principle, quite the reverse. The court addressed that principle as if it also applied in tax law, but it found that the proper application of the matching principle in these circumstances was merely to allow the premium amount as a deduction.[192] This judgment constitutes the one and only support for the Partial Deduction Approach.[193]

We may assume that, had it not been for the company deducting only the amount of the premium in calculating its "accounting earnings" in its financial statements, it is possible that, even in this case, this approach might not have been applied. In any event, it is difficult to predict how the court would have acted had the company not paid the premium amount to an outside insurer but had borne the future payments to the plaintiffs itself, and in its financial reports deducted the full amount of the nominal liability at a time when it was clear (by the very existence of the difference between that liability amount and the premium amount to an outside party) that the present value of the liability amount was some 18 per cent of its nominal value.

7.3.3 Administrative directives

Some of the administrative directives emphasize that fixing the date of deduction of liability is subject to compliance with the "all events test" condition and the "economic performance" condition, and implement the "all events test" by adopting the Absolute Certainty Degree or the High Certainty Degree requirements.[194] Other administrative directives deal with fixing defined cases, in which taxpayers will be given concessions in determining the deduction of liability as an expense (compared with case law which, in the main, has chosen solutions which defer the timing of the recognition for deducting liabilities as an expense).

Other administrative directives provided the "safe harbor method" of accounting for purposes of the recurring item exception in which a taxpayer will be treated as satisfying the requirement in Treas Reg §1.461–5(b)(1).[195] Thus, for example, in Rev. Rul. 67–127[196] and in other directives,[197] few concessions have been given in respect of the date of deduction of state property taxes as compared to the above-mentioned case law.[198] Rev. Rul. 80–182[199] grants a concession in determining the deduction of a liability as an expense in regard to gas and oil expiration companies. Rev. Proc. 92–29[200] provides the procedure for a developer of real estate to obtain IRS's consent to use an alternative to the general method under IRC§461(h) for determining when common improvement costs may be included in the basis of properties sold for purposes of determining the gain or loss resulting from sales. Under this alternative, subject to a few limitations, a developer may include in the basis of properties sold their allocable share of the estimated cost of common improvements without regard for whether the costs are incurred under IRC§461(h).

In Rev. Rul. 98–39,[201] a concession in determining the date of deduction of the liability as an expense is given in respect of "co-operative advertising services". In Rev. Proc. 2008–25,[202] a "safe harbor method" of accounting is provided for taxpayers using an accrual basis method of accounting that incur Federal Insurance Contributions Act (FICA) tax and Federal

Unemployment Tax Act (FUTA) tax ("payroll tax") liabilities[203] for compensation (including bonuses and vacation pay).[204]

Reading the administrative directives as a whole gives the impression that the main concern of IRS in dealing with time recognition of liability as an expense for tax purposes is one of administrative convenience more than any consideration relating to the time value of money.

7.3.4 Comments

The US academic commentary reflects a broad range of opinions relating to all aspects of the timing of the deduction of a liability as an expense.

In light of the time value of money consideration, in Halperin's opinion, the preferred solution is to create a parallel between the timing of recognizing income in the hands of the recipient, and the timing of allowing the expense in the hands of the payer.[205] For reasons of administrative convenience, Halperin believes that the recipe of deferring the timing for allowing the expense until the date it is actually paid, instead of limiting the amount of the deduction to the current value of the liability amount, is the proper method for avoiding unjust tax advantages. According to him, this solution is simpler and does not require any extensive knowledge regarding the future payment date, the future payment amount, market interest and other factors required to determine the amount of the expenses in present values.[206]

Cliff and Levine adopt a different approach. They are aware that if the taxpayer is granted the option of deducting the full value of the liability amount before this sum has actually been paid by him, then due to the time gap between deducting the amount of the expense and the expected actual payment date, he will somehow derive an economic advantage.[207] However, despite this advantage, it is inappropriate to adopt the solution of deferring the timing for allowing the expense until the date of actual payment, and keeping to GAAP produces preferable certainty.[208] They believe that considering the time value of money is not an all-encompassing obligation.[209]

Sunley speaks of a "pure" tax system unfettered by statutory limitations, and divorced from accounting theory, and raises the question of the present value of the amount of the expenses that ought to be deducted in respect of future payments.[210] He addresses the question of whether, in a "pure" tax system, the discounted present value of future costs should be computed using a pretax interest rate or an after-tax interest rate. According to him, under a pure income tax system, future costs should be discounted at a pre-tax interest rate, and the discounted present value should be included in the basis and deducted as related income comes in. Interest should be deducted as it accrues, and the recipient of the expense should pick up the interest as it accrues.[211]

Kaywood asserts that in the same transaction, where both parties report on the accrual basis, a time gap is created to the benefit of IRS, by which the income in the hands of the recipient will already become liable to tax, but the expense has yet to be recognized for the payer.[212] In his opinion, it would have been proper to match the date of the recognition of the income in the recipient's hands to the date of the timing of the allowance of the expense for the payer.[213]

Jensen states that it is difficult to reconcile the *Hughes* and *GD* cases. He asserts that the *GD* ruling constitutes a regression from the principle that a liability may be recognized as an expense even if it has not yet actually been paid, and it is possible that it may never actually be paid (which principle was recognized in the *Hughes* case).[214] He contends that the same arguments that led the Supreme Court to disallow the expense on the same date as it was claimed for the deduction by the *GD* case could, by the same degree, have certainly led to the disallowance of the expense in the *Hughes* case, since the possibility that claim forms would not be completed by the employees, which prevented allowing the expense in the *GD* case, does not necessarily appear to be more reasonable than the case of the winner of a prize, to which the liability in the *Hughes* case related. According to him, following the lack of uniformity between these two rulings, it is appropriate to limit their applicability only to the special facts that they addressed.[215]

On grounds of the time value of money, Dubetz justifies the statutory amendment (within which the "economic performance test" was inserted) that was intended to confront tax planning designed at "advancing" the deduction of expenses compared with the timing of their actual payment.[216] However, in his opinion, it was precisely because of considerations of the time value of money that the Supreme Court ought to have reversed the results differentiating the *GD* and *Hughes* cases. The duration of time between the fiscal year in which *GD* sought to deduct its liabilities in connection with the indemnity of the employees, and the date on which there was an expectation that they would actually be paid, was much shorter than the period of time between the date on which the casino (in the *Hughes* case) deducted the provision for a win at the casino, and the date of the actual payment of the win (which could continue for many years).[217] Therefore, in his opinion, the direction taken by the court in the *GD* case effectively overruled the precedent in the *Hughes* case, and gave IRS a weapon to reduce the phenomenon of creating tax advantages by means of advancing the timing of the recognition of expenses.

Malman states that disregarding the matching principle in determining taxable income will create a distortion in economic terms of income for tax purposes. Therefore, this accounting principle should also be applied to tax laws as standing alone, whatever the opinion might be regarding tax laws following GAAP.[218]

Gunn believes that the matching principle, of itself, has no importance from the tax standpoint.[219] Only for reasons of convenience, the use of the matching principle ought to be allowed, subject to IRS's power to disregard GAAP where applying it would lead to a breach of the "clearly reflect income" test in a manner that interprets the term "income" for this test differently than GAAP.[220]

Johnson believes that the deduction of a liability should not be allowed before it has actually been paid, unless the amount of the liability that is deducted would be reduced at a rate that reflects the prospect that such liability will not be paid, and at a rate that also reflects the present value of the liability amount with regard to the expected payment date.[221]

Klein criticizes the view that asserts that future expenses should not be deducted if they are not fixed and certain. He believes that the requirement of the High Certainty Degree (both with respect to the liability itself as well as regarding its amount as a condition for its deduction as an expense), while negating the use of evaluations, disregards the uncertainty existing in economics and creates a distortion in determining the income for tax purposes.[222]

Butler believes that the combination between IRC§461(h) (that resulted mainly from considerations of disallowing tax advantages in terms of the time value of money)[223] and the adoption of the Advance Approach has led to a tax distortion in the very same terms of time value of money.[224] This, as income is imputed to the taxpayer from an advance, while his expenses for creating that income (even if they have crystallized and become certain) will not be allowed for deduction on the same date following the non-fulfillment of the condition of "economic performance". From this standpoint, Butler states that it is actually IRS that enjoys the time value of money.[225] In another article,[226] Butler expresses the position that a middle road should be adopted that would negate legislation which disregards GAAP and greatly limits the difference between reporting based on the cash basis and reporting based on the accrual basis method for tax purposes. However, "adverse exploitation" of GAAP should be avoided in obtaining time value of money advantages, while cautiously applying IRS's powers under the "clearly reflect income" test according to IRC§446(b).[227] The tool that he proposes in balancing between using GAAP for tax purposes and preventing tax advantages based on time value of money is to use the present value method where use of GAAP would result in taxable income not meeting the test of "clearly reflecting income".[228]

Geier, who supports the Dualistic Doctrine, is of the opinion that the (accounting) matching principle should not be used for purposes of timing the recognition of allowable expenses.[229] In reviewing judicial history, she reaches the conclusion that the general integration of GAAP into tax laws was previously made for considerations of administrative convenience only.[230] The courts that chose to use accounting practice as an aid in measuring income for tax purposes (including the matching principle) did not address the tax values that are repugnant to those accounting rules.[231] Although the courts have not made do with the Accounting

Certainty Degree as a condition for determining the timing of the deduction of a liability as an expense, and have disallowed provisions for the deduction, this, from her point of view, is not enough.[232] According to her, allowing an expense in the present following a liability whose payment date will fall in the future erodes the tax value and its anti-tax-arbitrage value.[233] In her opinion, the only justification for tax accounting relying on GAAP derives from the administrative desire to prevent the taxpayer from keeping two sets of books. However, once the taxpayer is, in any event, required to make various adjustments for tax purposes, there is no reason for adjustments not to be made when dealing with the timing of the recognition of expenses, and for the timing of the recognition thereof being on the "cash basis" for tax purposes. In any event, it should be forbidden that administrative convenience, which makes it possible for a taxpayer to report for tax purposes on the accrual basis, will cause erosion in tax values, and the value of anti-tax arbitrage is sufficiently important to prevent the taxpayer from deducting liabilities whose payment date falls in the future.[234]

7.4 Timing of deduction of future expenses – Israeli tax law

Israeli legislation (like that of the UK and US) provides for a series of substantive conditions for deducting a liability as an expense for tax purposes.[235] In certain cases, it also provides the timing on which liabilities may be deducted for tax purposes.[236] However, as we have mentioned, our question relates to the timing of the recognition of a liability as an expense, assuming that the liability itself may be deducted by statute, and assuming further that, with respect to the timing of the deduction thereof, no specific statutory provision provides otherwise. With respect to this question, Israeli legislation is silent, and no general conditions are prescribed by statutory provision for the timing of the deduction of liabilities for tax purposes.[237] The Israeli case law may be summarized as having adopted the Accounting Certainty Degree and the Full and Immediate Deduction Approach. However, alongside this approach, we have already seen that the Israeli tax system, inspired by US case law, has not followed GAAP on the issue of the timing of the recognition of income from deposits and advances. Thus, it created an amalgam in which the accounting matching principle is upheld on the subject of the timing of deducting liabilities, whereas the realization principle is abandoned on the subject of the timing of the recognition of income from deposits and advances.

7.4.1 The case law

Israeli case law relating to the deduction of future expenses for tax purposes will also be divided into two: cases that deal mainly with the question of the required degree of certainty, and cases that deal with the time gap question.

7.4.1.1 The required degree of certainty

In the absence of any limitation existing in the ITO concerning the timing of deducting an expense, a liability may be deducted for tax purposes on the date on which the taxpayer deducts the expenses in his books, according to the method by which he keeps them. Therefore, with respect to a taxpayer who keeps his books according to GAAP and reports on the accrual basis method, the timing of deducting a liability for tax purposes will not be the date of their actual payment but the date on which he must bring these expenses into the calculation of his profit according to GAAP.[238] In light of this approach, Israeli case law has broadly and consistently supported the application of the accounting matching principle for tax purposes also with respect to all those taxpayers who report on the accrual basis method.[239] In relation to the possibility of deducting provisions for tax purposes, Israeli case law has relied on the rule laid down in *Southern Railway of Peru*[240] and has held, in a long line of cases, that it is possible to deduct a provision on account of a liability that was created in the past, even if the amount or the timing of the payment of the liability is uncertain. For this purpose, cases like *Nakid*,[241] *Arkia*,[242] *Tel Ronnen*,[243] *First Amisragas*,[244] *Deal*,[245] *Ramdo*[246] and *Aharon*[247] have made the deduction of the provision conditional on three conditions. First, that a reasonable prospect exists of the liability being paid in the future; second, that according to GAAP, the provision is to be made in calculating the profit/loss of the taxpayer; and third, that the circumstances of the case and the resources available to the taxpayer enable the determination of the liability with reasonable certainty.[248] The position that accepts the Accounting Certainty Degree as a condition for determining the timing of the deduction of the expense was eroded to a certain extent in the rulings of the district court in the *Second Amisragas* case,[249] and the *Pazgas* case,[250] and in the ruling of the Supreme Court in the *Amisragas-Pazgas* case.[251] In those cases the court ruled that the deduction of financing expenses that had accrued by reason of deposits that the gas companies had received and which they were required to repay to customers, did not meet the degree of certainty required. According to the court, where an empirical examination indicated that repayment of the liabilities occurred on average after 30 years, the time element of itself created the material doubt regarding the probability that the liability would indeed be realized. It thus appears that, in practice, the court added a further, fourth condition to the three mentioned above (that allowed a provision in the current year to be made) – the time factor. According to this condition, the prospect of the liability being realized in the future would be appraised not according to the status of the legal rights and obligations, but also according to considerations such as forgetfulness or lack of knowledge (of the consumer) as to what might happen to the consumers or the taxpayers during such a long period.[252]

7.4.1.2 The time gap question

The Israeli case law mentioned above has been unequivocal and consistent in adopting the Full and Immediate Deduction Approach. That is to say, once the liability meets the required degree of certainty, the full deduction thereof (in the nominal amount) will be allowed as an expense on that date, whatever its future payment date might be. The time factor that was added in the above-mentioned cases was a condition of the degree of certainty requirement, and was not intended to examine the taxpayer's economic benefit from this time element (in terms of the time value of money).

7.4.2 Comments

The Israeli academic commentary, like that of the UK, unanimously supports the view that as long as there is no contrary directive by law, the Accounting Certainty Degree will "suffice" as a condition for the timing of the recognition of the liability as an expense. This being so, the academic commentary supports the deduction of provisions as an expense, provided that the provision is required by GAAP, and the amount can be reached by an agreed evaluation with a high possibility that it would indeed be realized.[253] In addition, academic commentary overwhelmingly supports the Full and Immediate Deduction Approach of the liability, whatever the future date of its payment might be.[254]

7.5 Timing of deduction of future expenses – summary and comments

The question of the timing of the recognition of income is irrevocably connected with the question of the timing of the recognition of future expenses. Two questions were posed regarding the timing of the recognition of liabilities as an expense for tax purposes. One is that of the degree of certainty required as a condition for determining the timing of the recognition of a liability as an expense. The other is related to the time gap between the timing of the deduction and the timing of the expected performance.

With respect to the degree of certainty question: the UK tax system, consistent with the trend of maximizing the merger of tax accounting with GAAP, has "made do" with the Accounting Certainty Degree in order to allow the deduction of a liability as an expense. That is to say, in order to permit the deduction of a liability (as well as a provision) for tax purposes, it is sufficient that there be certainty with respect to the very existence of the liability that was created in the past, even if the amount of the liability or the date of its payment is not clear and absolute. This tax system enables ascertaining such an amount by means of evaluations and calculations.[255]

The US tax system has hovered between the High Certainty Degree and the Absolute Certainty Degree. In the spirit of the High Certainty Degree, we have found statements indicating that the "all events test" requires absolute certainty only with respect to the intrinsic existence of the liability. However, with respect to the amount of the liability, it is sufficient for the amount to be fixed with reasonable probability (although determination of this sum cannot be made on the basis of evaluations or assessments, as is the case when following GAAP).[256]

Nevertheless, in the spirit of the Absolute Certainty Degree, we have found statements adopting the "last link" test, and thereby requiring that certainty and lack of doubt apply not merely with respect to the very performance of the liability but also to its amount.[257] However, contrary to the UK, the US tax system has not "made do" with the Accounting Certainty Degree in order to allow a liability as an expense for tax purposes, and disallows the deduction of provisions. In negating the use of evaluations or assessments, this system has also led to a distinction being made between a liability to perform services and a liability to pay money.[258] By doing so, this system continues to give a "vote of non-confidence" to the application of GAAP in tax law.[259] Like the "clearly reflect income" test that could have been interpreted by means of an interpretation matching GAAP, but which the courts have preferred to interpret otherwise,[260] the case law, in interpreting the "all events test",[261] has chosen a construction that effectively overturns the possibility of deducting expenses on the dates that are required by the accounting matching principle.[262]

The Israeli tax system has generally "made do" with the Accounting Certainty Degree.[263] It has, therefore, allowed the deduction of provisions, and the fact that the amount of the provisions was set by means of evaluations did not of itself affect the matter. Nevertheless, although GAAP does not impute importance to the time factor with respect to the very need to make a provision,[264] the recent cases indicate that the longer the time period of the expected performance of the liability, the firmer is the tendency not to regard the liability as meeting the required degree of certainty.[265]

With respect to the time gap question: the UK and the Israeli systems support the Full and Immediate Deduction Approach by giving no weight to the timing of the actual payment as a factor in determining the timing of the deduction of or its amount.[266] In the US tax system, the focus on the question of the required degree of certainty has rendered the time gap question secondary.[267] On this question, most US cases have adopted the Full and Immediate Deduction Approach, although we have seen that some case law has adopted the Deferred Deduction Date Approach with one exception in which the Partial Deduction Approach was adopted.[268]

As mentioned above, in confronting the question of the timing of the deduction of a liability for tax purposes, tax laws must address two elements.

The first is the risk that, ultimately, the liability for which the deduction of the expense is requested will not fully or even partially materialize ("**the risk element**").

The second is the value at which it will be possible to deduct the liability that will be performed on a future date, where it is clear that the longer the period between the time of the deduction until the future date on which the liability is to be performed, the greater the period between the future nominal value of the liability and its present value ("**the time-difference element**").

In addressing these two elements, it seems that neither of the approaches that have been adopted in the tax systems reviewed is immune from criticism.

7.5.1 *Criticism of relying on the Accounting Certainty Degree*

As we saw, the UK tax system has adopted the Accounting Certainty Degree as a threshold condition for fixing the time on which a liability will be recognized as an expense for tax purposes. In doing so (together with adopting the Full and Immediate Deduction Approach), the tax system adopted in the UK completes a full, coherent model that is based on the spirit of the Singular Doctrine and the Consistent Approach according to which both the timing of the recognition of income and that of an expense will be fixed according to GAAP (provided there is no specific deviating statutory provision with respect to a particular transaction, or particular income, or a particular expense). The Israeli tax system similarly "suffices" with adopting the Accounting Certainty Degree as a threshold condition for determining the time of the recognition of a liability, but as distinct from the UK tax system, the system that prevails in Israel does not constitute a coherent model of the Consistent Approach since, as we have seen, on other matters that pertain to the timing of the recognition of income, the Israeli tax system has refrained from applying GAAP.[269]

It appears that both these tax systems which, in the spirit of the Consistent Approach, have "sufficed" with the Accounting Certainty Degree as a sufficient threshold condition for determining the timing of the recognition of liability as an expense, have not attributed the proper weight to the risk element that holds that the liability may not ever be discharged, at least at the time for which it was fixed, or if it is, not at the amount specified. We have already noted that alongside the advantage of convenience and efficiency in following GAAP in determining the timing of the recognition of income and expense for tax purposes, we must not forget the fact that GAAP, which was designed to protect relevant third parties, is guided by principles such as that of conservatism, which obligate adopting a policy of minimalization of assets and maximization of liabilities.[270]

We also mentioned that different tax values, such as those "equity", "neutrality" and the prevention of unjust tax advantages, are completely ignored by GAAP.[271] Therefore, in the "world of the GAAP", the risk element that income will not be covered on the future date constitutes a material threshold condition for its intrinsic recognition according to the realization principle.[272] In contrast, according to GAAP, no weight is attributed to the question of whether a risk exists (or possibly from the point of view of the taxpayer who is personally liable – a possibility) that he will even repay the liability that he has undertaken. Thus, according to GAAP, in measuring the profit, liabilities will be included that it is absolutely clear that the taxpayer (on account of his situation) will never be able to pay.[273] According to GAAP, the taxpayer, on measuring the profit, will also present liabilities that it is absolutely clear the beneficiaries will not be required to pay, at least not on their appointed date and/or in the amount presented.[274]

It seems that cases such as *Anise*[275] and *Herbert Smith*[276] demonstrate how following GAAP can create tax advantages by reducing the chargeable income on the basis of a liability that contains a great risk (and more precisely – a possibility) of not being paid in the future, at least in its full current amount.

However, most of our criticism with respect to the timing of the recognition of a liability as an expense in the UK and Israel does not actually relate to how those tax systems confront the "risk element" inherent in the question of performing a future liability, but actually relates to the time difference component.

7.5.2 *Criticism of the Full and Immediate Deduction Approach*

As stated, the UK and Israeli tax systems have adopted the Accounting Certainty Degree combined with the Full and Immediate Deduction Approach.[277] It appears that the combination of these two, in the spirit of the Consistent Approach, illustrates more than anything else how relying on GAAP can lead to erosion of tax values.

Thus, we may well ask, is it appropriate for a tax system to enable the reduction of the amount of the income that is liable to tax in a particular year to the full extent of the nominal amount that will be expended in the future, even where it is clear that when the liability is effectively performed, the real value of the nominal amount will be lower? Does the taxpayer not thereby enjoy the same thing twice, first from the very possibility of deferring tax to a future date on account of an expense whose certainty is not absolute, and second, from the reduction of income amounts represented in real terms, using values in future nominal figures (and not in real terms) of an anticipated payment?

It seems that advancing the timing of the recognition of a liability in nominal terms in the spirit of GAAP may infringe tax values such as the principle of neutrality, the principle of "horizontal equity", the principle of "efficiency" and the principle of "preventing unjustified tax advantages.

The principle of neutrality – applying the Full and Immediate Deduction Approach leads to the result that, in such transaction, when the taxpayer faces the possibility of paying the supplier a payment in current value and on an immediate date, or to pay him the same amount in real terms (and at higher nominal values) in the future, he will always prefer the second option. The tax that the taxpayer will pay in the year in which he has assumed the liability will be influenced not by the present value of the liability, but by the nominal (higher) value of the liability. Thus, the above tax system creates a tax advantage for making transactions in future installments, while exploiting the time differences in order to reduce the current earnings due to the use of nominal values for liabilities whose performance date falls in the future.

The principle of horizontal equity – adopting the Full and Immediate Deduction Approach carries with it the potential that two "identical" taxpayers who bore the same expense (in real values) or create the same income (in real values), will pay different tax in respect of precisely the same transaction and on precisely the same amount of profit. One taxpayer chooses to pay the expense in current values immediately, and take this amount into account in calculating his tax in the year in which he recognized the income. The other, who generated precisely the same income, asks to defer the timing of the payment of the expense to a future date, thereby determining the nominal amount thereof for payment in the future at a higher value than that of present value. This taxpayer, according to the Full and Immediate Deduction Approach, will on calculating his tax deduct the nominal value of the future payment, and thus the tax that he will pay in the year in which he generated the income will be lower in real terms than that which was paid by the first taxpayer.

For example, in the *Hughes* case,[278] the US Supreme Court adopted the Full and Immediate Deduction Approach, and allowed a deduction in a current year for the liability of a casino owner to pay a jackpot to an unknown winner at an unknown date in the future. Let us compare that to another casino owner who actually paid the same jackpot (in nominal terms) in the same current year. Would it make sense to argue that both casino owners should be entitled to deduct the same amounts as an expense for tax purposes in the same year, even though, economically, these nominal terms represented totally different real amounts?

The principle of efficiency and preventing unjustified tax advantages – it would appear possible to illustrate this erosion by the following example. A taxpayer purchases a product from a supplier for $90, and sells that product to a customer for $100. The customer pays $100 to the taxpayer immediately. However, the taxpayer's payment to the supplier is deferred until a future date, and is fixed at $100, reflecting $90 plus interest in real terms. According to the Full and Immediate Deduction Approach, in the year in which the income of $100 accrues to the taxpayer, he will be allowed an equal expense of $100, although he has a profit of $10 in real terms in that year (assuming that he had no other expenses).

Cases such as *Herbert Smith*[279] in the UK, *Pazgas*[280] in Israel, and *Burnham*,[281] *Crescent Wharf*,[282] *Hughes*[283] and *Gold Coast*[284] in the US illustrate how adopting the Full and Immediate Deduction Approach for tax purposes can lead to the result that the use of nominal future values of liabilities turns the calculation of taxable income completely upside-down in real terms.

7.5.3 *Criticism of the requirement of the High or the Absolute Certainty Degree*

In a tax system like that of the US, in which the Dualistic Doctrine applies, and there is an awareness of the difference between the objectives of financial accounting and those of the tax system, one would expect that greater weight would be attached to tax values in determining the timing of the recognition of a liability as an expense for tax purposes. However, in our opinion, the proposed solution of recourse to the High Certainty Degree or the Absolute Certainty Degree not only fails to advance tax values, but infringes tax values to an extent no less, if not greater, than what would result from adopting GAAP for determining the timing of recognition of a liability as an expense. This can be clarified as follows.

Harm to the value of "non-erosion of capital" – the requirement of the High Certainty Degree or the Absolute Certainty Degree leads, as we have seen, to the deferral of the timing of the recognition of future liabilities until the date on which they can be clearly and certainly quantified in monetary terms.[285] Such deferral is also made where there is complete certainty that the particular liability will be paid in the future. Thus, the approach leads to a lack of symmetry between the timing of the recognition of income and that of the recognition of liabilities in a manner whereby, in some cases, liabilities taken in order to create income will not be recognized in the year the income was earned, and the taxpayer will find that he is compelled to pay "turnover tax" on the income, and not on profit. This payment will erode the taxpayer's capital in terms of the interest that he is compelled to pay in order to finance the tax that has been imposed on the component that exceeds the amount of the profit he earned.

It would seem that the erosion is most extreme where the taxpayer's capital is eroded as a result of applying the requirement of the High Certainty Degree or the Absolute Certainty Degree to a liability to be performed in the future in regard to income that has yet to be received, and for which the timing of receipt also falls in the future. In such cases, erosion of the taxpayer's capital is most significant as he is required to use other sources in order to finance tax for income that has yet to be received, such tax being computed not on the profit that he purportedly earned in such a year, but on the turnover of such income.

The absence of a parallel between the timing of the recognition of income and that of the recognition of the liability undertaken to produce it thus creates a difference in time on account of which the taxpayer is required to finance tax, which, in the short or long term, is not tax on profit (but on turnover).

The erosion of the neutrality principle – the requirement of the High Certainty Degree or the Absolute Certainty Degree has led to a distinction between liabilities in the "nature of cash" and liabilities to perform services.[286] As we have seen, on the one hand, a cash payment liability already meets the requirement of certainty mentioned above at the stage at which it crystallized, and at such early date has already been allowed for deduction. On the other hand, the timing of the liability to perform services is deferred until a later date, in most cases until the "last link" of the chain has been performed.[287] In economic terms, there is no difference between a liability denominated in a cash amount and one that requires performing an act, where the cost of both of them is identical. Nonetheless, according to the requirements of the High Certainty Degree and the Absolute Certainty Degree, the value that is attributed to each of these liabilities in order to determine the tax amount that applies to a transaction will be different. The difference results from the time differential at which the liability will be recognized as an expense for tax purposes.

Eroding the tax value of preventing unjustified tax advantages – this tax value is not intended merely to prevent taxpayers from enjoying unjustified tax advantages, but is meant to apply to the tax authorities to the same extent. Adopting the High Certainty Degree or the Absolute Certainty Degree as a condition for determining the timing of the recognition of an expense can lead to an asymmetrical result. According to such requirements, the income will be recognized on the date on which it has been earned even if it has not been received in cash, and even if its expected receipt falls on some future date on which the liabilities that were used to produce it will similarly be paid in cash. In contrast, the timing of the recognition of precisely the same liabilities will be deferred until the future year in which the requirement of the High Certainty Degree or the Absolute Certainty Degree will be fulfilled.

This situation creates a tax advantage for the tax authorities in terms of time.[288] The taxpayer finds himself obligated to finance a tax payment not merely in respect of unrealized profits, but in respect of turnover (which has nothing whatsoever to do with profit), while the tax authority has the benefit of using money that does not in any way reflect the tax that it would have been entitled to receive had it been calculated only on the profit.

Violating the Proportionality Principle – over and above all of the foregoing, it appears that adopting the High Certainty Degree or the Absolute Certainty Degree as a solution for negating unjustified tax advantage in terms of time that may favor the taxpayer infringes the Proportionality Principle. This principle is founded on three criteria:[289] "the rational means test" that requires that the means selected serve the purpose for which they are intended;[290] "the less harmful means test", according to which means appropriate to obtaining the purpose will not be regarded as meeting the Proportionality Principle if other means could achieve the same goal with less harm;[291] "the relative means test" that may require the rejection of proper means selected for a proper goal, even if there are no other alternative means, if the harm to the tax values resulting from applying such means is extremely significant.[292]

It seems to us that adopting the High Certainty Degree or the Absolute Certainty Degree as a means to prevent tax advantages to taxpayers in terms of time does not meet any of the criteria of the Proportionality Principle.

As to the first test – "the rational means test" – the requirement of certainty is designed to confront the issue of the risk or the prospect of non-performance of the liability in the future.[293] It is doubtful if requiring the High Certainty Degree or the Absolute Certainty Degree as a condition for determining the timing of the recognition of liabilities as an expense for tax purposes constitutes a means to attain the goal of neutralizing tax advantages to the taxpayer in terms of time. We have already seen that using these means can lead to the deferral of the timing of the recognition of liabilities to perform services, but it is not able to "limit" the time difference between the actual payment and the timing of the recognition of a liability as an expense for tax purposes when we are dealing with a liability in clear and definitive monetary terms.[294]

Indeed, in cases where the liability was for a liquidated cash sum payable on a remote date, the US courts were compelled to allow the deduction of the liability according to the timing that created time advantages for the taxpayer.[295] Moreover, the isolated and unusual attempts by the courts to confront significant time differences between the timing of the deduction of a cash liability as an expense and the timing of actual payment were not, and could not have been, based on the requirement of the High Certainty Degree or the Absolute Certainty Degree, but on other constraints, mainly on the extended jurisdiction of IRS by virtue of IRC§446(b).[296]

Moreover, requiring the High Certainty Degree or the Absolute Certainty Degree served as a bar to recognizing a liability as an expense for tax purposes even where the time differentials between that timing and that of the performance were extremely short and insignificant.[297] This shows us that the requirement of the High Certainty Degree or the Absolute Certainty Degree with respect to the amount of the liability did not evolve simply as a means to deal with the question of the time differential and the tax advantages inherent therein, and even if they do help to serve that purpose, such assistance is selective and does not correlate to the duration of the period of the particular time differential.[298]

As to the second test – "the less harmful means test" – even if it is possible to consider the High Certainty Degree or the Absolute Certainty Degree to be a rational means for implementing the goal of preventing tax advantages to taxpayers that result from the time differential, nonetheless, other means that are somewhat less harmful to the tax values can achieve precisely the same goal. We have already seen that alongside adopting GAAP and the accrual basis method, there are also other methods, such as the cash basis method or hybrid methods that, with all their attendant weaknesses,[299] neutralize the time advantage to taxpayers without affecting tax values in the manner in which they are eroded by the High Certainty Degree or the Absolute Certainty Degree requirements. Moreover, the tool that IRS has in IRC§446(b) can be used as an efficient means to attain the same goal. Evidence of this is actually to be found in its use in the isolated and exceptional cases in which the court disqualified those tax advantages without the assistance of the High Certainty Degree or the Absolute Certainty Degree.[300] Additionally, as we will show below, there are other alternative means that, until now, have not even been considered (and which we believe directly address the question of tax advantages that are created from exploiting the time differential between the timing of recognizing a liability as an expense and that of the effective performance of that liability).[301] Thus, we believe that the requirement of the High Certainty Degree or the Absolute Certainty Degree, as a means to deal with tax advantages in terms of time, does not fulfill the second criterion of the Proportionality Principle, namely, the "less harmful test".

As to the third test – "the relative means test" – even if we were to say that adopting the High Certainty Degree or the Absolute Certainty Degree constitutes an efficient means of attaining the goal of preventing unjust tax advantages as a result of the time differentials, and even if we were to say that the harm caused by applying such means is no greater than that of other alternative means, it would still be very doubtful if adopting the High Certainty Degree or the Absolute Certainty Degree is consistent with the third criterion of the Proportionality Principle, namely, "the relative means test". As we have seen above, the UK tax system that, in principle, adopted the Accounting Certainty Degree for purposes of timing the recognition of liability as an expense, appears to have abandoned achieving the objective of preventing unjust tax advantages as a result of time differentials,[302] except in those cases where express statutory provisions have been provided.[303]

It appears that the injury caused by the UK tax system to tax values as a result of the apparent abandoning of the objective of preventing unjust tax advantages that result from time differentials, does not exceed the damage caused by confronting that goal by means of the High Certainty Degree or the Absolute Certainty Degree.

7.5.4 Criticism of the certainty requirement in correlation with the Income Approach and the Advance Approach

With respect to the timing of the deduction of liabilities in transactions where deposits or advances are received, it is submitted that the approaches adopted by the tax systems reviewed, as regard to the certainty requirement, should be rejected, at least in those cases where the Income Approach (in respect of deposits) and the Advance Approach (in respect of advances) are implemented.

We have seen that generally none of the tax systems reviewed has adopted an approach that allows advancing the deduction of future expenses in transactions where deposits or advances are received. In the UK tax system, the acceptance of the Loan Approach (in relation to deposits), and acceptance of the Deferral Approach (in relation to advances), coupled with the implementation of the matching principle in relation to the timing of the deduction of liabilities for tax purposes, collectively produce "a comprehensive picture" that, on matters of timing, integrates with the perception·of GAAP.

In contrast, the US and Israeli systems, which prefer (in several cases) the Income Approach (in relation to deposits), and the Advance Approach (in relation to advances), are the "obvious candidates" for advancing the deduction of future expenses in relation to deposits or advances that are recognized as "income" on the date of receipt. However, in the case law that adopts the Advance Approach, the Israeli tax system, has not found it appropriate to match the timing of the recognition of income from such an advance to the timing of the recognition of the liabilities that were used in obtaining it, nor has it found it appropriate to bring them forward. In any event, it has left in place the Accounting Certainty Degree requirement as regards the timing of the deduction of expenses.[304]

The US tax system has made much of favoring the adoption of the Advance Approach, and not only found it appropriate to advance the deduction of future expenses with respect to the liabilities incurred in order to obtain the deposit or advance (yet to be earned), but also demanded a degree of certainty that transcends the Accounting Certainty Degree in determining the timing of deduction. The adoption of the Income Approach and the Advance Approach, alongside the above perception relating to the timing of the deduction of liabilities, combine to produce a confusing and non-uniform global picture that attempts to prevent tax advantages in terms of timing, but in relation generally to deposits and advances creates tax distortions that are expressed in the payment of tax on turnover and not on "profit".[305] Notwithstanding the position held by GAAP with respect to the non-inclusion of contingencies in calculating profit,[306] and notwithstanding the overall conception of the tax system to the certainty requirement, it is submitted that in a tax system that seeks to tax the economic benefit of a deposit or an advance on the date on which they are received, these risks cannot be ignored, even if no degree of certainty exists in respect to them. Applying the "usual" requirement of certainty in determining the timing of deduction of liabilities undertaken in order to produce income from deposits or advances in cases in which those receivables are considered to be income on the date of receipt might mean that tax will be imposed on the full amount of the deposit or advance in the year in which it was received (and not on the "profit" inherent therein). Furthermore, this might mean that in the year in which it would be possible to deduct those liabilities, there may no longer be any income from which they can be deducted.

It is submitted that, at least in a case where a deposit or an advance is considered to be "income" before it has been earned, not only should deduction be allowed for liabilities that crystallized at a point of time in the past and regarding which the amount and timing of payment is known, but also for provisions on account of liabilities created in the past and for which lack of clarity exists with respect to the amount or timing of payment, and finally also for contingencies where a degree of uncertainty exists as to the intrinsic existence of the liability itself.[307]

From what has been said until now, we believe that none of the tax systems that have been reviewed has found an efficient remedy to prevent unjust tax advantages to taxpayers who seek to reduce their chargeable income for tax purposes based on the existence of a future liability whose performance is required to create the income, or who seek to defer payment of the tax in reliance on liabilities to be performed in the future. As we have seen, the UK tax system, subject to specific statutory provisions that exists with respect to the timing of the deduction of defined liabilities, has completely disregarded the "malady" and effectively allowed the exploitation of time both for deferring payment of tax (while "advancing" the deduction of liabilities), and also for effectively reducing it while using the nominal value of the future payment for deduction, in lieu of the present value. In contrast, the US tax system has certainly been aware of the "malady", but the remedy it has chosen has failed to cure it. Moreover, it has led to a long series of shortcomings that may well be even more serious than the illness that it seeks to cure.

While the tax systems reviewed have failed to remedy unjust tax advantages in a manner that addresses the problem without creating greater injury, we believe that such a remedy does indeed exist on the levels of both income and expense, as we will demonstrate in Chapter 8 below.

8   Alternative models

As we have seen above, the question of the timing of the recognition of income and an expense for tax purposes has two main implications.

First, the question of the effect of the timing of recognition of income on the timing of collection of tax, i.e. at what time taxes should be paid ("the Collection Question").

Second, on the level of quantification, that is, how to ensure that as a result of the time differences between the timing of the recognition of income or an expense as opposed to the respective dates on which the amount is actually received or paid, do not distort the determination of the amount of chargeable income ("the Quantification Question").[1]

We have already expressed our view that the Collection Question (the question of the timing of the tax) is secondary to that of quantifying the profit, and have sought to show that considerations of speedy collection do not, of themselves, justify deviating from GAAP where such a deviation requires that a price be paid in terms of violating tax values.[2] In contrast, the quantification (of the profit) is crucial to any tax system that seeks to be regarded as "fair", and lies at the basis of the tax values that we reviewed above.[3] Thus, if distortions arise with respect to the quantification of the taxpayer's annual income as a result of time differences between the date of receiving money and the time of recognizing it as income, or as a result of time differences between the performing of a liability and the recognition of that liability as an expense, then the tax values require that we confront the "malaise". As we explained earlier, this must be carried out in a manner consistent with the Proportionality Principle, in all of its three elements.[4]

As we have seen, the tax systems reviewed do not suggest an appropriate solution that prevents erosion of tax values (mainly the value of preventing unjust tax advantages) that can ensue from exploiting the time component for the benefit of the taxpayer, without concurrently causing real damage to other tax values that are no less important.

Adopting the accrual basis method offered by GAAP with respect to both the timing of the recognition of income and the timing of the recognition of expense (as was done, for example, in the UK tax system) leads to results that disregard the tax advantages that arise to the taxpayer in terms of time, not merely with respect to the timing of the payment of the tax, but also in regard to calculating the income upon which tax is imposed.[5] Using the "all events test" as a replacement for the "pure" accrual basis method (as was done in the US tax system), and adopting the realization principle taken from GAAP with respect to the timing of the recognition of income, while adopting the High Certainty Degree or the Absolute Certainty Degree requirements as a condition for recognizing a liability as an expense, leads to even more egregious results. As we have seen in the US tax system, the mixture inflicts a long line of harmful effects to other tax values.[6]

Moreover, with regard to deposits and advances, as we have seen above, both the Loan Approach and the Income Approach (in relation to deposits) as well as the Deferral Approach and the Advance Approach (in relation to advances) are inadequate and should be rejected as solutions to the question of the timing of the recognition of income from deposits and advances.

The tax systems reviewed have, in our opinion, failed to put in place apparatus to eliminate the tax advantages and disadvantages that can flow to taxpayers who report on an accrual basis, and act according to GAAP, from time differences between the recognition of income and expenses and the actual date of receiving the revenues or incurring the liabilities.[7] Moreover, none of the tax system reviewed presents a suitable reporting method that can be regarded as a systematic, coherent alternative to the accrual basis method.

In light of this failure, the question arises whether alternatives exist in which the accrual basis method could be implemented while eliminating tax advantages and disadvantages that can arise from time differentials. We will examine two alternatives that will be termed "the Comparative Value Taxation model" (hereinafter: "**the CVT model**") and "the Alternative Financing Interest model" (hereinafter: "**the SFC model**").

8.1 The Comparative Value Taxation model ("the CVT model")

As opposed to the existing approaches in the tax systems reviewed, an alternative model may be proposed for neutralizing the time component in calculating taxable income.

The CVT model seeks to tackle the two main problems that can arise from the time differences between a receipt or payment and its recognition as income or expense for tax purposes: the Collection Question and the Quantification Question.

With respect to the Collection Question, the CVT model seeks to make the recognition of income for tax purposes on the date of recognition according to GAAP, or on the date of actual receipt, whichever is earlier, and even if the income has not yet been earned on that date. This is done in the spirit of the Income Approach (in regard to deposits), and the Advance Approach (in regard to advances), in order that the State Treasury not suffer as a result of time differentials.

With respect to the Quantification Question, in order to eliminate distortions at the level of the various tax values,[8] the CVT model holds that at the specific point of time at which income or liabilities are recognized for tax purposes, the income and the expense will be quantified, taking into account the time component. The CVT model holds that the tax distortions created by following GAAP addressing or not addressing the time component should be prevented by entirely eliminating this component. In order to eliminate the time component, all the values relevant to calculating the income should be assembled together at one point along the timeline. According to the CVT model, the advantage or the disadvantage that may accrue to the taxpayer as a result of earning an income that has not yet been received, or in receiving a deposit or advance, does not originate in the actual earning or receipt, but in the terms by which the income or receivables, as well as the amount of liabilities, are taken into consideration. The CVT model examines whether the time component has caused a distortion in calculating the income and profit. In order to neutralize this possible distortion, the CVT model seeks to place all the relevant values (on the level of income as well as liabilities) on the same timeline.

In dealing with earned income from customers, the CVT model adopts the idea that any sale or service transaction ("the base transaction") in which a time lag exists between the supply date and the payment date (regardless of whether the payment precedes or is subsequent to the supply according to the base transaction) should be treated for tax purposes as comprising two transactions, one, the base transaction, and the other, a finance transaction with disguised interest ("the finance transaction").[9] As regards liabilities incurred for earning an income from customers, the CVT model also divides this expense into two parts, funds for sales or services, and interest for delaying the future payment. As regards unearned receivables, such as deposits or advances, the CVT model taxes the benefit accruing (if at all) from deposits or advances.

This model substantially resembles the Income Approach (in relation to a deposit), and the Advance Approach (in relation to advances), but with one main difference: according to this model, the tax is imposed in the year in which the payment is received not on the entire amount, but only on the profit component inherent therein. In order to achieve this objective, liability undertaken and value of future depreciation on equipment purchased in order to obtain such receivables is taken into consideration at their value on the date of receipt.

In the case of future liabilities (i.e. liabilities undertaken at present to be performed on a future date), here again, the CVT model divides these expenses into two parts, funds for sales or services and interest for delaying the future payment. According to this model, timing of recognition of income for tax purposes from the base transaction would be on the date upon which it is earned or on the date of its receipt, whichever is the earliest.

In both cases, in setting the amount of the taxable income (and expenditure) the time component is neutralized by using the capitalization mechanism. In cases in which income from customers is earned prior the date in which it is received, only the present value of future receivables and future payments is taken into consideration for calculating profits for tax purposes, and the rest of the nominal terms of receivables or payments are regarded as financing income or expenses. Where income from customers is received prior to the year it has been earned, the full amount of the advance will be included in the recipient's income at the time it is received, and in the same year the recipient, in calculating his income, is entitled to deduct not the full amount of his liabilities incurred for purposes of creating the income by reason of which the advance was received, but only the present value of the liabilities that are required for attaining the income. The difference between these two reflects the increase in the recipient's wealth in the same year.[10]

8.1.1 The CVT formula

A number of parameters are necessary to implement this model, namely the expected amount of the earned income and the date of its future receipt. In the case of unearned receivables (like deposits or advances), the following variables must be ascertained: the expected amount of the deposit repayment, the timing of the deposit repayment and the timing of the earning of the advance, the timing of making the taxpayer's other liabilities and the expected amount thereof,[11] and in all cases the rate of the market interest applicable to loans for the same term (between the date of earning an income and the future date of receipt, or between the date of receipt of the deposit and the repayment date thereof, or between the date on which the advance is received and the date of its earning).[12]

Having these parameters, the model may be expressed by means of the following formulae:

The base transaction formula

$$BT = \sum_{m=1}^{M} \frac{CFm}{(1 + im - Km)^{tm/12}} - \sum_{n=1}^{N} \frac{Ln}{(1 + in)^{yn/12}} - CO * d * \frac{x}{12}$$

The finance transaction formula

$$FT = \left[\sum_{m=1}^{M} CFm - \sum_{n=1}^{N} Ln - CO * d * \frac{x}{12} \right] - BT$$

Where,

BT = the base transaction, i.e. the taxable income in the relevant year (of earning the income or of receiving it).

FT = the finance transaction, i.e. the differences between the nominal terms of income or receivables and their values in real terms as well as the differences between the nominal terms of liabilities and their values in real terms, that reflect a disguised interest to be received or paid.

M = the total number of payments (cash flows) to be received by the taxpayer in a given transaction, whether those payments are deposits, advances or payments which are deferred as compared to "the earliest date of recognition of income".[13]

m = a counter (running from 1 to M) representing a specific payment (whether a deposit, an advance or a payment for "recognized income"[14] in a specific transaction to be received in the future).

N = the total number of "recognized liabilities" for the BT,[15] to be paid or performed by the taxpayer in the future in a given transaction.

n = a counter (running from 1 to N) representing a specific "recognized liability" as an expense,[16] in a given transaction.

CFm = the amount of the payment m.

t_m = the number of months between "the earliest date of recognition of income"[17] and the date of receipt of future payment m (in future payments for "recognized income"[18]) or the date of returning or earning (according to GAAP) m of unearned receivables (deposit or advance).[19]

i_m = the "market interest rate" on debit loans for the term of t_m.

k_m = the monthly interest rate that is added (if at all) to the deposit m. If no interest is added, then $k_m = 0$.

d = the annual depreciation rate applying in connection with the equipment given (if at all) to a deposit payer.

CO = the cost of the equipment to be placed at the disposal of the client as a condition for receiving a deposit. Where the taxpayer is not required to provide equipment, then $CO = 0$.

x = the number of months between the date equipment is placed at the disposal of the client as a condition for receiving a deposit and the date of return of the equipment.

Ln = the amount of liability n.

y_n = in relation to the liability n, the number of months between "the earliest date of recognition of liability"[20] and the date on which it is paid or performed.

i_n = the "market interest rate" on debit loans for the term of y_n.

8.1.2 The base transaction (BT)

According to this model, earned income that has not yet been received, as well as unpaid liabilities, should be divided into present value terms that reflect the net income accrued from the base transaction that should be taxed in the year earned. The rest of the future amount to be received or paid reflects a finance transaction that should be recognized as income or deducted as an expense over the years as financing income or expenses.

In dealing with unearned receivables like deposits or advances, the CVT model seeks to tax the economic advantage accruing (if at all) on the date on which the amount is received. However, the taxation in the year of receipt according to this model does not apply to the entire amount of the receivables, but only to the economic value of the advantage accruing to the recipient. In light of this, the formula examines the difference between the amount received and the liabilities undertaken by the taxpayer as a condition for receiving this amount, but the values of these liabilities are represented in the same terms as the CF terms (i.e. in present value):

The first component of the formula relates to each earned income that has not yet been received (hereinafter: "**unreceived earned income**"), and also relates to each receivable (such as deposit or advance) that has not yet been earned according to GAAP (hereinafter: "**unearned receivable**"). According to the CVT model, the income from the base transaction will be recognized for tax purposes on the earlier date earned according to GAAP and the date it is actually received, but in any case, one must take into account the time factor. By subtracting the present value of the future receivables, it may be seen that the longer the time gap between the timing of the earning and the timing of receipt, or the longer the time gap between the timing the deduction and the timing of the payment, the more the present value of those incomes or liabilities will decline.[21]

The second component of the formula relates to liabilities that are required for producing the unreceived earned income and the unearned receivable, and reflects the present value of the liability to repay the deposit ("the repayment amount"). It also reflects at present value any other deductible liabilities[22] that the taxpayer undertakes in order to provide services or goods in transactions in which he earned income or received a receivable (such as deposit or advance). As mentioned above,[23] disregarding the time gap between the date of the deduction of liabilities and the timing of the payment or performance erodes tax values and the time value of money concept. By subtracting the present value of the repayment amount from the deposit amount received, it may be seen that the longer the deposit life and the higher the difference between the interest paid (if at all) to the customer and "the market interest", the more the present value of the repayment amount will be reduced. The opposite also obtains: the shorter the duration of the "deposit life" and/or the difference between the interest that is added to the deposit and the "market interest", the lower the difference between the deposit amount and the present value of the repayment amount.

Assuming that GAAP measures the amount of the liability inherent in the deposit (according to the historic (nominal) cost or the current value thereof),[24] the difference between GAAP's measurements and the present value of the expected amount of repayment reflects the benefit that is not expressed according to GAAP. When dealing with advances, the attempt to impose tax on the "profit" (as distinct from tax on the full amount of the advance) on the date of receiving the advance can only be made after the future liabilities relating to this transaction are taken into account.[25] As we have already mentioned with respect to future liabilities, one must take into account the difference between the date on which they are brought into account in calculating profit, namely the month in which the advance is received and the date of the expected payment of the liabilities.

The third component of the formula is relevant in cases where a deposit is given to secure the equipment that the taxpayer must provide to the customer ("the duty to provide equipment").[26] Where the obligation to provide equipment applies, the economic value of this liability is equal to the difference between the value of the equipment as it will be when provided to the customer at the beginning of the "deposit life", and the value thereof on the date it is returned to the taxpayer at the end of the "deposit life". It can be said that, the value of "the duty to provide equipment" is the depreciation on the equipment in the years during which the equipment is provided, as long as the deposit remains in force.[27]

The question of reduction of the amount of the repayment (in the first component), or the reduction of the amount of the future liabilities (in the third component) that are deducted at a rate that reflects the present value of these amounts, having regard to the expected payment date, does not arise with respect to the deduction of depreciation of the equipment. This is because the assumption is that the payment in respect of the purchase of equipment has already been made in the year in which the deposit was received,[28] and the nominal deduction of the anticipated depreciation reflects the value in real terms (in the year in which the deposit was received).

8.1.3 *The finance transaction (FT)*

One might argue that taxing the base transaction of sales or services by using the present value of future receipts from customer income, and deducting liabilities at their present value on the date when income is earned or receivables are received, is a substitute for taxing them or deducting them in their future value on the date on which "they were recognized", according to GAAP, and is also a substitute for taxing them or deducting them at their future value on the date they are actually received or paid. Nevertheless, splitting each transaction where a time lag exists between date of recognition (of income or liability) and date of receipt or payment of cash flow, into two transactions (including a finance one) more precisely reflects the economic reality.

The gaps between the present value of income that is to be received in the future and its current value expresses a transaction whereby the tax-payer receives the income at its present value and immediately provides a loan to the customer to the full extent of the current value of the income, which will revert to the taxpayer (together with interest) on a future date that is fixed for the payment. The same applies with regard to a taxpayer who assumes a liability towards third parties, and instead of paying them on a later date, pays them immediately at their current value. To that end, the taxpayer takes a loan from the supplier to enable him to do this. The maturity date of the loan falls on the future performance date of the liabilities. As this difference between the current value of income and the future nominal value thereof reflects financing income, and since that difference between the current value of a liability and the nominal future value of payment reflects a financing expense, the FT formula reflects and expresses this differential, and in doing so also prevents differences between the taxpayer's cash flow and his income or expenses for tax purposes.

8.1.4 Date of taxation under the model

As was made clear above, the CVT model seeks to solve both the Collection Question as well as the Quantification Question. Thus, the desire to advance the date of recognizing the income to the earlier date on which it is actually earned or received, and the desire for the profit to be computed at that point on the time scale in economic values that are capable of being compared (for both the income and the expense), makes it necessary to split the transaction into two components, namely the base transaction and the finance transaction.

As mentioned above, because the objective of the CVT model is to solve the Collection Question, the income from the base transaction is recognized for tax purposes on the earlier date earned according to GAAP and the date it is actually received. Liabilities undertaken in order to produce this income would be matched at the same date of recognition of income from the base transaction.

The finance transaction should be recognized by a similar method used by GAAP, according to "the effective interest" method. As mentioned above, this method consists of calculating the amortized cost of a financial asset or a financial liability, and of allocating the interest income or interest expense over the relevant period.[29] For determining the relevant period for such allocation with respect to income that has been earned before it is received, the period for such allocation would lie between the date of the recognition of the income and the date on which it is actually received. In regard to income that has been received before it is earned (like deposits or advances), the period would be from the date on which it is received until it is recognized as income. In the case of liabilities, the period would run from the date of the recognition of the liability within the framework of the base transaction for tax purposes, until the date on which it is actually paid.

8.1.5 Waiver of the certainty requirement

As explained above,[30] liabilities may evolve at varying degrees of certainty. Liabilities may be certain, both in regard to their very existence, as well as in regard to the date of their performance and their amounts. Liabilities may be certain, but the actual date of their performance or their amount may be unknown ("provisions").[31] The very existence of some liabilities may be uncertain ("contingencies").[32] As mentioned above, in order to resolve both the Collection Question and the Quantification Question, the CVT model is willing to depart from GAAP. Like the Income Approach and the Advance Approach, in the case of unearned receivables, the timing of recognition of income from the base transaction would be at the date it is received. Nevertheless, unlike the Income Approach and the Advance Approach, in such a case the CVT model aims to tax upon receipt of the "value" of the base transaction, rather than at the date of receipt of its full amount. In order to do so, one must take into account the taxpayer's liabilities on that date, while waiving the requirement of certainty.

This "waiver" of the requirement of certainty signifies taking into account all the risks (including those which are uncertain) when determining the aggregate amount to be included in the duration component (i.e. the possibility that the liability will not be realized at all).[33] Following the waiver of the certainty requirement, the CVT model will demand that additional accounting be made in the future, to the extent that the liabilities have been deducted while taking into account the duration amount. This accounting will be made in real terms, in such a manner that if the liability is not realized in the future, then the income will be added to the unrealized amount of the liability that was deducted at the future value (FV) of the sum that was deducted in the year in which the income was earned or the deposit or advance were received. The same applies to a case where it transpires that the amount of the deduction that was made in the year of receipt does not reflect the full amount of the liability. In such a case a deduction of the full amount of the liability will be made in the future (in that future value), setting off the future value of that part of the deducted amount that was made in the year of the "beginning of the period" (that was based on the duration).

8.2 The Saving of Financing Costs model ("the SFC model")

In addition to the CVT model, another alternative model can also used to treat of the subject of the tax advantages or disadvantages that may arise as a result of time differentials between the date of recognizing income or expense and the date of actual receipt or payment.

While the CVT model seeks to relate to both the Collection Question[34] that can arise as a result of deferring the recognition of income or advancing the recognition of liabilities for tax purposes, and the Quantification Question,[35] the SFC model does not address the Collection Question at all. The purpose of the SFC model is solely to address the Quantification Question that may arise due to the derivative time differences between the date of the recognition of the income or the liability according to GAAP, and the actual date on which the income is received or the liability paid.

Put differently, while in the spirit of the Dualistic Doctrine and the Separating Approach,[36] the CVT model is prepared to deviate from GAAP and, in order to preserve the tax values, determine the timing of the recognition of income and expense differently from those set according to GAAP, this is not the intention of the SFC model.

The SFC model accepts GAAP as a given. In the spirit of the Singular Doctrine and the Consistent Approach, GAAP should not be deviated from to create a separate, unnecessary tax accounting.[37] More importantly, the SFC model not only follows GAAP in regard to the dates for recognizing income and expense, but even uses the tools of GAAP in order to determine the economic advantage that accrues to the taxpayer as a result of determining the timing of the recognition of income and expenses according to GAAP.

According to the SFC model, if a taxpayer does not treat receivables (such as a deposit or advance) as income on the date received, then this can be regarded as a double statement to the effect that these receivables have yet to be earned by him, and therefore are not his property, and that they belong to another person, although the taxpayer himself is the party that uses them. The same applies to a liability that has been recognized as an expense according to GAAP, despite the fact that it has yet to be paid. Here, too, the taxpayer's treatment can be regarded as comprising two statements, that is not only that this liability (although yet unpaid) "is no longer mine", but also, "I am using someone else's money" (as long as the recognized liability has not actually been performed).

The SFC model is established on those implied statements by the taxpayer by intrinsically recognizing income or expense on given dates that are other than the dates on which "the cash flows", and test the advantages that arise as a result of these time differentials.

While the CVT model uses a mechanism of capitalization in order to distinguish between the base transaction and the finance transaction, and to eliminate the value differentials by locating all the values at a single point along the "timeline", the mechanism of the SFC model is completely different.

According to the SFC model, it is possible to determine – at any given time, and regarding any transaction – the benefit or loss resulting from the time gap between recognition for tax purposes and actual receipt or payment, in terms of alternative interest.

In addressing the question of the "benefit" or "loss" related to the time gap, it ought to be remembered that this is a relative matter, for as soon as one asks what the "benefit" or "loss" is, one can ask "compared to what"? If, for example, a taxpayer receives a deposit and is required to repay it to the customer at the end of the term of the deposit, together with the interest that he would pay to a bank for a loan (hereinafter: "**the alternative debit interest**"), no "benefit" in the deposit accrues to him compared to alternative financing sources.

The same logic also applies to unpaid liabilities. If delaying the payment of a liability is subject to payment of interest at a rate that the taxpayer would pay to a bank for a loan, then there is no "benefit" in delaying performance of the liability when compared to the available alternative financing sources.

With regard to advances, if a taxpayer would have recognized income from an advance on the future date on which it is earned, but not at the nominal value at which the advance was given, but would have returned the advance to the customer with the alternative debit interest, and if on the same day the customer would have paid the income to the taxpayer in the amount of the repayment (which comprises both the principal of the advance and the alternative interest), then such an advance would not constitute a benefit. In terms of possible loss related to the time gap, if a taxpayer recognizes an earned income for tax purposes, although he has not yet received it, but is entitled to receive it at a future date with the interest that he would receive from a bank for a deposit (hereinafter: "**the alternative credit interest**"), no disadvantage in delaying the receivable accrues to him compared to alternative available financing.[38] It can thus be deduced that the time gap between date of recognition of income or liabilities for tax purposes, and the date of actual receipt or payment, has no financial advantage in and of itself, and all depends on the payment terms. In the absence of any economic difference between the Present Value ("PV") of the deposit or the advance on the date of its receipt, and the Future Value ("FV") on the date on which it is returned or earned, an advantage accrues to the taxpayer only when the actual receipt of the deposit or the advance saves the taxpayer alternative financing costs. This also applies to liabilities.

The SFC model tests at the "source" level whether, as a result of taking the deposit or the advance or deferring the loan, the taxpayer saves financing costs as against the alternatives that are available to him. It should be emphasized that the test according to the model is made at the "source" level only (the "passive" side of the balance sheet), while the "uses" that have been financed from those "sources" (that are included in the "active" side of the balance sheet) are of no interest at all to this model. That is to say, what the taxpayer has done with unearned receivable (like an advance or deposit), or the amount that he owes but has yet to pay, is of no concern to this model.

According to the model, a saving in financing costs on raising and using "outside capital" is a benefit that accrues to the taxpayer (if at all) as a result of the conditions of taking the deposit or the advance or deferring the date of discharging the liability. The question of what was done with the money that was raised, or what it was used for, is completely irrelevant. In any event, it is not relevant that those "uses" resulted in profits that are liable to tax. The "nature" of those profits, whether as "business" or "financing" or other profits, is also of no interest, since the assumption is that those "uses" would have been made regardless of whether the "sources" of the financing of the "outside capital" for the taxpayer were "cheap" or "expensive". That is to say, the "benefit" that was created (if at all) to the taxpayer on the terms of raising his "sources of outside capital" is the tax event that concerns the model, and the "uses" that were made of that capital are not relevant. This saving of the costs of alternative debt financing (to the extent that it arises) is the benefit that should be taxed, regardless of the uses that the taxpayer makes of those resources.[39]

Moreover, the SFC model treats only of the taxpayer's saving of alternative financing costs on unearned receivables and by deferring the date of the discharge of his liabilities, and ignores hypothetical losses (that in practice do not exist) in terms of alternative credit interest in cases were income is earned for tax purposes before it has been received.[40]

8.2.1 *The SFC ("multipart") formula*

The SFC model is intended to determine the benefit that accrues to the taxpayer in each year in which the taxpayer holds a deposit, an advance or a liability. This benefit (regardless of the uses the taxpayer makes of receivables)[41] is measured in terms of the savings those funds afford the taxpayer when compared to alternative financing costs. Accordingly, the annual benefit or loss arising from any deposit, advance or other liability yet to be performed, and any earned income yet to be received, may be expressed as follows:

$$\sum_{i=1}^{N} RLi * [1 + (AIRi - k_i)^{ti/12} - 1]$$

Where,

N = the total number of unearned receivables (like deposits or advances) and of unpaid liabilities that were deducted as expenses for tax purposes ("**unpaid deductible liabilities**"), to be performed by the taxpayer in the future.

i = a counter (running from 1 to N) representing a specific unearned receivable or unpaid deductible liability.

RLi = the amount (in terms of principal) of any specific unearned receivable (like a deposit or advance) or of any specific unpaid deductible liability.

k_i = the agreed interest, i.e. with respect to a deposit is the interest rate that is added (if at all) to the repayment of the deposit. Insofar as no interest is added to the deposit, $k = 0$. With respect to an advance, generally the advance does not include a liability to make a financial repayment, and in any event it is not an addition to the repayment amount and, therefore, in a case of advance, $k = 0$. With respect to unpaid deductible liability (L) is the interest rate that is added (if at all) to the payment of the liability. Insofar as no interest is added to the liability, $k = 0$.

$AIRi$ ("the alternative interest rate") = the average debit interest rate paid by the taxpayer to an unrelated third party in any year in which the deposit is in effect, or in which the balance of the advance exists, or in which there is unpaid deductible liability (hereinafter: "**given year**", "**fiscal year**" or "**relevant year**") on loans for the same period between the date of receiving the deposit or the advance and the date on which they are returned or earned for tax purposes or for the same period between the date of deducting unpaid deductible liability for tax purposes or recognizing a receivable earned income for tax purposes, and the date of payment or receipt. Generally, the $AIRi$ with respect to deposits (in light of the time gap between the date of their receipt and the date of their expected repayment) would be the average interest rate that the taxpayer would pay in that given year on long-term loans. Generally, the $AIRi$ on advances or unpaid deductible liability would be the average interest rate that the taxpayer would pay in that given year on short-term loans.[42] In cases where third-party loans from unrelated persons (for the same time period) are not available, the $AIRi$ would be equal to the annual "market interest" rate for the same time interval.[43]

t_i = the number of months that have elapsed from the date of commencement until the date of termination. For this purpose:

> "**Date of commencement**" with respect to deposits or advances that have been received before the fiscal year, or with respect to unpaid deductible liability that have been recognized for tax purposes before the fiscal year, the date of commencement means the beginning of the current fiscal year. With respect to deposits or advances that have been received during the course of the fiscal year, or with respect to

unpaid deductible liabilities that have been recognized for tax purposes during the course of the fiscal year, the date of commencement means the date of receipt or the date of recognition.

"**Date of termination**" means: the date during the course of the fiscal year in which the deposit is returned to the customer; the date on which, for tax purposes, the deposit or the advance is earned; or the date on which unpaid deductible liabilities have been paid. If the deposit or the advance has not been repaid or earned in that year, or the unpaid deductible liability has not been paid in that year, the date of termination will be the expiration date of that fiscal year.

8.2.2 *The SFC ("simple") formula*

$(R + L) * AIR / 365 - Ktot$

R = "the opening balance" in a given day (in terms of principal) of unearned receivables (like deposits or advances) received before the commencement of that day (less any sum that has been returned or earned before the beginning of the day), as well as the principal of any unearned receivables that was received during the day.

L = "the opening balance" in a given day (in terms of principal) of unpaid liabilities that were deducted as expenses for tax purposes ("unpaid deductible liabilities") before the commencement of that day (less any sum that has been paid before the beginning of the day), as well as the principal of such unpaid deductible liabilities that was recognized as an expenses for tax purposes during the day.

AIR ("the alternative interest rate") = the average debit interest rate paid by the taxpayer to an unrelated third party in any given year on loans from all sources. In cases where loans from unrelated persons are not available, the AIR will be equal to the annual average "market interest" rate applicable in a given year.[44]

$Ktot$ = the aggregate amount of all agreeable interest added on a daily basis to unearned receivables (like deposits or advances) (included in R) or to unpaid deductible liabilities (included in L).

8.2.3 *The benefit according to the SFC formula*

The model tests the benefit to the taxpayer in terms of savings of alternative financing costs. While the CVT model focuses on the cash flow, and requires splitting the base transaction and the finance transaction by using the present value or future value as compared to actually received payment, the SFC model is not concerned with comparing values of cash flow. The aim of the SFC model is to isolate the taxpayer advantage arising from the time gap between the date of recognition of income or liabilities for tax purposes and the date of actual received or payment.

This is achieved by calculating the alternative interest that the taxpayer would have been required to pay if he had not received a deposit or advance from the customer, or had not delayed payment to a supplier for the period between the date of the recognition of income or liability for tax purposes and the date of actual receipt or payment.

"There are no free loans",[45] and therefore, the assumption must be that if a customer gives the taxpayer a deposit or an advance, or a supplier agrees to defer the date of the taxpayer's date performing his liabilities on conditions that generate a saving in alternative financing costs for the taxpayer, this is not done without reason. Logic dictates that this real saving is given in return for it for some consideration. The taxpayer waived part of what he was owed in the transaction in which the deposit or advance was received, or agreed to pay a higher price in return for deferring the date for performance. The "shortfall" to the Treasury does not derive from a "genuine" discount to the customer or a "genuine" increase in the liability to the supplier. It derives from a quasi-barter transaction in which the taxpayer partially "waives" the price of the product or the service, in consideration for "cheap credit", or assumes a greater liability in exchange for "cheap credit".[46] From this standpoint, both the "multipart" SFC formula and the "simple" SFC formula are intended to effectively indemnify the Treasury.

8.2.3.1 *The benefit according to the "multipart" SFC formula*

The "multipart" SFC formula is intended to examine the benefit that accrued to the taxpayer in terms of saving of alternative financing costs at the level of the isolated transaction in which an unearned deposit or an advance has been received from a customer, or in which the performance of a deductable liability has been delayed. The formula should be implemented for each isolated transaction as such. By testing each transaction at the individual level, the formula examines each and every transaction in which revenue is received before it has been earned, on the date it is received, or on the date that discharge of the liability is deferred. It examines how much financing cost the taxpayer has saved (if at all) at the "level of the individual transaction" as a result of receiving the money before it was earned, or as a result of deferring the timing of the performance of the liability that he assumed, having regard to the specific conditions of each and every transaction. The assumption is that this "saving" of financing costs reflects a parallel "cheapening" of the price of the product or the service.[47]

The term $(AIR - k)$ reflects the difference between the AIR[48] and the interest that the taxpayer undertook to pay to the customer, together with the principal of the deposit he undertook to pay to his supplier, alongside the principal of his liability.[49] This expression, which reflects the interest saved by receiving the deposit or the advance from customer, or by delaying performance of liability, lies at the very heart of the proposed model. It reflects the amount of the benefit or disadvantage accruing to the taxpayer in any given year as a result of using funds that do not belong to him, or the inability to use funds to which he is entitled.[50]

Thus, for example, if the taxpayer received a £1,000 deposit four years ago, to be repaid in another 30 years, and in the relevant year the AIR at which the taxpayer raised long-term loans from outside sources was 7 per cent per annum, and the interest added to the deposit (k) is 2 per cent per annum, and up to that fourth year no repayments on account of the deposit have yet been made, and during such year the deposit remains in effect, then the formula leads to the result that in that given year the benefit that will be imputed to the taxpayer is:

$$PV^* \; [(1 + (AIR - k)^{t/12} - 1] = 1{,}000^* \; [(1 + (7\% - 2\%))^{2/12} - 1]$$
$$= 1{,}000^* \; [1.05 - 1] = 50$$

To this amount we naturally have to add the benefit that will be imputed to the taxpayer in respect of the deposit principal in each of the years in which the deposit exists and remains in effect until the date of its return or is earned, the benefit being appropriated, according to this model, to the relevant year.

Another example is where an advance of £1,000 is received on 30 June 2004 for services to be supplied in March 2006, and the alternative interest paid by the taxpayer from 2004 to 2006 in respect of a two-year loan was 10 per cent per annum. The benefit that will be imputed to the taxpayer according to the proposed model will be as follows:

In the year 2004: $PV^*[(1 + AIR)^{t/12} - 1] = 1{,}000^* \; [1.10^{6/12} - 1] = 48.8$

In the year 2005: $PV^*[(1 + AIR)^{t/12} - 1] = 1{,}000^* \; [1.10^{12/12} - 1] = 100$

In the year 2006: $PV^*[(1 + AIR)^{t/12} - 1] = 1{,}000^* \; [1.10^{3/12} - 1] = 24.11$

If a liability of £1,000 is recognized for tax purposes on 30 June 2004, but the actual payment (or other performance) will be made by the taxpayer in March 2006, and no interest is added to the payment of the debt, and the alternative interest paid by the taxpayer from 2004 up to 2006 in respect of a two-year loan was 10 per cent per annum, then the benefit that will be imputed to the taxpayer according to the proposed model will be the same as in the previous example (computed for an advance).

8.2.3.2 *The benefit according to the "simple" SFC formula*

The complex formula seeks to assess the benefit that accrues to a taxpayer at the level of the individual transaction, i.e. with respect to each and every transaction in which a receipt has been received that has not been recognized as income, or for which the date of the performance of the liability has been recognized as an expense. The benefit component to the taxpayer inherent in such transactions is the saving of finance costs. The simple SFC formula does not invade to the level of the individual transaction, but focuses on the overall cashflow of the taxpayer originating in revenues from customers that have not yet been included in the taxpayer's income for tax purposes, or which originate from deferring payments in respect of liabilities that have already been recognized as an expense for tax purposes (hereinafter: "**the untaxed cashflow**"). The formula tests the overall untaxed cashflow on a daily basis, and tests what sum the taxpayer has saved (if at all) throughout the year as a result of being able to use that cashflow without being required to borrow monies from other sources.

Let us say that, on a particular day, the taxpayer held receivables on which no tax had yet been paid, and liabilities to suppliers that had yet to be effectively discharged, in the aggregate sum of £1,000. And let us say that the overall interest that he had to pay to those customers or suppliers for those unearned receivables or deferred liabilities amounted to £10 (an average of 1 per cent on annual interest), and the average interest payable by the taxpayer to all his unrelated creditors (either those relating to long-term loans or short-term loans) was at the annual rate of 8 per cent. The benefit element that would apply to him in respect of that day would be:

$$1,000 * 8\% / 365 - 1\%/365 = 0.1916.$$

A similar calculation would be made for each date in the course of the year.

8.2.4 *The model and the irrelevance of taxation on the "uses"*

It should be emphasized that taxation according to the SFC model is imposed on the "sources" level, whatever the uses will be and whatever the taxation on those uses will be. The case of a deposit could be compared with a situation where, in order to secure his obligation under a contract, the customer lends the taxpayer, for a defined period, a machine that the taxpayer uses for his business. The case of an advance could be compared with a situation where a customer lends the taxpayer the same machine in order to secure the payment of a nominal amount of the consideration, after providing the goods or the services on a future date. The case of an unpaid liability could be compared with a situation where a supplier of machines lends the taxpayer the machine for a defined period in order to persuade the taxpayer to purchase it at a later date. In all cases (which will be called "the machine examples"), the assumption is that the machine has produced an additional income during this period, and this additional income is taxable.

If instead of lending a machine, the customer (in cases of deposits or advances) or the supplier (in cases of liabilities) lends the taxpayer a private car to use for his private needs without producing any income (hereinafter: "**the private car example**"), it is still clear that the taxpayer enjoys the economic benefit of using someone else's car without payment. In all examples, the question whether or not the use of the machine or the car would produce a taxable income has no relevancy in measuring the benefit that accrued to the taxpayer from this specific customer or supplier. This is because the use in producing income from the machine would have been liable to the same tax, whether or not it had been rented for the full rental fees, or whether it had been purchased by the taxpayer from his net income (after tax). Furthermore, the fact that the car does not produce any taxable income does not mean that the taxpayer does not gain an economic advantage by saving the full rental fee for the car.

As compared to the cases of deposits or advances or delaying the performance of liabilities, the benefit that accrues to the taxpayer in the machine and the car examples can be measured against the difference between the rental fees actually paid by the taxpayer for them, and the rental fees that he would have paid for the same machine or car for the same defined periods. There is no economic difference between these examples and the cases of deposits or advances or unpaid liabilities. The saving of alternative interests should itself be regarded as a taxable economic advantage, regardless of the taxation imposed (or not) on the uses that the taxpayer makes of those resources.

8.2.5 The model ignores the "losses" in deferring receipt of earned income

On the face of it, the logic of the SFC model applies not only in cases of unearned receivables and deferred liabilities (with regard to the saving of the alternative debit interest), but also vice versa with regard to unreceived earned income. By delaying the receiving date to a later date than the date of earning the income (via the realization principle), the taxpayer loses an alternative credit interest that he would have been able to produce if there were no such time gap. In other words, by giving the customer a zero-rate interest for delaying the payment date from the date of delivering the goods or supplying the services (in case where no interest is added to the receivable), then by recognizing the full amount of the income prior to the date of receipt, the taxpayer loses the alternative credit interest that would have accrued to him if no time gap existed between those dates.

It can be argued that the same logic by which the SFC model examines at the "source" level whether a deposit or advance or deferment saves the taxpayer financing costs also demands checking whether deferring receipt of income that has already been earned causes the taxpayer a loss at the "source" level. According to this argument, the question of the benefit that can accrue to the taxpayer (at the "source" level) due to his ability to raise "outside capital" (by means of the "instrument" of deposits or advances or deferring the discharge of his liabilities) raises the question as to the possibility that he will incur a loss (also at the "source" level) as a result of the fact that he earned income, but deferred the timing of its receipt to a later date.

On the face of it, the time difference between the date of the recognition of the income until the later date of receiving the amount from the customer reflects a credit period that was granted to the customer during which the taxpayer could have earned that amount that was recognized by him as income. Had the income been received by him on that date, he could have made use of it. In other words, from the moment he earned the income until the date on which he received the money, the taxpayer "lost" the difference between the interest that he collected, if at all, from the customer in respect of that time difference, and the interest that he could have earned had the consideration actually been paid to the taxpayer on the date on which the income was earned.

On the face of it, there would appear to be a balance or symmetry between the "benefit" that is caused to the taxpayer from receiving deposits, advances and deferring liabilities where alternative financing costs are saved by the taxpayer, and the "loss" incurred in terms of alternative interest as a result of deferring the timing of receipt of the amount in respect of the income that has been earned.

We say, "on the face of it" because this is not so in practice. In our opinion, no such balance or symmetry exists between the "benefit" in saving alternative financing costs (in cases of deposits, advances and deferring the discharge of liabilities) and the "loss" in obtaining alternative yields (in the case of recognizing income before the time of actually receiving it). As we have already stated, "there are no free loans".[51] The assumption is that a taxpayer who has received a deposit or an advance from the customer that appears to be "interest free", or at lower rate than the alternative interest that would be paid on "outside credit" ("the interest saves"), would have been prepared to reduce the price of the product or the service by the "interest saves" component. The same applies with respect to the willingness of the taxpayer to add the same "interest saves" to the principal amount of the liability which he received credit from the supplier. Therefore, in circumstances where the taxpayer has saved alternative financing costs, imputing the "benefit" to that taxpayer according to the SFC model is intended, in practical terms, "to indemnify" the Treasury for the cost of a shortfall in the price of the product or the service, such shortfall being parallel to the "interest saved".

The very same logic by which "there are no free loans" also leads to the conclusion that where the taxpayer has earned the income before it has been received, he should be regarded as having granted credit to the customer, where the cost of the credit (as long as it is not paid by the customer as an addition) is included in the price of the product or the service. In such a case, no "loss" is to be imputed to that taxpayer from not receiving alternative interest since he has already received the interest component (that constitutes part of the price of the product or the service). Had such a "loss" been imputed to the taxpayer, then, according to the SFC model, the Treasury's income would have been eroded, since, in practice, the price of the product or the service would have been reduced for tax purposes to below the amount that was actually paid. In such a case where the income has been earned before it has been received, it might be more appropriate to split that part which reflects the base transaction from that part of the income that has been earned and that reflects the financial transaction (or the interest component), and to spread its recognition over the period between the date it was earned and the date it was received.

In any case, it is inconceivable that by means of recognizing a "loss" from not receiving an alternative yield, part of the income that has been earned (and which reflects the interest component that is inherent therein) will be totally struck out. Moreover, a taxpayer who advances credit to one of his customers (at "low" or "zero" interest) can finance that credit from outside financing ("foreign funds"), thereby receiving "protection" of the "sources" in respect to that income that has been earned.[52] Therefore, it is submitted that recognizing a notional "loss" as a result of not earning an alternative yield in the period of granting credit to customers means "double protection".

This is not the case where the taxpayer saves alternative financing costs when he receives a deposit or advance or defers the date of performing a liability. In such a case, at the "source" level, it is actually the State purse that suffers by the reduction of the price of the product or the service, without the amount of that discount (that reflects the "interest saved") being taxable. This being so, the SFC model only treats the aspect of the saving to the taxpayer of alternative financing costs on receiving unearned receivables and deferring the date of the discharge of his liabilities, and does not address the hypothetical loss from recognizing income before it has been received.

8.2.6 The SFC model and erosion of tax

It could be argued that the benefit component that is calculated according to the SFC model in regard to unearned receivables (like deposits or advances) and in regard to unpaid liabilities does not provide a real answer to the advantages that they might create. This is because the more time that elapses from the year in which the receivable is received or the unpaid liability is recognized for tax purposes, the greater the distortion created by the calculation of the additional income in terms of the AIR on the principal of the receivable or the liability (and not on the estimated values thereof as at the beginning of the relevant year). This argument of tax erosion holds that in each relevant year the taxpayer saves the financing costs not merely on the principal of the deposit or the advance, but also on the estimated value of that principal.

However, it is submitted that this is not so, and that in each year the additional income must be calculated only on the principal. The model seeks to tax one thing only – the annual saving in alternative financing costs, that is to say, how much the taxpayer has saved at the "source" level by the very fact that he used resources that do not belong to him for his own purposes. The ability of the taxpayer to make use of what he has earned in the past does not constitute a "saving" of financing costs. Even if a receivable is received a number of years before the relevant fiscal year, or a liability is recognized for tax purposes long before the fiscal year, and the value thereof at the beginning of the relevant year is higher than the principal value, the assumption is that this saving to the taxpayer in alternative financing costs has already been added to the taxpayer's income in the past (i.e. as from the date on which the receivables were received or the liabilities were recognized, until the year which preceded the relevant fiscal year). From this it follows that this "saving" that has been added to the taxpayer's income has become "his property". That is to say, the taxpayer "has acquired" his right to such addition (on which tax has been paid in the past), and this right will not be taken into account in determining the saving of the AIR that has accrued to him in the relevant year. This resembles the possibility that at the end of the year preceding the relevant year, the taxpayer will repay the principal of the deposit or the advance (plus the agreed interest (k)) that is due to the customer (if at all), or pay the liability to the supplier (plus the agreed interest (k). In all these cases, the tax payer retains the "saving" achieved up to that year (i.e. $AIR - k$). Under this construction, the taxpayer's benefit in the relevant year from the possibility of making use of the addition that has accrued on the receivable principal or the unpaid recognized liability principal does not constitute a saving of alternative financing costs, but a benefit that derives from the use of funds that have become the taxpayer's property before the relevant tax year began.[53]

8.2.7 *Date of taxation under the SFC model*

As indicated in the formula set out above, the tax, if any, that is due on any benefit inherent in the unearned deposit or advance or unpaid recognized liability must be paid on an annual basis throughout the entire life of the deposit, from the date it is received until its return or until it has been earned ("the deposit life"), and for the entire life of the advance from the date of its receipt until it is earned ("the advance life"), and for the entire life of the unpaid recognized liability from the date of its recognition as an expense for tax purposes until it is paid or performed ("**the unpaid liability life**"). The reasons for this are as follows:

As stated above, if the deposit or the advance, or the delaying of per-formance of a liability contains a benefit, then this benefit, in substance, is financial, and as in an ordinary loan GAAP dictates that financing income should be appropriated throughout the period it was obtained by using the effective interest method.[54] There is no reason for not following this method in relation to a benefit created by a deposit or an advance, or by delaying liability performance.[55]

Moreover, from the standpoint of the objective of preventing unjust tax advantages and addressing the Quantification Question (as opposed to the Collection Question), it is immaterial whether negating "the tax advantage" will be on an annual basis or on another date (such as the date of receipt), provided that the tax will be paid in real terms that do not violate the tax values that we described above.[56] In light of this, imposing tax on the AIR saving at the beginning of the life of the deposit or the advance life or the liability, and thus preferring the Treasury as a creditor (as against other interested parties) by providing it with the option to collect tax on "profit" (from the saving finance benefit) that has yet to accrue, would contradict the Proportionality Principle that requires a proper balance between the objective and the means for achieving it.[57] Therefore, the Proportionality Principle requires favoring the view that spreads "income" from any benefit created (if at all), as against the view that taxes such benefit in advance.[58]

8.2.8 The model compared to the Loan and the Income Approaches

The difference between the SFC model and the Loan Approach is clear. Where the Loan Approach, relying on GAAP, does not impose tax on the benefit accruing to the recipient of the deposit (to the extent that it arises), and in this way tax values could be violated,[59] the model singles out for taxation only the benefit accruing to the recipient.

The difference between the SFC model and the Income Approach is more complex, as both approaches seek to address the absence of tax on the accrued benefit that may result from a deposit. However, despite this identical goal, the means employed to achieve it according to the SFC model are clearly different from those of the Income Approach. These different means can be distinguished as follows:

While the Income Approach is a product of *ad hoc* judicial decisions, and encompasses various, sometimes contradictory tests that seek to distinguish between regarding the deposit as a loan and viewing it as income,[60] the SFC model is not be based upon *ad hoc* judicial rulings, but presents a uniform legislative solution.

While the Income Approach taxes the entire amount of the deposit – both the liability component as well as the benefit component – and by doing so violates the tax value of non-erosion of capital,[61] the SFC model concentrates on taxing only the benefit.

While some of the tests that have been laid down in the Income Approach are unrelated to the question of whether or not the recipient acquires any financial benefit,[62] the SFC model is entirely focused on examining the financial benefit.

While the Income Approach is highly concerned with the reasons for the deposit,[63] these reasons are of no concern at all to the SFC model, since it is only interested in whether the taxpayer has "profited" as a result of the deposit (in terms of saving alternative financing costs).[64]

While the Income Approach imposes the entire tax on the date on which the deposit is received,[65] the annual accounting under the SFC model is more in accord with a beneficial financial transaction, since the financial advantage thereof is expressed in low-cost financing sources. The SFC model gives expression to the fact that the financial benefit from a deposit that is given on preferential terms is not created "at the very outset" or at the end of the process, but is distributed throughout the period.

As has been noted, the Income Approach is an ideal example of non-compliance with the Proportionality Principle. The proper objective of preventing unjust tax advantages has led to the drastic "solution" of taxing the entire principal of the deposit, although it is clear that all or part of it does not enrich the taxpayer. The result is that the "remedy" for the malady of unjust tax advantages leads to the more serious malady of imposing tax on something which is not income at all.[66] In contrast, the SFC model concentrates on the malady and seeks to cure it without causing other, more serious damage.

8.2.9 The model compared to the Deferral and the Advance Approaches

The difference between the SFC model and the Deferral Approach is clear. The SFC model is predicated on the assumption that the Deferral Approach that relies on GAAP leaves an arbitrage, in which the recipient of an advance could receive low-cost financing that constitutes an untaxed component of his income and, in this way, tax values could be violated.[67] The SFC model seeks to prevent this by imposing tax on that arbitrage (to the extent it exists).

The objective of the SFC model resembles that of the Advance Approach, which is preventing unjust tax advantages. The difference is expressed in the means employed to achieve the same goal. The SFC model does not create a theoretical financial transaction that, on the face of it, also necessitates treating the payer of the advance in a way that justifies his taxes for theoretical financing income.[68] It does not impose tax on the present value (PV) of a payment based on a "theoretical" future value, and it seeks to examine the benefit in terms of the specific taxpayer in light of the saving that he gains in relation to alternative financing costs in accordance with his own values.[69] The distortion of calculating tax based on the total turnover of the advance, which violates the tax value of non-erosion of capital, does not exist in the SFC model.[70] For the same reason, the advantage from the standpoint of the tax authorities' cash flow is similarly annulled.[71] The SFC model does not fail on the neutrality principle, in that it does not create a different tax law for advances as opposed to loans.[72] From this standpoint, the SFC model does not violate the horizontal equity principle that applies equally to a party who receives an advance, and one who receives a loan.[73] But principally, the means proposed in this model accomplishes, to a large extent, the desirable goal of preventing unjust tax advantages without involving the potential payment of tax in advance on the turnover in connection with "profit" that has not yet arisen, in deviation from the Proportionality Principle.[74]

8.2.10 The model compared to the timing requirements for recognition of expenses

The various tax systems have determined, as we have seen, the different levels of certainty that are required as a condition for determining the timing of the recognition of a liability as an expense for tax purposes. Acceptance of the standard of the Accounting Certainty Degree of a liability as a condition for determining the timing of its recognition as an expense, together with the Full and Immediate Deduction Approach (as customary in the UK and Israeli tax systems), leaves the door open not merely to deferring the payment of the tax in reliance on a liability that has yet to be fulfilled, but also opens the door to reducing the amount of the tax in real terms. This is so because deducting in the present a liability at its future nominal value means reducing the taxable income in the present year as a result of the amount of the future nominal liability at a value that is higher than its real value on the date of the deduction.[75] In other words, integrating the Accounting Certainty Degree requirement and the Full and Immediate Deduction Approach leads to an intermingling of future values of liabilities on calculating chargeable income in the relevant year. The income (that has been received in that year) is presented at its real value, and expenses, which reduce that income and relate to liabilities having a future repayment date, are presented in their future nominal terms, which are higher than their value in real terms as of the date of the deduction.

The SFC model does not deal with this anomaly through the CVT model according to which the deductible value of the liability will decrease in the relevant year by means of the mechanism of capitalization. According to the SFC model, a deferred liability is the same as a loan that has been granted to the taxpayer by the supplier. If the interest rate on that loan is lower than the average interest rate payable by the taxpayer, then taking the loan on those conditions saves the taxpayer the interest differential. This tax payment on the interest differential throughout the period between the date of the recognition of the liability until the date on which it is performed can be compared for tax purposes to the status of a taxpayer who has deducted a liability in the year in which it both crystallized and was paid (by using a loan).

A taxpayer who seeks to deduct a liability for tax purposes in the relevant year, despite the fact that the payment date thereof will fall in the future, is to be treated as a person who asserts that he holds financial resources (to the extent of the nominal amount of the liability that he deducted as an expense) that, in fact, do not belong to him (but to the supplier towards whom the liability was incurred). The very fact that they are still in his possession (until the date of actual payment) means that he is to be regarded as a person who has received credit. If the interest rate on this credit is lower than the average interest that a taxpayer pays, then the taxpayer will pay tax on this saving at the source level.

According to the SFC model, the problem does not lie in bringing forward the timing of the recognition of the liability as an expense, nor does it lie in the values at which the expense was deducted. The CVT model seeks to determine the value of the expense to which the future liability relates according to PV. According to the SFC model, the benefit that will be imputed to the taxpayer is only the saving of his financing costs, and the ability to use money (at low interest having regard to his ability to raise money) that was advanced to him as a credit by the supplier.

As we have seen, adopting the requirement of the Absolute Certainty Degree or the High Certainty Degree (in the US tax system), which are prima facie designed to be used as means to prevent unjust tax advantages, has led to a long line of failures, including distorting the income of taxpayers in the year in which it accrued to them by assuming liabilities having a future performance date, the non-economic distinction between a liability to pay cash and the liability to perform services, and the like.[76]

Adopting the SFC model renders unnecessary the need to defer the timing of the recognition of the liability as an expense, and prevents most of the failures involved from doing so. From this standpoint, the SFC model provides an answer to the tax value of preventing unjust tax advantages by means of allowing the deduction of future expenses at terms that do not reflect their true value. Although the expense will be recognized on the date on which the liability crystallized at the nominal value of the amount of future payment, nonetheless, treating that liability as a loan that was granted to the taxpayer by the supplier will ensure that in each year in which the liability remains unpaid, the taxpayer will be taxed on the difference between the interest that is added to the amount of the liability (if at all) and the interest that he would have been required to pay on the same debt had he received it from a "normal" creditor. For example, if we apply the model to cases such as those discussed in *Burn-ham*[77] and *Mooney Aircraft*,[78] then, first and foremost, it is inconceivable that three different results were obtained in three cases that were substantially the same in relation to the timing of the recognition of the liability as an expense, and the amount to be recognized as such. Moreover, and this is the main point, presenting the total amount of the liability in its future nominal value in the financial statements drawn according to GAAP, despite the fact that the timing of the payment thereof in the amount presented above occurred many years later, was considered to be a statement by the taxpayer that he received an interest-free loan from the creditor. Therefore, the benefit of saving the interest from the date on which the liability was created and its registration should be treated as an expense until the date on which it was paid, and should be treated and taxed as financial income.

If we apply the model to the same case as that debated in the *Ford Motor* case,[79] then, in the spirit of the logic of the SFC model, which follows GAAP, the taxpayer should be told that it is inconceivable that for purposes of its financial statements the amount of the liability will be presented to the world at large in its value in real terms, but for tax purposes it will be presented in its nominal value.[80] The taxpayer should also be told that even in the absence of recognizing the amount of the liability to the insurance company, he should be required to present the liability in its future nominal value according to GAAP. That statement will be deemed to be an admission on his part that he received credit bearing no interest for a lengthy period, and that this constitutes a taxable advantage according to the formula under the SFC.

8.3 Selecting one of the two models

The two alternative models that we have presented – the CVT model and the SFC model – are, in our opinion, preferable to all the tax solutions provided by the tax systems reviewed as a way of confronting the elimination of the effects of the passage of time. The tax systems reviewed enable taxpayers to defer the timing of the recognition of income, or bring forward the timing of the recognition of a liability as an expense (and incidentally defer the timing of the tax payments, and, more seriously, create a result that leads to profit being calculated for tax purposes in other than real terms).[81] As opposed to this, the above two models seek to neutralize the effect of the time dimension on the collection of tax and on calculating the amount that is liable to tax. The tax systems reviewed attempt to confront the effect of time both with respect to the Collection Question and the Quantification Question by means of inconsistent and *ad hoc* case law that deviates from GAAP, and is based on tests that are unrelated to measuring the economic advantages and disadvantages arising from the time differentials between the recognition of income and expense and those of the cash flow.[82] The two models seek to offer a consistent solution that is based on economic logic which prevents erosion to the tax value of preventing unjust tax advantages, but conversely attempts to treat the "malaise" on the basis of the Proportionality Principle, causing the minimum possible damage to other tax values.[83] In addition, the CVT model and the SFC model are far preferable to the cash basis method or the hybrid method, which, in our opinion, do not reflect proper standards of determining an addition to wealth or profit.[84]

Although, in this sense, there is similarity between the two alternative models, nonetheless, there are significant differences between them.

8.3.1 *The targets of the two models*

From our standpoint, the difference between the CVT model and the SFC model with respect to the timing of the recognition of income and liabilities reflects a conceptual difference between the two following global approaches.

The CVT model seeks to constitute a proper solution to the two fundamental questions that have been presented, and that may create time differentials between the time of recognizing income and liabilities for tax purposes and the date of the actual receipt or payment, that is, the Collection Question and the Quantification Question.[85] In light of this, the CVT model is willing to advance the timing of the recognition of income of the base transaction to the earliest possible date between the timing of the recognition of the income and that of the receipt of the payment. In contrast, the SFC model does not seek to tackle the Collection Question. It follows that, according to this model, the dates of the recognition of the income, both with respect to the base transaction and also in regard to the additional income for tax purposes that is added according to the model and is intended to reflect the inherent benefit (if at all) resulting from the above time differences, match and are consistent with GAAP.

The CVT model, as mentioned, seeks to confront the Collection Question together with the Quantification Question of the profit at each point of time and regards the "speedy collection interest" as sufficiently important to justify deviating from GAAP in all aspects relating to the timing of the recognition of income. However, contrary to the Income Approach and the Advance Approach, it seeks that from the standpoint of timing, this deviation will not lead to a distortion of income. In contrast, the SFC model does not regard the "speedy collection interest" as one that is sufficiently important to justify deviating from GAAP,[86] and from this it follows that it does not "advance" any income compared with the timing that is fixed for its recognition according to GAAP.

The CVT model, in the spirit of the Dualistic Doctrine and the Separating Approach or the Selective Consistent Approach, regards GAAP as reflecting a regulatory rule that prevents some of the purposes of tax laws, and where tax values justify this there is nothing to prevent deviating from it for tax purposes. In contrast, the SFC model, in the spirit of the Singular Doctrine and the Consistent Approach, regards the linking of GAAP as of importance for the purpose of upholding tax values (such as "efficiency" and "certainty"). Moreover, where the model seeks to prevent unjust tax advantages that result from the time differentials, it limits the deviation from GAAP only for the purpose of preventing a distortion in quantifying the profit, and not for considerations of collection. Moreover, this model even uses GAAP to determine the substance of the advantage or disadvantage that arises from these tax differentials, and to determine their extent.[87]

8.3.2 *Identifying the benefit component and the solution*

The SFC model seeks to identify and isolate the benefit that arises from the time gap between the date of recognition of income or expenses and the date of cash flow, where the time difference creates a saving in alternative financing interest. Its solution is to tax that benefit of saving in terms of alternative interest.

The CVT model seeks to identify and isolate the benefit that arises from the time gap between the date of recognition of income or expenses and the date of cash flow, where the time difference creates a calculation of income for tax purposes on nominal values (not in real terms). Its solution is to eliminate the value differentials by placing all the values at a single point along the timeline. Thus, the two models offer different interpretative methods for identifying the benefit component.

8.3.3 *Date of taxation*

The SFC model regards savings derived from alternative financing inter-est as financing income or expenses created throughout the "deposit life", "advance life" or "unpaid liability life".[88]

The CVT model is a kind of "upgrade" to the Income Approach (with respect to deposits), and to the Advance Approach (with respect to advances). This model seeks to impose tax on the earliest date between the date of recognition of income and the date of receipt of cash flow. The difference, however, between this model and the approaches mentioned above is that this model seeks to achieve a result whereby taxing "at the very beginning" will be of the "profit" component inherent in the transaction, and not of the gross turnover. In order to find this "profit" component, a distinction must be made between the base transaction that will be taxable "at the very beginning" and the financial transaction that will be recognized as income throughout the period from the date of taxing the base transaction until the date "completing" the transaction by recognizing the income or by receiving the income or by performing the liability.

8.3.4 Disadvantages

Notwithstanding the fact that the two alternative models are preferable to those that have been adopted by the tax systems reviewed, these models are themselves not immune from criticism. Their disadvantages will be examined briefly.

8.3.4.1 Disadvantages of the SFC model

8.3.4.1.1 THE NEED FOR ASSESSMENTS

Apparently, the model is based, to a certain extent, on evaluations and assessments mainly as to duration of the "advance life", the duration of the "deposit life" and the duration of "the unpaid liability life", and assessments of the determination of the AIR or the market interest.

With respect to this criticism, we would respond as follows – It has already been said that modern economic life dictates the use of evaluations and assessments.[89] This is preferable to the alternative of disregarding assessments and evaluations, where doing so would lead to absurd results.[90] Moreover, in this model, the need to make use of evaluations and assessments is relatively limited. According to this argument, practically every existing approach (such as the Loan Approach and the Income Approach, as well as the Deferral Approach and the Advance Approach) could be attacked on its merits, since all of them are based to some degree on assumptions and assessments.

8.3.4.1.2 DIFFICULTIES IN APPLICATION

The model appears to be difficult to apply, as it requires the determination of individual income for each taxpayer, depending on the alternative interest rate that applies to him.

With respect to this criticism, we would respond as follows – The model measuring the additional income or expenses in terms of alternative interest is not complicated at all. With respect to every taxpayer, a relatively simple formula can ascertain the average interest that the taxpayer paid or received in each relevant year in respect of "outside financing". Moreover, the problem of complexity should not necessarily prevent the rectification of tax distortions.[91]

8.3.4.1.3 TAX EROSION

It would appear that the benefit component that is calculated according to this model does not provide a real answer to the advantages that could flow from deposits or advances or delaying payments of liabilities. This appears to be so for two reasons. First, the more remote the relevant year from the date on which the advance or deposit was received or the liability was undertaken, the more likely that the calculation of the benefit (in the guise of a saving of the alternative interest) on the principal of the amount received would cause tax erosion. Second, this model does not take into account the possibility that the deposit will not be returned at all, or that the sale or service in respect of which the advance was received will not be provided, or the liability will not be performed.

As regards this criticism, we would respond as follows – First, as seen at para 8.2.6 above, the additional income that accrued in the past in the form of saving in alternative financing costs should be regarded, for application of this model in the relevant year, as the taxpayer's property. From this it follows that the use of the "additional" income by the taxpayer during the relevant year (as distinct from the use of the principal in the same year) does not signify the use of funds that do not belong to him. Once taxation is imposed on the saving (in the past), this saving should be regarded for future uses as the taxpayer's capital, and he should not be taxed on the saving of alternative financing costs with respect to his own capital.

Second, regarding the possibility that the deposit may never be returned, there may indeed be cases in which, at the "end of the day", the refund amount will not be returned to the payer.[92] Similarly, one cannot discount the possibility that, in certain cases, the sale or the service on account of which the advance was received will not be supplied, and the advance itself will not be repaid.[93] In the same vein, there is always a possibility that a liability may never be performed.[94] Nevertheless, this probability should not have any impact on the SFC model. It can be argued that there is no such thing as an outstanding liability that will be repaid with absolute certainty. Nevertheless, the catastrophic possibility of the taxpayer going bankrupt, or that another event will prevent payment of the liability, does not generally prevent the deduction of the liability in full as an expense for tax purposes.[95] In addition, we must remember that if we wish to take this possibility into account within the scope of this model, then the weight that will be imputed to that probability will require complex statistical formulae, which will necessarily increase the criticism of the complexity of the model.

8.3.4.1.4 ABSENCE OF SYMMETRY

According to the model, there seems to be no symmetry between the "benefit" of saving alternative interest and losing such alternative interest. The model desires to tax the "benefit" that accrues to the taxpayer in terms of saving alternative financing costs (in transactions in which revenues are received that are not recognized as "income" on the date they are received, like a deposit or an advance, or where the taxpayer's liabilities are deferred). In a case where the taxpayer recognizes income prior to its being received by him, on the face of it, a "loss" has been caused to the taxpayer in terms of alternative financing yield. According to this argument, the SFC model should recognize a loss that, on the face of it, has been caused to the taxpayer as a result of his willingness to receive at a later date (and at interest lower than the credit interest that he receives in the bank) income that he is entitled to receive and which he has included in calculating his chargeable income.

We would respond to this argument as follows – There is no basis for a comparison between the cases. We have already clarified that "there are no free loans", and therefore the assumption is that if the taxpayer has chosen to receive a deposit or advance on interest terms that are low, and the customer has agreed to this, then the price of the product or the service to the customer has been reduced in recognition of the "interest saving" that has accrued to the taxpayer.

The same applies to deferring the payment date of the taxpayer's liabilities. The assumption is that the supplier would not have agreed to defer the performance date of the taxpayer's liabilities unless the amount of the liabilities payable increased. The saving of the financing costs to the taxpayer where a deposit or advance is received is on account of reducing the taxpayer's income, and in the case of a deferral of liabilities to the supplier, that saving is on account of an increase of the principal amount of the taxpayer's liability. According to exactly the same logic of "no free loans", the result of the case where income has been earned and has been recognized for tax purposes prior to being actually received need not be one that causes a "loss" to the taxpayer, as when the taxpayer elects to grant his customer cheap credit without adding any interest to the transaction separately. The assumption is that the "interest component" has already been worked into the price of the product or the service (to which the income earned relates, but has yet to be received), and no financing damage has been caused to the taxpayer as a result.

With respect to a transaction of this kind, it can at the most be argued that the recognition date of the "interest component" inherent in the product or service price must be spread throughout the "customer credit" period. It cannot be challenged on a claim of apparent "symmetry" that holds that this interest component must be reduced from the amount of the taxpayer's income. That is to say, where income has been earned but has yet to be received, the loss of alternative interest is only theoretical, and does not reflect a genuine shortfall that has accrued to the taxpayer. Therefore, it should not form part of the calculation provided by the model.[96]

8.3.4.2 *Disadvantages of the CVT model*

8.3.4.2.1 THE NEED FOR ASSESSMENTS AND SPECULATIONS

Apparently, the CVT model requires the making of evaluations and assessments, mainly with respect to the volume of the liabilities that are related to the transaction, and these include liabilities that have not yet arisen. Although, as stated above, modern economic conditions dictate the use of evaluations and assessments,[97] in this model the need for using assessments far exceeds the need to do so in the SFC model. In this respect, the SFC model is more efficient and simpler to implement than the CVT model.[98]

8.3.4.2.2 UNFAIR PREFERENCE OF THE STATE TREASURY AS A CREDITOR

It would appear that the taxation of the benefit component at the outset, according to this model, contradicts the idea that "profit" from the time value of money is created with the passage of time. We have already stated that advancing the payment of tax (the "speedy collection interest") should not be regarded as a "value" in itself.[99] According to the CVT model, it is possible that the tax paid "at the very outset" is paid in respect of "profit" that in retrospect never existed. Thus, for example, if the taxpayer is precluded from supplying the service or the product for which the advance was received and the same is repaid to the payer, then the "profit" on which the tax is paid in the CVT model would never have arisen. Similarly, if the taxpayer is required to repay a deposit that he received after a period of time that is much shorter than the one on which the "profit" resulting from that deposit was calculated, then again, it is possible that the tax that has been paid in advance would have been paid on "profit" that never materialized.

Although the CVT model is preferable in this respect to the Income Approach and the Advance Approach, this still does not ensure a situation of not granting priority to the tax authorities over other creditors. In this respect as well, the SFC model is more efficient and simpler to implement than the CVT model.

8.3.4.2.3 UNNECESSARY DEVIATION FROM GAAP

While the CVT model changes the character of deposits and advances from "liabilities" according to GAAP into "income" for tax purposes, the

SFC model imposes tax on the benefit component inherent in these receivables without deviating from GAAP.

As stated above, applying the Proportionality Principle requires the conclusion that the tax system must not use such means to accomplish the objective of achieving the tax values (including preventing unjust tax advantages) that would result in the damage to other values being even greater.[100] Where the prevention of violating tax values can be accomplished by means that do not necessitate deviation from GAAP (e.g. the SFC model), the CVT model will not be regarded as meeting the Proportionality Principle.[101]

In light of this consideration it is submitted that the SFC model is preferable to the CVT model.

8.4 Impact on tax revenues

The impact of the SFC model on Treasury revenues depends on how the particular tax system operated before that model was adopted.

In a tax system that adopts the accrual basis method for tax purposes, enables recognition of unpaid liabilities and uses the Loan Approach (with respect to deposits) or the Deferral Approach (with respect to advances) (such as in the UK), application of the SFC model will increase Treasury revenues. This is the case because this model permits the recognition of unpaid liabilities according to the Accounting Certainty Degree and the Full and Immediate Approach, and permits classification of deposits and advances as liabilities on the date they are received, similar to the Loan Approach and the Deferral Approach, but adds a tax component that does not exist in these approaches, namely, taxation of the saving in the financing costs to the taxpayer.[102]

As regards the US tax system that applies the Absolute or the High Certainty Degrees (as a prerequisite for recognition of unpaid liabilities for tax purposes), and applies the Income Approach (with respect to deposits) or the Advance Approach (with respect to advances), it can be said that, first, there is no certainty that the application of the SFC model will lead to a reduction in Treasury revenues due to the limitations of the Absolute or the High Certainty Degrees, the Income Approach and the Advance Approach (hereinafter: "**limitations of the strict approaches**").

Second, even if applying the SFC model leads to a reduction in taxes in the short term, it is doubtful that this will be the result in the long term (hereinafter: "**collection in the short and long terms**").

Third, even if there is a reduction in tax collection, such reduction is justifiable in light of the relevant tax values (hereinafter: "**the value consideration**").

We will address these considerations as follows.

8.4.1 *The limitations of the strict approaches*

In the US tax system, where the Income Approach has been adopted with respect to deposits, the courts have employed diverse tests to distinguish between deposits classified as "income" on the date of their receipt, and deposits classified as "liabilities" for tax purposes.[103] On occasion, the test employed according to the Income Approach for such a distinction was a "broader filter" (enabling a long list of deposits to be classified as loans).[104] At times, the test that was used by the Income Approach to make such distinction was a "narrower filter" (generating the classification of a greater number of the deposits as income).[105] One way or the other, the Income Approach (apart from classifying some deposits as "income" on the date they are received) has left a series of deposits as "liabilities" for which it has also left the potential advantage inherent in them to the recipient of the deposit (of a saving in financing costs).[106] With respect to advances, in cases where the Advance Approach has been adopted, its adoption has been limited. Although the Advance Approach in the US has been applied through court rulings, it has been severely limited by legislative provisions as well as administrative directives.[107]

With respect to unpaid liabilities, we have seen that the adoption of the High Certainty Degree or the Absolute Certainty Degree as a prerequisite for recognition for tax purposes in the US tax system[108] has been limited only in regard to liabilities to perform future services, and not in cases where the liability is for a liquidated cash sum that is payable on a remote date.[109]

The SFC model applies to all classes of transactions in which deposits or advances are received, or payments or performance for which liabilities are undertaken are delayed. The model taxes the economic benefit of such transactions. The general application of this model leads to the conclusion that there will not necessarily be a reduction in Treasury revenues in tax systems that have employed the Income Approach, the Deferral Approach and the High Certainty Degree or the Absolute Certainty Degree requirements.

8.4.2 *Collection in the short and long terms*

Deferring the date of the recognition of income to the date on which it is earned, and recognition of liabilities according to GAAP although they have not yet been paid, is done according to the SFC model "in exchange" for payment of tax on account of the time component (on the saving of alternative interest). It follows that it is doubtful that in the long term there will be a loss of tax to the Treasury even in cases were the Income Approach and the Deferral Approach classified deposits and advances as "income" on the date they were received, or where the High Certainty Degree or the Absolute Certainty Degree, as a prerequisite for recognition of liabilities for tax purposes, deferred the date of recognition of liabilities for tax purposes.

8.4.3 *The value consideration*

A tax system that aspires to "fairness"[110] and that wishes to uphold tax values (including the value of non-erosion of the taxpayer's capital)[111] will find it hard to justify imposing tax in advance on an amount received (according to the Income Approach and the Advance Approach), or deferring the recognition of liabilities and imposing tax on turnover by abandoning the matching principle, while having at its disposal a tool such as the SFC model that safeguards tax values without eroding the taxpayer's capital.

In light of the foregoing, it is submitted that, in the UK, adopting the SFC model will lead to increased tax revenues. In the US and Israel, adopting the model may lead to some short-term reduction in tax revenues with respect to certain classes of deposits, advances and unpaid liabilities, but to a long-term increase of those tax revenues.

9   Conclusions

This book has explored the question of the timing of the recognition of income and expenses for tax purposes. This question has two main implications.

The first is in regard to collection, that is, at what time the tax should be paid in respect of income or a receipt that will accrue to the taxpayer ("**the Collection Question**");

The second question relates to quantification, that is, how to ensure that the time difference between recognition of income or expenses and the respective dates of actual receipt or payment do not result in a distortion in determining the amount of the annual taxable income or annual profit ("**the Quantification Question**").

In Chapter 2 it was established that the main goal of GAAP is to provide precise information (to the extent that this is possible) to shareholders, investors and other relevant parties concerning the financial condition of the taxpayer. In order to achieve this goal, GAAP is aided by a series of principles that assist it to quantify and measure the results of business activity over a certain time span. In general, according to GAAP, the recognition of income is mainly based on the "realization principle", and the recognition of a liability as an expense is mainly based on the matching principle.

According to the realization principle and the earned requirement, in most cases income will be regarded as earned on the date of supplying the goods or providing the services. The date of payment for such goods or services is, in most cases, irrelevant for fixing the date of earning the income. In light of this principle, monies received as a deposit by a person who is required to return them (as a financial refund) in the future, or that are taken as an advance against future sales or services, are not deemed as "income" on the date of receipt. They are deemed income only when the obligation to repay the deposit has been cancelled, or when the advance has been earned.

According to GAAP, this timing (based upon the realization principle) also dictates the measurement of the income in nominal terms on the date they were earned, and at that point in time the calculation of profit, according to the matching principle, is done by matching the liabilities that were undertaken in order to produce the "income" to the earned income. Liabilities that would be recognized in calculating the profits according to GAAP (mainly based upon the matching principle) will be also measured in nominal terms on the date of recognition, even if the date of actual payment or performance of such liabilities would be in the future.

Before deciding whether to adopt these financial accounting principles of timing into tax law, we must bear in mind, as seen in Chapter 3, that the goal of tax laws is different from the goal of GAAP. One of the main aims of taxation is to collect funds on a fair basis to finance the public good. In light of this, over and above the particular tax legislation existing in the UK, the US and Israel, these tax systems seek to uphold a number of minimum requirements in order to be deemed "fair". These requirements (**"tax values"**) include, *inter alia*, the principles of non-erosion of capital, tax equity, tax neutrality, tax certainty, efficiency and prevention of unjust tax advantages. These tax values are of no concern to GAAP. Adopting GAAP for timing the recognition of income in tax law, while ignoring the effect of the time value of money, could violate these tax values by imposing tax on "income" that has been fixed in unrealistic terms.

Chapter 4 establishes that despite the different objectives of GAAP and tax laws, the governing doctrine in the UK tax system posits that "income is income", and what is appropriate for determining income for the purposes of investors, creditors, shareholders or other third parties is certainly appropriate for tax purposes. According to this doctrine (**"the Singular Doctrine"**), subject to specific statutory provisions that apply in particular cases that require otherwise, tax law should use the timing and measurement tools created by GAAP for recognition and measurement of "income" for tax purposes. This doctrine produces the practicable position that we called **"the Consistent Approach"**, which supports the adoption of GAAP in order to resolve questions and make up deficiencies in the field of tax laws.

In the US federal tax system (and lately in Israel), the governing doctrine argues that in light of the different objectives of GAAP and tax law, tax laws are to be regarded as necessitating accounting solutions that match tax values (including, for purposes of timing, recognition of income and its quantification) (**"The Dualistic Doctrine"**). This doctrine produces two alternative positions in relation to tax accounting. The first posits that tax accounting should be based on different rules from those of GAAP (**"The Separating Approach"**), the second finds cases or conditions in which tax accounting follows GAAP (mainly for considerations of convenience), and cases or conditions where this is inappropriate (notwithstanding the absence of contradictory statutory provisions), by reason of which an "accounting solution" is needed to safeguard tax values (mainly preventing unjust tax advantages) ("**The Consistent Selective Approach**").

The UK tax system, based upon the Singular Doctrine and the Consistent Approach, favors strict conformity in the reporting method (according to GAAP) ("the accrual basis method"), and greatly limits IRS ability to deviate from GAAP. By doing so, it seeks to ensure uniformity and certainty, although possibly at the "price" of eroding tax values in those cases where GAAP dictates solutions that do not necessarily coincide with the essential purpose of the tax laws.

The US tax system, on the one hand, exhibits flexibility in regard to the reporting method, and enables reporting and recognition of income for tax purposes according to the accrual basis method, as well as according to other, alternative reporting practices that are not based upon GAAP, like the cash basis method and the hybrid method. However, this tax system also grants to HMRC broad discretion to deviate from the principles of GAAP (as well as other methods of reporting) for the sake of maintaining tax values, thereby seeking to ensure "fiscal justice", albeit at the price of compromising uniformity and certainty.

The Israeli tax system allows (in the absence of relevant legislation) maximum flexibility regarding the reporting method, although support may be found both for the Singular Doctrine as well as the Dualistic Doctrine.

None of the tax systems reviewed has succeeded in creating tax accounting as a regulated theory that constitutes a substitute for the accrual basis method created by GAAP. None of the alternative methods of accounting that has been examined or mentioned in regard to the tax systems reviewed, like the cash basis method or the hybrid methods, can be regarded as a coherent, systematic and efficient method for measuring income for tax purposes. In the absence of any methodical alternative accounting method for tax purposes, the creation of tax accounting mainly by means of *ad hoc* rulings not only violates tax values, but also harms the administrative convenience of both the taxpayer and the tax authorities themselves. Hence, for both ethical and practical considerations, the Dualistic Doctrine does not stand up to scrutiny. However, the Singular Doctrine and adopting GAAP's accrual basis method, as is, for timing recognition of income for tax purposes are also not immune from criticism for eroding tax values (like the principles of tax neutrality, efficiency and preventing unjust tax advantages).

A balance must be sought to embrace the strengths of the two opposing doctrines, and at the same time seek to neutralize their disadvantages. Applying the **Proportionality Principle** (in all its tests, i.e. the rational means test, the less harmful means test and the relative means test) ensures that deviating from GAAP to accomplish the objective of preserving tax values (including preventing unjust tax advantages) remains an alternative to be used only where it will not cause greater harm to other values, and only in the absence of alternative means for achieving the same purpose.

Chapter 5 shows that the UK tax system, following GAAP, adopts the approach that a deposit is a liability that does not constitute income as long as the recipient is bound to repay it, whatever the future repayment date or repayment terms may be. There is no reference to the economic benefits inherent in holding and using the deposit, and deriving from the conditions or timing of its repayment. The latter, on the face of it, does not affect the question of the recognition of the deposit or any part thereof as income (**"the Loan Approach"**).

In the US and Israeli tax systems, support can be found for the Loan Approach. However, support can also be found for an opposite approach that, despite GAAP, would adopt classification methods that have been independently created by the courts to classify a deposit as "income" on the date of its receipt (**"the Income Approach"**). This tax accounting, created by *ad hoc* judicial rulings on the subject of the classification of deposits, is such that when one test or another supports classifying an item received as a "deposit", the court adopts that test in disregard for any inherent component of a benefit, and rules that the entire amount received is to be regarded as untaxable liability. In contrast, when the test points in the direction of regarding an item as an "advance", the entire item received is classified as "income", without separating the benefit component from the part that should rightly be treated as a liability, no different from any other loan.

It is submitted that the Loan Approach should be rejected for violating the tax values of tax neutrality, efficiency and preventing unjust tax advantages and the Income Approach should be rejected for violating tax values like the principles of non-erosion of capital and tax certainty, as well as for violating the Proportionality Principle.

As shown in Chapter 6, the UK tax system is the most constant and coherent of the three systems examined. Consistent with GAAP, it determines that as long as advances have yet to be earned, they should not be regarded as "income" for tax purposes (**"the Deferral Approach"**). In doing so, this tax system evinces coherence between this system's approach to advances, and the manner in which it addresses deposits.

The US tax system, which deviates from GAAP (mainly from the realization principle), determines that advances are to be taxed in the year in which they are received, disregarding liabilities to sell goods or provide services against those advances in the future, and disregarding the potential obligation to repay them (**"the Advance Approach"**).[1] It seems that one of the factors that led to the US case law to adopt the Advance Approach is the instinctive understanding of the courts that the taxpayer's ability to make use of advance resources creates an economic advantage that justifies the imposition of tax. Ultimately, IRS's considerations of convenience (which take preference over those of the taxpayers) justify the imposition of tax on the date on which cash is exchanged, without the any need for IRS to carry out complex calculations regarding the spread of income. The same instinctive response brought the Israeli case law to the same conclusion, and to the adoption of the Advance Approach (despite the fact that the Israeli legislature has not granted ITA any power similar to that granted to IRS under IRC§446(b)).

It is submitted that the Deferral Approach should be rejected for violating some pertinent tax values (e.g. principles of horizontal equity, tax neutrality, efficiency and preventing unjust tax advantages), and that the Advance Approach should equally be rejected for violating other pertinent tax values (e.g. principles of non-erosion of capital and tax neutrality), and for eroding the Proportionality Principle.

As seen in Chapter 7, the UK tax system requires reporting for tax purposes according the accrual basis method, and adopts the Loan Approach (with respect to deposits) and the Deferral Approach (with respect to advances). Consistently maximizing the merger of tax accounting with GAAP, the UK system uses GAAP criteria in order to fix the timing of the deduction of a liability as an expense (the "**Accounting Certainty Degree**"). By doing so, and by adopting the "Full and Immediate Deduction Approach", the UK system takes no notice of the Quantification Question and allows the creation of tax advantages derived from the gap between the timing of deduction in nominal terms and the timing of actual payments.

The US tax system and the Israeli tax system, which exhibit flexibility in regard to the reporting method for tax purposes, permit reporting by the accrual basis method, the cash basis method, as well as other practices. These systems, in which support can be found for the Income Approach (with respect to deposits) and the Advance Approach (with respect to advances), have not considered the possibility of advancing the deduction of liabilities for deposits and advances to the date on which those receivables are considered "income" even though they have not yet been earned. Moreover, in the US tax system, by using the "**Absolute Certainty Degree**" or the "**High Certainty Degree**" as a prerequisite for allowing a deduction of liability, the date for recognizing it as an expense for tax purposes may differ from the date according to the Accounting Certainty Degree requirement.

It is submitted that the Accounting Certainty Degree, combined with the **Full and Immediate Deduction Approach** requirement for fixing the date of recognition of liability as an expense for tax purposes, violates the tax value of preventing unjust tax advantages. It is also submitted that the Absolute Certainty Degree the High Certainty Degree as a prerequisite for allowing a deduction of liability does not provide an appropriate answer to the Quantification Question. The combination of the Absolute Certainty Degree or the High Certainty Degree with the Full and Immediate Deduction Approach should be rejected for violating other pertinent tax values (e.g. principles of non-erosion of capital and tax neutrality), but most of all, for eroding the Proportionality Principle.

Chapter 8 demonstrates alternatives to the approaches and requirements adopted by the tax systems reviewed as regards timing recognition of income and liabilities for tax purposes. Among those alternatives is the SFC model that we have proposed. This model seeks to identify and isolate the benefit that arises from the deposit, the advance or the delaying of the performance of a liability, where the time difference creates a saving in alternative financing costs. The solution is to tax that saving throughout the "deposit life" or the "advance life" or the "unpaid liability life".

In the "physical universe," said Einstein, time is a relative concept that depends on the speed of the observer,[2] and this relativity of time is measured in comparison to the absolute concepts of nature (kinematics' invariants).[3]

This study has sought to demonstrate that, in the "fiscal universe", in connection with timing recognition of income for tax purposes, the value of time also becomes a relative concept that depends on the perception of the observer, and this relativity must be measured against the absolute concepts of tax values.

With respect to the perceptions of this observer – As we have seen, there are those who look at the value of time and say that, for tax purposes, time does not even constitute the "starting point", and the passage of time has nothing to do with the measurement of income. Such observers (who obviously adhere to the Loan Approach, the Deferral Approach and the Full and Immediate Deduction Approach) hold that tax laws should generally be indifferent to the component of time in relation to the timing and measuring of income that is created over time.[4]

As opposed to this, there are those who look at the value of time and say that time constitutes the "finishing point", and the passage of time, itself, can create income liable to tax. These observers (who are adherents of the Income Approach, the Advance Approach and the Deferred Deduction Date Approach or the Partial Deduction Approach) assert that the existence of a time gap between the date an amount is received and the date of recognition of income, or the existence of a time gap between the date an amount is paid and the date of recognition of liability is sufficient to create tax rules that differ from GAAP, and that may result in the taxation not of profits, but of amounts received.[5]

With respect to the measurement against the concepts of tax values – The observation here is that "fiscal time" is a "starting point", but not a "finishing point". It is a "starting point", since unlike supporters of the Loan Approach, the Deferral Approach, and the Full and Immediate Deduction Approach, we are not indifferent to time and we accept that it

228 The timing of income recognition in tax law

must be taken into account for tax purposes. It is not the "finishing point", since, unlike supporters of the Income Approach, the Advance Approach and the Deferred Deduction Date Approach or the Partial Deduction Approach, we believe that "time" of itself is insufficient to justify deviating from GAAP and creating tax accounting that transforms "liabilities" into "income" for tax purposes.

If reliance on GAAP leads to the possibility that tax is imposed only on nominal terms of income (and not on the value of income in real economic terms), thereby eroding tax values (such as preventing unjust tax advantages), then the prevention of this erosion is indeed a worthy cause that justifies the creation of a solution that taxes the benefits caused by the passage of time. Tax values and the Proportionality Principle demand rejecting the existing solutions for the question of the timing of recognition of income and liabilities in the tax systems reviewed.

The question of the timing of the recognition of income, as we perceive it, encompasses two subsidiary questions, the Collection Question and the Quantification Question. While the various tax systems have addressed the issues that arise in connection with the timing of the recognition of income (and expenses) in legislation, in case law or in the professional literature, they have not distinguished between these two subsidiary questions, and have regarded them as part of an overall problem.

One would imagine that the ardent supporters of the Singular Doctrine, who seem indifferent to the dimension of time, would not wish to be associated with obtaining unjustifiable tax advantages and infringing other tax values. But according to them, in the absence of a proper alternative to GAAP, following GAAP is to be regarded as the lesser of two evils in all aspects relating to the effect of time on the value of money.

In contrast, it appears that the ardent supporters of the Dualistic Doctrine, who have supported sweeping deviations from GAAP and have emphasized the value of time, did not do so in order to solve the Collection Question by advancing the Treasury's "speedy collection interest". Advancing that interest is not, of itself, a tax value (nor does it even approximate one). Moreover, charging tax at a particular point along the axis of time on something that does not constitute profit at that point of time could intrinsically affect other tax values and could harm legitimate public interests that the tax regime was intended to advance from the outset. This is not so with reference to the Quantification Question. The (current) indifference of GAAP to time differences in relation to the values at which income or expenses are recorded provides most of the ammunition to the supporters of the Dualistic Doctrine.

In our opinion, applying the SFC model serves both doctrines (the Singular Doctrine and the Dualistic Doctrine) at the same time. A solution in the form of the payment of tax on the benefit that is caused in cases where quantifying the income for tax purposes is made in nominal terms will enable the broad adoption of GAAP for tax purposes (almost entirely) in all the transactions and for all classes of income (subject to exceptions that will be specifically provided for in legislation) and subject to the application of the SFC model. Moreover, the very existence of this model will constitute a response to the Quantification Question that has arisen by the very use that GAAP makes of nominal terms in addressing the question of timing.

In our view, the SFC model strikes the proper balance among the various considerations that guided the conflicting approaches that we have addressed in this book. Making an adjustment for tax purposes to income and expenses calculated according to GAAP by applying one (simple) formula in the form of the SFC model, constitutes an appropriate means for advancing the objective of preventing unjust tax advantages at the level of the values at which the income is quantified, in the spirit of the Proportionality Principle.

The goal of preventing wrong and injustice in our world (including the world of tax) is worth fighting for, whatever the prospects of achieving it may be. However, as in every such struggle, it must be remembered that the goal, however worthy, does not justify the use of all and every means. The objective of preventing unjust tax advantages and avoiding the erosion of tax neutrality and tax equity is one that justifies the search for a way to prevent the possibility of exploiting GAAP for the purposes of paying tax on terms that are unrealistic.

Nevertheless, however worthy the goal may be, a question (no less, and perhaps even more important) remains as to the means that are to be used for achieving it. If one seeks to prevent a wrong, one must not use means that are totally unrelated to the wrong that is to be put right, and the means employed should not cause greater harm to other values than preventing the wrong itself. One must use means that serve to right the injustice, without inflicting harm to other important values and objectives. It is in this spirit that we have written this book, and it is this idea that stands behind the proffered SFC model.

Notes

1 Introduction

* Primo Levi, *If This Is a Man* (Abacus, new edn, January, 1991), 19.
1 In this book, this situation will be referred to as "**unreceived earned income**".
2 In this book, the term "**deposits**" refers to funds that a taxpayer receives that are intended to secure property belonging to the recipient or to secure the fulfillment of contractual obligations of the depositor, both being characterized by the fact that the recipient of the deposit is under an obligation to return it to the depositor at a given time or upon the fulfillment of certain conditions.
3 In this book, the term "**advance payments**" refers to funds received by a taxpayer for the sale of goods or for services that will be provided in the future (i.e. on a date later than that on which the payment is made).
4 In this book, this type of situation will be referred to as "**unpaid recognized liabilities**".

2 Accounting background

1 In the US, the power to determine professional directives in accounting (e.g. the US GAAP) is conferred as a rule on the **FASB**, and the professional organizations that preceded it. (See Accounting Series Release No 150, "Statement of Policy on the Establishment and Improvement of Accounting Principles and Standards" (1973) (ASR#150)). While FASB standards are mandatory, they do not cover all accounting issues, and even when there is a governing standard, there is not necessarily a unique permissible result for a set of facts. As indicated by the words "generally accepted" in GAAP, the standards started as a loose system of consensual rules that left considerable discretion in reporting. The FASB standards, however, are commonly very detailed as to where to draw lines. Under its authority, the **EITF** has also issued a not inconsiderable number of directives (mainly in relation to specific fields). Various supervisory bodies in the US also publish professional directives that reflect their position or interpretation with respect to accepted accounting standards, although the directives issued by those bodies do not necessarily reflect accepted accounting principles themselves, and are not necessarily binding on firms that are not subject to those particular supervisory bodies. Nonetheless, as distinct from the statutory situation in the UK, the tax laws, in and of themselves, do not define which bodies are empowered to issue accounting standards that will similarly be binding for tax purposes. Moreover, the US tax legislation approach to the various types of accounting standards is, to put it mildly, ambivalent. On the authority to determine accounting standards in the US, see Eric G. Press and Joseph B. Weintrop, "Accounting-Based Constraints in Public

and Private Debt Agreements," 12 J Acct & Econ 65 (1990). For other relevant US legislation, see para 4.4.1 below.

2 For the meaning of "International Accounting Standards", see Regulation (EC) No 1606/2002 of the European Parliament and the Council of 19 July 2002 on the application of international accounting standards.

3 In the UK, s 256(1) of the Companies Act 1985 (Inserted by ss 4(1) and 5(1) of the Companies Act 1989) stated that "'accounting standards' means statements of standard accounting practice issued by such body or bodies as may be prescribed by regulations". The Accounting Standards Board ("**ASB**") is the body authorized for purposes of s 256, and is the Board that is charged with determining the Accounting Standards whose application is required to meet the above criteria of "true and fair view". Since 2005, following a statutory change in ss 50–54 FA 2004 and Sch 10 and ss 80–84 FA 2005 and Sch 4 of the Companies Act 1985 (International Accounting Standards and Other Accounting Amendments), and following Regulations 2004, SI 2004/2947, the Companies (1986 Order) (International Accounting Standards and Other Accounting Amendments) Regulations (Northern Ireland) 2004 SR 2004/496, the International Accounting Standards ("**IAS**") have been adopted for purposes of UK law, with the intention of granting equivalent binding effect to the standardization of the International Accounting Standards Board ("**IASB**") (the IAS Standards), similar to that granted to UK GAAP. As a rule, the standards prescribed by the ASB and IASB are the same, although certain differences exist, mainly in relation to small companies, for which the ASB has laid down a series of more flexible standards. The IAS, like the International Financial Reporting Standards (**IFRS**), and similar to the related interpretations (SIC-IFRIC Interpretations) that are issued by the IASB, were thus adopted in the UK following the entering into effect of the above legislation. Subject to the Standards adopted by the European Commission, which adopted all of the existing IAS (except for two exceptions to IAS#39, Chapter 2, n 18, and International Financial Reporting Standards No 1, "First-time Adoption of International Reporting Standards" (IFRS#1) and International Financial Reporting Standards No 5 "Non-current Assets Held for Sale and Discontinued Operations" (IFRS#5)). According to the provisions of ss 50–54, FA 2004, in cases where the European Commission has not adopted it, the company is entitled, at its discretion, to act according to the un-adopted standard or according to the UK GAAP. In December 2004, the ASB issued a number of Notes designed to consolidate the UK GAAP with the IAS, and, *inter alia*, Financial Reporting Standards No 25 "Financial Instruments: Disclosure and Presentation" (FRS#25) and Financial Reporting Standards No 26 "Financial instruments: Measurement" (FRS#26) were issued, these being parallel to the International Accounting Standard No 32, "Financial Instruments: Disclosure and Presentation" (Issued Dec 2003) (IAS#32), and IAS#39, id. See, e.g. BIM31025. For other UK relevant legislation, see para 4.3.1.

4 In Israel, supervisory bodies such as the Securities Authority or the Ministry of Finance, by virtue of various enactments (e.g. the Securities (Periodical and Immediate Reports) Regulations, 5730–1970; the State Health Insurance (Supervision and Control over the Finances of Sick Funds) Regulations, 5756–1995 and others), published regulations and/or directives regarding the form of accounting presentation of the reports deliverable to those supervisory bodies. However, in Israel, as in the US, regulations or directives such as these do not necessarily reflect accepted accounting practices, and do not apply to or obligate firms that are not subject to those supervisory bodies. Accounting standardization in Israel is carried out by the Israeli Accounting Standards Board ("**ISB**") by virtue of the authority of the Institute of Certified Public

Accountants in Israel to determine binding auditing procedures for accountants (under the Auditors (Behavior Unbefitting the Profession) Regulations, 5725–1965). From this it follows that wherever, in civil legislation (e.g. the Companies Law, 5759–1999), financial reports audited by an accountant are required, and this means that these reports must be prepared in accordance with the Israeli GAAP. According to Israeli Accounting Standard No 29 (Issued 7/2006) of the Institute of Certified Public Accountants in Israel, International Accounting Standards (IAS) apply in Israel. For the power to determine accounting standards in Israel, see Y. Samet, *Financial Accounting – Theory and Practice – vol. 1* (Ahiyosef Publishers, Netanya, Is, 1990), pp 11–16. For other relevant Israeli legislation, see para 4.5.1.

5 In the following chapter the accounting background is related to as a single field, assuming that for the purpose of this chapter there is no material difference between US GAAP and IFRS, the two major financial reporting regimes. In the interest of simplicity, the two regimes will henceforth be referred to as financial accounting or GAAP. Where needed, the difference between the two financial reporting regimes will be noted.

6 IASB is an independent accounting standard-setter based in London, UK, which develops, in the public interest, a single set of high quality, understandable and enforceable global accounting standards (IAS and IFRS).

7 FASB is a private organization that develops, in the public interest, generally accepted accounting principles (GAAP) within the United States (US GAAP). See Chapter 2, n 1.

8 See official web sites of IASB and FASB: http://www.iasb.org/; http://www.fasb.org/.

9 Such as employees, suppliers, customers, governmental agencies and the general public; for IFRS see the International Accounting Standards Board (IASB) Framework adopted in April 2001 for the Preparation and Presentation of Financial Statements published by the Commission of the European Communities (Brussels, November 2003), and comments concerning certain Articles of the Regulation (EC) No 1606/2002 of the European Parliament and the Council of 19 July 2002 on the application of international accounting standards and the Fourth Council Directive 78/660/EEC of 25 July 1978 and the Seventh Council Directive 83/349/EEC of June 1983 on accounting ("**IASB Framework**") at paras 12–13; for US GAAP, see Statement of Financial Accounting Concept No 1, "Objectives of Financial Reporting by Business Enterprises" (Issued 11/78) ("SFAC#1"), sec 37.

10 The financial position of an enterprise is described by providing information about the economic resources controlled by the enterprise, its financial structure, its liquidity and solvency, and its capacity to adapt to changes in the environment in which it operates. Performance is the ability of an enterprise to earn a profit on the resources that have been invested in it. Information about the amounts and variability of profits helps in forecasting future cash flows from the enterprise's existing resources and in forecasting potential additional cash flows from additional resources that might be invested in the enterprise. In addition, the users of financial statements seek information about the investing, financing and operating activities that an enterprise has undertaken during the reporting period, which helps them to assess how well the enterprise can generate cash and how it uses those cash flows. See IASB Framework, Chapter 2, n 9, ss 16–18.

11 IASB Framework, ibid, sec 14.

12 IASB Framework, ibid, sec 46 (for the same principle in former UK GAAP, see Statement of Standard Accounting Practice No 1 "Presentation of Financial Statements" (Superseded by FRS#9) (SSAP#1) (Issued May 1999)).

13 For the prudence concept, see IASB Framework, Chapter 2, n 9, sec 37; for US GAAP, see Statement of Financial Accounting Concept No 4, "Objective of Financial Reporting by Nonbusiness Organizations" (Issued 12/80) (SFAC#4), sec 171; see also Robert R. Sterling, *Conservatism: The Fundamental Principle of Valuation in Traditional Accounting* (Accounting Foundation, University of Sydney, Aus., Abacus, 2nd edn, 1967), p 109; for the same principle in former UK GAAP, see Financial Reporting Standards No 18 "Accounting Policies" (FRS#18) (Issued 2000) and Statement of Standard Accounting Practice No 2 "Disclosure of Accounting Policies" (Superseded by FRS 18) (SSAP#2), (Issued Nov 1971), sec 14.

14 Previously known as conservatism, see, e.g. SSAP#2, ibid.

15 US GAAP Accounting Principles Board (APB) Opinions No 4, "Accounting for 'Investment Credit' (Amending No 2)" (APB#4), sec 27 recognizes three levels of accounting principles: first, Pervasive Principles, which relate to financial accounting as an entirety, and which make up the fundamentals for the other principles (i.e. Understandability, Materiality, Neutrality, Substance over form, True and fair view); second, Broad Operating Principles, which assume registration procedures, measuring and the engagement of the financial accounting (i.e. Going Concern, Accrual, Consistency and Prudence); third, Detailed Principles, which indicate the practical execution in a given case of accounting principles from the two higher levels. See also Statement of Financial Accounting Standards No 48 "Revenue Recognition with Right of Return Exists" (Issued 6/81) (SFAS#48); for International GAAP, see the IASB Framework, Chapter 2, n 9, at ss 25, 29–30, 35, 46 (for former UK GAAP, see FRS#18, Chapter 2, n 13; Financial Reporting Standards No 5 "Reporting the Substance of Transactions" (FRS#5) and BIM31045). However, it should be pointed out that there are accounting practices that do not participate in the above-mentioned hierarchy, see Levis D. McCullers and Richard G. Schroeder, *Accounting Theory Text and Reading* (St. Paul, MN, USA, Wiley. John & Sons, Inc., 2nd edn, 1982), pp 13–14.

16 Nevertheless, it should be noted that prudence does not justify deliberate overstatement of liabilities or expenses or deliberate understatement of assets or income, because the financial statements would not be neutral and, therefore, not have the quality of reliability; see IASB Framework, Chapter 2, n 9, sec 37.

17 See IASB Framework, ibid, sec 70(a).

18 Capital gains on the sale of an asset is a surplus from the realization of an asset used by the firm in its business, the sale of which, however, does not constitute part of its business, see International Accounting Standard No 16 "Property, Plant and Equipment" (IAS#16). Fair value gain may refer to an increase in the valuation of the firm's Investment Property according to International Accounting Standard No 40 "Investment Property" (IAS#40). It may also refer to an increase in the market value of marketable securities according to International Accounting Standard No 39 "Financial Instruments: Recognition and Measurement" (IAS#39).

19 International Accounting Standard No 18 "Revenue" (IAS#18) treats only revenue recognition, while gains are dealt with in other standards; IAS#18 defines revenue as "the gross inflow of economic benefits during the period arising in the ordinary course of activities of an entity when those inflows result in increases in equity other than increases relating to contributions from equity participants," see IAS#18, sec 7.

20 For example, unrealized gains from revaluation of marketable securities, the recognition of which is deferred until realized. For a detailed discussion of the realization principle and the earned requirement, see para 2.3.2.

21 IASB Framework, Chapter 2, n 9, sec 22.
22 Stanger, Vander Kam and Polifka, "Prepaid Income and Estimated Expense: Financial Accounting versus Tax Accounting Dichotomy," 33 Tax L Rev 403, 405 (1980) (citing SFAS#5); Erik M. Jensen, "The Supreme Court and the Timing of Deductions for Accrual Basis Taxpayers," 22 Ga L Rev 229, n 14 (1988).
23 For other reporting methods not supported by GAAP, see paras 4.2 and 4.4.1.
24 See S. Shuv, *New Financial Accounting: IFRS – vol. 1* (Globes Publishing House, Tel Aviv, 2007), pp 501–505.
25 See IAS#18, Chapter 2, n 19, sec 14; in US GAAP, the realization principle was first implemented in APB Statement No 4, stating that "revenue is generally recognized when both of the following conditions are met: (1) the earning process is complete or virtually complete, and (2) an exchange has taken place". Later on this principle was rephrased by Statement of Financial Accounting Concept No 5, "Recognition and Measurement in Financial Statements of Business Enterprises" (Issued 12/84) (SFAC#5), which states that revenues are not recognized until they are "(1) realized or realizable and (2) earned", see SFAC#5, sec 83. (For former UK GAAP, see SSAP#2, Chapter 2, n 13, and FRS#18, Chapter 2, n 13, and BIM31031.)
26 Y. Barkai, *Accounting and Monetary Reporting – vol. 2* (Bar-Or Publishing House, Ramat Hsharon, Is, 2003), p 22.
27 Staff Accounting Bulletin No 101 "Revenue Recognition – Questions arising from time to time and their answers" (SAB#101) states that the timing of recognition of income occurs when the following conditions are met: the price has been determined (or can be determined at the time of the exchange); payment of the consideration is not subject to the sale to others by the buyer; the risks are transferred to the buyer in such a way that his obligations are not influenced in cases of theft, loss or damage; the buyer is a different economic entity from the seller; the seller does not have further material execution obligations to bring the goods up to the condition that they can be resold; the number of returns in the future can reasonably be determined. In such transactions where the right to return or to cancel is at the buyer's disposal, the realization principle is only perfected when the one-sided right to return or cancel lapses. For these conditions and for exceptions, see also IAS#18, Chapter 2, n 19.
28 See IAS#18, Chapter 2, n 19, sec 14; for US-GAAP, see SAB #101, Chapter 2, n 27 (for former UK GAAP, see SSAP#2, Chapter 2, n 13, FRS#18, Chapter 2, n 13, and BIM31031).
29 See John H. Myers, "The critical event and Recognition of Net Profit" The Accounting Review 34 (October 1959), pp 528–32.
30 When the product is completed, the uncertainty as regards the cost of production is removed, and the sale price is determined. If the delivery expenses and the bad debt risk are assessed, it might be appropriate to recognize revenue at the completion of production. This method is used in certain industries, e.g. production of minerals and mineral products; see Mike Bonham et al, *International GAAP 2005* (Croydon, Surrey, UK, Ernst & Young, LexisNexis Publishing House, 2004), pp 997–1015.
31 This is the most widely used basis as at this point most of the uncertainties are eliminated (except return of goods and bad debt risk). Usually the contract for sale of goods is entered into after the goods are produced and the delivery takes place shortly thereafter. But sometimes the contract is entered into before the goods are produced, and the delivery takes place in a future moment. In such cases the sale is considered to be at the point of delivery. This stems from

the language of SFAC#5: "Revenues are not recognized until earned . . . If sale or cash receipt (or both) precedes production and delivery . . . revenues may be recognized as earned by production and delivery", see SFAC#5, Chapter 2, n 25, sec 83. The language of SFAC#5 leaves the impression that US GAAP requires delivery in order to recognize revenue. IFRS is more flexible in that regard. IAS#18 views as the critical point the passing to the buyer of significant risks and rewards associated with the ownership of the goods, see IAS#18, Chapter 2, n 19, sec 14. See also Bonham et al, ibid.

32 This basis is appropriate when there are significant uncertainties after the delivery point. For example, if significant uncertainty as regards collectivity exists, a possible approach would be to defer revenue recognition until collection is reasonably assured. In addition, if a right to return goods exists, revenue recognition might be deferred beyond the delivery date (e.g. after the return possibility expires) unless certain conditions are fulfilled; for US GAAP, see Statement of Financial Accounting Concept No 48, "Revenue Recognition When Right to Return Exists" (SFAC#48), sec 6.

33 See IAS#18, Chapter 2, n 19, sec 18.

34 According to the clarifications in SAB#101, Chapter 2, n 27, the key consideration in this issue is if the reporting body sells or can sell the components separately. See also Emerging Issues Task Force (EITF) 00–21 "Revenue Arrangements with Multiple Deliverables" on determining cases where complex contracts can be divided into accounting units.

35 See IAS#18, Chapter 2, n 19, sec 1.

36 According to IAS#18, the transfer of risks and rewards is a critical condition for revenue recognition. The Standard presents four typical examples of situations in which the risks and rewards are not transferred: (a) when the seller retains an obligation for unsatisfactory performance; (b) the goods require installation and the installation is a significant part of the contract which is not yet completed by the seller; (c) the buyer has the right to rescind the purchase; or (d) the receipt of the revenue is contingent on the derivation of revenue by the buyer. See IAS#18, Chapter 2, n 19, paras 14–16. See also S. Shuv, Chapter 2, n 24.

37 IAS#18 requires that: (a) the amount of revenue can be measured reliably; (b) it is probable that the economic benefits associated with the transaction will flow to the entity; (c) the costs incurred or to be incurred can be measured reliably; and (d) the entity does not retain effective control or managerial involvement, see IAS#18, Chapter 2, n 19, sec 14. For US GAAP, see SAB#101, Chapter 2, n 27, which states that the timing of recognition of income occurs when the following conditions are met: (a) the price has been determined (or can be determined at the time of the exchange); (b) payment of the consideration is not subject to the sale to others by the buyer; the risks are transferred to the buyer in such a way that his obligations are not influenced in cases of theft, loss or damage; (c) the buyer is a different economic entity from the seller; (d) the seller does not have further material execution obligations to bring the goods up to the condition that they can be resold; (e) the number of returns in the future can reasonably be determined.

38 See Bonham et al, Chapter 2, n 30. An exception to this rule is provided by IAS#16 in the case of exchange of property, plant and equipment for non-monetary assets; see IAS#16, Chapter 2, n 18, sec 24. IAS#16 does not determine if the fair value of the non-monetary asset received in exchange for property, plant and equipment represents revenue or gain. A similar example is provided by International Accounting Standard No 38 "Intangible Assets" (IAS#38) in regards to exchange of intangible assets, see IAS#38, ss 45–47.

39 See IAS#18, Chapter 2, n 19, sec 26; for US GAAP, see SAB#101, Chapter 2, n 27

(for former UK GAAP, see Statement of Standard Accounting Practice No 9 "Stock and long terms contracts" (SSAP#9)).

40 Ibid.

41 According to the language of IAS#18, the revenue is recognized "by reference to the stage of completion of the transaction". See IAS#18, Chapter 2, n 19, ss 20–21.

42 The stage of completion may also be determined by estimating the services performed to date as a percentage of total services to be performed or by surveys of work performed, see IAS#18, Chapter 2, n 19, sec 24.

43 IAS#18 requires that: (a) the amount of revenue may be measured reliably; (b) it is probable that the economic benefits will flow to the entity; (c) the stage of completion may be measured reliably; and (d) the costs incurred and to be incurred can be measured reliably. See IAS#18, Chapter 2, n 19, sec 20.

44 See IAS#18, Chapter 2, n 19, ss 29–30.

45 According to IAS#39, Chapter 2, n 18, the effective interest method consists of calculating the amortized cost of a financial asset or a financial liability, and of allocating the interest income or interest expense over the relevant period. The effective interest rate is the rate that exactly discounts estimated future cash payments or receipts through the expected life of the financial instrument or, when appropriate, a shorter period to the net carrying amount of the financial asset or financial liability. When calculating the effective interest rate, an entity shall estimate cash flows considering all contractual terms of the financial instrument, but shall not consider future credit losses. The calculation includes all fees and points paid or received between parties to the contract that are an integral part of the effective interest rate, transaction costs, and all other premiums or discounts. There is a presumption that the cash flows and the expected life of a group of similar financial instruments can be estimated reliably. However, when it is not possible to estimate reliably the cash flows or the expected life, the entity should use the contractual cash flows over the full contractual term of the financial instrument. See IAS#39, Chapter 2, n 18.

46 See IAS#18, Chapter 2, n 19.

47 Ibid.

48 International Accounting Standard No 11 "Construction Contracts" (IAS#11).

49 Ibid.

50 The Boards refer to the fair value as a legal layoff price, which is the price that the reporting entity would have to pay an unrelated party to assume legal responsibility for performing all of its remaining obligations, ibid.

51 A contract might be recognized either as an asset or as a liability. It will be recognized as an asset if the remaining rights exceed the remaining obligations, and recognized as a liability if the remaining obligations exceed the remaining rights, ibid.

52 According to the measurement method, the contract asset or liability is measured according to the amount that the entity expects to receive or pay in order to transfer its remaining contractual rights and obligations to the other party. At the inception date, revenue may arise if the current exit price of the rights obtained exceeds the current exit price of the obligations incurred. In this case, profit will arise if the current exit price of rights obtained less the current exit price of obligations incurred exceeds the contract acquisition expenses. In contrast, under the customer consideration method, the contract rights are measured at the amount of consideration stated in the contract. At contract inception, the total performance obligations are measured at an amount equal to the customer consideration. Therefore, under this method, neither revenue nor profit may arise at the inception date, ibid.

53 Ibid.

54 For example, the "comprehensive income statement" according to which extraordinary income can be recognized even though it has not yet been earned. See Accounting Principles Board (APB) Opinions No 9, "Reporting the Results of Operations" (APB#9), sec 17; Statement of Financial Accounting Concept No 6, "Elements of Financial Statements, a Replacement of FASB Concepts Statement No 3 (incorporating an amendment of FASB Concepts No 2)" (Issued 12/85) (SFAC#6), sec 70; Statement of Financial Accounting Standards No 14, "Financial Reporting for Segments of a Business Enterprise" (Issued 12/76) (SFAS #14).

55 Like in cases of "extraordinary" items as described in Leopold A. Bernstein, *Accounting for Extraordinary Gains and Losses* (New York, Ronald Press, 1967), pp 15–79 and Weldon Powell, "Extraordinary Items," The Journal of Accountancy (January, 1966), at p 31.

56 Like the instrument of "Price Earning Ratio," which is the inverse of an interest rate. Investors are willing to pay more than the inverse of the available interest rate because of the assumption that the earnings will grow, but even when earnings are assumed to grow, the price earnings ratio comes from an assumed perpetual interest rate plus the growth factor: Price = earnings / (interest rate – rate of growth of earnings). See James C. Van Home, *Financial Management and Policy* (Prentice Hall, NJ, USA, 5th edn, 1980), p 32.

57 Stanger, Vander Kam and Polifka, Chapter 2, n 22 (citing SFAS#5); and Jensen, Chapter 2, n 22.

58 See Jay M. Smith and K. Fred Skousen, *Intermediate Accounting Comprehensive Volume*, 11 Edition (Southwestern Publishing: Cincinnati, OH, USA, 1992), p 579. See also Y. Barkai, *Accounting and Monetary Reporting – vol.1* (Bar-Or Publishing House, Ramat Hsharon, Is, 2003), p 7, which adds that the basic differentiation between a liability and equity is that a liability is generally intended to be redeemed at a defined moment in time, whereas the financial resources at the firm's disposal derived from capital are at its disposal for the long term and there is no legal obligation to return them, even though in today's economic reality, this distinction is sometimes blurred, and today many forms of liabilities for an undefined period can be found (such as shareholders loans), together with different forms of equity (such as preferred shares that can be redeemed at a given date) for an undefined period.

59 IASB Framework, Chapter 2, n 9, sec 91, and see the same definition in International Accounting Standard No 37, "Provisions, contingent liabilities and contingent assets" (IAS#37), sec 10. A similar definition is determined by the US GAAP, in SFAC#6, Chapter 2, n 43, sec 35–36, stating: "Liabilities are probable future sacrifices of economic benefits arising from present obligations of a particular entity to transfer assets or provide services to other entities in the future as a result of past transactions or events."

60 H. Dubroff, M.C. Chail and M. Norris, "The Relationships of Clear Reflection of Income to Generally Accepted Accounting Principles," 47 Alb L Rev 354, at p 359, n 20 (1983).

61 See IASB Framework, Chapter 2, n 9, sec 95; for US GAAP, see Statement of Financial Accounting Concepts No 6, "Elements of Financial Statements" (SFAC#6), sec 146; see also Miguel A. De Caprilles, "Modern Financial Accounting" (Pt 1), 37 NYUL Rev 1001, 1015–1019 (1962); (for former UK GAAP, see SSAP#2, Chapter 2, n 13; FRS#18, Chapter 2, n 13; BIM31031 and BIM31115).

62 Y. Samet, Chapter 2, n 4, at p 36.

63 Such as insurance, rent, property taxes and interest.

64 SFAS#5 and Jensen, Chapter 2, n 22, at n 13.

65 Financial Reporting Standards No 13, "Derivatives and other Financial

Instruments: Disclosures" (FRS#13) permits development expenditure, under certain conditions, to be deferred to future periods. Financial Reporting Standards No 10, "Goodwill and Intangible Assets" (FRS#10) requires expenditure on the purchase of an intangible asset to be spread over the expected useful economic life of the asset.

66 See IAS#37, Chapter 2, n 59, sec 10 (for former UK GAAP, see Financial Reporting Standards No 12, "Provisions, contingent liabilities and contingent assets" (FRS#12)).

67 International Financial Reporting Standards No 3, "Business Combinations" (IFRS#3); and International Financial Reporting Standards No 5, "Non-current Assets Held for Sale and Discontinued Operations" (IFRS#5).

68 A. Azbetzki, *Financial Accounting – vol 1* (Boursi Legal Publishers, Tel Aviv, 2001), p 453.

69 IAS#37, Chapter 2, n 59 (for former UK GAAP, see SSAP#9, Chapter 2, n 39 and Statement of Standard Accounting Practice No 21, "Accounting for leases and hire purchase contracts" (SSAP#21)).

70 IAS#37, ibid (for former UK GAAP, see FRS #12, Chapter 2, n 66).

71 Ibid, capitalization will be made (if the time value influence is material) by using the present value discount rates before tax representing the present value for the monetary value of time and of the same risks characterizing the liability that are not expressed in the best assessment of the expected expenditure.

72 Profits from the expected realization of assets are not taken into account, even when the expected realization is tightly linked to the event that was the reason for the provision. See Azbetzki, Chapter 2, n 68, pp 454–5.

73 Not exceeding the amount of the provision. See Azbetzki, ibid.

74 The warranty clause might in an extreme case be interpreted as if the seller did not transfer the significant risks and rewards or as if the seller did not fulfill all of the obligations. Under such interpretation, no revenue is recognized; see S. Shuv, Chapter 2, n 24.

75 Ibid.

76 See IAS#37, Chapter 2, n 59, sec 10. For US GAAP, see SFAC#5, Chapter 2, n 25 (for former UK GAAP, see FRS#18, Chapter 2, n 13).

77 See IAS#37, ibid. The "uncertainty" moves between the expected or probable and the remote, and should be valued and assessed in this spectrum.

78 Examples of provisions include, *inter alia*, provisions: for warranties; for returns; in connection with pending lawsuits; for post-retirement benefits; for onerous contracts; and for restructuring. In all of these cases, the event for which the taxpayer is expected to reduce its future resources was created in the past and the timing and amount of the obligation are uncertain.

79 Examples of contingent liabilities include, *inter alia*, guarantees that the firm provided on behalf of a third party, and lawsuits whose outcome is unknown.

80 Barkai, Chapter 2, n 58, at p 8.

81 See IAS#37, ibid, paras 84–6; and Azbetzki, n 68, at p 728.

82 According to IAS#39, Chapter 2, n 18, it will always start with the historic cost of an asset or liability, but for some transactions it may subsequently re-measure those assets or liabilities at their fair value (as defined in IAS#39, sec 98). See also CFM12075 and CFM12055.

83 IASB and FASB started using the term "fair value" at the beginning of the 1990s. For definition of "fair value", see IAS#39, ibid.

84 It should be noted that present value might be used either as a standalone measuring method or as a technique to estimate the fair value under the fair value method. For example, present value is used as a standalone method in International Accounting Standard No 36, "Impairment of Assets" (IAS#36),

which uses the present value method for estimating usage value, while it is used as a technique to estimate the fair value under the "fair value method" in IAS#40, Chapter 2, n 18, one of the techniques for investment property fair value estimation. For use of this method, see also Statement of Financial Accounting Standards No 114, "Accounting by Creditors for Impairment of a Loan – an amendment of FASB Statements No's 5 and 15" (Issued 5/93) (SFAS#114); Statement of Financial Accounting Standards No 87, "Employers' Accounting for Pensions" (Issued 12/85) (SFAS#87); Statement of Financial Accounting Standards No 106, "Employers' Accounting for Postretirement Benefits other than Pensions" (Issued 12/90) (SFAS#106); and Accounting Principles Board (APB) Opinions No 21, "Interest on Receivables and Payables" (APB#21).

85 Nevertheless, SFAC#5, Chapter 2, n 25, sec 67 mentioned that five different attributes of assets (and liabilities) are used in present practice: historical cost (historical proceeds), current cost, current market value, net realizable (settlement) value and present (or discounted) value of future cash flows.

86 SFAC#5, ibid, paras 66–67; and IASB Framework, Chapter 2, n 9, sec 100.

87 For example, there are a number of standards proscribing the use of the PV method: payments for retirement and damages to employees – Statement of Financial Accounting Standards No 74, "Accounting for Special Termination Benefits Paid to Employees" (Issued 8/83) (SFAS#74); monetary assets and liabilities acquired within the framework of the acquisition of a company – Accounting Principles Board (APB) Opinion No 16, "Business Combinations" (APB #16); interest on receivables and payables – APB#21, Chapter 2, n 84; lease payments for capital leases – Accounting Principles Board (APB) Opinion No 13, "Amending APB No 9, Application to Commercial Banks" (APB#13); receipts from insurance policies – Statement of Financial Accounting Standards No 60, "Accounting and Reporting by Insurance Enterprises" (Issued 6/82) (SFAS#60); employer's liabilities for pensions – Statement of Financial Accounting Standards No 87, "Employers' Accounting for Pensions" (Issued 12/85) (SFAS#87); abandoned assets – Statement of Financial Accounting Standards No 90, "Regulated Enterprises – Accounting for Abandonment's and Disallowances of Plant Costs (an amendment of SFAS No 71)" (Issued 12/86) (SFAS#90); commissions on bank loans – Statement of Financial Accounting Standards No 91, "Accounting for Nonrefundable Fees and Costs Associated with Originating for Acquiring Loans and Initial Direct Costs of Leases" (Issued 12/86) (SFAS #91); disclosure of the appropriate value of financial instruments – Statement of Financial Accounting Standards No 107, "Disclosure about Fair Value of Financial Instruments" (Issued 12/91) (SFAS#107); accounting provisions by creditors for loans whose value has been eroded – SFAS#114, Chapter 2, n 84; valuation of options issued to employees – Statement of Financial Accounting Standards No 123, "Accounting for Stock Based Compensation" (Issued 12/04) (SFAS #123), etc.

88 Examples where the PV method cannot be used are: convertible bonds – Accounting Principles Board (APB) Opinion No 14, "Accounting for Convertible Debt and Debt Issued with Stock Purchase Warrants" (ABP #14); assets and liabilities for a term up to one year – ABP#21, Chapter 2, n 84; reserves for deferred taxes Statement of Financial Accounting Standards No 109, "Accounting for Income Tax" (Issued 2/92) (SFAS#109), etc.

89 See, e.g. AICPA (American Institute of Certified Public Accountants), "Official Releases: Statement of financial Accounting Standards No 98 – Accounting for Leases", 8–88 JA 151, 158 (August 1988); AICPA, "Official Releases: FASB No 144—SOP 01–6—Auditing Interpretation", 3–02 JA 81, 95–6 (March 2002); AICPA, "Official Releases: Statement No 10 of the Governmental Accounting

Standards Board – Accounting and Financial Reporting for Risk Financing and Related Insurance", 4–90 JA 114, 118 (April 1990); and AICPA, "Official Releases: Ethics Notice . . . Statements of Position 98–7 and 98–9", 3–99 JA 90 (March 1999).

90 For the classification of current items (assets and liabilities) and long-term items, see International Accounting Standard No 1, "Presentation of Financial Statements" (IAS, 1997) (IAS#1), sec 53.

91 See IAS#1, ibid, sec 60, and in US GAAP, see Accounting Research Bulletins No 43, "Restatement and Revision of Accounting Research Bulletins" (ARB, 1953) (ARB#43).

92 Samet, Chapter 2, n 4, p 532.

93 APB#21, Chapter 2, n 84.

94 APB#21, sec 3(C) stated as follows: "Except that paragraph 16 covering statement presentation of discount and premium is applicable in all circumstances, this section is not intended to apply to . . . Amounts intended to provide security for one party to an agreement (for example security deposits, retain ages on contracts)".

95 See also CFM12015 and CFM12055.

96 Such as deposits to secure the return of equipment or the performance of an agreement whose return is linked to the agreement's termination.

97 When an unlimited right to return the deposit to the client exists ("on call" obligation) and the rate of the holding can be determined, SFAS#48, Chapter 2, n 15 states that, according to the matching principle, the income from the gap is approximately the expected size of the return from the sales that will be registered parallel therewith.

98 See IAS#39, Chapter 2, n 18.

99 For example, the discounted cash flows technique (i.e. the present value of the future cash flows), which refers to the current fair value of other financial instruments that are substantially the same, etc.

100 For IFRS, see IAS#39, Chapter 2, n 18.

101 See para 2.3.2.

102 See IAS#18, Chapter 2, n 19; for US GAAP, see SAB#101, Chapter 2, n 27.

103 Accounting Principles Board (APB) Opinions No 6, "Status of Accounting Research Bulletins" (APB#6), sec 38; AICPA, *Contemporary Accounting: A Refresher Course for Public Accountants* (Arthur Leland, ed, 1945), paras 2–17; William A. Paton, *Essentials of Accounting* (New York, USA, Macmillan Co, 1949), p 315; W.A. Paton and A.C. Littleton, *An Introduction to Corporate Accounting Standards* (Ann Arbor, MI, USA, American Accounting Association, 1940), p 59; Laurie L. Malman, "Treatment of Prepaid Income – Clear Reflection of Income or Muddied Waters", 37 Tax L Rev 103, 105 (1981); and Donald E. Kieso and Jerry J. Weygandt, *Intermediate Accounting* (New York, USA, John Wiley & Sons, 4th edn, 1983), pp 73–4.

104 Harold Dubroff, "The Claim of Rights Doctrine", 40 Tax L Rev 729, 771 (1985); Dubroff summarizes the accounting theory on this issue as follows: "Under generally accepted accounting principles (GAAP) income is recognized when 'earned'. Since prepaid income is payment for goods or services to be supplied in the future, it is not earned in the year of receipt. Therefore, items such as prepaid rent or magazine subscriptions are not treated as income when received, but as revenue in the future period when earned. These amounts are carried as unearned revenue until the earnings process is complete. Similarly, in order to properly match expenses with revenue, GAAP treats costs associated with future revenue as prepaid assets and the expenses is deferred to future years".

105 As described in para 2.3.

106 APB#6, Chapter 2, n 103; and Paton, Chapter 2, n 103, at p 315.

107 APB#4, Chapter 2, n 15; and Paton, ibid, at pp 465–6.

108 Barkai, Chapter 2, n 58, at pp 16–41.

109 In any case, APB#21, Chapter 2, n 84 removes from its application the measuring at present value of current liabilities derived from transactions with suppliers in the ordinary course of business that do not exceed one year.

110 For revenue recognition requirements, see para 2.3.

111 As described in para 2.5.1 and IAS#39, Chapter 2, n 18.

112 No doubt, the price of the goods or services to be provided in the future should be higher than what a customer is willing to pay in advance for those goods or services. This principle reflects the time value of money; see R. Brealey et al, *Principles of Corporate Finance* (9th edn, 2008), p 89.

113 It should be noted that the above-mentioned discussion does not refer to credit sales and credit purchases. In such cases the fact that the transaction of goods and services takes place before the actual payment is taken into consideration by GAAP and, if material effect of the credit component is present, the time value of money is taken into account.

3 Tax values

1 See para 2.1.

2 Academic commentary defines "public goods" according to two features: non-exclusivity – that is, an impossible or very expensive product to supply to one person as opposed to another; and non-rivalry – the fact that another person enjoys the product does not make it more expensive. It is argued that products exist that cannot be supplied by the market – namely, public products – and it is the role of the state to supply those products. For further discussion on the subject of "public goods", see: Mancur Olson, *The Logic of Collective Action: Public Goods and the Theory of Groups* (1965), p 45; Anthony de Jasay, *Social Contract, Free Ride: A Study of the Public Goods Problem* (1989); A. Lizzeri and N. Persico, "The Provision of Public Goods under Alternative Electoral Incentives", American Economic Review 91, 225–39 (March 2001); and Herbert J. Kiesling, *Taxation and Public Goods: A Welfare-Economic Critique of Tax Policy Analysis* (University of Michigan Press, 1992).

3 Adam Smith, *An Inquiry into the Nature and Causes of the Wealth of Nations*, p 825 (R.H. Campbell and A.S. Skinner, eds, *Liberty Classics*, 1981) (1776) (Book V, Ch II, Pt II).

4 For the aspect of "fairness" in taxation in the UK tax system, see G. Macdonald and D. Martin, "Tax and Accounting A Response to the 2003 Consultation Document on Corporation Tax Reform", Tax Law Review Committee, The Institute for Fiscal Studies (February 2004) TLRC Discussion Paper No 4, http://www.ifs.org.uk/comms/dp4.pdf ("**The Macdonald-Martin Committee No 4**"), ss 3.1–3.2. For using the justice criterion as an instrument for interpretation of tax law as a deeming provision, see, e.g. *CIR v Hinchy* [1969] 3 All ER 39, 90, 95; *Marshall v Kerr* [1982] STC 30, HL at p 32; Simon's Direct Tax Service/Binder 2 General Principles Procedures, Schedules A, B and C/Part A1 General principles/Division A1.3 The construction and application of tax legislation/A1.304 "ascertaining the intention generally".

5 For the aspect of "fairness" in taxation in the US federal tax systems, see *Thor Power Tool Co v Commissioner* 563 F2d 861 (7th Cir 1977); R. Musgrave, *The Theory of Public Finance* (New York, 1959); J.E. Stiglitz, *Economics of the Public Sector* (3rd edn, New York, W.W. Norton, 2000); A. Gunn, "Matching of Costs and Revenues as a Goal of Tax Accounting", 4 Va Tax Rev 1, 4 (summer 1984); J. Schoenblum, "Tax Fairness or Unfairness? Consideration of Philosophical

Bases for Unequal Taxation of Individuals", 12 Am J Tax Pol'y 221 (1995); and
L. Kaplow and S. Shavel, "Fairness versus Welfare", 114 Harv L Rev 961 (2001).

6 For the aspect of "fairness" in taxation in the Israeli tax system, see ITA(H)
804/06, 806/06 *Ricenbach and Kavizal v Haifa Assessing Officer*, Taxes (August
2008), E-212; *"The Report of the Public Committee for Reform in Income Tax"* ("Ben
Bassat Committee") (Ronnen Ltd, 2000), pp 8–9; Y. Edrey, "A General Tax Base
for Israel", 12 Mishpatim (1982) 431; J. Gross, *The New Israeli Tax Law* (3rd
edn, Tagidim Ltd, Tel Aviv University, 2003), pp 2–9; A. Shenhav, "Tax Expenditures in the Israeli Tax system: Legal Aspects, Economic Aspects and Lines for
Reform", Taxes (April 1998) A-1; and A. Nov, "The Tax System and the
Encouragement of Investments", Taxes (February 2005), A-1–A-3.

7 In this sense a comparison may be drawn between the tax values and the
particular legislative sections in each and every country on the one hand, and
the existing treatment in another regulatory system which we examined –
namely GAAP, i.e. the comparison between pervasive principles and detailed
principles (see Chapter 2, n 15).

8 See para 5.2, first passage.

9 See para 5.4, first passage.

10 See para 5.3, first passage.

11 For the purposes of our discussion it is sufficient to say that even if no clear
definition exists of the concept of "income", all three tax systems reviewed do
not aspire to erode the capital, but impose the tax only on the increased element thereof. According to the formula that was made in the early 1920s, known
as the Haig-Simons formula, income is measured according to the increase in
the taxpayer's consumption ability (including additions to savings) over a
given timeframe. That increase is equal to money and the equivalent of money
received by the taxpayer during the course of that timeframe, less the present
value of his future refunds and future costs, and also on his net income from
savings in that period, including an increase in the value of his assets. For the
source of the Haig-Simons formula and the comprehensive tax basis theory,
see Henry C. Simons, *Personal Income Taxation: the Definition of Income as a
Problem of Fiscal Policy* (Chicago, University of Chicago Press, 1938), pp 50–51;
Robert M. Haig, *"The Concept of Income – Economic and Legal Aspects"*, *The
Federal Income Tax* (New York: Columbia University Press, 1921), p 7. For a
classic critical description of the "comprehensive tax basis theory", see Boris I.
Bittker, "A Comprehensive Tax Base as a Goal of Income Tax Reform", 80 Harv
L Rev 925 (1967). For a description of the rise and fall of the importance of the
"comprehensive tax basis theory", see Michael A. Livingston, "Reinventing
Tax Scholarship: Lawyers, Economists, and the Role of the Legal Academy", 83
Cornell L Rev 365 (1998).

12 See paras 5.2–5.4, first passage only.

13 For the value of horizontal equity in the UK tax system, see Taxation
Magazine/2005 Volume 155/Issue 4021, 18 August 2005/Editorial/"Post-
marital tax"; Simon's Direct Tax Service Budget Bulletin/Extract from the
Financial Statement/Economic and Fiscal Strategy Report/5 Building a Fairer
Society/"Modernising the tax system", sec 5.1.1.7.

14 For the value of horizontal equity in the US federal tax system, see D. Shapiro,
"Tax Accounting for Prepaid Income and Reserves for Future Expenses, in two
Compendium of Papers on Broadening the Tax Base Submitted to Comm on
Ways and Means", 86th Cong, 1st Sess (Comm. Print 1959) 1133; R. Sappideen,
"Imputation of the Corporate and Personal Income Tax: Is It Chasing One's
Tail?", 15 Am J Tax Pol'y 167, 171–5, 190–4 (1998); Michael J. Graetz, "The David
R. Tillinghast Lecture: Taxing International Income: Inadequate Principles,
Outdated Concepts, and Unsatisfactory Policies", 54 Tax L Rev 261, 301–3

(2001); Stephen B. Land, "Defeating Deferral: A Proposal for Retrospective Taxation", 52 Tax L Rev 45, 49–51 (1996); Charles E. McLure, Jr, "Taxation of Electronic Commerce: Economic Objectives, Technological Constraints, and Tax Laws", 52 Tax L Rev 269, 380 (1997); I. Bittker, "Equity, Efficiency, and Income Tax Theory: Do Misallocations Drive Out Inequities?", 16 San Diego, L Rev 735 (1979); L. Kaplow, "Horizontal Equity: Measures in Search of a Principle", 4 Nat'l Tax J 139 (1989); M.J. Grates and D.H. Schenk, *Federal Income Taxation: Principles and Policies* (3rd edn, New York, 1995), p 31; R. Musgrave, "Horizontal Equity, Once More", 43 Nat'l Tax J 113 (1990); L. Kaplow, "A Note on Horizontal Equity", 1 Fla Tax Rev 191 (1992); R. Musgrave, "Horizontal Equity: A Further Note", 1 Fla Tax Rev 354 (1993); P.R. McDaniel and J.R. Repetti, "Horizontal and Vertical Equity: The Musgrave/Kaplow Exchange", 1 Fla Tax Rev 607 (1993); and E.M. Zolt, "The Uneasy Case for Uniform Taxation," 16 Va Tax Rev 39, 86–98 (1996).

15 For the value of horizontal equity in the Israeli tax system, see Gross, Chapter 3, n 6, pp 6–7; Shenhav, Chapter 3, n 6, p 12; Y. Margaliot, "Examination of the Recommendations of Ben Bassat Committee in the Light of Tax Policy", Taxes (June 2000), A-56, A-62–A-63; and O. Granot, "Purposeful Interpretation in Tax Law: from Declaration of Principles into Practical Practice", Taxes (April 2004), A-79, A-87.

16 For the value of vertical equity in the UK tax system, see Chapter 3, n 13.

17 For the value of vertical equity in the US federal tax system, see Schapiro, Chapter 3, n 14, pp 1142–4; McDaniel and Repetti, Chapter 3, n 14, p 607; Sappideen, Chapter 3, n 14, pp 201–3; Joseph M. Dodge, "Theories of Tax Justice: Ruminations on the Benefit, Partnership, and Ability-to-Pay Principles", 58 Tax L Rev 399, 401, 451, 458 (2005); Deborah H. Schenk, "A Positive Account of the Realization Rule", 57 Tax L Rev 355, 393 (2004); Graetz, Chapter 3, n 14, at pp 301–3; Land, Chapter 3, n 14, at pp 49–51; and McLure, Chapter 3, n 14, at p 383.

18 For the value of vertical equity in the Israeli tax system, see Gross, Chapter 3, n 6, at pp 6–7; Margaliot, Chapter 3, n 15, at pp 62–3; Shenhav, Chapter 3, n 6, at p 12; and Granot, Chapter 3, n 15, at p 87.

19 For the value of neutrality in the UK tax system, see Tolley's Tax Planning/15 Electronic Commerce/UK tax developments; The Macdonald-Martin Committee No 4, Chapter 3, n 4, sec 3.1–3.2; Specialist Tax Regulatory Materials, Issued by Inland Revenue, "International Accounting Standards – The UK Tax Implications" (published on 1/9/2005); BIM31001; Simon's Tax Planning/PART D Companies/Chapter 19 Incorporation/1 "Introduction"; Simon's Direct Tax Service, Chapter 3, n 13, ss 5.1.1.9–5.1.2.0.

20 For the value of neutrality in the US federal tax system, see Christina I. Smith, "Challenging the Treasury: United Dominion Industries, Inc v. Unites States", 17 Akron Tax J 61, 97 (2002); Sappideen, Chapter 3, n 14, pp 171 and 176; William D. Andrews, "Tax Neutrality Between Equity Capital and Debt", 30 Wayne L Rev 1057, 1058–9 (1984); Douglas A. Kahn, "Comments on Tax Neutrality Between Equity Capital and Debt", 30 Wayne L Rev 1081, 1082 (1984); and Gunn, Chapter 3, n 5, at p 23.

21 For the value of neutrality in the Israeli tax system, see Margaliot, Chapter 3, n 15, at p 59; Nov, Chapter 3, n 6, at pp 6–9; Shenhav, Chapter 3, n 6, at pp 10–11; and Granot, Chapter 3, n 15, at p 87.

22 For the value of certainty in the UK tax system, see Tolley's Tax Planning/15 Electronic Commerce/UK tax developments; *WT Ramsay v CIR* [1981] STC 174, 179; *Willows v Lewis* [1982] STC 141, 147; Simon's Direct Tax Service, Chapter 3, n 13, sec 5.1.1.3.

23 For the value of certainty in the US federal tax system, see D. Ghosh and T.L.

Crain, "Structure of Uncertainty and Decision Making: An Experimental Investigation", 24 Decision Sciences 789 (1993); J.T. Casey and J.T. Scholz, "Boundary of Vague Risk Information on Taxpayer Decision", 50 Organizational Behavior and Human Decision Processes 360 (1991); J.T. Casey and J.T. Scholz, "Beyond Deterrence: Behavioral Decision Theory and Tax Compliance", 25 Law & Soc'y Rev 821 (1991); and William A. Klein, "The UCLA Tax Policy Conference: Tailor To The Emperor With No Clothes: The Supreme Court Tax Rules For Deposits and Advanced Payments", 41 UCLA L Rev 1685, 1734–5 (1994).

24 For the value of certainty in the Israeli tax system, see Gross, Chapter 3, n 6, at p 8; Nov, Chapter 3, n 6, at pp 3–4; and Granot, Chapter 3, n 15, at p 87.

25 For an opinion that certainty is not necessarily needed in tax law, see D.A. Weisbach, "Ten Truths about Tax Shelters", 55 Tax L Rev 201 (2002).

26 For the value of efficiency (including collection and enforcement) in the UK tax system, see Tolley's Tax Planning, Chapter 3, n 19; The Macdonald-Martin Committee No 4, Chapter 3, n 4, sec 3.1–3.2; Specialist Tax Regulatory, Chapter 3, n 19; BIM31001; Simon's Tax Intelligence/2006/Issue 12, 30 March 2006/ Extract from the Financial Statement; Simon's Direct Tax Service, Chapter 3, n 13, sec 5.1.1.2 and 5.1.1.5.

27 For the value of efficiency (including collection and enforcement) in the US federal tax system, see Lynn A. Stout, "The Unimportance of Being Efficient: An Economic Analysis of Stock Market Pricing and Securities Regulation", 87 Mich L Rev 613 (1988); Sappideen, Chapter 3, n 14, at pp 168–70, 193–7; Daniel I. Halperin, "Will Integration Increase Efficiency? The Old and New View of Dividend Policy", 47 Tax L Rev 645, 647 (1992); Klein, Chapter 3, n 23, pp 1734– 5; Calvin H. Johnson, "The Illegitimate 'Earned' Requirement in Tax and Non Tax Accounting", 50 Tax L Rev 373, 401–5 (1995); and Karl S. Coplan, "Protecting the Public Fisc: Fighting Accrual Abuse with Section 446 Discretion", 83 Col L Rev 378, 405–11 (1983).

28 For the value of efficiency (including collection and enforcement) in the Israeli tax system, see Ben Bassat Committee, Chapter 3, n 6, at pp 8–9; Gross, Chapter 3, n 6, at p 8; Nov, Chapter 3, n 6, at pp 9–11; and Granot, Chapter 3, n 15, at p 87.

29 For preventing unjust tax advantages in the UK tax system, see The Macdonald-Martin Committee No 4, Chapter 3, n 4, sec. 3.1–3.2; Specialist Tax Regulatory, n 19; BIM31001; *Furniss v Dawson* [1984] STC 153; *Magnavox Electronics v Hall* [1985] STC 260; [1986] STC 561; *Young v Phillips* [1984] STC 520; *Hatton v CIR* [1992] STC 140; *Countess Fitzwilliam v CIR* [1993] STC 502; *CIR v McGuckian* [1997] STC 908; *Pumahaven Ltd v Williams* [2002] STC 1423; *Barclays Mercantile Business Finance Ltd v Mawson* [2003] STC 66; Simon's Direct Tax Service/Binder 2 General principles procedures, Schedules A, B and C/Part A1 General Principles/Division A1.3 The construction and application of tax legislation/A1.315 "Artificial documents and transactions".

30 For preventing unjust tax advantages in the US federal tax system, see R. Rice, "Judicial Techniques in Combating Tax Avoidance", 51 Mich. L Rev 1021, 1041, 1043 (1953); Johnson, Chapter 3, n 27, at 401–5; *Compaq Computer Corp v Commissioner* 2001 WL 1662035, Doc 2002–184, 2002 TNT 1–5 (2 January 2002); D.P. Hariton, "The Compaq Case, Notice 985, and Tax Shelters: The Theory Is All Wrong", 2002 TNT 19–30 (28 January 2002); L.A. Sheppard, "Should Riskless Profit Equal Economic Substance?" 2002 TNT 11–2 (14 January 2002); M. Kane, "Compaq and IES: Putting the Tax Back into After-Tax Income", 94 Tax Notes 1215 (4 March 2002); W.A. Klein and K.J. Stark, "Compaq Computer Corporation v Commissioner – Where is The Tax Arbitrage?" 2002 TNT 48–50 (12 March 2002); D.N. Shaviro and D.A. Weisbach, "The Fifth

Circuit Gets It Wrong in Compaq v Commissioner?" 2002 TNT 19–31 (29 January 2002); D.N. Shaviro, "Economic Substance, Corporate Tax Shelters, and the Compaq Case", 2000 TNT 132–80 (10 July 2000); and G.K. Yin, "Getting Serious About Corporate Tax Shelters: Taking A Lesson from History", 54 SMU L Rev 209 (2001).

31 For preventing unjust tax advantages in the Israeli tax system, see D. Gliksberg, *The Boundaries of Tax Planning* (Hebrew University of Jerusalem, 1990); and A. Zuckerman, "Anatomy of a Judgment: the Life and Death of Section 86 of the Ordinance", Taxes (October 2003), A-54.

32 See Sam K. Kaywood, Jr, "Comment: The Deficit Reduction Act of 1984: Reform for Deferred Payment Accounting", 35 Emory LJ 507, 507–10 and n 12 (1986).

33 Daniel I. Halperin, "Interest in Disguise: Taxing the Time Value of Money", 95 Yale LJ 506 (1986).

34 For Halperin's opinion, see also para 7.3.4.

35 Deborah A. Geier, "The Myth of Matching Principle as a Tax Value", 15 Am J Tax Pol'y 17, 25–6 (1998).

36 See paras 4.4.4 and 7.3.4.

37 Geier, at p 91; for Geier's opinion, see also paras 4.4.4 and 7.3.4.

38 For other common tax values, such as simplicity or transparency, which are not relevant for our purposes, see George Warskett, Stanley Winer and Walter Hettich, "The Complexity of Tax Structure in Competitive Political Systems" 5th vol Nun 2, International Tax and Public Finance (Springer, Netherlands, May 1998), pp 123–51; K. Edmiston, M. Shannon and V. Neven, "Tax Structures and FDI: The Deterrent Effects of Complexity and Uncertainty", Fiscal Studies, 24 (3), 341–359 (2003), 341; Draft United Nations Manual on Anti-Corruption Policy (http://www.unodc.org/pdf/crime/gpacpublications/manual.pdf).

39 For other tax subjects or values which are totally unrelated to financial accounting, the tax authorities in the UK (**"HMRC"**) relate to 11 possible categories (i.e. government policy, transfer prices, structural, tax avoidance, tax neutrality, capital elements, fiscal incentives, symmetry, realisability, tax capacity and "true reflection"). See "International Accounting Standards – The UK Implications (Finance Act 2004 Update)", Inland Revenue (Issued 15 September 2004); Specialist Tax Regulatory Materials, Issued by Inland Revenue, "International Accounting Standards – The UK Tax Implications" (published 1 September 2005); BIM31001; and The Macdonald-Martin Committee No 4, Chapter 3, n 4, at sec 3.1–3.2.

40 The Macdonald-Martin Committee No 4, ibid, at sec 3.4–3.5, adding that this interest is also pure financial accounting.

41 See paras 2.3 and 2.4.

42 Halperin, Chapter 3, n 33, at pp 519–24.

43 Geier, Chapter 3, n 35, and reference there.

44 On the cash basis method, see paras 4.2.2, 4.4.1.3, and 4.4.2.1.

45 For the definition of the "matching principle", see para 2.4.

46 Take, for example, the case that Halperin, Chapter 3, n 33, at pp 519–24 speaks of regarding employees' wages. The desire to "match" the date of deduction of the wages by the employer and recognition of income of the employee, even "at the price" of deferring the deduction of the expense to the employer on a cash basis method, disregards the fact that such an employee's employment created income from other sources for the employer in the year in which it was made, against which, according to this approach, the expense that created it would not be allowed in that year.

4 Between GAAP and fiscal accounting

1 See para 2.1 and the first passage of Chapter 3.
2 Ibid.
3 *Thor*, Chapter 3, n 5.
4 Discussed in Chapter 2.
5 Gunn, Chapter 3, n 5, at pp 12–13.
6 Gunn, ibid.
7 Coplan, Chapter 3, n 27, at pp 405–11.
8 J. Silk, "Advanced Payments – Prepaid Income: Recent Developments; an Old Problem Put to Rest", 30 NYU Inst 1651, 1652 (1972).
9 Johnson, Chapter 3, n 27, at pp 401–5.
10 Ibid.
11 As mentioned in para 2.4.
12 *Kleinrock's TaxExpert Analysis and Explanation*, from January 2002 through 2009 (Rockville, MD, Kleinrock Publishing, 2001) (http://www.lexis.com/research/ retrieve?_m=12004a25270587265163ed931d1550c&_src=248035.3006719&_cat= 3006719&tcfrmsrc=1&_tcid=248035&_fmtstr=TOC&tcact=initial&svc=toc&_ stateList=svc&wchp=dGLzVtz-zSKAI&_md5=3885b19bdbf20cec7d99d3234bd c5d4b), sec 501.4.
13 Geier, Chapter 3, n 35, at p 145.
14 Geier, ibid.
15 The Macdonald-Martin Committee No 4, Chapter 3, n 4, at ss 3.5–3.6.
16 The Macdonald-Martin Committee No 4, at ss 2.10–2.25.
17 Ibid.
18 Ibid, at sec 3.7–3.10 and 3.12.
19 Ibid, at sec 3.8.
20 Ibid, at sec 2.2, 2.3 and 2.4.
21 Dubroff, Chail and Norris, Chapter 2, n 60, at p 359, n 57, p 389, n 66 and at pp 404–6.
22 Klein, Chapter 3, n 23, at 1685–6 and at pp 1701–2.
23 For "certainty" and "efficiency" as tax values, see paras 3.1.4–3.1.5.
24 See Chapter 2.
25 See paras 2.3 and 2.4.
26 Ibid.
27 For this awareness, see para 4.3.3.
28 For statutory adjustments in the UK Tax Acts departing from GAAP, see para 4.3.1.2.
29 With regard to questions of classification of income, see our discussion in para 4.3.2 on the case of *Tapemaze Ltd v Melluish* [2000] STC 189; (2000) 73 TC 167.
30 Inserted by ss 4(1) and 5(1) of the Companies Act 1989.
31 The requirement of the "true and fair view" was first included as a standard for financial statements in the Companies Act 1947, which amended in this respect the expression "true and correct". This concept of "true and fair view" was adopted by the EC in the Fourth Directive and this Directive was adopted in UK legislation in the scope of the Companies Act 1981, and underwent consolidation in the framework of the Companies Act 1985. Additional changes made within the scope of the Seventh Directive were adopted in 1989, and also encompassed amendments to the provisions prescribed in ss 226–7 of the Companies Act and Schs 4 and 4A to that Act.
32 Inserted by s 19(3) of the Companies Act 1989: repealed by ss 16 (7), 64, Sch 8 of the Companies (Audit, Investigations and Community Enterprise) Act 2004.
33 s 836A, ICTA 1988 and s 42, FA 1998 as amended by s 103, FA 2002.
34 BIM31004.

35 BIM31027.
36 Ibid.
37 See Chapter 4, n 33.
38 For this pervasive principle, see Chapter 2, n 15. See also Lakshmi Narain, "The Use of Accounts for Tax – Back to Basis – Account for Tax", Tax Journal (17 March 2003).
39 As to the expression "clear reflection" in US tax law, see our discussion in paras 4.4.1.2 and 4.4.2.3.
40 SSAP#2, Chapter 3, n 13.
41 FRS#18, Chapter 2, n 13.
42 See Chapter 2.
43 See para 2.1.
44 BIM74001.
45 BIM74005.
46 BIM74001 and BIM74005.
47 For statutory adjustments in the UK Tax Acts departing from GAAP, see, e.g. ss 90, 579 and 592(4), ICTA 1988; s 43, FA 1989; ss 74(1)(f)(g), 348–350 and 817(2), ITCA 1988 (until 2005–06); ss 33, 45–7 and 74, ITTOIA 2005 (from 2005–06); s 17 of Chapter 25 of FA 2002, in all aspects relating to the reporting of profits or losses resulting from derivatives.
48 *Heather v PE Consulting Group Ltd* (1972) 48 TC 293, 322.
49 *ECC Quarries Ltd v Watkis* (1975) 51 TC 153, 173.
50 See, e.g. *Patrick v Broadstone Mills Ltd* (1953) 35 TC 44; *Heather*, Chapter 4, n 48; and *Willingale v International Commercial Bank Ltd* [1978] STC 75.
51 *Owen v Southern Railway of Peru Ltd* (1956) 36 TC 602, 646; in the context of the question as to whether the amount of the provision that had been included in the computation of the company's profit/loss, Lord Radcliffe stated: "I think that one is bound to say that reference to an auditors duty under the Companies Act take us into a field that is not exactly the same as that in which the annual profits of trade should be ascertained for the purposes of Income Tax".
52 *Lothian Chemical Co v Rogers* (1926) 11 TC 508.
53 *Chancery Lane Safe Deposit and Offices Co Ltd v CIR* (1965) 43 TC 83.
54 *Odeon Associated Theaters Ltd v Jones* (1971) 1 WLR 442; 48 TC 257.
55 *Absalom v Talbot* (1944) 26 TC 166.
56 *CIR v Newcastle Breweries Ltd* (1927) 12 TC 927, 951, HK.
57 *Gardner, Mountain and D'Ambrumenil Ltd v CIR* [1947] 1 All ER 650; 29 TC 69.
58 *Rownson, Drew and Clydesdale Ltd v CIR* (1931) 16 TC 595.
59 *Cowen and Cowen's Ideal Trading Stamp Co (Glasgow) Ltd v CIR* (1934) 19 TC 155.
60 *Hall (JP) and Co Ltd v CIR* [1921] 3 KB 152; 12 TC 382.
61 *New Conveyor Co Ltd v Dodd* (1945) 27 TC 11.
62 *Gunn v CIR* (1955) 36 TC 93.
63 *Rownson, Drew and Clydesdale Ltd*, Chapter 4, n 58.
64 For example, in the case of assessees who charged rent on the storage of their customers' whiskey bottles, the court tended to recognize income from that rent on a cash basis, and not spread the income over the period of the lease, see *Dailuaine-Talisker Distilleries Ltd v CIR* [1930] SC 878.
65 *Symons v Lord Llewedyn-Daries Personal Representative and others* (1982) 56 TC 630.
66 *Gallagher v Jones; Threlfall v Jones* [1993] STC 537; (1993) 66 TC 77.
67 SSAP#21, Chapter 2, n 69.
68 *Threlfall*, at p 128I.
69 *Threlfall*, at p 123B, in relating to this, the court states: "I find it hard to

understand how any judge-made rule could override the application of a generally accepted rule of commercial accountancy which (a) applied to the situation in question, (b) was not one of two or more rules applicable to the situation in question and (c) was not shown to be inconsistent with the true facts or otherwise inapt to determine the true profits or losses of the business".

70 *Johnston v Britannia Airways Ltd* (1994) 67 TC 99.
71 *Britannia Airways*, at p 123E.
72 *Herbert Smith (A Firm) v Honour* (1999) 72 TC 130.
73 See also BIM31100.
74 *Tapemaze*, Chapter 4, n 29.
75 Ibid, at p 199.
76 See also BIM31105.
77 See BIM31002, BIM31003, BIM31019 and BIM31026.
78 *Britannia Airways*, Chapter 4, n 70.
79 BIM31095. HMRC nonetheless adds that on other subjects (such as the distinction between capital and income), this judgment is not to be regarded as obliging tax legislation to follow GAAP.
80 See BIM31001, BIM31004 and BIM31120.
81 Statement of Practice 3/91.
82 Such reporting was standard for practitioners of certain free professions before the enactment of the FA 98.
83 BIM74010.
84 BIM40080.
85 BIM42215.
86 As to those subjects where such a deviation may be made, see Chapter 3, n 39.
87 In BIM31003, the example that was given for that Directive is a prosaic and "innocent" example that relates to not allowing expenses that are substantially of a capital nature.
88 See also BIM56410.
89 CIOT, The Chartered Institute of Taxation, Application of International Accounting Standards to consolidated tax base by Technical Department, "Submission by the CIOT to the European Commission" (6 May 2003), http://www.tax.org.uk/showarticle.pl?id=1776 ("**The CIOT Application**").
90 The CIOT Application, sec 2.
91 The CIOT Application, sec 9.
92 G. Macdonald and D. Martin, "Aligning Tax and Accounting Profits – The Need to Review Current Legislation", Tax Law Review Committee, The Institute for Fiscal Studies (November 2004), TLRC Discussion Paper No 5, http://www.ifs.org.uk/comms/dp5.pdf ("**The Macdonald-Martin Committee No 5**") and The Macdonald-Martin Committee No 4, Chapter 3, n 4, sec 1.11.
93 The Macdonald-Martin Committee No 4, Chapter 3, n 4, sec 2.9, although there is a certain difference here between Discussion Paper No 4 – which recommends amending s 42, FA 1998 in a manner whereby deviating from GAAP for tax purposes will only be made by way of legislation – and Discussion Paper No 5, sec 1, from which it appears that the committee does not limit the deviation only to specific legislation and, on the face of it, "makes do" with the publication of the circumstances in which a deviation will be made by HMRC.
94 The Macdonald-Martin Committee No 4, Chapter 3, n 4, sec 1.7, 2.6. It is unclear whether the term "the existing precedents" means those preceding the 1998 legislation or those which existed on the date the Report was issued in 2003.
95 For example: Lakshmi, Chapter 4, n 38; and A. Stobart, "Tax Deductibility of Provisions", Tax Journal (11 March 2003).

96 USCS §26 441.
97 USCS § 26 7701.
98 USCS § 26 451.
99 Mentioned in IRC§451 (e.g. in the case of the taxpayer's death, as regards bonuses to workers, insurance payments deriving from loss of damage and the like).
100 USCS §26 446.
101 Treas Reg § 1.446–1, 26 USCS 446.
102 Treas Reg § 1.446–1(c)(2)(i), 26 USCS 446.
103 IRC §447(c)(1), 26 USCS 447.
104 IRC §447(c), 26 USCS 447.
105 IRC§ 447(d)(1), 26 USCS 447.
106 Although some guidance may perhaps be garnered from the nature of Treas Reg 1.446–1(a)(2), which provides that: "A method of accounting which reflects the consistent application of generally accepted accounting principles in a particular trade or business in accordance with accepted conditions or practices in that trade or business will ordinarily be regarded as clearly reflecting income, provided all items of gross income and expense are treated consistently from year to year."
107 In s 836A, ICTA 1988 and s 42, FA 1998.
108 Subject to specific exceptions in which the US federal legislator has dictated a particular reporting method like those mentioned in para 4.4.1.1.
109 As mentioned in para 4.3.1.
110 The Administrative Procedure Act, 5 USC§706(2)(A) (1994) ("**APA**").
111 The standards according to which the courts will examine and review the decisions of the administrative agency set in the APA are as follows: "To the extent necessary to decision and when presented, the reviewing court shall decide all relevant questions of law, interpret constitutional and statutory provisions, and determine the meaning or applicability of the terms of an agency action. The reviewing court shall ... (2) hold unlawful and set aside agency action, findings, and conclusions found to be (A) arbitrary, capricious, an abuse of discretion, or otherwise not in accordance with law; ... (E) unsupported by substantial evidence in a case subject to sections 556 and 557 or this title or otherwise reviewed on the record of an agency hearing provided by statute; or (F) unwarranted by the facts to the extent that the facts are subject to trial de novo by the reviewing court".
112 Jennifer C. Root, "The Commissioner's Clear Reflection of Income Power under 446(b) and the Abuse of Discretion Standard of Review: Where Has the Rule of Law Gone, and Can We Get It Back?" 15 Tax J 69, 101(2000); in her research relating to this provision, *inter alia*, Root states (at p 101): "The APA has given guidance as to the definition of the abuse of discretion standard of review. The standard was created with the purpose to reinstate judicial review over administrative agency determinations. The Supreme Court has noted that under the standard, a court can only invalidate a determination when the determination is irrational or not based upon all the relevant factors that should have been taken into account. In no way does this standard of review allow a court to invalidate a determination simply because it would have come to a different conclusion than the agency. Furthermore, when looking to the continuum of review granted to courts, the abuse of discretion standard limits the power of the courts to the greatest extent when compared to the other standards. Thus, the reversal of an agency determination when the court is limited to the abuse of discretion standard of review should be rare and only occur in the most extreme of cases."
113 *Cherokee Motor Coach Co v Commissioner* 135 F2d 840 (6th Cir 1943).

114 Treas Reg § 1.451–2(a), 26 USCS 451.
115 See also our discussion on this subject in para 4.4.2.1.
116 See para 2.3.
117 See para 2.4.
118 See para 2.3.
119 Treas Reg § 1.446–1(a)(2), 26 USCS 446; *Potter v Commissioner* 44 TC 159 (TC 1965).
120 See para 4.4.2.2.
121 See also para 4.4.2.3.
122 See para 2.4.
123 We will address this difference in the level of liabilities and expenses in para 7.3.
124 IRC§ 453(e), 26 USCS 453.
125 IRC §453(g), 26 USCS 453.
126 IRC §453(d), 26 USCS 453.
127 IRC§ 453(d)(3), 26 USCS 453.
128 *Roy v Commissioner* 69 F2d 786 (5th Cir 1934).
129 *Wiseman v Scruggs* 281 F2d 900 (10th Cir 1960).
130 IT 1819, II-1 CB 73, which was declared obsolete by Rev Rul 71–498, 1971–2 CB 434.
131 *Frank Lyon Co v US* 435 US 561 (US 1978).
132 Treas Reg §1.453–1(b)(3), 26 USCS 453.
133 *Tombari v Commissioner* 299 F2d 889 (9th Cir 1962); 35 TC 250 (TC 1960).
134 The concept of "qualifying indebtedness" generally includes debts relating to the asset, such as: a mortgage or other debt that is secured by the asset, and any other debt which is not secured by the asset, but which the buyer assumes the debt as relating to the asset purchased.
135 The term "related parties" is defined in IRC§1239(b), 26 USCS 1239 as follows:

"(1) a person and all entities which are controlled entities with respect to such person,
(2) a taxpayer and any trust in which such taxpayer (or his spouse) is a beneficiary, unless such beneficiary's interest in the trust is a remote contingent interest (within the meaning of section 318(a)(3)(B)(i) [26 USCS § 318(a)(3)(B)(i)]), and
(3) Except in the case of a sale or exchange in satisfaction of a pecuniary bequest, an executor of an estate and a beneficiary of such estate".

136 See our discussion in para 2.3.3.
137 *Sam W Emerson Co v Commissioner* 37 TC 1063, 1068 (TC 1962); and *Fort Pitt Bridge Works v Commissioner* 24 BTA 626, 641 (BTA 1931).
138 Notice 89–15, 1989–1 CB 634, Q&A-19.
139 Notice 89–15, ibid, Q&A-40.
140 IRC § 460(b)(2), 26 USCS 460.
141 IRC § 460(b)(4), 26 USCS 460.
142 Treas Reg § 1.451–3(d), 26 USCS 451.
143 *Atkinson Co of California v Commissioner* 82 TC 275 (TC 1984).
144 Treas Reg § 1.451–3(d)(5)(i)(ii), 26 USCS 451.
145 Treas Reg § 1.451–3(d), 26 USCS 451.
146 IRC § 454(b), 26 USCS 454.
147 For other statutory adjustments in the US federal Tax Acts departing from GAAP, see, e.g., IRC§174, which provides specific tax accounting rules with regard to research and experimental expenditures; IRC§175, which provides for specific accounting rules in relation to expenses expended by an agriculturalist for soil or water conservation; IRC§451(d), with regard to insurance

proceeds received by the taxpayer reporting on a cash basis for damages; and IRC§451(e), which provides for specific accounting rules with regard to the sale of livestock due to drought or flood. See also Treas Reg 1.446–1–1.446–4 and Treas Reg § 1.447–1.

148 Treas Reg § 1.446–1(c)(1)(iv), 26 USCS 446.
149 Treas Reg § 1.446–1(c)(1)(iv)(b), 26 USCS 446.
150 Treas Reg § 1.446–1(c)(2)(ii), 26 USCS 446.
151 *Sea Shipping Co Inc v Commissioner* 1 TC 30 (TC 1942).
152 *Central R Co of New Jersey v Commissioner* 35 BTA 501 (BTA 1937).
153 *Pierce Ditching Co v Commissioner* 73 TC 301 (TC 1979).
154 *Pierce Ditching*, ibid.
155 On the term "true and fair view" in the UK tax system, see paras 4.3.1.1 and 4.3.2.
156 *Helvering v Schimmel* 114 F2d 554 (8th Cir 1940).
157 *Adams v Commissioner* 155 F2d 246 (3rd Cir 1946); and *Bazley v Commissioner* 332 US 752 (1947).
158 *Peninsula Steel Products and Equipment Co v Commissioner* 78 TC 1029, 1047 (TC 1982).
159 *Muhleman v Hoey* 124 F2d 414 (2nd Cir 1942).
160 *Fischer v Commissioner* 14 TC 792 (TC 1950); and *Madigan v Commissioner* 43 BTA 549 (BTA 1941).
161 Ibid.
162 *Moran v Commissioner* 67 F2d 601 (1st Cir 1933); 26 BTA 1154 (BTA 1932).
163 *Sowell v Commissioner* 302 F2d 177 (5th Cir 1962); and *Cohen v Commissioner* 39 TC 1055 (TC 1963).
164 *Tufts v Commissioner* 6 TC 217 (TC 1946).
165 *Carter v Commissioner* 40 TC 654 (TC 1980).
166 Rev Rul 70–331, 1970–1 CB 15.
167 *Lavery v Commissioner* 158 F2d 859 (7th Cir 1946).
168 *Bright v US* 926 F2d 383 (5th Cir 1991).
169 *Lavery*, Chapter 4, n 167.
170 *Bright*, Chapter 4, n 168; *Kahler v Commissioner* 18 TC 31 (TC 1952).
171 *Fischer*, Chapter 4, n 160.
172 *Bones v Commissioner* 4 TC 415 (TC 1944).
173 *Boutire v Commissioner* 36 F3d 1361 (5th Cir 1994).
174 *Commissioner v Adams* 54 F2d 228 (1st Cir 1931).
175 *Commissioner v Fox* 218 F2d 347 (3rd Cir 1955).
176 *William Hardy Inc v Commissioner* 82 F2d 249 (2nd Cir 1936).
177 *Commissioner v Security Flour Mills Co* 135 F2d 165 (10th Cir 1943).
178 See para 2.3.2.
179 As we have seen in our discussion in para 4.3.1.
180 As we have seen in para 4.4.1.4.
181 *Frank's Casing Crew and Rental Tools v Commissioner* TC Memo 1996–413 (US Tax Court Memos 1996).
182 This deviation will be dealt with at length in para 7.3.
183 *Reuben H Donnelley Corp v US* 257 F Supp 747 (SDNY 1966).
184 *Campana Corp v Commissioner* 210 F2d 897 (7th Cir 1954).
185 *Key Homes Inc v Commissioner* 271 F2d 280 (6th Cir 1959).
186 *Cloverleaf Creamery Co Inc v Davis* 97 F Supp 121 (ND Ala 1951).
187 *US v Safety Car Heating & Lighting Co* 297 US 88 (US 1936).
188 See para 2.3.2.
189 *New Hampshire Fire Ins Co v Commissioner* 2 TC 708 (TC 1943).
190 *Clifton Mfg Co v Commissioner* 137 F2d 290 (4th Cir 1943).
191 *Hunt v Commissioner* TC Memo 1989–335 (US Tax Court Memos 1989).

192 That will be discussed at length in para 6.3.2.1.
193 Like other types of income, taxpayers who report for tax purposes according to the accrual basis method recognize, according to GAAP, capital gains, according to the realization principle and to the earned requirement, when the taxpayer's right to receive the income from the sale of the asset from the purchaser arises, subject to material restrictions not being imposed over the taxpayer's right, see in this connection para 2.3 and *Kaufman v Commissioner* TC Memo 1964–127 (US Tax Court Memos 1964). Nonetheless, transactions exist in which payment of the consideration in respect of the asset sold is deferred to a later date and, as a result, the value of the asset sold is not quantifiable or estimable on the date of the sale. The Open Transaction Doctrine is designed to solve problems of this kind, in that it enables the taxpayer to impute the future consideration that will be received by the taxpayer firstly to the cost of the asset, as existed in his hands, so that all of the surplus above the cost of the asset will be regarded as profit in the hands of the taxpayer. This doctrine was first developed in *Burnet v Logan* 283 US 404 (US 1931). In that case, the taxpayer held shares in a mining company from 1 March 1913 to 11 March 1916. On 11 March 1916, the shareholders of the company sold their holdings to another corporation for cash and future consideration that would be paid to the shareholders according to the mine's business results. The future payments were made in 1917, 1918 and 1919, and the taxpayer, who reported his income according to the cash basis, argued that the monies that had been received by him would not constitute his income until the date on which the consideration received from the mining of the quarry reached the cost of the shares that had been sold by him. The court in that case ruled that, as it was not possible to determine with reasonable certainty the market value of the parties' bargain with regard to the future consideration that would derive from the quarry's profits, the income from the sale of the shares would not be recognized to the extent that the revenues that were received did not exceed the cost of the taxpayer's shares as it existed on 1 March 1913. It appears that the application of this doctrine is limited to those cases in which the value of the transaction is not absolutely quantifiable, and it is not practicable to cases in which it is possible to apply IRC§453 (which was discussed in para 4.4.1.4), which lays down a special arrangement for transactions in which the consideration is received in installments.
194 That will be discussed at length in para 5.3.1.4.
195 That will be discussed at length in para 6.3.2.
196 With respect to the determination of tax accounting in the US as regards the timing of the recognition of expenses and the deviation thereof from GAAP, see para 7.3.
197 Geier, Chapter 3, n 35, at p 20.
198 *Garth v Commissioner* 56 TC 610, 619 (TC 1971).
199 Ibid, at pp 619–23.
200 *Public Service Co v Commissioner* 78 TC 445, 456 (TC 1982).
201 L. Stuart, "The Taxation of Economic Reality: The Role of Anti Abuse Rules in Tax Administration", 431 Pli/Tax 1215, 1227 (1998).
202 *Fort Howard Paper Co v Commissioner* 49 TC 275, 286–7 (TC 1967).
203 *Pierce Ditching*, Chapter 4, n 153, at p 306.
204 *Public Service*, Chapter 4, n 200.
205 See para 4.3.1 regarding the legislative change in 2002 in s 42, FA 1998.
206 *Caldwell v Commissioner* 202 F2d 112 (2nd Cir 1953).
207 *Asphalt Products Co v Commissioner* 796 F2d 843 (6th Cir 1989).
208 *Osterloh v Lucas* 37 F2d 277, 278 (9th Cir 1930).

209 *Glenn v Kentucky Color and Chemical Co* 186 F2d 975 (6th Cir 1951).
210 *Fong v Commissioner* TC Memo 1984–402 (US Tax Court Memos 1984).
211 *Electric Controls and Service Co. Inc. v Commissioner*, TC Memo 1996–486 (US Tax Court Memos 1996).
212 *Franklin County Distilling Co v Commissioner* 125 F2d 800 (6th Cir 1942).
213 The Supreme Court in *Security Flour Mills Co v Commissioner* 321 US 281 (US 1944); and for the court of appeals ruling see Chapter 4, n 177.
214 *Commissioner v Blaine, Mackay, Lee Co* 141 F2d 201 (3rd Cir 1944).
215 *Hallmark Cards Inc v Commissioner* 90 TC 26 (TC 1988).
216 *Collegiate Cap & Gown Co v Commissioner* TC Memo 1978–226 (US Tax Court Memos 1978); see also Rev Rul 86–35, 1986–1 CB 218.
217 *Key Homes*, Chapter 4, n 185.
218 See, e.g. *Highland Farms v Commissioner* 106 TC 237 (TC 1996).
219 See paras 2.3 and 2.4.
220 *Caldwell*, Chapter 4, n 206.
221 *Asphalt Products*, Chapter 4, n 207.
222 *Franklin County*, Chapter 4, n 212.
223 *Kahuku Plantation Co v Commissioner* 132 F2d 671 (9th Cir 1942).
224 *Koehring Co v US* 190 Ct Cl 898 (Ct Cl 1970).
225 *Resale Mobile Homes Inc v Commissioner* 965 F2d 818 (10th Cir 1992).
226 *Reading and Bates Corp v US* 40 Fed. C1 (Fed CL 1998).
227 *Key Homes*, Chapter 4, n 185.
228 See, e.g. *Grays Harbor Motorship Corp v US* 71 Ct Cl 167 (Ct Cl 1930); *Lomas & Nettleton Financial Corp v US* 486 F Supp 652 (ND Tex 1980); *Lynn L Smith v Commissioner* TC Memo 1983–472 (US Tax Court Memos 1983); *National Bank of Fort Banning v US* 79–2 USTC P9627 (MD Ga 1979); and *WW Enterprises Inc v Commissioner* TC Memo 1985–313 (US Tax Court Memos 1985).
229 Dubroff, Chail and Norris, Chapter 2, n 60, at pp 363–4; and Eric M. Jensen, "The Deductions of Future Liabilities by Accrual-Basis Taxpayers: Premature Accruals, the All Events Test, and Economic Performance", 37 U Fla L Rev 443, 445 (1985).
230 *Commissioner v Hansen* 360 US 446 (US 1959).
231 *Becker v US* 21 F2d 1003 (5th Cir 1927).
232 *Hygienic Products Co v Commissioner* 111 F2d 330 (6th Cir 1940); *Hansen*, Chapter 4, n 230.
233 *Zimmerman Steel Co v Commissioner* 130 F2d 1011 (8th Cir 1942); and *Burck v Commissioner* 533 F2d 768 (2nd Cir 1976).
234 *Ferrill v Commissioner* 684 F2d 261 (3rd Cir 1982).
235 *Thomas v Commissioner* 92 TC 206 (TC 1989).
236 *Dunn v US* 468 F Supp 991 (SDNY 1979); *Owens v Commissioner* 568 F2d 1233 (6th Cir 1977); and *Thomas*, Chapter 4, n 235.
237 *Tog Shop v US* 916 F2d 720 (11th Cir 1990); and *Thor*, Chapter 3, n 5, at p 532.
238 *St Paul Union Depot Co v Commissioner* 123 F2d 235 (8th Cir 1941); and *Hamilton Industries Inc and others v Commissioner* 97 TC 120 (TC 1991).
239 *Thor*, Chapter 3, n 5, at p 533; and *Root*, n 112, at pp 110–14.
240 See, e.g. *Dana Distributors Inc v Commissioner* 874 F2d 120 (2nd Cir 1989); *Knight-Ridder Newspapers Inc v US* 743 F2d 781 (11th Cir 1984); *Michael Drazen v Commissioner* 34 TC 1070 (TC 1960); *Reco Industries Inc v Commissioner*, 83 TC 912 (TC 1984); and *RCA Corp v US* 664 F2d 881 (2nd Cir 1981).
241 For a different opinion, see *Mulholland v US* 28 Fed Cl 320 (Ct Cl 1993), where it was said that the court's power to examine the actions of IRS is not limited merely to "abuse of discretion", the court does have the power to examine the matter from scratch (on de novo review) and the court is also entitled to rely

on additional evidence to examine whether the accounting method used by the taxpayer in keeping his books indeed properly reflects his income.

242 Francis M. Allegra, "Section 482: Manning the Contours of the Abuse of Discretion Standard of Judicial Review", 13 Va Tax Rev 423, 481–2 (1994).

243 *Thor*, Chapter 3, n 5, at pp 538–9; and Root, Chapter 4, n 112, at pp 102–3.

244 *Fruehauf Corp v Commissioner* 356 F2d 975 (6th Cir 1966).

245 Ibid.

246 *Cross Oil Co v Commissioner* TC Memo 2001–126 (US Tax Court Memos 2001).

247 *Stephens Marine Inc v Commissioner* 430 F2d 679 (9th Cir 1970).

248 *Austin v Commissioner* TC Memo 1997–157 (US Tax Court Memos 1997); *RCA*, Chapter 4, n 240; and *Ansley-Sheppard-Burgess Co v Commissioner* 104 TC 367 (TC 1995).

249 *US v Catto et al.* 384 US 102 (US 1966).

250 *Russell v Commissioner* 45 F2d 100 (1st Cir 1930).

251 *North American Coal Corp v Commissioner* 97 F2d 325 (6th Cir 1938).

252 *Franklin County*, Chapter 4, n 212.

253 Root, Chapter 4, n 112, at p 114. According to Root, the solution must be to allow a broader judicial review of decisions of the authorities according to IRC§446(b) by raising the standard of the review from a check on whether the decision was unlawful only, to a review standard of intervention and reversal of the decision; also in cases where the decision, while lawful, was erroneous.

254 For example, in *Hughes v Commissioner* 476 US 593, 602–3 (US 1986), in addressing one of the basic principles of GAAP, the Supreme Court took the trouble to explain: "Proper financial accounting and acceptable tax account-ing, to be sure, are not the same . . . the Commissioner may impose a method that does clearly reflect income . . . the Commissioner has broad discretion, that financial accounting does not control for tax purposes, and that the mere desirability of matching expenses with income will not necessarily sustain a taxpayer's deduction."

255 *Brown v Helvering* 291 US 193 (US 1934).

256 *London Butte Gold Mines v Commissioner* 116 F2d 478 (10th Cir 1940).

257 *South Date Farms Inc v Commissioner* 138 F2d 818 (5th Cir 1943).

258 *Dixie Pine Products Co v Commissioner* 320 US 516 (US 1944).

259 *Security Flour*, Chapter 4, n 213.

260 *DD Oil Co v Commissioner* 147 F2d 936 (5th Cir Tex 1945).

261 *Capital Warehouse Co v Commissioner* 171 F2d 395 (8th Cir 1948).

262 *US v Consolidated Edison Co* 366 US 380 (6th Cir 1960).

263 *Prichard Funeral Home Inc v Commissioner* TC Memo 1962–259 (US Tax Court Memos 1962).

264 *Hagen Advertising Displays Inc v Commissioner* 407 F2d 1105 (6th Cir 1969).

265 *Lincoln Electric Co v Commissioner* 444 F2d 491 (6th Cir 1971).

266 *Burck*, Chapter 4, n 233.

267 *US v General Dynamics Corp* 481 US 239 (US 1987) (*"GD"*).

268 *Frank's Casing Crew*, Chapter 4, n 181.

269 *Cleveland Trencher Company v Commissioner* 1998 US App LEXIS 26043 (6th Cir 1998).

270 For other cases in which GAAP has been rejected for tax purposes on the ground that it does not properly reflect the income, see, e.g. *Electric & Neon Inc v Commissioner* 56 TC 1324 (TC 1971); *Jiminez v Commissioner* 496 F2d 876 (5th Cir 1974); *Streight Radio, & Television, Inc v Commissioner* 280 F2d 883 (7th Cir 1960); and *Continental Illinois Corp v Commissioner* 998 F2d 513 (7th Cir 1993).

271 See, e.g. paras 5.3.2 and 6.3.3. These directives have been exploited more than once, in light of this case, specifically in order to determine "pseudo" GAAP

standards, and not merely because the case law that has evolved from case to case, from an *ad hoc* accounting standpoint, has created such absolute uncertainty and gross deviation from GAAP to the extent that it is actually IRS, in its various directives, which has been required on occasions to "pull back" the tax laws in the direction of GAAP.

272 Dubroff, Chail and Norris, Chapter 2, n 60, p 359, n 57 and p 389, n 66.
273 Ibid, at pp 404–6.
274 For other support of the Singular Doctrine, see AICPA, "Conformity of Tax and Financial Accounting", 132 JA 75 (1971); and Walter C. Cliff and Philip J. Levine, "Interest and Accrual and the Time Value of Money", 34 Am UL Rev 107, 113–18 (1984).
275 Geier, Chapter 3, n 35, at pp 22–3.
276 Geier, ibid pp 25–6.
277 Geier, ibid p 91.
278 Geier, ibid pp 95–6. On this matter, see also Gunn, Coplan and Johnson in para 7.3.4.
279 Geier, ibid p 145.
280 Geier, ibid.
281 Silk, Chapter 4, n 8, at p 1652.
282 In the original draft of the 1913 Act, the underlying basis of tax laws rests on the cash basis method. Under Revenue Act 1916, Ch 463, ss 8(g) (individuals) and 13(d) (corporations), 39 Stat 756, 763, 771 (1916), the legislator was willing "to accommodate" firms that keep their books on a GAAP basis to use for tax purposes not the cash basis method, but that same reporting method that was being used by them for accounting purposes.
283 Gunn, Chapter 3, n 5, at pp 18–22.
284 Coplan, Chapter 3, n 27, at pp 405–11.
285 Kleinrock, Chapter 4, n 12, sec 501.4.
286 Ibid, sec 505.3.
287 Johnson, Chapter 3, n 27, at pp 401–5.
288 *Eisner v Macomber* 252 US 189, 207 (1920) (holding stock dividend not taxable); see also *Edwards v Cuba RR* 268 US 628 (1925) (holding government subsidy not taxed because not earned); Sol Op 132, I-1 CB 92 (1922) (reversing prior position, service ruled recoveries under suits for slander or libel of personal nature and for alienation of affection are not income because they are not derived from labor, capital or both).
289 *Commissioner v Glenshaw Glass Co* 348 US 426, 431 (US 1955) (holding punitive damages taxable).
290 On the principle of conservatism or prudence, see para 2.1.
291 Johnson, Chapter 3, n 27, at p 404.
292 Ibid.
293 For statutory adjustments in the UK Tax Acts that prescribe in special transactions accounting treatment for tax purposes that deviates from GAAP, see para 4.3.1.2.
294 For statutory adjustments in the US Tax Acts that prescribe in special transactions accounting treatment for tax purposes that deviates from GAAP, see para 4.4.1.5.
295 The Income Tax Ordinance (New Version), 5721–1961 (**ITO**).
296 For statutory adjustments in Israeli Tax Acts departing from GAAP, see para 4.5.1.2.
297 Although according to Income Tax (Bookkeeping Management) Regulations, 5733–1973 combined with the VAT (Bookkeeping Management) Regulations, 5736–1976 ("**the Bookkeeping Management Regulations**"), taxpayers of various classes have been obliged (mainly according to the type of the branch,

size and existence of stock) to maintain books for tax purposes in certain ways. Nonetheless, this bookkeeping management has not been construed as binding for timing recognition of income and expenses.

298 A. Namdar, *Tax Law (the Substantial Law)* (Hoshen Le'Mishpat, Tel Aviv, 1985), p 258; and Y. Edrey and A. Dotan, "Taxation of Rental in Advance in Income Tax", Legal Research D (1986) 79, 81.

299 Such as s 25, ITTOIA 2005.

300 Such as IRC§446.

301 In the past, within the scope of Bill No 69, sec 24 was included, according to which the accrual basis method will be the default for reporting for tax purposes as long as it has not been stated to the contrary in legislation. However, this bill did not become law.

302 s 131(c) of the ITO and Income Tax (Reports and Additional Reports by a Body of Persons) Regulations, 5724–1963.

303 The Income Tax (Adjustments by Reason of Inflation) Law, 5745–1985.

304 The Income Tax (Adjustments by Reason of Inflation) Law, ibid; this statute has been abolished as of 2008 for reasons that are not relevant to the specific provision relating to this study.

305 Income Tax Ordinance Bill (No 166) (On Application of International Financial Reporting Standards – Temporary Provision for the 2007 and 2008 Fiscal Years), 5768–2008.

306 For Israeli Accounting Standard No 29, see Chapter 2, n 4.

307 The maximum marginal tax rate in 2008.

308 The assumption is that taxpayers who create income to which the section applies report to the tax authorities on the cash basis method.

309 Note that this section, after 2003, lost its relevance almost completely since in that fiscal year the tax rates applicable to capital gains were limited to rates significantly lower than the marginal rates applying to individuals.

310 According to Income Tax Appeal (**ITA**) (TA) 62/85 *Kiriat Yehudit Industrial Section Ltd v Accessing Officer for Large Enterprises (**AOLE**)*, 14 PDA 24, this section applies to income from rent of its various kinds, whether it can be classified as passive income according to sec 2(6) of the ITO or as an active (business) income according to s 2(1) of the ITO.

311 Section 17 of the ITO provides: "For the purpose of ascertaining the chargeable income of any person there shall be deducted all outgoings and expenses wholly and exclusively incurred during the tax year by such person in the production of the income, including . . ."

312 ITA (J) 29/79 *Jerusalem Central Printing Ltd v Jerusalem Assessing Officer* 5741(a) Tax Cases 45, and Supreme Court Appeal ("**CA**") 510/80 *Jerusalem Assessing Officer v Central Printing, Publishing Company Ltd* 36(4) PD 589.

313 The Land Taxation (Appreciation and Purchase) Law, 5723–1963.

314 Part E (sec 88–105) of the ITO.

315 For other statutory adjustments in the ITO departing from GAAP, see, e.g. s 3(b) of ITO, (which creates "income" from the forgiveness of debts); s 85 of ITO (which creates "income" from the sale of business stock even if this has not been realized in a case where the stock belongs to a business that has ceased to operate, or has been transferred to be used as fixed property and the like); s 100 of ITO (which regards fixed assets and investments as if they had been sold if the designation thereof is other than stock); and so on.

316 CA 494/87 *Hashomrim Group Safety and Security Ltd v Assessing Officer (TA3)* Taxes (October 1992), E-54.

317 Ibid, at p E-57.

318 Ibid, at p E-69; and, to quote: "The Ordinance does not provide when income

is to be regarded as earned or accrued. The timing is the result of the account-ing methods according to which the return is made."

319 CA 190/58 *Assessing Officer TA3 v Nakid Company Ltd* 13 PD 1453.

320 *Central Printing, Publishing Company*, Chapter 4, n 312, at p 594.

321 CA 57/79 *Haifa Assessing Officer v Israeli Shipyards Ltd* 11 PDA 49, 54.

322 ITA (TA) 176/82 *Moshe Ginzburg Ltd v Assessing Officer TA1*, Taxes (January 1987), E-117.

323 ITA (H) 138/87 *Tambour Ltd v Haifa Assessing Officer* 16 PDA 163.

324 See, e.g. CA 860/75 *Isranil Ltd. v Assessing Officer TA3*, 31(2) PD 729; CA 600/75 *Tel Ronnen Contractors and Builders Ltd v AOLE*, 9 PDA86; CA 5024/90 *Bohadana v Customs and VAT Director* Taxes (August 1993), E-62, E-66; ITA (TA) 1067/99 *Barr v Assessing Officer TA4* Taxes (February 2002), E-245; ITA (TA) 539/81 *Zuckerman v Kfar Saba Assessing Officer* 12 PDA 167; and ITA (TA) 1278/02 *Car Fruit Holon Ltd v Assessing Officer TA3*, Taxes (December 2005), E-143.

325 ITA (H) 129/91 *Dumbo Ltd v Haifa Assessing Officer* 21 PDA 507; here, the district court accepted the view that in light of the legislation's silence on the point, the taxpayer should be allowed to file income tax returns based on the "cash basis" despite the fact that it was a company that carried out work and repairs with regard to gas and oil systems, and maintained inventory for the purpose of that work. The court held that the tax authorities are under a duty to prove that companies of this kind are bound to prepare reports on an accrual basis (i.e. according to GAAP), and having failed to discharge that burden of proof, there was nothing to prevent reporting on the cash basis as being the "admission ticket" for purposes of the tax laws.

326 ITA (TA) 171/81 *Raznitzki v Assessing Officer TA3*, 12 PDA 455; here the district court ruled that there is nothing to stop a firm that "for its own purposes" keeps its books on the accrual basis method (whether or not it is required to do so) from reporting on a cash basis method for tax purposes, as long as it is not prohibited from doing so by law.

327 We would note that it is doubtful if it is possible to use these district court cases as a basis for drawing far-reaching conclusions relating to firms that have stock that is not just "materials" or "stock of work in progress".

328 ITA (TA) 181/84 *Gil Bernstein v Assessing Officer TA4*, 15 PDA 179 (on the subject of depreciation).

329 ITA (TA) 1207/00 *Yaacobi and Sons Ltd v Assessing Officer TA3*, Taxes (October 2003), E-244.

330 ITA (TA) 1009/99 *Pi Glilot Oil Terminals and Pipes Ltd v AOLE* Taxes (June 2005), E-135 (on the subject of defining rent as an income expense or capital expense).

331 CA 7493/98 *Sharon v National Assessing Unit* Taxes (February 2004), E-55 (on the subject of defining "goodwill").

332 For another approach, see ITA (H) 55/91 *Hacharat Ltd v Haifa Assessing Officer* Taxes (December 1992), E-187. Here, on the subject of the classification of "assets" as fixed property or stock, use was made of GAAP to "make up the deficiency" for purposes also of classification required for tax purposes.

333 ITA (TA) 43/95 *Israel American Gas Company Ltd v AOLE* Taxes (October 2001), E-96 (**the third *Amisragas case***").

334 CA 6557/01 and CA 9391/01 *American Israeli Gas Company Ltd & Pazgas Marketing Company Ltd v AOLE* Taxes (December 2006), E-1 (**the *Amisragas-Pazgas case***").

335 Despite of the fact that ITA has not been granted the statutory powers that were granted to IRS, such as those contained in IRC§446(b).

336 Israel Income Tax Circular (hereinafter "**IITC**") 39/93.

337 IITC 12/94.
338 IITC 12/2003, this instruction was made on the ground that it is inconceivable that the same accountant who audited the company's financial accounts and believed that GAAP requires it to report on an accrual basis method would sign a tax return on a cash basis method that is contrary to GAAP.
339 Namdar, Chapter 4, n 298, at p 258.
340 A. Raphael and Y. Mehulall, *Income Tax Laws*, vol 1 (5th edn, Shocken Publishing, Jerusalem and Tel Aviv, 1995), p 576.
341 A. Witkon and Y. Neeman, *Tax Laws* (4th edn, Shocken, 1969), p 118.
342 Y. Strauss, "On Accounting Principles and the Income Tax Ordinance Rules", 18 the Accountant 135 (1968).
343 See, e.g. M. Shekel, "Reporting Methods: Accrual or Cash, Response to Circular 12/2003", 328 Yeda Le'Meida 23 (January 2004); A. Raphael and D. Ephrati, *Income Tax Laws, vol 1* (Shocken Publishing, Jerusalem and Tel Aviv, 1984), pp 574–6; A. Klimovski, "Accounting Rules and Legal Principles in Income Tax Laws", Tax Quarterly 424 (December 1965); Y. Witkon, "Income Tax Cases and Accounting Principles", 15 the Accountant 5 (1965); H.S. Lovenberg, "Accounting Principles and Income Tax Laws in Caselaw", 18 the Accountant 125 (1968); but A. Rosenberg, "Advance Income – Why is the Tax Liability for Reporters on an Accrual basis", Taxes (September 1989), A-45–48, supporting the Consistent Selective Approach by stating that GAAP may be deviated from with regard to all aspects of the taxation of advance payments.
344 For the Principle of Proportionality, see S. H. Bice, "Rationality Analysis in Constitutional Law", 65 Minn L Rev 1 (1980); Robert F. Nagel, "Rationalism in Constitutional Law", 4 Constitutional Commentary 9 (1987); in US case law: *Widmar v Vincent* 454 US 263 (US 1981); *Craig v Boren* 429 US 190 (US 1976); in Canadian case law: *R v Oakes* [1986] 1 SCR 103.
345 For a discussion regarding the application of the Proportionality Principle in the UK, see *R v Secretary of State for the Home Department* (2001) 3 All ER 433. This case not only outlines the key features of the Proportionality Principle and illustrates its application in a concrete case, but there is also some discussion of how it departs from the unreasonableness test.
346 See, in Canada, *R v Edwards Books and Art* [1986] 2 SCR 713.
347 See, in Canada, *R v Vaillancourt* [1987] 2 SCR 636; *Rocket v Royal College of Dental Surgeons* [1990] 2 SCR 232.
348 See, in Canada, *Oakes*, Chapter 4, n 344.
349 For the Proportionality Principle and the tests mentioned above, see also A. Barak, *Interpretation in Law, vol 3, Constitutional Interpretation* (Nevo Publishing, Tel Aviv, 1994), p 536.
350 For the definitions of these questions, see Chapter 1.
351 As regards to the Collection Question, see para 4.6.3.1.
352 See, e.g. the Macdonald-Martin Committee No 4, Chapter 3, n 4, paras 4.1.2 and 4.3.4; and Klein, Chapter 3, n 23, paras 4.1.2 and 6.3.4.
353 IASB Framework, Chapter 2, n 9, sec 13 (the IASB Framework "justifying" this disadvantage by the fact that accounting principles describe in the main the financial results of past events, and do not necessarily supply non-financial data).
354 McCullers and Schroeder, Chapter 2, n 15, at pp 2–3 and 12–13, saying that accepted accounting principles "do not mean that GAAP is based on what is most appropriate or reasonable in a given situation but simply that the practice represents a consensus".
355 John E. Hilsenrath, "On the Books, More Fact and Less Fiction", NY Times, 16 February 1997, § 3, at pp 1 and 5.

356 Hilsenrath, ibid.

357 Thomas F. Keller and Stephen A. Zeff, *Financial Accounting Theory II* (New York, USA, McGraw Hill Book Company, 1969), p 3.

358 Thus, e.g. AICPA, "The Code of Professional Ethics" (http://www.aicpa.org/about/code/et_203.html#et), in Rule 203 states that, in the absence of a clear accounting directive and unusual circumstances, a departure from GAAP can be made in practice, and this necessarily leaves a broad margin for improvisation.

359 See para 3.1.

360 Ibid.

361 See, e.g. measuring of provisions in para 2.4.1.

362 See para 2.6.

363 See, e.g. Gunn, paras 4.1.1 and 4.4.4; and Coplan, paras 4.1.1 and 4.4.4.

364 See, e.g. Johnson, para 4.4.4; Kleinrock, para 4.4.4; and Geier, para 7.3.4.

365 See, e.g. Johnson, paras 4.1.1 and 4.4.4; and Geier, paras 3.2, 7.3.4 and 6.3.4.

366 See, e.g. Gunn, paras 4.1.1 and 4.4.4; and Klein, paras 4.1.2 and 6.3.4.

367 See in the beginning of this Chapter 4.

368 As defined in Chapter 1.

369 *Thor*, Chapter 3, n 5.

370 This being either in order to extend their power in relation to the non-acceptance of reports prepared according to GAAP, or in order to achieve an interpretation that advocates measuring the income in a manner that advances recognition of the income or defers recognition of the expenses. See, e.g. para 4.4.2.

371 This assumption of itself is not immune to criticism, and is worthy of separate study.

372 See para 3.1.4.

373 See para 3.1.5.

374 It is sufficient if we show the gamut of the various conflicting tests that have been adopted in US case law in relation to the classification of deposits (see para 5.3.1) or the various conflicting approaches relating to the timing of the recognition of liabilities as an expense (see para 7.3.2) in order to understand that as long as no regulated system is in place for measuring income for tax purposes, following the Dualistic Doctrine will create a lack of uniformity and lack of consistency in the tax laws themselves.

375 Nevertheless, it is worthy of note that, in this context, it seems that Geier's position is otherwise, see paras 3.2 and 4.4.4.

376 For the Haig-Simons' definition of "income", see para 3.1.1 and Chapter 3, n 11.

377 For the definition of "income" in GAAP, see IASB Framework, Chapter 2, n 9, sec 70(b), and para 2.2.

378 Young K. Kwon, "Accrual versus cash-basis accounting methods: An agency-theoretic comparison", 8 Journal of Accounting and Public Policy 4 (winter 1989), pp 267–81.

379 Tim Berry, "Q&A: Cash basis vs. accrual accounting", http://www.allbusiness.com/business-planning-structures/business-plans/4353766-1.html.

380 Glenn P. Schwartz, "How many trades must a trader make to be in the trading business?" 22 Va Tax Rev 395, 441 (winter 2003) (citing the Staff of Joint Common Taxation, 105th Cong).

381 See, e.g. *Burck*, Chapter 4, n 233, at p 769; and Coplan, Chapter 3, n 27, at p 411, n 166.

382 Melissa Bushman, "Cash Basis Versus Accrual Basis Accounting", http://www.associatedcontent.com/user/38548/ Melissa_bushman.html.

383 Regarding this argument, see also The Macdonald-Martin Committee No 4,

in paras 4.1.2 and 4.3.4; Klein, in paras 4.1.2 and 6.3.4 infra; Dubroff, Chail and Norris, in para 4.4.4; Root, Chapter 4, n 112, at pp 80–3; Richard M. Lipton, "We Have Met the Enemy and He is us: More Thoughts on Hyper Lexis", 47 Tax L Rev 1, 1–2 (1993); and Linda A. Schwartzstein, "Smoke and Mirrors: Tax Legislation Uncertainty and Entrepreneurship", 6 Cornel J. L. and Pub Pol'y 61, 62 (1996).

384 Regarding administrative convenience, see the Macdonald-Martin Committee No 4, in paras 4.1.2 and 4.3.4; Klein, in paras 4.1.2 and 6.3.4; Gunn, in paras 4.1.1 and 6.3.4; and Coplan, in paras 4.1.1 and 4.4.4.

385 As we said in para 4.1.3, according to the Consistent Approach deviation from GAAP by means of legislation (but only by means of legislation) is not precluded.

386 As mentioned in para 4.6.3.2.

387 As explained in para 4.6.3.1.

388 For these tax values, see para 3.1.

389 See para 2.6.

390 As defined in Chapter 1.

391 As we will see in Chapter 8.

5 Timing of recognition of income from deposits

1 B. Bittker and L. Lokken, *Federal Taxation of Income Estates and Gifts*, vol 2 (Boston: Warren, Gorham and Lamont, 1989), sec 5.2 at 5–17; *Matarese v Commissioner* TC Memo 1975–184 (US Tax Court Memos 1975); Glen A. Kohl, "The Identification Theory of Basis", 40 Tax L Rev 623, 634 (1985); and William D. Popkin, "The Taxation of Borrowing", 56 Ind LJ 43 (1980).

2 See para 2.5.1.

3 For alternative approaches, see Chapter 8.

4 Although one may reach the conclusion that a deposit is equal to a loan according to s 56, ICTA 1988 dealing with certificates of deposit.

5 s 18, ICTA 1988.

6 s 87, FA 1996 relates to financial debts (except for debts for sales or services) on cheap conditions between connected parties, which are repayable on demand. As regards deposits to which this study relates, even if it is a deposit granted on favorable repayment terms (from the standpoint of the recipient of the deposit), this provision has no relevance with regard to a deposit between non-related parties. See CFM15209, and as to the definition of "connected" parties for purposes of s 87, FA 1996, see CFM5600–CFM5616.

7 *Morley v Messrs Tattersall* (1938) 22 TC 51.

8 *Jay's the Jewellers Ltd v CIR* (1947) 29 TC 274.

9 *Elson v Prices Tailors Ltd* [1963] 1 All ER 231; 40 TC 671.

10 See para 6.2.1.

11 *Anise Ltd v Hammond* (2003) SSCD 258 (Sp C 364).

12 *Prices Tailors*, ibid.

13 BIM31110 summarizes the tax law in the UK in connection with deposits simply, briefly and clearly, and we can do no better than repeat it here: "When a deposit is received the business will not have carried out the actions necessary to earn the money. This applies whether or not the deposit will be forfeited if the transaction is not carried through. The deposit should be recognized either when the good or services are provided or when it is reasonably certain that no good or services will ever be provided and the deposit will be forfeited".

14 See, e.g. BIM56420, stating that in a case where lease rentals are secured by a

security deposit, then "it should be remembered that interest on that deposit is likely to arise over the lease period, so that any provision should normally be limited to the 'capital repayment' element of the payments under the finance lease."

15 For example, *Helvering v Clifford* 309 US 331, 334 (US 1940).

16 IRC§61 implicitly refers to "income", "gain" and other items that would increase the taxpayer wealth. See also A. Eid, "Tax–Free Security: Federal Income Taxation of Customer Deposits After Commissioner v Indianapolis Power and Light Co 110 S.CT 589 (1990)", 66 Wash L Rev 267, 268 (1991).

17 See Bittker and Lokken, Chapter 5, n 1, sec 5.2 at 5–17, and Eid, ibid, at p 268.

18 Bittker and Lokken, ibid, sec 6.1–6.2; William D. Andrews, *Basic Federal Income Taxation* (Aspen Law and Business, 5th ed. 1993), 369; H. Alaghband, "Comment: Abolition of the Completed Contract Method under Fire: A Study in Legislative Compromise", 32 Am U L Rev 1009, 1020 (1983); and Eid, ibid, at p 268.

19 *Al-Halkim v Commissioner* 53 TCM (CCH) 352 (1987).

20 According to IRC§7872, where an interest-free loan is granted, the absence of interest means, in effect, the existence of disguised interest when the economic value reflects possibly a gift, or consideration for services or part of the purchase price, whereas in effect "it is always present", and this disguised interest will be taxable in the hands of the lender and recognized as an expense by the borrower. In the same vein, see in UK tax law: s 87, FA 1996, Chapter 5, n 6, and in the Israeli tax law sections 3(i) and 3(j) of the ITO (Chapter 5, n. 137). None of these statutory provisions was applied with regard to customer's deposits or advances.

21 *US v Ivey* 414 F2d 199, 202–03 (5th Cir 1969) (loan proceeds non-taxable); *Thompson v Commissioner* 322 F2d 122, 129–30 (5th Cir 1963) (stating that because of an obligation to pay back the loan, borrowed funds create no addition to the wealth of the borrower, and upon payment, the debtor cannot deduct the amount paid from income); *Consolidated Hammer Dry Plate & Film Co v Commissioner* 317 F2d 829, 832 (7th Cir 1963); and *Commissioner v Tufts* 461 US 300 (US 1983) (stating that: "When a taxpayer receives a loan, he incurs an obligation to repay that loan at some future date. Because of this obligation, the loan proceeds do not qualify as income to the taxpayer").

22 See *Shuster v Helvering* 121 F2d 643 (2nd Cir 1941); and *Gatlin v Commissioner* 34 BTA 50 (BTA 1936).

23 This question in substance resembles that which arose in the UK in *Messrs Tattersall* (Chapter 5, n 7) and *Jay's Jewellers* (Chapter 5, n 8).

24 *Boston Consol Gas Co v Commissioner* 128 F2d 473 (1st Cir 1942).

25 Boston Consol, at 476; as to the meaning of this difference as regards the classification question, see in this chapter.

26 Ibid.

27 *Commissioner v Langwell Real Estate Corp* 47 F2d 841 (7th Cir 1931).

28 *Warren Service Corp v Commissioner* 110 F2d 723 (2nd Cir 1940).

29 See also Bittker and Lokken, Chapter 5, n 1, para 6.1 at 6–2.

30 *Jay's Jewellers*, Chapter 5, n 8 and para 5.2.1.

31 See BIM31110, and Chapter 5, n 13.

32 See *Messrs Tattersall*, Chapter 5, n 7; and *Anise*, Chapter 5, n 11.

33 See para 6.3.

34 *Warren*, Chapter 5, n 28.

35 *Boston Consol*, Chapter 5, n 24.

36 *Clinton Hotel Realty Corp v Commissioner* 128 F2d 968 (5th Cir 1942).

37 In addition, this amount was to have been refunded to the tenant in the event of the property being destroyed.

38 *Commissioner v Lyon* 97 F2d 70 (9th Cir 1938).
39 Based on the explanation given in para 6.3.2.1, in our opinion, the court in Lyon erred in finding that the *North American Oil* (Chapter 6, n 48) case justified a result whereby an advance on account of income that had yet to be earned was liable to tax on the date it was received.
40 *US v Williams* 395 F2d 508 (5th Cir 1968).
41 Ibid, at p 510.
42 Ibid, at p 511.
43 *Adams v Commissioner* 58 TC 41 (TC 1972), upholding that a mining property lesser who received advances from the lessee which were not evidenced by a note and treated the advances on his books as advance royalties, did not receive a loan but advance payments which were income when received.
44 *Astor Holding Co v Commissioner* 135 F2d 47 (5th Cir 1943).
45 Ibid, at p 50.
46 *Heininger v Commissioner* 133 F2d 567 (7th Cir 1943); in that case, it was held that amounts that were described as "deposits" received by a dentist in connection with the sale of false teeth, and which ought to have been refunded to the client if he was not satisfied, should be regarded as advances taxable on the date they were received, and not as deposits, relying on the fact that those sums had been deposited in the taxpayer's ("ordinary") bank account and he controlled them and could have used them.
47 *Hogle v Commissioner* 132 F2d 66 (10th Cir 1942).
48 *Blum v Higgins* 150 F2d 471 (2nd Cir 1945).
49 *James v US* 366 US 213 (1961).
50 *Estate of Holzwarth v Commissioner* TC Memo 1965–304 (US Tax Court Memos 1965).
51 *Commissioner v First Sec Bank Inc* 405 US 394 (1972).
52 *Hedrick v Commissioner* 154 F2d 90 (2nd Cir 1946); *Gilken Corp v Commissioner* 176 F2d 141 (6th Cir 1949); and *Davis v US* 226 F2d 331 (6th Cir 1955).
53 *Hirsch Improvement Co v Commissioner* 143 F2d 912 (2th Cir 1944).
54 Ibid, at p 915.
55 *Van Wagoner v US* 368 F2d 95 (5th Cir 1966).
56 This relying on the "trilogy" discussed in para 6.3.2.3.
57 *Fairchild v Commissioner* 462 F2d 462 (3rd Cir 1972) (upholding that money advanced to a taxpayer is income where the money is used by him as his own, and if at the time of the receipt he has no intention to make repayment).
58 *In re Point Loma Dev Corp* 1971 US Dist Lexis 14687 (D Cal 1971).
59 See also *New England Tank Industries Inc v Commissioner* 413 F2d 1038 (1st Cir 1969) (holding that without evidence that a loan was intended, advance construction payments (from the US Government) in order to finance the purchase of facilities to be leased to the US were income. The only test that was used was the intention test).
60 *Arlen v Commissioner* 48 TC 640 (TC 1967).
60a *City Gas of Florida Co v Commissioner* 689 F2d 943 (11th Cir 1982).
61 Eid, Chapter 5, n 16, at p 270.
62 Martin J. Burke and Michael K. Friel, "Tax Free Security: Reflections on Indianapolis Power and Light", 12 Rev of Tax'n of Individuals 157, 167 (1989).
63 For example, *Van Wagoner*, Chapter 5, n 55.
64 Eid, Chapter 5, n 16, at p 273.
65 For example, *Arlen*, Chapter 5, n 60.
66 *City Gas of Florida Co v Commissioner* 689 F2d 943 (11th Cir 1982).
67 The trilogy will be discussed in para 6.3.2.3.
68 *City Gas*, ibid; the court disregarded the remaining tests that had previously been proposed, and expressly rejected the control and use test, saying (at

p 945) "where the amount paid is intended to secure property of the taxpayer against damages or loss, or to secure the performance of conditions or other non income-producing covenants of a contract, and the sum is to be returned to the payer, the payment is a nontaxable security deposit, notwithstanding the fact that the taxpayer had temporary use of the money".

69 Ibid, at pp 945–6.

70 Ibid, at pp 946–8. And in the court's words (p 948): "The test to be applied in this case is whether, under all the circumstances, the primary purpose of the payments at issue was prepayment of income items or whether the primary purpose was to secure the performance of non-income producing covenants."

71 IRS in Rev Rul 72–519, 1972–2 CB 32 explained that test as follows: "That is, when the purpose of the deposit is to guarantee the customer's payment of amounts owed to the creditor, such a deposit is treated as an advance payment, but when the purpose of the deposit is to secure a property interest of the taxpayer the deposit is regarded as a true security deposit."

72 See also Dubroff, Chapter 2, n 104, at pp 737–8, stating: "If the primary purpose is security for future performance of general covenants of an agreement (for example, the obligation of lessee to insure the property) or to secure against damage to property, it is nontaxable even though the deposit may, as well, be applied to defaults in payment of income items."

73 *Indianapolis Power & Light Co v Commissioner* 857 F2d 1162 (7th Cir 1988) (*"IPL"*).

74 *IPL*, at p 1170.

75 *Commissioner v Indianapolis Power & Light Co* 493 US 203 (US 1990).

76 *IPL*, at 1168, and in the court's words: "the crucial point is not whether his use of the funds is unconstrained during some interim period. The key is whether the taxpayer has some guarantee that he will be allowed to keep the money."

77 Ibid, and, in the language of the court, in addressing the profit obtained as a result of using the monies of the deposits: "Again, the same could be said of a commercial loan, since, as has been noted, a business is unlikely to borrow unless it believes that it can realize benefits that exceed the cost of servicing the debt. A bank could hardly operate profitably if its earnings on deposits did not surpass its interest obligations; but the deposits themselves are not treated as income. Any income that the utility may earn through use of the deposit money of course is taxable, but the prospect that income will be generated provides no ground taxing 'the principal'." And at p 1171 the court added: "We recognize that IPL derives an economic benefit from these deposits. But a taxpayer does not realize taxable income from every event that improves his economic condition. A customer who makes this deposit reflects no commitment to purchase services, and IPL's right to retain the money is contingent upon events outside its control. We hold that such dominion as IPL has over these customer deposits is insufficient for the deposits to qualify as taxable income at the time they are made."

78 *IPL*, at 1173.

79 *IPL*, at 1173–1174.

80 Ibid; and Eid, Chapter 5, n 16, at p 277.

81 *IPL*, ibid; Eid, ibid, at p 277.

82 *Oak Industries Inc v Commissioner* 96 TC 559 (TC 1991) (*"NST"*).

83 *NST*, at p 569, and in the court's words: "The subscriber was contractually obligated to pay for monthly services in advance and at termination to pay all monthly fees due and surrender the decoder. The security deposit was intended to secure faithful performance of the terms of the agreement by the subscriber. NST was only permitted to keep the security deposit if the subscriber breached his obligations under the agreement."

264   *Notes*

84 Ibid, and at p 570 the court noted that: "The fact that NST could use the deposits 'as it sees fit' and was not required to segregate the deposits in a separate account is not dispositive in determining whether NST had 'complete dominion' over the deposits. NST's control over the use of the deposits was no different than the control exercised by a borrower over loan proceeds in a commercial loan situation. It follows that NST's unconstrained use of the deposits during the interim period before the time of refund is not crucial in determining whether NST had 'complete dominion' over the deposits. Instead, the key is whether NST had some guarantee that it would be allowed to keep the money."

85 Ibid, at p 573; and in the court's words: "The fact that NST did not have to account to depositors for earnings or interest on the deposits is also not 'especially significant' in determining whether the deposits are taxable income. Once again, in a commercial loan situation, a borrower is under no obligation to account the lender for earnings from the loan proceeds and generally borrows with an expectation of earning more income on the loan proceeds than interest paid the lender. NST will be required to pay tax on income that the deposits earn but that is no grounds for taxing the deposits."

86 Ibid; in this case the court was, in our opinion, laboring under an error. The fact of the payment of tax on the "use" does not justify disregarding the economic advantages at the level of "sources". See para 8.2.4.

87 Ibid, at p 574, stating that: "The lender in effect has taken repayment of his money (as was his contractual right) and has chosen to use the proceeds for the purchase of goods or services from the borrower."

88 Ibid, at p 577, and therefore the court concluded that: "Accordingly, we hold that the security deposits received by NST are not includable in petitioners' taxable income because NST did not enjoy 'complete dominion' over the deposits when the deposits were made."

89 *Houston Industries Inc v US* 125 F3d 1442 (11th Cir 1997).

90 Ibid, stating at p 1444 that: "The Supreme Court, however, has provided a number of tests for gross income. Gross income includes all 'undeniable accessions to wealth, clearly realized, and over which the taxpayers have complete dominion' . . ."

91 Ibid; and subsequently, the court further ruled that: "In fact, the utilities, burdened by additional accounting and administrative responsibilities, derived little or no benefit under this system. Moreover HL&P accounted for full interest on the overrecoveries and petitioned to initiate a repayment when the overrecovery balance became excessive. Under these circumstances, HL&P acted as a custodian of these funds."

92 *Florida Progress Corp v Commissioner* 114 TC 587 (TC 2000); as to the ruling of the appeals court, see Chapter 6, n 158.

93 See para 6.3.2.1.

94 Ibid, at p 599.

95 *Karns Prime & Fancy Food Ltd v Commissioner* 494 F3d 404 (3rd Cir 2007).

96 Ibid, at p 407.

97 Ibid, at p 410; and in the court's words: "The logic of the Supreme Court's holding in Indianapolis Power applies here. According to that decision, if the taxpayer has some guarantee that it will be allowed to retain the funds, then it has complete dominion over the money . . . Such is the case here. Karns, and Karns alone, was at all times in control of whether it would meet the Supply Agreement. Therefore, the funds provided to Karns were in substance a projected rebate for products to be supplied, analogous to an advance payment, and as such were taxable income."

98 *Westpac Pacific Food v Commissioner* 451 F3d 970 (9th Cir 2006).

99 *American Valmar International Inc v Commissioner*, 229 F3d 98 (2th Cir 2000); and see para 6.3.2.4 and Chapter 6, n 156.

100 Ibid, and in the court's words in pp. 102–103: "As in Indianapolis Power, the deposits by Valmar's customers were not commitments to purchase a specified quantity of goods. Indeed, the Tax Court found that 'at the time ... Valmar received funds from customers; it did not necessarily have instructions as to how those funds were to be used.' Just as in Indianapolis Power, where 'IPL's right to keep the money depends on the customer's purchase of electricity, and upon his later decision to have the deposit applied to future bills', Valmar's right to use at least some of the excess funds in the customer account depended on whether customers requested additional goods or a refund. Moreover, the 'question ... cannot be resolved simply by noting that respondent derives some economic benefit from receipt of these deposits.' The test is, therefore, not whether the funds inure exclusively to the customer's benefit. Rather, the proper test is whether Valmar had an obligation to use them for the customer or repay any excess, or, conversely, whether it had the right to use them on its own behalf ..."

101 *Iowa Southern Utilities Co v US* 841 F2d 1108 (Fed Cir 1988).

102 *Wood v US* 863 F2d 417 (5th Cir 1989).

103 *US v D'Agostino* 145 F3d 69 (2nd Cir 1998); and *US v Peters* 153 F3d 445 (7th Cir 1998).

104 See, e.g. *Allen v Beazley*, 157 F2d 970 (5th Cir 1946); *Michigan Retailers Ass'n v US* 676 F Supp 151 (WD Mich 1988); *Ford Dealers Advertising Fund Inc v Commissioner* 456 F2d 255 (5th Cir 1972); *Rittenhouse v Commissioner* TC Memo 1965–245 (US Tax Court Memos 1965); and *Roberson v Commissioner* TC Memo 1996–335 (US Tax Court Memos 1996).

105 *Lehew v Commissioner* TC Memo 1987–389 (US Tax Court Memos 1987).

106 *Firetag v Commissioner* 2000 US App Lexis 25428 (4th Cir 2000).

107 *Dana Distributors*, Chapter 4, n 240.

108 *Colonial Wholesale Beverage Corp v Commissioner* 878 F2d 23 (1st Cir 1989).

109 *Wilson v Commissioner* TC Memo 1986–140 (US Tax Court Memos 1986).

110 *Fred Nesbit Distributing Co v US* 604 F Supp 552 (SD Iowa 1985).

111 In addition, the possibility of allowing the expense on account of that liability to customers was denied relying on the "all events test" that will be discussed in para 7.3.2 and Chapter 7, n 157.

112 *Highland Farms*, Chapter 4, n 218.

113 The court in *Highland Farms* distinguished between that part of the initial receipt paid in advance with regard to the period of the tenant's stay throughout the term and with respect to that part it was ruled (in light of the "trilogy" that will be discussed in para 6.3.2) that it was taxable in the year in which it was received, while the balance of the receipt that was to return to the tenant or his successors upon the termination of the agreement by the tenant or upon his death was held to be a non-taxable loan.

114 Rev Rul 68–19, 1968–1 CB 42.

115 But according to this Rev Rul 68–19, at the time when the deposit will be regarded as income, the landlord will be able to deduct any expenses by reason of financing losses, since the entire amount will be regarded as rent that had been received in the same year.

116 Rev Rul 72–519, 1972–2 CB 32.

117 According to the control and use test, adopted in Rev Rul 72–519, the Rule also determines that payments made by a water company's customers that are termed as "deposits" and that are paid to secure the payment of the water

bills will be taxed on the date they are received as advances where there is no limitation on the water company's use of those monies, despite the fact that the company pays interest to the customers on these "deposits".

118 Rev Rul 75–152, 1975–1 CB 144 (superseded 1979–2 CB 210).
119 Dubroff, Chapter 2, n 104, at pp 737–8.
120 *Boston Consol*, Chapter 5, n 24.
121 Bittker and Lokken, Chapter 5, n 1, sec 5.5.3.
122 Ibid.
123 Bittker and Lokken, ibid, at sec 5.5.3, n 14.
124 Eid, Chapter 5, n 16, at pp 278–9.
125 Eid, ibid, at pp 279–80. As evidence she submits a series of cases, in which "deposits" have been classified as taxable advances, either according to the control and use test or according to the purpose or other tests, and which, if they were tested according to the complete dominion test, would have produced the opposite results.
126 i.e. only in those cases where by law the supplier is under a duty to repay the deposit, and where the customer has not undertaken to purchase the services.
127 For proper use of this test, Eid, at pp 282–3 mentions the cases of *Williams*, Chapter 5, n 40, and *Adams*, Chapter 5, n 43.
128 Klein, Chapter 3, n 23, at pp 1694–5; and see also Klein's comments in para 6.3.4.
129 *IPL*, Chapter 5, n 75, at p 210.
130 Klein, at pp 1715–16.
131 Klein, ibid.
132 Geier, Chapter 3, n 35, at pp 129–30.
133 Geier, at pp 130–2; in order to demonstrate her argument regarding the false premise of *IPL*, Geier (at pp 136–9) gives an example of a deposit with no interest for a period of 30 years, which according to IPL might be classified as a liability rather than income, although its present value is only 17.5% of the capital. According to Geier's approach, such a deposit should be recognized as income from day one.
134 As to the non-deductibility of a "contingent liability" according to US law, see the discussion in para 7.3.2.
135 Geier, at p 135.
136 This being necessitated by the definition of the term "income" in s 1 of the ITO, and from ss 2 and 3 of the ITO.
137 In s 3(i) of the ITO, tax is imposed, *inter alia*, on a borrower who has acquired a benefit in respect of a loan on favorable interest terms compared with a loan at "market conditions" (as defined in the regulations, one whose conditions are CPI-linked +4% annual interest). However, this provision does not apply to every loan relationship, but only to beneficial loans that have been granted in relation to an employer–employee relationship (as a result of wages), to a service-supplier/customer relationship (as a result of a payment for services) and to the relationship of a controlling shareholder with a company (as an addition to or in lieu of dividends). Under s 3(j) of the ITO, tax is imposed on a lender (!) in respect of a beneficial loan granted by him to a third party (in relation to the benefit inherent therein as compared to the "market interest"). This provision is designed to impose sanctions on persons who effect shifting of income by means of granting beneficial loans to third parties. Section 3(j) does not apply to loans to which s 3(i) applies, nor to loans granted on commercial grounds (such as a supplier's credit, customer's credit and the like) and, accordingly, does not apply to consumer deposits either. The provisions of ss 3(i) and 3(j), like those in s 87, FA 1996 in UK law (Chapter 5, n 6), and similar to IRC§7872 in the US Tax law (Chapter 5, n 20), do not have the force

to determine the timing recognition nor the classification conditions of deposits as income.

138 ITA (TA) 392/82 *American Company for Gas Transportation Ltd v AOLE*, Taxes (May 1988), E-157 (**"the First Amisragas case"**).

139 ITA (TA) 43/95, 31/96, *American Israeli Gas Company Ltd v AOLE*, Taxes (April 2001), E-69 (**"the Second Amisragas case"**).

140 ITA (TA) 24/96 *Pazgas Marketing Company Ltd v AOLE*, Taxes (June 2001), E-105.

141 At the same time it should be noted that while the controlling perception relating to the classification of the deposits in those cases was the Loan Approach, the low return prospects, although not negating the "loan" character of the deposit, influenced the courts in those cases to determine that the recipient of the deposit should not be allowed to deduct the financing differentials added to the deposit as an expense. In this respect reference should be made to our discussion in para 7.4.1.

142 The *Third Amisragas* case, Chapter 4, n 333 (which was published in 7 September 2001).

143 The *Amisragas-Pazgas* case, Chapter 4, n 334.

144 The court specifically mentioned the US cases of *Hirsch Improvement*, Chapter 5, n 53, *City Gas*, Chapter 5, n 66, and *IPL*, Chapter 5, n 75, which have been discussed in para 5.3.1.

145 As regards this doctrine, see our discussion in para 6.3.2.1.

146 The *Second Amisragas* case, Chapter 5, n 140, at p E-120.

147 Income Tax Ordinance Accounts Codex issued by the Income Tax and Property Tax Commission (Ronnen Press) (**"the Codex"**). This Codex reflects the administrative interpretation of ITA.

148 As clarified in para 6.3.2.1 and Chapter 6, n 58, in our opinion, the ITA Codex erred in finding that the Claim of Right Doctrine justified a result whereby an advance on account of income that had yet to be earned was liable to tax on the date it was received.

149 Sec 2.4.1 of the Codex.

150 Sec 2.3.3 and 2.3.4 of the Codex.

151 M. Shekel, "Classification of Deposits in the Amisragas Case – Reliance on Foreign Rules that do not Even Exist", Taxes 20–2 (April 2006), A-1.

152 See para 4.4.2.3.

153 Following our discussion in para 4.6.3.2, it appears that from the standpoint of the courts' approach to the issue of classifying deposits in the US, there is nothing more apt to illustrate the shortcomings of "the Dualistic Doctrine", since if the issue of a deposit were brought before the US courts today, there is no certainty that any kind of deposit will indeed be classified as such, or despite a duty to repay it, be classified as "income".

154 In para 4.6.3.

155 In para 5.2.1.

156 *Messrs Tattersall*, Chapter 5, n 7.

157 *Anise*, Chapter 5, n 11.

158 In para 5.3.1.

159 As mentioned in paras 3.1.5 and 3.1.6.

160 Nevertheless, according to our discussion in para 7.3.2.1 it seems that in most cases where a deposit contains a cash payment liability, this liability will be recognized as an expense.

161 As defined in para 4.6.1.

162 Ibid.

163 As mentioned in para 3.1.1.

164 See Chapter 8.

6 Timing of recognition of income from advances

1 Malman, Chapter 2, n 103, at p 105.
2 See para 2.5.2.
3 For alternative approaches, see Chapter 8.
4 See para 4.3.1.
5 As clarified in para 4.3.2.
6 *Sun Insurance Office v Clark* (1912) 6 TC 59.
7 *John Cronk & Sons Ltd v Harrison* (1936) 20 TC 612.
8 See also *Absalom v Talbot*, Chapter 4, n 55.
9 *Chibbet v Brookfield (Harold) & Sons Ltd* [1952] 2 All ER 265, 33 TC 467, 475.
10 BIM40080.
11 See para 2.3.2.
12 *Lincolnshire Sugar Co Ltd v Smart* [1937] 1 All ER 413; 20 TC 643.
13 *Prices Tailors*, Chapter 5, n 9.
14 *Johnson v WS Try Ltd* (1946) 27 TC 167.
15 *WS Try*, ibid, at 185. See also *Hall (JP)*, Chapter 4, n 60.
16 *Gardner, Mountain*, Chapter 4, n 57.
17 Ibid, at 93; see also Yellow Tax Handbook 2005–2006/PART II/Inland Revenue Interpretations/"RI 30" (regarding commissions of insurance companies).
18 *John and E Sturge Ltd v Hessel* [1975] STC 183.
19 *Symons v Weeks and others* [1983] STC 195.
20 SSAP#9, Chapter 2, n 39.
21 *Odeon*, Chapter 4, n 54.
22 *Lincolnshire Sugar*, Chapter 6, n 12.
23 *Prices Tailors*, Chapter 5, n 9.
24 *Weeks*, Chapter 6, n 19, at pp 237–8.
25 *Tapemaze*, Chapter 4, n 29.
26 See Financial Reporting Standards No 2, "Accounting for subsidiary undertakings" (FRS#2) and para 2.5.2.
27 *Tapemaze*, Chapter 4, n 29, at p 203.
28 *Tapemaze*, ibid, at p 201.
29 See BIM31110, BIM31090, BIM40700, TO5435 and CTM51210.
30 The Macdonald-Martin Committee No 5, Chapter 4, n 92.
31 See para 4.3.4.
32 *CIR v John Lewis Properties Plc* [2003] 75 TC 131; [2003] STC 117.
33 See The Macdonald-Martin Committee No 5, Chapter 4, n 92, at sec 2 and in respect of s 43A–G, ICTA 1988.
34 As we saw in para 4.4.
35 Ibid.
36 See our discussion in paras 4.4.1.2 and 4.4.2.3.
37 S Rep No 1622, 83d Cong, 2d Sess 61–62 (1954) in IRC§452(e) "prepaid income" was defined as any "amount (includable in gross income) which is received in connection with and is directly attributable to a liability which extends beyond the close of the taxable year in which such amount is received." "Liability" was defined as "a liability to render services, furnish goods or other property, or allow the use of property".
38 Internal Revenue Act 1954, Pub L No 591 Ch 736.
39 Internal Revenue Act 1955, Pub L No 74–143 69 Stat 134.
40 Stanger, Vander Kam and Polifka, Chapter 2, n 22, at p 409; and Malman, Chapter 2, n 103, at p 109.
41 26 CFR 1.446–1(c)(1).
42 For the timing of recognition of income according to GAAP, see para 2.3.
43 See, e.g. *European American Bank and Trust Company v US* 940 F2d 677 (1991),

stating: "For a taxpayer on an accrual method of accounting, it is the right to receive the income, not the actual receipt that determines its inclusion in income for tax purposes."

44 For the absence of material uncertainty as a condition under GAAP for recognition of income, see para 2.3.2. For the same condition under the "all events test" in Treas Reg 1.446–1(c), see the *European American Bank* case, ibid, and regarding this condition in respect of some specific services provisions, see IRC§448(d)(5)(a).

45 26 CFR 1.451–5.

46 This concession is made on the condition that we are dealing with a taxpayer who reports on the accrual basis method and receives advances in connection with goods that are sold by him during the ordinary course of business, or a taxpayer who sells goods within the framework of building, installing, constructing or manufacturing of items pursuant to a long-term contract. If other services are to be performed, the rule generally only applies to the portion of the goods applicable to supplying the goods.

47 For example, according to Reg 1.446–6(a), an inducement fee received by a taxpayer in connection with becoming the holder of a non-economic REMIC residual interest must be included in income over a period reasonably related to the period during which the REMIC is expected to generate taxable income or net loss allocable to that taxpayer. The taxpayer must recognize an inducement fee over the remaining expected life of the REMIC in a manner that reasonably reflects the after-tax costs and benefits of holding the non-economic residual interest.

48 *North American Oil Consolidated v Burnet* 286 US 417 (US 1932).

49 The Decree was affirmed by the court of appeals in 1922.

50 Ibid, at p 424; the determination of the general rule, as stated by the court, was: "If a taxpayer receives earnings under a claim of right and without restriction as to its disposition, he has received income which he is required to return, even though it may still be claimed that he is not entitled to retain the money, and even though he may still be adjudged to restore its equivalent".

51 Dubroff, Chapter 2, n 104, at p 733.

52 Dubroff, at p 737, declaring this presumption under the title: "doctrine inapplicable to non-income items".

53 *American Tel & Tel Co v Commissioner* TC Memo 1988–35 (US Tax Court Memos 1988), where it was held that amounts collected by a telephone company from customers who had no credit constituted deposits that were not liable to tax and not advances that were liable to tax, if those sums that had not been demanded by those customers were meant to pass to the state, and not to the taxpayer company. *Prima facie*, in regard to those sums, although the three conditions of the doctrine existed, the component that provided "the character of income" for those sums was lacking.

54 *Patel v Commissioner* TC Memo 1998–306 (US Tax Court Memos 1998), where it was held, *inter alia*, that the taxpayer who received sums for his own account from a foreign resident, and used them "as his own", although in effect, he did not regard them as amounts that belonged to him and acted more like a trustee, would not be regarded, according to the Claim of Right Doctrine, as liable to tax in respect thereof, due to the absence of the character of "income".

55 *Roberts v US* 734 F Supp 314 (ND Ill 1988). Here, it was held, again in the same spirit, that taxpayers are not deemed to be persons who have received "income" despite having received amounts for their own business account and, on the face of it, could have used the same, when those taxpayers were not aware of receiving them, and did not use them as belonging to them.

56 For example, *Air-Way Electric Appliance Corp v Guitteau* 123 F2d 20 (6th Cir 1946).
57 See also Dubroff, Chapter 2, n 104, at p 732.
58 For case law in the US that wrongly interpreted the Claim of Right Doctrine as supporting the Advance Approach as defined below, see, e.g. the *Lyon* case, Chapter 5, n 38; and the *Michigan* case, Chapter 5, n 104. For the same incorrect interpretation by Israeli case law and Israeli Tax Authorities ("ITA"), see, e.g. the *third Amisragas* case, Chapter 4, n 333 and the ITA Codex, Chapter 5, n 149.
59 C.E. Lister, "The Use and Abuse of Pragmatism: The Judicial Doctrine of Claim of Right", 21 Tax L Rev 263, 272 (1996).
60 Malman, Chapter 2, n 103, at pp 117–18.
61 Dubroff, Chapter 2, n 104, at pp 770–1.
62 Bittker and Lokken, Chapter 5, n 1, at sec 6.3.2, 6.15; Dubroff, Chail and Norris, Chapter 2, n 60, at p 359.
63 See para 5.3.1.4.
64 Like, e.g. the *Houston Industries* case, Chapter 5, n 89; and the text in para 5.3.1.5.
65 See our discussion in para 5.3.1.5.
66 *Inductotherm Industries Inc v US* 351 F3d 120 (3rd Cir 2003).
67 Ibid, and in the court's words on p 124: "As to the Doctrine's second prong (no disposition restriction on the sale proceeds), Inductotherm, having commingled the funds instead of blocking them, placed itself in a position of complete dominion over those funds (at least during the 1991 tax year). In this context, the Executive Order was 'a potential or dormant restriction . . . which depends on the future application of rules of law to present facts [and therefore was] not a "restriction on use" within the meaning of *North American Oil v Burnet*' . . . The Government was entitled to prosecute Inductotherm for failure to comply with the Executive Order. However, as with any regulation or criminal law, the Government had the discretion not to pursue Inductotherm's Executive Order violation. Thus, Inductotherm's control over the Furnace A proceeds was analogous to that of the James."
68 *Houston Industries*, Chapter 5, n 89.
69 *Penn v Robertson* 115 F2d 167 (4th Cir 1940).
70 *Hanna v Commissioner* 156 F2d 135 (9th Cir 1946).
71 *Dominion Resources Corp v US* 219 F3d 359 (4th Cir 2000).
72 See, e.g. *US v Lewis* 340 US 590 (US 1951); *Healy v Commissioner* 345 US 278 (US 1953); *Bramlette Bldg Corp v Commissioner* 424 F2d 751 (5th Cir 1970); and *Carlstedt Associates Inc v Commissioner* TC Memo 1989–27 (US Tax Court Memos 1989).
73 *James v US* 366 US 213 (US 1961).
74 *Brown*, Chapter 4, n 255.
75 In regard to this decision in the *Brown* case, see para 7.3.2.1.
76 *Brown*, at p 204.
77 The *Brown* case clearly decided that insurance agents could not take a present deduction, and in effect, establish a reserve for expected future cancellations. This is still the law. See para 7.3.2.1. In Rev Rul 75–541, 1975–2 CB 195, IRS ruled that an accrual basis loan corporation that receives a commission from an insurance company, from which it obtains life insurance coverage for its borrowers, must report the entire commission as income for the taxable year in which the insurance coverage is arranged, even though, in the event of a loan prepayment and termination of insurance coverage, it may be required to refund or abate a portion of the commission.
78 *Automobile Underwriters Inc v Commissioner* 19 BTA 1160 (BTA 1930).
79 *Bradstreet Company of Maine v Commissioner* 23 BTA 1093 (BTA 1931) (fees for furnishing financial information).

80 *Northern Illinois College of Optometry v Commissioner* 1943 Tax Ct Memo LEXIS 144 (US Tax Court Memos 1943) (tuition fees paid in advance).
81 *South Tacoma Motor Co v Commissioner* 3 TC 411 (TC 1944) (contract entitling purchaser to certain services that might be called for and performed after the year of sale).
82 *Your Health Club Inc v Commissioner* 4 TC 385 (TC 1944) (advance receipts for health and gym services).
83 *US v Boston and PRR Corp* 37 F2d 670 (1st Cir Mass 1930).
84 *Gates v Helvering* 69 F2d 277 (8th Cir 1934).
85 *Renwick v US* 87 F2d 123 (7th Cir 1936).
86 *Lyon*, Chapter 5, n 38.
87 *Clinton Hotel*, Chapter 5, n 36.
88 *Clinton Hotel*, ibid; *Astor Holding*, Chapter 5, n 44; *Grauman's Greater Hollywood Theatre v Commissioner* 37 BTA 448 (BTA 1938); *Grand Cent Public Market Inc v US* 22 F Supp 119 (D Cal 1938); and *South Date Farms*, Chapter 4, n 257.
89 In para 5.3.1.
90 See, e.g. *Clinton Hotel*, Chapter 5, n 36; *Astor Holding*, Chapter 5, n 44; and *Hirsch Improvement* Chapter 5, n 53.
91 *Heininger*, Chapter 5, n 46.
92 *Northern Illinois College*, Chapter 6, n 80.
93 *South Tacoma Motor*, Chapter 6, n 81.
94 *Andrews v Commissioner* 23 TC 1026 (TC 1955).
95 *Schaefer v Commissioner* TC Memo 1959–229 (US Tax Court Memos 1959).
96 For example, *Your Health Club*, Chapter 6, n 82; *National Airlines Inc v Commissioner* 9 TC 159 (TC 1947); and *Moritz v Commissioner* 21 TC 622 (TC 1954).
97 *Streight Radio*, Chapter 4, n 270.
98 *London Butte*, Chapter 4, n 256.
99 For the same statement, see *DD Oil Co*, Chapter 4, n 260.
100 *Beacon Publishing Co v Commissioner* 218 F2d 697 (10th Cir 1955).
101 Ibid, at p 700. In the same spirit, see *Watkins v US* 287 F2d 932 (1st Cir 1961).
102 *Automobile Club of Michigan v Commissioner* 353 US 180 (1957) (*"Michigan"*).
103 See para 2.3.2 and Chapter 2, n 39.
104 *Michigan*, at p 183 and p 188.
105 *Beacon Publishing*, Chapter 6, n 100.
106 *Bressner Radio Inc v Commissioner* 267 F2d 520 (2nd Cir 1959).
107 e.g. *North American Oil*, Chapter 6, n 48 and *Brown*, Chapter 4, n 255.
108 *Bressner*, Chapter 6, n 106, at p 526.
109 *Bressner*, at p 528; but see the statement in the *RCA* case in para 6.3.2.4 and Chapter 6, n 143.
110 *American Automobile Association v US* 367 US 687 (US 1961) (*"AAA"*).
111 Ibid, at p 688.
112 Ibid, at p 691. Klein, Chapter 3, n 23, at p 1703, mentions that the court didn't offer any explanation why the computation of income should focus on individuals rather than on averages or aggregates.
113 Ibid, at p 692. The court's majority further stated at p 693: "It may be true that to the accountant the actual incidence of cost in serving an individual member in exchange for his individual dues is inconsequential or, from the viewpoint of commercial accounting, unessential to determination and disclosure of the overall financial condition of the Association ... however ... When their receipt as earned income is recognized ratably over two calendar years, without regard to correspondingly fixed individual expense or performance justification, but consistently with overall experience, their accounting doubtless presents a rather accurate image of the total financial structure,

but fails to respect the criteria of annual tax accounting and may be rejected by the Commissioner."

114 As mentioned in para 6.3.1.

115 *AAA*, at p 697.

116 *AAA*, Stewart J dissenting opinion, added at p 714: "the enforcement of such a hybrid accounting method may result in a distortion of actual income".

117 *Schlude v Commissioner* 372 US 129 (US 1963) (*"Schlude"*).

118 Ibid, at pp 135–6.

119 See para 6.3.1.

120 *Artnell Company v Commissioner* 400 F2d 982 (7th Cir 1968). In *Artnell*, the taxpayer purchased the Chicago White Sox baseball franchise from the seller in the middle of the baseball season, and the middle of the seller's tax year. The seller had deferred that part of its receipts from season tickets, advanced single admission tickets, season parking books and television and radio broadcasting rights, which were allocable to games to be played after 31 May. As each game was played, the taxpayer took as income that part of the deferred income allocable to that game. The court approved the deferral system employed, despite the fact that it seemed to violate two principles of the trilogy. First, while *AAA* implied that deferral would be allowed only on income for which there was a "correspondingly fixed individual expense or performance justification", it would seem that the taxpayer in *Artnell* could do no more than pool all of his expenses and allocate a ratable share to his income for each game. Second, while *Schlude* emphasized that the accounting method there was unacceptable in part because the taxpayer did not attempt to estimate cancellations and take this into income, the court-approved accounting method in *Artnell* did not estimate customer cancellations, i.e. not appearing at the games, for which no services would ever be rendered or expenses incurred.

121 *Boise Cascade Corp v US* 208 Ct Cl 619 (Ct Cl 1976) *530 F.2d 1367* here, the taxpayer performed engineering, architectural and construction services. Depending on the contracts, payments were in some cases due prior to the annual period in which the associated services were performed. When the taxpayer billed for services prior to the year of their performance, he credited the amount in an account designated "unearned income". As these services were performed over the course of the following year, the taxpayer debited the "unearned income" account and credited a "service revenues" account. When the taxpayer performed services prior to the year in which he was entitled to bill or receive payment, he credited the "service revenues" account. The amount in the "service revenues" account was reported as gross income. There was no doubt that this method was in accordance with GAAP. The court reversed IRS's requirement to include the "unearned income" as an income for tax purposes, by reading the trilogy to allow a deferral of income if a taxpayer's obligations were fixed and definite, and not subject solely to customer demand. Here the court found such fixed and definite obligations, since the taxpayer had to perform its services in constructing electric power plants in coordination with other contractors and under rigid schedules.

122 *Artnell*, at pp 983–4; and *Boise Cascade*, at 1369–71. See also J.M.B. "Note & Comment RCA Corp. v US: The Taxation of income from future services", 1 VA Tax Review 189, 192 (1981).

123 See, e.g. *Collegiate Cap*, Chapter 4, n 216. In this case, the court decided that a taxpayer in the business of graduation apparel may defer taxation of prepaid income because there is certainty of performance, which is the delivery date of graduation apparel, the taxpayer permitted cancellation of orders up to the time of performance, and certain categories of expenses were not deducted

until the year when income to which they were related was earned. In that case, the court emphasized that it was bound in its decision, because appeal would be to the Seventh Circuit, which had decided *Artnell*. See also *Morgan Guaranty Trust Co v US* 218 Ct Cl 57 (Ct Cl 1978).

124 *Tampa Bay Devil Rays Ltd v Commissioner* TC Memo 2002–248 (US Tax Court Memos 2002). Here it was ruled, relying on *Artnell*, that a partnership that owned a baseball team and kept its books on the accrual basis could spread its income from advances that it received in connection with the sale of subscriptions for the period to which the subscriptions related, such finding emphasizing, in the main, the fact that the payer of the advance for the subscription had a right to a refund of a proportionate part of the advance that he paid, if he cancelled the annual subscription during the playing season. Having regard for the fact that this ruling was only given recently, and taking into account the fact that the taxpayer used the advance monies, it is, as we will see below, highly exceptional.

125 For the narrow view of the *Artnell* exception, see, e.g. *TFH Publications Inc v Commissioner* 72 TC 623 (TC 1979); *Springfield Productions Inc v Commissioner* TC Memo 1979–23 (US Tax Court Memos 1979); *Allied Fidelity Corp v Commissioner* 66 TC 1068 (TC 1976); and *Standard Television Tube Corp v Commissioner* 64 TC 238 (TC 1975).

126 *Veenstra & De Haan Coal Co v Commissioner* 11 TC 964 (TC 1948).

127 *Consolidated Hammer*, Chapter 5, n 21.

128 In this vein, see Stanger, Vander Kam and Polifka, Chapter 2, n 22, at p 413.

129 *Fifth and York Company v US* 234 F Supp 421 (D. Ky. 1964). In this case, a merchant sold vehicles on the "two for one" basis, and in 1954, made agreements under which, for consideration he received in that year, he undertook, to supply purchasers of 1954 models with vehicles of the 1955 model (against trade-in of the 1954 model). Relying on this liability, the merchant sought to spread his income proportionately, assigning one-half of the consideration that he had received in 1954 to 1954, and the balance to 1955. The court extended the trilogy and dismissed the taxpayer's rights to spread recognition of his income from selling vehicles, holding that the taxpayer's right to income crystallized in its entirety at the time the agreements were signed in 1954. The fact that in the scope of those agreements the taxpayer assumed the liability did not justify spreading recognition of the income from the sale of 1954 vehicles to the following year, and did not justify a provision in respect of this liability as long as the liability had not crystallized by means of a demand from the vehicle purchaser to make the substitution (which demand had only been included in 1955).

130 *Boeing Co v US* 338 F2d 342, 350 (Ct Cl 1964).

131 *McAllister v Commissioner* 417 F2d 581 (9th Cir 1981).

132 *Hagen Advertising*, Chapter 4, n 264.

133 Nevertheless, as we saw in para 6.3.1, Reg 1.451–1 cancelled, in most of the cases, the application of the Advance Approach to the sale of goods.

134 *New England Tank*, Chapter 5, n 59.

135 *Adshead v Commissioner* TC Memo 1976–196 (US Tax Court Memos 1976).

136 *Franklin Life Ins Co v US* 399 F2d 757 (7th Cir 1968).

137 *George Blood Enterprises Inc v Commissioner*, TC Memo 1976–102 (US Tax Court Memos 1976).

138 Ibid, at pp 445–6.

139 In para 7.3.2.1.

140 Ibid, at p 447, and in the court's words: "Commissions are taken into income when received even though there is a possibility that some portion of the amount might have to be refunded to the insurance company if the policy is

canceled. *Van Wagoner v US*, 368 F2d 95 (5th Cir 1966). This conclusion is consistent with numerous cases holding that amounts received under a claim of right are includable in income when received even though at some later date some of the amounts may have to be refunded. See *North American Oil Consolidated v Burnet*, 286 US 417 (1932)". As we mentioned in para 6.3.2.1, according to our understanding, the Claim of Right Doctrine does not justify the recognition of advances as income.

141 *Prichard*, Chapter 4, n 263.

142 *RCA*, Chapter 4, n 240.

143 *RCA*, at pp 882–3. The court faced three major issues in deciding the validity of RCA's deferral of advances: first, whether the trilogy authorized IRS to reject any deferral of income from future services not fixed specifically in time, no matter how accurately it matches revenues and expenses, and if not, whether use of statistical projections prevents an accounting method from being "purely artificial"; second, whether the repeal of IRC§452 precludes use of the accounting method employed by RCA; and, third, whether the method used by RCA clearly reflects income. Regarding IRS's authority to reject any deferral of income, the court held that the trilogy empowers IRS to reject a deferral method that is "purely artificial", but does not authorize the rejection of a method that clearly reflects income, regardless of whether the time for performance of future services is uncertain. The court rejected IRS's argument that the decisive factor in the trilogy was the unspecified time for the performance of future services. Regarding repeal of IRC§452, the court next addressed whether IRS had the authority to reject any method of accounting that defers the inclusion of payments for future services, unless there exists a specific statutory exception. IRS argued that the Supreme Court, in *AAA* and *Schlude*, had interpreted this repeal as empowering the Commissioner to reject any such deferral method in the absence of a contrary statutory provision. The court rejected IRS's argument. The court believed that repeal of the deferral sections did not constitute a general prohibition against deferral of prepaid service income. Regarding the third question, whether the methods used by RCA "clearly reject income", the court rejected IRS's argument that RCA had a burden to prove not only that its accounting method as a whole worked with precision, but also that each component of the method did so. The court determined that RCA's projections estimated its expenses with reasonable accuracy, and therefore concluded that IRS had abused its discretion under IRC§446 in imposing a different accounting method on RCA.

144 Ibid, at pp 887–8; the court also stated that the *Bressner* ruling (Chapter 6, n 106) no longer had force.

145 *Chesapeake Financial Corp v Commissioner* 78 TC 869 (TC 1982).

146 Ibid, at p 877.

147 Ibid, at pp 878–81. The court stated that the taxpayer incurred expenses both before and after the receipt of income, while deferring all of the income until the date of permanent funding. Accordingly, the taxpayer had not attempted to match income with expenses. On this point, the court did not reject the outcome of *Artnell* and *Boise Cascade*, but interpreted them as requiring the taxpayer to show "at a minimum . . . the year in which the services are to be rendered and that the income deferred is recognized as the services are rendered and the correlative expenses incurred. Petitioner misses this threshold by a significant marrying".

148 *Johnson v Commissioner* 184 F3d 786 (8th Cir 1999).

149 *Bob Wondries Motor Inc v Commissioner* 268 F3d 1156 (9th Cir 2001).

150 But see Rev Proc 92–98, 1992–2 CB 512 and Rev Proc 97–38, 1997–2 CB 479, in para 6.3.3.

151 *Philmon v US* 1999 US Dist LEXIS 14258 (MD Fla 1999).

152 *Park Chester Beach Club Corp v Commissioner* 335 F2d 478 (2nd Cir 1964).

153 *Popular Library Inc v Commissioner* 39 TC 1092 (TC 1963).

154 *Chester Farrar v Commissioner* 44 TC 189 (TC 1965).

155 And see also *Standard Television Tube Corp*, Chapter 6, n 125; and *Allied Fidelity Corp*, Chapter 6, n 125.

156 *American Valmar*, Chapter 5, n 99.

157 *Houston Industries*, Chapter 5, n 89.

158 *Florida Progress Corp v Commissioner* 348 F3d 954 (11th Cir 2003), and see also para 5.3.1.5.

159 See also, in the same spirit, *Cinergy Corp v US* 55 Fed Cl 489 (Fed Cl 2003). IRS has announced in Rev Rul 2003–39, 2003–1 CB 811 that it will follow this treatment and not argue for inclusion when the utilities receive the over-recoveries with an obligation to repay.

160 *Stendig v US* 843 F2d 163 (4th Cir 1988). Here, it was held that rent received by a partnership reporting on an accrual basis method, which was required to deposit it in a reserve fund in order to receive government financing for "low income financing projects", ought to have been included in the partnership's income, despite the fact that there were restrictions on using the reserve monies. This finding was based on the fact that this had a material effect on the partnership on making decisions pertaining to use of the reserve monies. The fact that it was only a remote possibility that expenses paid out of the reserve would not be for the use of the beneficiaries was thought to be insufficient in order to subtract the full payment of the reserve amount from the partnership's income in the year in which the monies to which the reserve related were received.

161 *Firetag*, Chapter 5, n 106; here it was held that the fact that a receipt having the character of "income" that had been deposited in the court coffers did not change the conclusion that the taxpayer was bound to recognize it as income for tax purposes on the date on which it was received.

162 *Iowa Southern Utilities*, Chapter 5, n 101. Here it was held that where there was no duty of the taxpayer to return advance monies that had been deposited in a separate account, this advance would be regarded as income on the date of its receipt.

163 Like Rev Rul 84–31, 1984–1 CB 127, which stated: "All the events that fix the right to receive income generally occur when (1) the payment is earned through performance, (2) payment is due to the taxpayer, *whichever happens earliest*" (emphasis added).

164 Rev Proc 71–21, 1971–2 CB 549.

165 Rev Proc 71–21, sec 3.02.

166 Rev Proc 71–21, sec 3.03(a).

167 *Barnett Banks of FL Inc v Commissioner* 106 TC 103 (TC 1996).

168 *Signet Banking Corp v Commissioner* 118 F3d 239 (4th Cir 1997).

169 Relying mainly on the fact that in *Barnett Banks* the holder of the card was entitled to a proportional refund of the service fees if he cancelled his engagement with the issuing company.

170 This decision in *Signet Banking* was mainly based on the reason that the holder of the card was not entitled to any refund in respect of the annual membership fees that he had paid in advance, and these membership fees were described not as consideration for an annual future service, but as consideration for the issue of the card and the creation of a "credit limit".

171 *American Express Company v US* 262 F3d 1376 (Fed Cir 2001).

172 *American Express*, at p 1383. The basis of this finding was that when interpreting a term that is included in the procedural directives of the tax authorities,

preference should be given to the interpretation offered by the tax authorities for the procedural directives that they themselves had issued.

173 Rev Rul 2004–52, 2004–1 CB 973.

174 Rev Rul 78–212, 1978–1 CB 139.

175 If a coupon is given to a specific customer, the seller has *prima facie* received an item in respect of the sale, which may subsequently be expected to be reduced by using the coupon. In this context, Treas Reg §1.451–4 and Rev Proc 72–36, 1972–2 CB771 provide that the seller may, notwithstanding the adoption of the Advance Approach, make certain provisions in respect of such coupons, which will be deductible for income tax purposes.

176 Rev Proc 92–98, 1992–2 CB 512.

177 Rev Proc 97–38, 1997–2 CB 479.

178 See paras 7.3.2.1 and 7.3.3.

179 Provided the spread will only relate to that part of the amount received in advance to the extent of the sum which the taxpayer has undertaken to pay (within 60 days of receiving the money) to the (unrelated) third party, for purchasing an insurance policy that will cover the taxpayer's liability to provide that warranty.

180 That is to say, the spread in those cases is conditional, *inter alia*, on the future payments to the insurer in respect of the warranty services being capitalized, in a manner whereby there will be attributed to the taxpayer's income an amount that reflects the economic advantage that accrues to him from the very fact that he has received money in advance, against the taking of a liability the payment date of which is in the future. The calculation of the capitalization is done under Rev Proc 92–97, 1992–2 CB 510.

181 Regarding Rev Proc 97–38, Kleinrock, Chapter 4, n 12, wrote in sec 505.4.2.2 as follows: "In the ideal income tax, economic accrual of both the payment and the future cost would resolve the accounting questions, but the ideal is often impossibly hard to achieve. The service warranty income method of Rev. Proc. 97–38 is inspired by the concept of economic accrual but prescribes a simpler approach."

182 *Bob Wondries*, Chapter 6, n 149. This case concerned a group of car dealers who sold warranty services together with the vehicles sold, and who were entitled to be included in Rev Proc 92–98. They requested that in calculating the amount available for spread in respect of warranty services that they had sold to vehicle purchasers, the capitalized amount that they had paid to a third party (the insurer) to purchase insurance should be calculated in a manner whereby the formula of the capitalization would apply as if the payment that they had made to the insurer started from the beginning of the year in which the advance payment was received (to which the spread applied). This would create symmetry between the period for which the spread applied, and the period for which the current value of the future payments to the insurer for the warranty were calculated.

183 Ibid, at p 1161, stating: "Yet matching of income and related expense does not necessarily result in a clear reflection of income for tax purposes. Taxpayer must recognize prepaid income when received, even though this would mismatch expenses and revenues in contravention of generally accepted commercial accounting principles."

184 Rev Proc 2004–34, 2004–1 CB 991.

185 According to sec 4.01, this procedure will apply if the advance payments are for all kinds of services; the sale of goods (other than for the sale of goods for which the taxpayer uses a method of deferral provided in Treas Reg §1.451–5(b)(1)(ii)); the use (including by license or lease) of intellectual property; the occupancy or use of property if the occupancy or use is ancillary to the

provision of services; the sale, lease or license of computer software, guaranty or warranty contracts ancillary to an item or items described in sec 4.01; subscription (other than subscription for which an election under IRC§455 is in effect), whether or not provided in a tangible or intangible format; memberships in an organization (other than memberships for which an election under IRC§456 is in effect); or any combination of items described above.

186 See sec 4.01 of Rev Proc 2004–34, the definition of "advance payment". Section 5 states: "A taxpayer that chooses to defer inclusion must include an advance payment in gross income in the year of receipt to the extent it is either included in an applicable financial statement or earned in that year and must include the remaining amount of the advance payment in gross income in the next succeeding taxable year . . ."

187 Rev Proc 2004–34, in sec 5.01.

188 According to sec 4.02, the spread under Rev Proc 2004–34 does not apply if the advance payments are for rent (other than that paid for the use of intellectual property, computer software and property ancillary to the provision of services); insurance premiums to the extent governed by the taxation of insurance companies; payments with regard to financial instruments, such as debt instruments, deposits, letters of credit, notional principal contracts, options, forward contracts, futures contracts, foreign currency contracts, credit card agreements and financial derivatives, including purported prepayments of interest; payments with regard to service warranty contracts in which the payments are included in income over the life of the obligation; payments with regard to warranty and guaranty contracts under which a third party is the primary obligor; certain payments with regard to non-resident aliens and foreign corporations; payments in property transferred in connection with the performance of services to which Code sec 83 applies. According to sec 5.02(5), this procedure does not apply and a taxpayer using the deferral method must include in gross income for the taxable year of receipt all advance payments (including those for transactions specified in sec 4.01) in cases of the taxpayer's death, merger and in cases where in that taxable year, the taxpayer's obligation with regard to the advance payments is satisfied.

189 Rev Proc 2004–34, sec 5.02(3), although in sec 5.02(4) it has been stated that with respect to that part of the advance that is paid for a transaction to which the directive applies, that part will be spreadable pursuant to the directive (until not later than the end of the ensuing year), provided that the determination of such proportionate part will be made on the basis of objective criteria.

190 Rev Proc 2004–34, sec 5.02(3)(b).

191 It should, however, be noted that in IRC§§455(c) and (e), a spread is allowed of registration fees for subscribers without limitations from the standpoint of the period.

192 AICPA, Chapter 2, n 103, pp 2–17.

193 J.K. Lasser and Maurice E. Peloubet, "Tax Accounting Versus Commercial Accounting", 4 Tax L Rev 343, 347 (1949); see also Chester M. Edelman, "Is Income Tax Accounting 'Good' Accounting Practice?" 24 Taxes 112, 121–2 (1946).

194 George O. May, "Accounting and the Accountant in the Administration of Income Taxation", 47 Colum L Rev 377, 388–9 (1947) (arguing that payment in advance for goods or services is not intended to be income under revenue statutes).

195 James H. Heffner, "Claim-of-Right and Other Tax Doctrines Are Distorting Proper Accounting", 5 J Tax'n 20, 20–1 (1956) (critiquing court decisions relying on the Claim of Right Doctrine instead of GAAP).

196 Murray H. Rothaus, "A Critical Analysis of the Tax Treatment of Prepaid

Income", 17 Md L Rev 121, 130–3 (1957) (claiming that immediate tax is legally unjustified).

197 S. Ralph Jacobs, "Changing Attitudes toward Accrual Concepts", 16 Inst, On Feb Tax'n 579, 586, 597 (1958) (arguing that a "hybrid" accounting method, half cash and half accrual, distorts income).

198 William M. Emery, "Time for accrual of Income and Expenses", 17 Inst on Feb Tax'n 183, 189 (1959) (stating: "income tax accounting cannot be dissociated from generally accepted accounting principles").

199 Donald Shapiro, "Tax Accounting for Prepaid Income and Reserves for Future Expenses", in 2 Compendium of Papers on Broadening the Tax Base Submitted to Comm on Ways and Means 86th Cong, 1st Sess, 1133, 1141, 1152 (Comm Print 1959) (while recognizing that immediate tax avoids judgments and estimates and produces a more uniform result among taxpayers, ultimately recommending legislation allowing deferral).

200 Robert A. Behren, "Prepaid Income Accounting Concepts and the Tax Law", 15 Tax L Rev 343, 366 (1960) (stating: "The arguments advanced in favor of the tax rule for prepaid income are not sufficiently strong to overcome the Congressional intent that taxable income be based on income determined under generally acceptable accounting principles").

201 Johannes R. Kramer, "Taxation of Advance Receipts for Future Services", Duke LJ 230, 258 (1961) (claiming that statute and proper accounting require deferral).

202 Robert A. Behren, "Schlude Holds Prepaid Income Taxable on 'Receipt'; Rationale is Uncertain", 18 J Tax'n 194, 199 (1963).

203 Robert H. Aland, "Prepaid Income and Estimated Future Expenses: Is a Legislative Solution Needed?" 54 ABA J 84, 89 (1968) (advising: "Correlation between generally accepted accounting principles and principles of tax accounting in the prepaid income and estimated future expense area").

204 John S. Nolan, "The Merit in Conformity of Tax to Financial Accounting", 50 Taxes 761, 767 (1972) (stating: "The Sixteenth Amendment authorizes a tax on 'income' without apportionments, and for a business taxpayer, this means net income, a concept which accounting standards are designed to measure").

205 Daniel C. Weary, "IRS Creation of Hybrid Methods: Prepayments and the Cash Method; Prepayments and the Accrual Method", 35 Inst On Feb Tax'n 59, 76 (1977).

206 J. Silk, Chapter 4, n 8, at p 1653.

207 Dave Stewart and R. Glen Woods, "Analysis of the Trend toward Deferring Recognition of Prepaid Income", 59 Taxes 400 (1981) (proposing a statutory amendment under which the taxpayers would not pay tax on receipts until earned).

208 Robert Scarborough, "Payments in Advance of Performance", 69 Taxes 799, 809, 818 (1989) (advocating deferral, and also shifting tax on interim investment income back to the prepayment payer).

209 Joseph M. Dodge, *The Logic of Tax: Federal income tax theory and policy* (St Paul Minn: West Pub, 1989), p 209 (describing literature on tax accrual accounting as "based on the feeble premise that tax accrual rules should 'conform' to business accounting rules").

210 Stanger, Vander Kam and Polifka, Chapter 2, n 22, at p 426. While they provide no fundamental assessment of the correctness of the trilogy, they do note that the promulgation of Rev Proc 71–21 moves in the direction of financial accounting principles with regard to income deferral. There had been no corresponding movement with regard to accrual of expenses, and they recommend that Congress remedy this situation by creating greater conformity between the two areas.

211 William L. Raby, "Meaning of 'Accrued' – Accounting Concepts Versus Tax Concepts", 92 TNT 223–97 (18 November 1992).
212 Lee A. Sheppard, "Equipment Leasing Shelters for Corporate Customers", 95 TNT 52–6 (16 March 1995).
213 Malman, Chapter 2, n 103, at pp 114–15.
214 Malman, ibid, at pp 117–18.
215 Malman, ibid, at pp 151–2. The example given at p 152 is a contract requiring the taxpayer to clean a customer's widget five times during the contractual period. This approach, suggests Malman, meets financial accounting purposes by reporting income when earned, and tax purposes by reporting income in an appropriate taxable period.
216 *JMB*, Chapter 6, n 122, at pp 193–4.
217 Ibid.
218 Coplan, Chapter 3, n 27, at pp 382–4.
219 Ibid.
220 Lister, Chapter 6, n 59, at p 283; and see also para 6.3.2.1.
221 Bittker and Lokken, Chapter 5, n 1, at sec 6.3.2.
222 Dubroff, Chapter 2, n 104, at pp 770–1.
223 i.e. in the *Michigan* case, Chapter 6, n 102.
224 i.e. in *Schlude*, Chapter 6, n 117 and *AAA*, Chapter 6, n 110.
225 Bittker and Lokken, Chapter 5, n 1, at para 6.3.2, pp 6–15; and Dubroff, Chapter 2, n 104, at p 770.
226 Dubroff, ibid, at p 771.
227 Lister, Chapter 6, n 59, at p 289.
228 Halperin, Chapter 3, n 33, at pp 515–17.
229 See para 2.5.2.
230 This is mainly the case where the recipient is a tax-exempt entity and the payment from the payer's standpoint is not a deductible expense. Thus, e.g. a person who pays university tuition fees a year in advance will receive a discount compared with a person who does not. This discount reflects the interest component on the credit advance to the university by the very making of the payment in advance, and the discount is exempt from tax in the hands of the payer, while another payer, who does not pay in advance and who will deposit the amount of the tuition fees in an interest-bearing investment, will probably pay tax on the yield (also on that part of the yield which is equivalent to the discount).
231 Halperin, at p 518; for Halperin's view, see also para 3.2.
232 Kleinrock, Chapter 4, n 12, at sec 505.3.1; for the Haig-Simons definition of "income", see Chapter 3, n 11.
233 Gunn, Chapter 3, n 5, at pp 18 and 21–2. According to Gunn, where both the seller and the buyer have high tax rates and the buyer can deduct as an expense the amount of the advance, although the timing of the deduction thereof is deferred until the future, adopting the Deferral Approach reflects more closely tax neutrality (since, in such a case, there is supposed to be an overlap between the timing of the recognition of the income with the seller and the timing of the recognition of the expense with the customer). However, when the buyer cannot deduct as an expense in the liabilities in relation to which the advance was paid, it is actually adopting the Advance Approach that reflects the neutrality of the tax (as the buyer is indifferent, while the seller will receive preference in receiving the advance as against similar sellers who do not take advances). However, if the seller himself is exempt from tax, then he will also be indifferent, and again the very act of the spread will not harm the principle of neutrality.
234 Gunn, at pp 23–5.

235 Reed Schuldiner, "A General Approach to the Taxation of Financial Instruments", 71 Tax L Rev 243, 296 (1992).
236 Ibid; see in Chapter 6, n 261 Johnson's reference to Schuldiner theory.
237 Klein, Chapter 3, n 23, at pp 1689–91.
238 Ibid, at p 1696.
239 Ibid, and see Klein comments in para 5.3.3.
240 Ibid, at p 1710.
241 Ibid, at pp 1712–13.
242 Ibid, at p 1698.
243 Ibid, at p 1699.
244 Ibid, at p 1707.
245 Ibid, at pp 1701–2.
246 Ibid, at pp 1705–6.
247 Ibid, at pp 1708–7.
248 For these tax values, see para 3.1.
249 Klein, at pp 1731–2. For the timing of deduction of future liabilities in the US, see para 7.3.
250 Johnson, Chapter 3, n 27, at pp 380–1.
251 Ibid, at p 380-1.
252 Ibid, at 384–5.
253 Ibid, at 388–9. Such disposal according to Johnson can be regarded for GAAP as no more than contingent liability, no provision will be registered in the books (see paras 2.4.2 and 2.4.3) and it is not deductible for tax purpose (see para 7.3.2).
254 Ibid, at pp 384–9, this in light of the fact that the recipient enjoys the full amount of the nominal value of the advance, while adopting the Deferral Approach will lead to a result whereby the income that will be imputed to the recipient will only be equal to the present value of the nominal advance sum.
255 See paras 2.5 and 2.6 and, for instance, SFAS#114 and APB#21, both Chapter 2, n 84.
256 Ibid, at p 400. In this aspect he mentioned the "Comprehensive Income Statements". For this method, see Chapter 2, n 54.
257 Ibid, at pp 402–3.
258 While Johnson adds that in the same year the recipient is entitled to deduct, in calculating his income, the present value of the recipient's liabilities that are required for attaining the income, and the difference between these two is that which reflects the increase in the recipient's wealth.
259 Ibid, at pp 391–2. Regarding the requirements for deductions of expenditures, see para 7.3.
260 Ibid, at pp 410 *et seq*.
261 In addressing Schuldiner's proposition that taxing the advance on the date of its receipt, on the one hand, and the lack of the payer's possibility of deducting the sum that has been paid as an advance, on the other, will lead to over-taxation of the transaction and harm tax neutrality, Johnson responds, *inter alia*, that even if we start from the assumption that the customer will not be entitled to deduct the advance on the date of its payment in calculating his own income, there is no reason for the recipient of the advance to benefit from this fact.
262 Geier, Chapter 3, n 35, at pp 113–14.
263 Ibid, at p 115.
264 Ibid, at p 134, e.g. Geier relates to Rev Proc 71–21 (para 6.3.3) as an unnecessary tax treatment of prepaid income, but can be treated as a reasonable deviation from tax values.
265 Geier, at pp 144–5; for Geier's views, see also paras 3.2, 4.1.4, 4.3.4, and 7.3.4.

266 See para 4.5.1.2.4.
267 See para 4.5.1.2.5.
268 For the timing of the deduction of liabilities undertaken in respect of these two types of advances, see Chapter 7, n 304.
269 ITA 61/85 *Yatziv Cooling Engineering and Air Conditioning Ltd v Assessing Officer TA1*, 17 PDA 295.
270 The *First Amisragas* case, Chapter 5, n 138.
271 ITA 83/85 *Aharon and Co v Haifa Assessing Officer* 14 PDA 307.
272 The *third Amisragas case*, Chapter 4, n 333.
273 The *Amisragas-Pazgas* case, Chapter 4, n 334.
274 See our critique relating to these cases, in para 5.4.3.
275 IITC 9/87; in para 12 of this Administrative Provision, it is stated that "the judgment may be applied to any deposit or advance of a similar kind".
276 A. Raphael, "The Date of the Liability of Advance Payments", 21 The Accountant 25 (1971).
277 Rosenberg, Chapter 4, n 343.
278 In a similar vein, see Y. Vita, "Transactions by Means of Coupons – Timing of Recognition of the Income", Taxes (May 1989), A-52.
279 Nevertheless, as we have seen, pursuant to administrative directives, a limited spread is possible.
280 As to the adoption of the Dualistic Doctrine and the Consistent Selective Approach in the US, see para 4.4.2.3.
281 As to this see paras 4.4.2 and 6.3.2.1.
282 Mainly in cases where services or goods will be delivered in the future, on dates that are unclear (where it is easier to calculate from the standpoint of spreading).
283 See our discussion in para 4.6.3.
284 For the values of efficiency, and preventing of unjust tax advantages, see paras 3.1.5 and 3.1.6.
285 As to the meaning of the "base transaction", see para 3.2.
286 See, e.g. Gunn, Chapter 3, n 5, at pp 39–40; and Geier, Chapter 3, n 35, at pp 160–1.
287 See Halperin's view in para 3.2.
288 Geier, ibid.
289 See para 7.5.4.
290 See para 7.3.2.1.
291 See, e.g. Schuldiner, Chapter 6, n 235, at p 296; and Klein, Chapter 3, n 23, at p 1707.
292 Within the meaning of para 3.1.1.
293 See para 4.6.3.1.
294 As to these tax values, see para 3.1.
295 As stated in paras 7.3.2.1 and 7.5.4.
296 Take, e.g. a case where a taxpayer seeks to receive an advance for a service that he will provide in another five years. It is quite easy to change the form of the transaction whereby the same taxpayer will receive a loan in the amount of the advance requested, which he will be required to repay in another five years, and at the same time make an agreement whereby, on the expected date of the loan repayment, consideration will be paid to the taxpayer in respect of a future service, the estimated termination date of which will fall in the same period.
297 This "appearance" may be improved upon. Thus, e.g. it can be determined that the seller of the service will receive a loan with favorable overdraft interest from the bank, secured by the principal of a deposit which the recipient of the service will make in the bank and which bears lower credit interest (than that of the overdraft). On the date of the expected repayment of the loan, the

seller will be entitled to receive, in return for the service, the principal amount of the loan plus the favorable interest.

298 "A loan is a loan" stated Klein, Chapter 3, n 23, at p 1722.

299 This tax disadvantage set against the alternative transaction of a loan results both from the fact that the Advance Approach imposes tax on the full advance turnover, and also that the alternative of a loan will not create potential for payment of tax in advance in respect of profit that has yet to be created. See Klein, ibid, at p 1707.

300 For the Proportionality Principle tests, see para 4.6.1.

301 See Chapter 8.

7 Timing of the deduction of future expenses

1 As we have seen in paras 2.3 and 2.4, GAAP as a rule (subject, however, to exceptions) prefers to determine a "thin borderline" (which is principally attained by the intrinsic combination of the realization and the matching principles) in which the timing of the recognition of the income is deferred until the date closest to that on which it is certain that it has actually been attained. At the same time that income has been recognized, the liabilities assumed by the firm in order to create that income will similarly be recognized.

2 See, e.g. in the UK, Chapter 7, n 12, in the US, Chapter 7, n 67, and in the Israeli tax system Chapter 7, n 235.

3 See, e.g. in the UK, Chapter 7, n 13, in the US, Chapter 7, n 68, and in the Israeli tax system Chapter 7, n 236.

4 Like in a case of "contingencies", as defined in para 2.4.2.

5 Like in a case of provision, as defined in para 2.4.1.

6 However, like the higher levels of certainty, the Accounting Certainty Degree will not allow the deduction of a liability that has not yet crystallized, and which is termed a "contingency" according to GAAP.

7 i.e. consistent with GAAP. For the meaning of the Singular Doctrine, see para 4.1.2.

8 As described in para 2.4.

9 Malman, Chapter 2, n 103, at 142.

10 And the application thereof by means of the Separating Approach or the Consistent Selective Approach (as defined in para 4.1.3).

11 See, e.g. *Michigan*, Chapter 6, n 102, at p 189, n 20; and *AAA*, Chapter 6, n 110, at p 691.

12 Under Sch D Cases I and II for corporation tax and Sch A for income tax s 21(3), ICTA 1988: "All expenses wholly and exclusively incurred for the purpose of the trade, profession or vocations are allowable other than those specifically mentioned". Under ss 348–50, ITCA 1988, until 2005–06 the expenses specifically mentioned as not allowable are: private living expenses, private living accommodation, reserves for repair expenditure as opposed to provisions for known liabilities, non-trading losses, capital payments (but not interest), improvement to premises, notional interest, reserves as opposed to actual provisions for bad debts, estimated losses, expenditure which will be subject to an insurance recovery, annuities or other annual payments (other than interest), or other deductions from total income which are specifically mentioned. From 2005–06, s 74, ITTOIA 2005 is relevant for calculation of profits under Sch D Cases I and II for corporation tax.

13 For provisions which determined certain timing for the deduction of certain liabilities, see, e.g. s 24, FA 2003.

14 See para 4.3.

15 Certain exceptions to this rule can be found in The General Insurance Reserves (Tax) Regulations 2001, SI 2001/1757 that were enacted according to s 107, FA 2000. According to s 107, FA 2000, a general insurer may elect to deduct for tax purposes its provisions for extinguishing unpaid liabilities in a sum lower than the amount of the provisional amount included in its "ordinary" financial reports, and where the amount of the provision that has been deducted for tax purposes in respect of the future liabilities has been made according to the best evaluation and this sum does not exceed 5% of what has actually been paid in respect of those liabilities, and no future exposure thereto will apply. In the alternative, such an insurer may elect to deduct as allowable for tax purposes a sum higher than that stated above in respect of a liability that he expects to be forced to pay in the future (but in any event no more than the amount of the provisions in its "ordinary" financial statements), although in such a case, it is exposed to its becoming apparent in the future that the provision in respect of those liabilities has exceeded the amount required, in which case this difference will be added to its income for tax purposes with the concurrent liability for interest on the additional tax amount that is added consequent upon the adjustment. In substance, this statutory provision relates to "the unearned premium provision (UPP)", not as a general provision for future liability, but effectively as the spreading of the income from the insurance premium and payment of the interest on the amount of the excess provision which is being made according to the above Regulations is designed to reflect the tax benefit that accrues to the insurer as a result of that deferral of tax. See GIM6020, "Technical provisions: Unearned Premium Provision".

16 From this standpoint, worthy of note is the difference between the overall reference to GAAP as made for income and companies' tax, and the approach of the UK Estate Duty Law, which as a rule prescribes the present value method in relation to the deduction of a future liability according to s 162(2), IHTA 1984. In this respect, see IHTM28070; IHTM28110; Simon's Direct Tax Service/ Binder 7 Inheritance tax/Part 14/ Transfers on Death/ Division 14.1 Charge on Death/14.146 "Liability to make future payments" and Simon's Direct Tax Service/Binder 7 Inheritance Tax/Part 18/Valuation/Division 18.2 Principles of Valuation/ 18.277 "Liabilities".

17 As defined in para 7.1.1.

18 As defined in para 7.1.2.

19 *Southern Railway of Peru*, Chapter 4, n 51. As mentioned in para 4.3.2.1, this case placed limited faith in accounting theory generally and the ability to assess the amount of the provision in particular.

20 Ibid, at p 643.

21 Ibid, at pp 644–5; the learned judge added that there is doubt whether accounting theory could impact the determination of the profit for purposes of tax law, although he fell short of determining what the rules were that would show the amount of the provision as complying with the condition of "reliable enough". It is worthwhile noting that Lord Radcliffe was more than a little surprised in relation to the attempt to include in the provision amount, at current values, the full risk that might be borne by the company if all of its employees were dismissed, since this risk related overall to periods of some decades.

22 See para 2.4. This distinction matches that made by GAAP between "provisions" that are to be taken into account in calculating the profit/loss and are allowable for deduction according to this rule, and "contingent liabilities" that are not taken into account in calculating the profit/loss (although it is possible to make a note to the accounts with respect thereto) and which may not be deducted according to this case.

23 *Britannia Airways*, Chapter 4, n 70.

24 The provision figure was calculated according to the average obtained from the cost of the general overhaul of the last ten engines which had undergone overhaul, and this average cost figure gave the average costs of a general overhaul for each flight hour. This average cost per flight hour was multiplied in each year by the number of hours that each plane had flown in that year, and the result constituted the annual provision figure for the required overhaul.

25 HMRC in BIM46550 make a distinction between aircraft that are owned by the taxpayer and those that are leased. With respect to leased aircraft, HMRC is prepared to regard the existence of a liability yet to be performed in the future as justifying (together with the fulfillment of the remaining conditions) the deduction of the provision, whereas in relation to an aircraft owned by the taxpayer, in their opinion, there was no requirement by statute to carry out an overhaul at any given period of time (as a condition for the permit) in order to create such a liability within the meaning of FRS#12. According to HMRC, only a contractual commitment met this condition and, therefore, in their view, only when a contract was signed regarding the repairs and the work to be carried out, only then could a provision be made with regard to the contractual liability yet to be performed.

26 *Jenners Princes Street Edinburgh Ltd v CIR* (1998) SSCD 196 (Sp C 166).

27 In fact, in the year in which the provision was entered, the company had yet to acquire a commitment towards the contractor in the future (as a result of the past events) and, *prima facie*, there was no room to recognize the provision.

28 HMRC now accepts the idea that such provision is allowable for tax purposes (see BIM46550).

29 *Herbert Smith*, Chapter 4, n 72.

30 See also *BSC Footwear Ltd v Rklgway* (1971) 47 TC 495.

31 BIM46550 justifiably (to my mind) pointed out that the amount of the provision that had been allowed for deduction in this case did not meet the general accounting tests set in Financial Reporting Standards No 12, "Provisions, contingent liabilities and contingent assets" (FRS#12) with respect to the factors that should be taken into consideration in calculating the provision under GAAP, including the time value of money: see para 2.4.1.

32 *Smith v Lion Brewery Co Ltd* (1910) 5 TC 568.

33 *Sun Insurance*, Chapter 6, n 6 (allowing deduction equal to 40% of the yearly premium receipts as a provision by insurance companies for estimating losses on unexpired risk).

34 *Titaghur Jute Factory Ltd v CIR* [1978] STC 166 (allowing provision for statutory leaving of gratuities for its employees in India in respect of their previous services).

35 *CIR v Lo & Lo (a firm)* [1984] STC 366 (allowing deduction of reserves as provisions for benefits to which employees were entitled on termination of their employment contract).

36 For example, *Clayton v Newcastle-under-Lyme Corp* (1888) 2 TC 416 (not allowing provisions for future repairs and renewal); and *RTZ Oil and Gas Ltd v Elliss* (1987) 61 TC 132 (disallowing provisions by company engaged in the exploitation of a North Sea oilfield for anticipated future expenditure on the completion of the exploitation in "cleaning up" the sea bed on the ground that this will be capital when incurred).

37 See Tolley's Corporation Tax 2005–06/64 Trading Income/"Contingent and future liabilities," 64.28; Tolley's Tax Guide 2005–06, 20.11; Yellow Tax Handbook 2005–2006/PART II/Inland Revenue Interpretations/ "RI 30".

38 In the terms of GAAP, such liabilities could have been treated as "contingencies", see para 2.4.2.

39 *Navel Colliery Co Ltd v CIR* (1928)12 TC 1017 (not allowing provisions for

reconditioning works charged in the account in the period before the works began).

40 *Merchant (Peter) Ltd v Stedeford* (1948) 30 TC 496.

41 In the *Merchant* case, which was held before *Southern Railway of Peru*, Chapter 4, n 51, the court dismissed the company's appeal against the Commissioners' rejection to allow deducting of provision to replace utensils provided by the factory owner by holding that legal liability would only arise if the factory owner made a claim for breach of contract. I think (with all due respect) that the court was wrong in this matter, because no one should have to wait for a claim for breach of contract in order to decide that the liability is fixed (in the present). To my understanding, in this case such provision ought to have been allowed for deduction, on the basis that all the conditions were met: see para 2.4.1.

42 *Monthly Salaries Loan Co Ltd v Furlong* (1962) 40 TC 313 (not allowing deduction of provisions in respect of future cost of collecting debts, stating that there was no general accounting practice as regards such a deduction and there was no necessity for such deduction under accounting practice).

43 *H Ford & Co Ltd v CIR* (1926) 12 TC 997 (not allowing provisions for monies claimed against the company which it disputed).

44 *Spencer (James) & Co v CIR* (1950) 32 TC 111 (not allowing the deduction of provisions in respect of future payment of damages regarding accidents to employees because liability had not yet been established).

45 *CIR v Niddrie & Benhar Coal Co Ltd* (1951) 32 TC 244 (not allowing provision for a liability not admitted, but finally settled by subsequent agreement).

46 *Worsley Brewery Co Ltd v CIR* (1932) 17 TC 349 (not allowing the claim of the company to deduct the fee it paid for services provided by an accounting firm between 1925 and 1928 regarding the company's accounts during the seven years before 1925, by spreading this fee over the seven accounting periods before 1925. The court held that the liability for the fees was incurred in 1925 and not in any earlier year).

47 *Albion Rovers Football Club Ltd v CIR* (1952) 33 TC 331 (not allowing deduction of provisions charged by a football club by the end of the football season in respect of its liabilities to the players to pay them wages not only for the playing season, but also for the non-playing period of the contract. The House of Lords held that the fact that the club had assumed liability for all of the playing season period (including the non-playing season) did not make the total payment for that period a proper deduction for the year in question, and the sums related to the non-playing season, which started during the following tax year, were expenses of that following year).

48 *Collins (Edward) & Sons Ltd v CIR* (1924) 12 TC 773 (not allowing provisions for anticipated losses in the future arising from a subsequent fall in prices because the amount claimed was not a loss which had been suffered in the tax year in question).

49 *JH Young & Co v CIR* (1925) 12 TC 817.

50 *Whimster & Co v CIR* (1925) 12 TC 813 (not allowing a provision for future loss arising from a fall in charter hire rates).

51 *CIR v Hugh T Barrie Ltd* (1928) 12 TC 1223 (in respect of provisions for anticipated losses in the future arising from a subsequent fall in prices).

52 In the same spirit, see *Meat Traders Ltd v Cushing* (1997) SSCD 245 (Sp C 131) (not allowing provision for future anticipated operating losses).

53 *Paisley Cemetery Co v Reith* (1898) 4 TC 59.

54 *London Cemetery Co v Barnes* (1917) 7 TC 92 (in respect of the liability of cemetery companies that received lump sums for the future maintenance of graves).

55 *Vallambrosa Rubber Co Ltd v Farmer* (1910) 5 TC 529.
56 *Duple Motor Bodies Ltd v Ostime* (1959) 59 TC 537.
57 *Threlfall*, Chapter 4, n 66.
58 But in respect to "provisions", see BIM46550 as mentioned in Chapter 7, n 31.
59 See para 2.4.
60 See, e.g. *Vallambrosa Rubber*, Chapter 7, n 55; and *Duple Motor*, Chapter 7, n 56.
61 As indicated by BIM42201, until the judgment in the *Threlfall* case was handed down, and relying on the above-mentioned cases, HMRC believed that a "tax principle" existed that in every case, the expenses for tax purposes should be deducted on the date they crystallized (regardless of the date of payment) and they would not be treated for tax purposes according to accounting practice (applying the spread principle matching the timing of the recognition of the income). In any event after *Threlfall*, HMRC's position today is to adhere absolutely to GAAP in all aspects relating to the timing of the recognition of an expense as a liability whose payment date falls in the future. See Yellow Tax Handbook: 2005–2006, Part II/Inland Revenue Interpretations/"R1 231" (June 2001).
62 See BIM46510; BIM46540; BIM46555; BIM42201; BIM42215; BIM46565; Inland Revenue, Tax Bulletin, Issue 44, December 1999, 707–9; Yellow Tax Handbook 2005–2006/PART II/Press Release etc./12 April 1995 ICAEW "Relationship between accountancy practice and tax computation in the light of *Gallagher v Jones* and *Johnson v Britannia Airways Ltd*. Guidance note" (TAX 10/95)/ Provisions; Inland Revenue, Tax Bulletin, Issue February 1999, 624 as regards changes in accounting practice superseding the decision in *Britannia Airways*; Inland Revenue, Tax Bulletin, April 1999, at pp 636–9; and Inland Revenue, Tax Bulletin, Issue 15, February 1995, p 189.
63 As regards this condition, Stobart, Chapter 4, n 95, believes that, currently, after the Consistent Approach has been applied (mainly according to legislation) and clear accounting principles have been determined with respect to the measuring of provision amounts (as seen in para 2.4.1), there is no longer any room for this condition (which originated in the cases from the 1950s).
64 With respect to HMRC's position on this issue, see Chapter 7, n 61.
65 See: Yellow Tax Handbook 2005–2006, Part II/Inland Revenue Interpretations/ R1 231 (June 2001) Interaction of Tax and Accountancy Deferred Revenue Expenditure/ "Our Understanding of the Law"; 2003–2004 Chiltern's Yellow Tax Guide Archive/ Part I Income tax, Corporation Tax, Capital Gains Tax/ Commentary on Statutes/ Income and Corporation Taxes Act 1988/Part IV Provisions relating to the Schedule D Charges/74 "General rules as to deductions not allowable" (B3. 1202); Tolley's Corporation Tax 2005–06/64, Chapter 7, n 37; Tolley's Income Tax 2005–06/82 Trading Income/ "Contingent and future liabilities", 82.45; Tolley's Tax Guide 2005–06/20 How are Business Profits Calculated?/ "General Rules for Computing Trading Profits" (ICTA 1988, s 74; FA 2004, ss 50 and 51; FA 2005, ss 80, 84 and Sch 4; ITTOIA 2005, ss 29, 33, 34)/ "Provisions for Future Liabilities" 20.11.
66 Ibid.
67 Under IRC§162(a): "There shall be allowed as a deduction all the ordinary and necessary expenses paid or incurred during the taxable year in carrying on any trade or business". For UK tax law, see Chapter 7, n 12, and for Israeli tax law, see Chapter 7, n 235.
68 See, e.g. IRC§467, in which, in relation to rent, it is provided that both parties to the lease transaction (the landlord and the tenant) should report rent for tax on the accrual basis – whatever the system may be by which they keep their books. In IRC§468, special provisions have been set relating to the deduction of liabilities of mines and quarries, including deduction of provisions with

respect to the expected costs relating to the deduction and rehabilitation of the mines upon their closure. In IRC§1272–1274, the OID method was adopted with respect to the sale of assets in return for a note. The OID system separates the component relating to the principal of the payment for the item sold and the interest component resulting from the fact that the note is slated for future payment. For the OID method, see also Chapter 7, n 82.

69 In relation to statutory provisions in UK law that determined certain timing for the deduction of certain liabilities, see, e.g. Chapter 7, n 13. In relation to statutory provisions in Israeli law that determined certain timing for the deduction of certain liabilities, see, e.g. Chapter 7, 236.

70 See Chapter 7, n 68.

71 IRC§461(a).

72 IRC§461(a) states as follows: "The amount of any deduction or credit allowed by this subtitle shall be taken for the taxable year which is the proper taxable year under the method of accounting used in computing taxable income".

73 Like those mentioned in IRC§461(i) that relate to the questions of timing of the expense in certain cases like the death of the taxpayer, tax shelters and the like.

74 For IRC§446(b) and the condition of "clearly reflect income", see paras 4.4.1.2 and 4.4.2.3.

75 Treas Reg §1.461–1(a)(2), 26 CFR §1.461–1(a)(2) (1986) stated: "under an accrual method of accounting", a liability (as defined in §1.446–1(c)(1)(ii)(B)) is incurred, and generally is taken into account for Federal Income Tax purposes, in the taxable year in which all the events have occurred that establish the fact of the liability, the amount of the liability can be determined with reasonable accuracy, and economic performance has occurred with respect to the liability.

76 18 July 1984, Pub. L 98–369, Div A, Title I, § 91(a), (e), 98 Stat 598, 607.

77 The Deficit Reduction Act of 1984, Pub L No 98–369, §92(a), 91(a) Stat 598–610 (1984) (codified at IRC §461(h) USCS S26 461(h). See also Treas Reg §1.461–1(a)(2)(i), 26 CFR § 1.461–1(a)(2) (1986).

78 IRC§461(h)(2)(a).

79 IRC§461(h)(2)(b).

80 IRC§461(h)(2)(c), although according to this provision, if the taxpayer makes immediate payment to an insurance company to cover such commitment (in present value), such expense will be recognized at the time it is so made.

81 IRC§461(h)(2)(d); nevertheless IRC§461(h)(5), as originally enacted, provided that this rule did not apply to any item to which IRC§166(C) or (F) (relating to reserves for bad debts), IRC§463 (relating to vacation pay), IRC§466 (relating to discount coupons) or any other provisions of IRC which specifically provide for a deduction for a reserve for estimated expenses. Subsequent changes in law deleted all references to specific sections of the IRC so that IRC§461(h)(5) now provides that IRC§461(h) shall not apply to any item for which a deduction is allowable under a provision of the IRC that specifically provides for a deduction for a reserve for estimated expenses. See Pub L 100–203, §10201(b)(5) and Pub L 99–514, §§805(c)(5) and 823(b)(1).

82 The OID method involves the re-characterizing of a deferred payment transaction in accordance with the time value of money. If, for example, the consideration includes a note, and such a note has a principal value of 100, but a present value of 60, then the OID method dictates that that only 60 will be realized for tax purposes in connection with the transaction, and the remaining 40 will be characterized as interest for tax purposes. With respect to the present value of the note – this will be deemed to be consideration for the item sold and, with respect to which a taxpayer reporting on a cash basis may continue

to defer the date of the recognition thereof until the payment date (the making of the actual payment). However, with respect to the interest component in the note – both the recognition of the income therefrom (in the hands of the recipient of the note) as well as recognition of the expense thereof (in the hands of the maker of the note) – this will be made on an accrual basis even if either of the parties is a taxpayer that reports on a cash basis. As to the dilemmas faced by the Senate Committee when it discussed the 84 Reform with respect to the time of the deduction of future liabilities, see Kaywood, Chapter 3, n 32, pp 541–3, 545 and 550.

83   Treas Reg §1.461–4 (g)(6), 26 CFR §1.461–4 (g)(6) (1986).

84   Thus, e.g. Treas Reg §1.461–5(b)(5)(ii) provides that, in the case of a liability for taxes, the matching requirement of the recurring item exception is deemed satisfied.

85   i.e. allowing deduction in the present year not only of absolute liabilities, but of provisions accounted for in the company's books by reason of liabilities having been created in the past, even if the amount or future payment thereof is not known (and, in this connection, has made do with evaluations or calculations); see para 7.2.1.1.

86   As defined in para 7.1.1.

87   For the meaning of these expressions, see para 7.1.

88   *Bauer Bros Co v Commissioner* 46 F2d 874 (6th Cir 1931).

89   *Brown*, Chapter 4, n 255, at p 201; in this case, the subject matter related to commissions taken by an insurance agent in respect of policy sales and that agent's commitment to return the commissions so taken in the event of the policies being cancelled. The insurance agent sought to deduct from his income in the fiscal year provisions he made to return expected commissions (in the event of the policies being cancelled).

90   *Brown*, at pp 195–7.

91   *Dixie Pine*, Chapter 4, n 258.

92   Nevertheless, in Rev Rul 67–127, 1967–1 CB 113, a concession has been given as compared to the *Dixie Pine* case, as to state property tax, by confirming that a taxpayer is not required to postpone a deduction of property taxes accruable in the preceding taxable year until the year of payment under protest.

93   *Harold v Commissioner* 192 F2d 1002 (4th Cir 1951) (allowing a strip miner to deduct a reserve for restoring the strip-mined land, although this reserve was based upon estimation. It appears that the characteristic of this exception lies in the fact that the liability on account of which the provision was made originates in statute, as distinct from a voluntary liability created by agreement between the parties). See also *Denise Coal Co v Commissioner* 271 F2d 930 (3rd Cir 1959).

94   *Ohio River Collieries Co v Commissioner* 77 TC 1369 (TC 1981) (allowing a strip-mining company to deduct the estimated cost of reclamation work it was required to perform upon completion of mining). As in the *Harold* case, the restoration liability of Ohio River's was made by law. Under the 84 Reform, IRC§468 was added, which, amongst other things, statutorily adopts the case law mentioned, and allows a deduction of provisions on account of statutory mining liabilities to bear the costs relating to restoration of land upon completion of the mining and quarrying works.

95   *Pacific Grape Products Co v Commissioner* 219 F2d 862 (9th Cir 1955) (allowing the deduction of the estimated cost of labeling and preparing goods for shipping and brokerage fees to be paid the following year).

96   *Schuessler v Commissioner* 230 F2d 722 (5th Cir 1956) (a provision was allowed for a deduction that was made by a taxpayer engaged in the sale of gas furnaces, and which was designed to cover the costs (as he had estimated them) of

a liability given by him to his customers to turn furnaces on and off for a period of five years). It seems difficult to explain this judgment given the other cases that addressed the question of allowing the provisions for deduction, and it seems that, to a large degree, this judgment was affected by the fact that it had indeed been proven to the court that such liability to customers actually helped the taxpayer sell more than his competitors.

97 *Beacon Publishing*, Chapter 6, n 100, and see our discussion in para 6.3.2.4.

98 *Jefferson Memorial Gardens Inc v Commissioner* 390 F2d 161 (5th Cir 1968) (allowing a deduction of a provision in the amount estimated by the taxpayer (15% of its income), which was designed to cover a liability to develop and build graves in respect of an advance received in connection with the sale of the burial plot. It appears that the court's willingness to deviate in this case from the prevailing rule that a provision will not be allowed as a deduction for tax purposes may be explained in light of the fact that the amount to which the expense related had been deposited in a special trust fund). But see also Chapter 7, n 107.

99 *Bituminous Casualty Corp v Commissioner* 57 TC 58 (TC 1971) (indicating that if, at the time the provision was accounted for, it was clear that it reflected amounts that would certainly not be retained by the taxpayer, since, even if they were not demanded in the future to be paid to a third party or to the payer, then they would be transferred to the State by statute they would be allowed as a deduction for tax purposes).

100 *Harrison v Heiner* 28 F2d 985 (D Pa 1928).

101 *Vang v Lewellyn* 35 F2d 283 (3rd Cir PA 1929).

102 *Quality Roofing Co v Commissioner* 16 BTA 1370 (BTA 1929).

103 *Lucas v American Code Co* 280 US 445 (1930).

104 *Commissioner v Old Dominion SS Co* 47 F2d 148 (2nd Cir 1931).

105 *Commissioner v Southeastern Express Co* 56 F2d 600 (5th Cir 1932).

106 *Strother v Commissioner* 55 F2d 626 (4th Cir 1932).

107 *Acacia Park Cemetery Ass'n v Commissioner* 67 F2d 699 (7th Cir 1933); here and in *Commissioner v Cedar Park Cemetery Ass'n* 183 F2d 553 (7th Cir 1950) where deduction of a provision was claimed that was designated for precisely the same purpose as in the *Jefferson Memorial* case (Chapter 7, n 98), but the amount had not been deposited in a special trust account designed for that purpose, the provision was not allowed as a deduction. See also *Green Lawn Memorial Park Inc v McDonald*, 164 F Supp 438 (D Pa 1958).

108 *Security Flour*, Chapter 4, n 213.

109 *Stevenson v US* 250 F Supp 647 (SD NY 1965) (which held that a taxpayer selling records could not deduct for tax purposes a provision that he had made to cover his liability to customers to supply a free record bonus despite the fact that the provision was required according to GAAP, since a liability could not be deducted as an allowable expense for tax purposes without clear proof confirming not merely the existence of the absolute commitment with reasonable certainty, but also the amount of the liability itself. Evaluations concerning the expected production costs to supply those records were insufficient).

110 *Bell Electric Co v Commissioner* 45 TC 158 (TC 1965).

111 *Peoples Bank & Trust Co v Commissioner* 415 F2d 1341 (7th Cir 1969) (where it was held that a bank cannot deduct as an expense in the current year interest that had accrued in respect of customers' deposits falling due (together with the applicable interest thereon) only in the ensuing year, since there was no certainty relating to those deposits being repaid only at the end of the term; from this it followed that it was not sufficiently certain that the bank would indeed be compelled to meet its obligation).

112 *All-Steel Equipment Inc v Commissioner* 467 F2d 1184 (7th Cir 1972).
113 *Continental Illinois,* Chapter 4, n 270 (where it was held that the fact that the
    bank was exposed to repayment of part of the interest to the customers did
    not enable a deduction of the resulting amount of exposure for tax purposes.
    In the court's opinion, this did not amount to the required degree of certainty
    according to the "all events test", and from this it followed that it was not
    possible to recognize it as a deductible expense).
114 *Fox v Commissioner* TC Memo 1987–209 (US Tax Court Memos 1987) (where it
    was held that a taxpayer was not entitled to deduct a payment liability where
    the very liability was subject to a legal argument in court).
115 *Diversified Fashions Inc v Commissioner* TC Memo 1988–239 (US Tax Court
    Memos 1988).
116 *Exxon Mobil Corp v Commissioner* 114 TC 293 (TC 2000) (in this case it was held
    that a partnership reporting on an accrual basis, which engaged in oil produc-
    tion and made provisions relating to its estimated expenses for equipment
    replacement and repair, as well as in connection with its expected costs for
    vacating its installations and restoring the soil, would not be entitled to
    deduct these provisions for tax purposes as an expense).
117 See, e.g. *Continental Pipe Mfg Co v Poe* 59 F2d 694 (9th Cir 1932); *Buffalo Union
    Furnace Co v Helvering* 72 F2d 399 (2nd Cir 1934); *Crown Cork & Seal Co v US* 73
    F2d 997 (2nd Cir 1934); *Shapleigh Hardware Co v US* 81 F2d 694 (8th Cir 1936);
    Air-Way Electric, Chapter 6, n 56; *Louisville Provision Co v Commissioner* 155 F2d
    505 (6th Cir 1946); *Canton Cotton Mills v US* 119 Ct Cl 24 (Ct Cl 1951); *Wayne
    Title & Trust Co v Commissioner* 195 F2d 401 (3rd Cir 1952); *Streight Radio,*
    Chapter 4, n 270; *Commissioner v Milwaukee & Suburban Transport Corp* 366 US
    965 (US 1961); and *Juniata Farmers Co-op Ass'n v Commissioner* 43 TC 836 (TC
    1965).
118 See para 7.3.2.2.1 and Chapter 7, nn 167–177.
119 *Frederick Villa Franca v Commissioner* 359 F2d 849 (6th Cir 1965) (future costs of
    teaching dance lessons; citing the trilogy of prepaid income cases).
120 *Spencer, White & Prentis Inc v Commissioner* 144 F2d 45 (2nd Cir 1944) (esti-
    mated future cost of restoration of premises adjoining construction site).
121 *Harris v Commissioner* TC Memo 1969–49 (US Tax Court Memos 1969)
    (estimated future cost of research services).
122 *Bell Electric,* Chapter 7, n 110 (future services under warranty agreements).
123 e.g. *Pioneer Auto Serve Co v Commissioner* 36 BTA 213 (BTA 1937) (automobile
    service contracts); and *Diversified Auto Services Inc v Commissioner* TC Memo
    1982–108 (US Tax Court Memos 1982) (future costs under automobile rust
    proofing warranty contracts).
124 Regarding GAAP definitions of these items, see paras 2.4.1 and 2.4.2. See in
    this connection Michael L. Schler, "Sales of Assets after Tax Reform: Section
    1060, Section 338(h) (10) and more", 43 Tax L Rev 605, 666–76 (1988). This
    article, examines, *inter alia,* the significance of not permitting expenses by
    reason of contingent liabilities in the context of the question of a sale of assets
    (that fall in the net of the provisions of ss 1060 and 338(h)(10) of the IRC) and
    the sale price of those assets was impacted by the fact that the purchaser had
    assumed a liability whose amount was unknown, and which was imposed on
    the seller in relation to the assets sold. The article which deals in this context
    with the question of the imputation of the sale proceeds and the sale costs,
    both from the seller's standpoint and also from the more distant standpoint of
    the buyer, goes beyond the subject of our discussion, although the questions
    raised on the subjects of the manner of imputing the sale price and the pur-
    chase price of a product the sale of which embodies the existence of a contin-
    gent liability, forms another facet of the difficulty that arises in all matters

relating to the way in which tax laws address the areas of uncertainty in modern economic life.

125 *Commissioner v Brooklyn Radio Services Corp* 79 F2d 833 (2nd Cir 1935).

126 *American Hotels Corp v Commissioner* 134 F2d 817 (2nd Cir 1943).

127 *David J Joseph v Commissioner* 136 F2d 410 (5th Cir 1943).

128 *Baltimore & OR Co v Commissioner* 78 F2d 456 (4th Cir 1935).

129 *Stiver v Commissioner* 90 F2d 505 (8th Cir 1937).

130 *Rhodes v Commissioner* 100 F2d 966 (6th Cir 1939).

131 *Shoolman v Commissioner* 108 F2d 987 (1st Cir 1940).

132 *Bickerstaff v Commissioner* 128 F2d 366 (5th Cir 1942).

133 *Crescent Wharf & Warehouse Company v Commissioner* 518 F2d 772 (9th Cir 1975); in this case, following the injury of an employee, when the statutory liability (under California State legislation) itself had become absolute, the employer sought to deduct as an expense a provision that he had made in his books in relation to those employees who were entitled to receive the indemnity sum, although that amount had not yet been paid to them and was, of itself, not certain and absolute.

134 *Milwaukee & Suburban Transport Corp v Commissioner* 283 F2d 279 (7th Cir 1960).

135 *AAA*, Chapter 6, n 110.

136 *Consolidated Edison*, Chapter 4, n 262. In that case, it was also held that even if an advance is taxable on the date it is received, despite the fact that the right to receive it is in dispute, this does not mean that the expected expense relating to that advance will be allowed as a deduction. See also Chapter 7, n 137.

137 In the *Milwaukee & Suburban Transport* case and the *Consolidated Edison* case. In IRC§461(f), the US legislator sought to clarify that in cases where there was a dispute in relation to the very existence of the liability, the timing of its deduction for tax purposes would be deferred until the dispute ended, and the existence of the liability would no longer be in dispute. However, within the framework of this provision, the legislator sought to repeal by statute the rule in the *Consolidated Edison* case, and provide a statutory answer to the problem that had come about following the cases that created a lack of correlation between income and expense. This section, which was designed to "serve" the matching principle provides, *inter alia*, in IRC§461(f)(4), that even where the liability is in dispute in the particular circumstances, if payment has actually been made in respect thereof, that payment will be allowed as a deductible expense. However, an analysis of this section reveals that it has absolutely nothing to do with the matching principle, since, as we have seen in para 2.4, the "matching" referred to by the accounting principle is not between the timing of the actual payment and the timing of the recognition of the income, but between the timing of the recognition of income and that of the recognition of the liability that served to create that income.

138 In the *AAA* case, Chapter 6, n 110.

139 As stated, in 1984, IRC§461(h) was added, according to which the "all events test" cannot exist unless all of the economic conditions for performance relating to that liability have been fulfilled. For the stricter interpretation of the requirement of IRC§461(h)(2)(A)(I), see, e.g. *IES Indus v US* 253 F3d 350, 353 (8th Cir 2001); *Yankee Atomic Elect. Co v US* 112 F3d 1569 (Fed Cir 1997); and *Sealy Corp v Commissioner* 107 TC 177 (TC 1996).

140 *Hughes*, Chapter 4, n 254; here, a Nevada casino operated, *inter alia*, a number of "advanced" gaming machines in which, in addition to the wins gained when a number of symbols showed, provided an additional win under a particular combination. The amount of that additional win accumulated over an unknown number of years until it came up by chance. According to the

Nevada Gaming Commission Regulations, the casino owner did not draw for himself the amounts that had been deposited in those "advanced" machines under the accrued win amount. According to GAAP, the casino owner was required to record in his books and reduce in the calculation of his profits a provision on account of the liability to pay the accrued win amount, the amount thereof being the same as that which the casino owner would pay the winner (if there was such a winner) at the end of the year. The casino owner sought to deduct this provision as recorded in his books as a deductible expense.

141 See para 7.3.1 in relation to Treas Reg § 1.461–1(a)(2); IRS went on to argue that if the casino were to close, discontinue its business, sell its business or go bankrupt, or stop gaming on those machines, then this liability would never be realized.

142 IRS had successfully employed such arguments in a similar case involving another Nevada casino in *Nightingale v US* 684 F2d 611 (9th Cir 1982).

143 Although, as mentioned, the court in *Hughes*, Chapter 4, n 254, at pp 603–4 reiterated the rule that in the US, tax accounting did not follow GAAP, and recognized the powers of IRS to order the taxpayer to deviate (for tax purposes) from GAAP.

144 *General Dynamics Corp*, ("**GD**"), Chapter 4, n 267.

145 According to Rev Rul 79–338, 1979–2 CB 212, an accrual basis corporation that has a self-insured medical care program administered by an independent administrator may not currently deduct estimated liability for medical services rendered during the year for which claims have not been certified eligible for payment by medical insurance administrators prior to the end of this year.

146 Jensen, Chapter 2, n 22, at p 241.

147 The shortfall resulted as a result of the non-filing of claims by the insured parties who were entitled to payment of the indemnity amount.

148 Another ground on which the Supreme Court relied pertained to the provision contained in 26 USCS § 832(b)(5) that related to insurance companies and allowed them (on certain conditions) to deduct provisions that they had made in respect of insurance claims "that had occurred but had yet to be reported". The court deduced from this section that if the "all events test" were interpreted in a broad manner, this would render the provision contained in IRC§832(b)(5) redundant, contrary to the rule of interpretation whereby "the legislator does not mince his words without reason".

149 *American Code*, Chapter 7, n 103; and *Security Flour*, Chapter 4, n 213.

150 *GD*, Chapter 4, n 267, at pp 242–3, and in the majority opinion words: "Last link in the chain of events creating liability for purposes of the all events test".

151 See in the same vein: *Brown*, Chapter 4, n 255, at pp 201–2; and *AAA*, Chapter 6, n 110, at p 693.

152 *GD* ibid, at p 249; the minority view continued in this connection by saying: "Unfortunately, the court today ignores the pragmatic roots of the 'all events' test and instead applies it in an essentially mechanistic and wholly unrealistic manner. Because the liability in this case was fixed with no less certainty than the range of expenses both routinely accrued by accrual method taxpayers and approved as deductible for tax purposes by this court and other courts in a variety of circumstances, I respectfully dissent."

153 Jensen, Chapter 2, n 22, at p 245.

154 *Crescent Wharf*, Chapter 7, n 133. It is submitted that the *GD* ruling rejected the result of the *Crescent Wharf* case since, according to "the last link" in the chain of events, it would not be possible to deduct the provision for an indemnity

amount by reason of the employees' injury as long as the employer had not received the formal demand from the State.

155 *Hughes*, Chapter 4, n 254. It is submitted that the *GD* ruling rejected the result of the *Hughes* case since, according to "the last link" in the chain of events, the casino's commitment to pay the accrued win amount has not yet occurred, as long as any gambler had not won the amount of the win. In the same spirit, see Michael Dubetz, "Case Comment: United States v General Dynamics: The Deduction of Estimated Liabilities by Accrual Method Taxpayers: The All Events Test and Economic Performance", 49 Ohio St LJ 1439 (1989).

156 *Challenge Publications Inc v Commissioner* 845 F2d 1541 (9th Cir 1988). In this case, the court of appeals rejected a magazine publishing company's appeal and accepted the position of IRS that negated the deduction of the provision as an expense by ruling that a provision that it had made on the basis of an evaluation of the number of magazines that would be returned to it does not fulfill the "all events test". The court ruled, base on the *GD* case, that the first condition in the "all events test" required that the very existence of the liability be absolute and certain, and the second condition of the "all events test" required that even if the liability had indeed been created in the past, it would not be possible to deduct a liability whose amount had been fixed (as in the particular case) on the basis of statistical evaluations or assessments. In addressing the taxpayer's claim that this position completely negated the "matching principle", the court simply responded that "matching of income and expenses is not an additional requirement of the 'all events' test". See the same results in *World Airways Inc v Commissioner* 564 F2d 886 (9th Cir 1977), where the taxpayer was not allowed to allocate the reasonably foreseeable cost of statutorily mandated aeroplane repairs to the periods in which the plane mileage revenues were accumulated.

157 *Dana Distributors*, Chapter 4, n 240, In this case (as mentioned in para 5.3.1.5), the distributor's request to deduct the provision to repay a deposit that had been received in connection with the sale of a container or packaging (which was to have been returned to the consumer upon the return of the bottle or the packaging) was denied. Based on the *GD* case, the timing of the recognition of the expense in connection with these refunds should be deferred until the year in which the containers were indeed actually returned, in a manner whereby its obligation to repay the deposit would be completely certain and absolute. For the same results, see *La Salle Portland Cement Co v Commissioner* 4 BTA 438 (BTA 1926); *Beadleston & Woerz Inc v Commissioner* 5 BTA 165 (BTA 1926); and *Wilson Furs Inc v Commissioner* 29 BTA 319 (BTA 1933). According to Rev Rul 78–273, 1978–2 CB 163, an accrual method beverage distributor cannot utilize a reserve for State-mandated deposits on non-refillable containers upon which refundable deposits are paid by the retailer. Such deposits must be included in income when received and can be deducted only when empty containers are returned.

158 *Arkla Inc v US* 1992 US, App Lexis 18461 (1992) (in this case, based on the *GD* case, the court disallowed a provision that the company had claimed in 1977–79 to cover a liability to the Department of Energy).

159 *Cleveland Trencher*, Chapter 4, n 269 (relying on the rule in *GD*, allowance of a liability for commission as an expense for deduction was denied when the court of appeals ruled that at the end of the fiscal year in which that expense had been claimed, it had not been proven that the provider of the services who is entitled to that commission had indeed, at that stage, fulfilled all of his liabilities down to the very last, in a manner which made the liability absolute and certain).

160 *Gold Coast Hotel &Casino v US* 158 F3d 484 (9th Cir 1998). Here, a casino

owner had created a customers' club in which the club members were entitled to accumulate points the more they used the casino. According to the rules of the members' club, once 1,200 points had been accumulated, the member was entitled to prizes. The taxpayer sought to deduct as an expense at the end of each year a provision to the extent of the financial value of the points accumulated by the club members in that year, and which had not yet been realized as prizes, such value being fixed according to the value of the prizes that the points conferred, divided by the number of points that had been accrued, but had yet to be used. At the same time, the taxpayer registered at the end of each year as income the points' cash value that had been deducted in the past as expenses in respect of the points accumulated by the club members in the preceding years, and which had not been converted into prizes.

161 Ibid, at pp 486–7.

162 Ibid, at p 487. To my mind, this distinction seems somewhat bewildering, mainly given the fact that, in the *GD* case, the taxpayer had demanded the expense only after that third party had already provided the service.

163 Ibid, with regard to the possibility that the casino would never be demanded to pay the prize, the court went on to state (at 487) that: "... the potential nonpayment of an incurred liability exists for every business that uses an accrual method, and it does not prevent accrual ... The existence of an absolute liability is necessary; absolute certainty that it will be discharged by payment is not."

164 In *Resale Mobile Homes*, Chapter 4, n 225, the Supreme Court rejected the taxpayer's argument that the test prescribed in the *GD* case should also be applied to the matter of the timing of recognition of the income, it being held there that the income of the taxpayer who kept his books according to GAAP and reported on the accrual basis method should be recognized for tax purposes upon the right to receive the income crystallizing, and that timing will not be deferred until the date that is concurrent with the date on which the income is actually received, when the last event required as a condition for obtaining the payment is fulfilled.

165 As mentioned in para 7.3.2.1.2.

166 As defined in para 7.1.2.

167 *US v Anderson* 269 US 422 (US 1926); here, the Supreme Court held that it was not possible to make a correct calculation of the taxpayer's chargeable income for income tax purposes in 1916 without factoring into the calculation its liability to pay the Federal Munitions Sales Tax, as all of the circumstances that created the obligation to pay it had crystallized in their entirety in 1916. In light of this, it was held that this liability would be deducted as an expense in calculating the profit in that year, despite the fact that the dispatch of the charge notice and timing of the payment would occur in the succeeding year.

168 *Laurens Steel v Commissioner* 442 F2d 1131 (3rd Cir 1971) (deduction in current values were allowed for future payments to a fund providing supplemental unemployment benefits to lay off workers).

169 *Franklin County*, Chapter 4, n 212 (deduction in current values were allowed even though the identity of the ultimate creditor was unknown; the key factor being that the obligation to pay was fixed in the year the court allowed the deduction).

170 *Cyclops Corp v US* 408 F Supp 1287 (D Pa 1976) (deductions in nominal values allowed for accrued liabilities under an unemployment benefit plan; amounts became sufficiently absolute and irrevocable during the tax years in dispute).

171 *Inland Steel Co v US* 677 F2d 72 (1st Cir 1982) (deductions in nominal values allowed for accrued liabilities under an unemployment benefit plan).

172 *Washington Post Co v US*, 186 Ct Cl 528 (Ct Cl 1969) (same as in the *Inland Steel* case, ibid).
173 *Reynolds Metals Co v Commissioner* 68 TC 943, 960 (TC 1977) (suggesting that the result might differ if the time period is so long as to make liability a "partial nullity").
174 *Cooper Communities Inc v US* 678 F Supp 1408 (D Ark 1987); here, it was held that a dealer in building units could deduct as an expense a liability to pay commission that he owed to the salesman of those units that he had sold in the building, and whose construction had been completed, despite the fact that the commission itself would actually be paid to that salesman some 16 to 19 months after the day on which the sale had been completed. IRS argued that the liability was subject to the right to cancel payment of the commission in the event of the cancellation of a sale agreement by the unit purchasers, and, therefore, it should not be regarded as a liability that met the certain and absolute requirement on that date. This argument was rejected as the court was satisfied that the performance of the sale agreements with the unit purchasers was not a precondition for the taxpayer paying the commission to the salesman.
175 *Crescent Wharf*, Chapter 7, n 133.
176 *Hughes*, Chapter 4, n 254, at pp 604–5.
177 *Gold Coast*, Chapter 7, n 160.
178 As defined in para 7.3.2.
179 *Burnham Corp v Commissioner* 878 F2d 86 (2nd Cir 1989).
180 Calculated on the basis of the formula of 16 × 12 × $1,250 = $240,000.
181 As we saw in our discussion in para 7.3.1, in some of the cases addressed by IRC§461(h), the deferral extends until the date of actual payment, while in others, the deferral subsists until the date which it is probable by definition would be close to the date of actual payment.
182 *GD*, Chapter 4, n 267.
183 As mentioned in para 7.3.2.1.3.
184 As defined in Treas Reg §1.461–1(a)2. See para 7.3.1.
185 As defined in IRC§446(b). See para 4.4.1.
186 *Mooney Aircraft Inc v US* 420 F2d 400 (5th Cir 1969).
187 For a case that criticized *Mooney Aircraft*, see *In re Dow Corning Corp* 270 BR 393 (Bankr. ED Mich 2001).
188 *Hodge v Commissioner* TC Memo 1973–64 (US Tax Court Memos 1973).
189 *Ford Motor Corp v Commissioner* 102 TC 87 (TC 1994).
190 *Burnham*, Chapter 7, n 179.
191 *Ford Motor*, ibid, at pp 103–4.
192 Geier, Chapter 3, n 35, p 112 attacks this approach that regards the matching principle as one that should be brought into account for tax law purposes, and criticizes the opportunity that was lost, according to her, to determine in this case that anti-arbitrage tax value supersedes the matching principle in any event.
193 As we have seen, in similar cases in which there was a substantial time gap between the date of the crystallization of the liability and the deduction thereof sought as an expense, and the date of expected payment, the courts chose to adopt the Full and Immediate Deduction Approach or, alternatively, the Deferred Deduction Date Approach.
194 See, e.g. Notice 91–10 1991–1 CB 317, Rev Rul 98–39 1998–33 IRB 4, Rev Rul 2007–3, 2007–1 CB 350.
195 For Treas Reg §1.461–5(b)(1), see para 7.3.1.
196 Rev Rul 67–127, Chapter 7, n 92.
197 See, e.g. Notice 90–64, 1990–2 CB 347, Announcement 91–89 (IRB 1991), Rev Proc 92–28, 1992–1 CB 745, Rev Proc 94–32, 1994–1 CB 627, etc.

198 See also Rev Rul 2003–90, 2003–2 CB 353, relating to the year of deduction of California franchise tax.
199 Rev Rul 80–182, 1980–2 CB 167.
200 Rev Proc 92–291, 1992–1 CB 748.
201 Rev Rul 98–39, 1998–2 CB 198.
202 Rev Proc 2008–25, 2008–13 IRB 686.
203 Under 26 USCS prec § 3301.
204 And see also Rev Rul 96–51, 1996–2 CB 36, and Rev Rul 2007–12, 2007–1 CB 685. relating to the year of deduction of a liability for payroll tax.
205 Halperin, Chapter 3, n 33, at p 520.
206 Halperin, at pp 525–526.
207 Cliff and Levine, Chapter 4, n 274, at pp 138–9.
208 Ibid, at p 123.
209 Ibid, at pp 138–9. In this context, they state that Staff of Joint Comm on Taxation, 98th Cong, 2nd Sess, Proposals Relating to Tax Shelters and other Tax Motivated Transactions 67–70 (discussing accrual of deductions prior to economic performance) (1984) and Treasury Department, General Explanations of Administration's Revenue Proposals in Fiscal Year 1985 Budget 109–11, 65–67 (1984) discussed the 84 Reform and rejected the proposal (relying on the theory of time value of money) not to enable the allowance of financing expenses at all on an accrual basis method.
210 Emil M. Sunley, "Observations on the Appropriate Tax Treatment of Future Costs", 23 Tax Notes 719, 720–721 (20 February 1984).
211 See also Donald W. Keifer, "The Tax Treatment of a 'Reverse' Investment: An Analysis of the Time Value of Money and the Appropriate Treatment of Future Costs", 26 Tax Notes 925 (4 March 1985) (supporting Sunley with helpful tables); William A. Klein, "Tax Accounting for Future Obligations: Basic Principles", 36 Tax Notes 623 (10 August 1987) (supporting Sunley with helpful spreadsheets); and Theodore S. Sims, "Environmental 'Remediation' Expenses and a Natural Interpretation of the Capitalization Requirement", 47 Nat'l Tax J 703, 705–11 (1994) (supporting Sunley with calculus). On the other hand, according to Halperin (Chapter 3, n 33), discounting at pre-tax rates would allow income streams to go untaxed. According to Halperin, in a system in which investments are available that systematically give returns in excess of post-tax interest; using pre-tax interest rates to discount future payments included in the tax basis often leads to tax benefits that are more valuable than the payments themselves are worth.
212 Which as been described in para 7.3.1.
213 Kaywood, Chapter 3, n 32, at p 554.
214 Jensen, Chapter 2, n 22, at p 246.
215 Ibid.
216 Dubetz, Chapter 7, n 155.
217 In addition, Dubetz mentions the fact that in the *Hughes* case, the taxpayer had a certain ability to control the timing of the actual payment of the win amount (e.g. by determining higher standards for winning on the same machines at the casino), but the employer in the *GD* case did not have such an ability.
218 Malman, Chapter 2, n 103, at pp 146–7. For the same opinion, see also Aidinoff and Lopata, "Section 461 and Accrual-Method Taxpayers: The Treatment of Liabilities Arising from an Obligation to be Performed in the Future", 33 Tax L Rev 789, 796–7 (1980); and Stanger, Vander Kam and Polifka, Chapter 2, n 22, at p 404.
219 Gunn, Chapter 3, n 5, at pp 12–13; in the same spirit, see also William L. Raby and Robert F. Richter, "Conformity of Tax and Financial Accounting", 139 J A 42

(March 1975); and Ted J. Fiflis, Homer Kripke and Paul M. Foster, *Accounting for Business Lawyers: Teaching Materials* (St. Paul, Minn, USA, West Group, 3rd edn, 1984), p 45.

220 Gunn, at pp 34–5.

221 Johnson, Chapter 3, n 27, at pp 391–2; and see references to Johnson's view also in paras 4.1.1, 4.4.4 and 6.3.4.

222 Klein, Chapter 3, n 23, at pp 1686–7; and see references to Klein's view also in paras 4.1.2, 5.3.3 and 6.3.4.

223 On IRC§461(h) reflecting mainly considerations of time value of money, see para 7.3.1.

224 Gordon T. Butler, "Section 461(h): Tax Fairness and Deduction of Future Liabilities", 26 U Mem L Rev 97, 101–2 (1995).

225 Butler, at pp 110–12. According to Butler, IRC§461(h) was superfluous due to the fact that even before that section was enacted, the tax authority had sufficient tools (i.e. the "all events test" and the "clear reflection test") to combat the phenomenon of the time value of money. As evidence of this, it can be seen that the ruling in the *Ford Motor* case (Chapter 7, n 189), which was handed down some 10 years after that Reform, did not even need the provision contained in IRC§461(h), and reached its conclusions based on the provision contained in IRC§461(b).

226 Gordon T. Butler, "Economic Benefit: Formulating a Workable Theory of Income Recognition", 27 Seton Hall L Rev 70 (1996).

227 Butler, ibid, n 226, at pp 73–5; and Butler, ibid, at n 224, p 128.

228 Butler, ibid, n 224, at pp 130–1.

229 Geier, Chapter 3, n 35, at pp 22–3; and see references to Geier's view also in paras 3.2, 4.1.1, 4.4.4 and 6.3.4.

230 Geier, at p 24. Moreover, she noted (at pp 83–5) that this integration was made at the time accounting theory had still not been formulated into a scientific theory, but reflected only different practices.

231 Geier, at pp 74–5.

232 Ibid, at pp 25–6.

233 Ibid, at p 91.

234 Ibid, at pp 95–6.

235 See, e.g. the first passage of s 17, ITO, Chapter 4, n 311 (which resembles in substance s 21(3), ICTA 1988) and s 32 of the ITO (which resembles in substance s 348, ITCA 1988). For UK tax law, see Chapter 7, n 12, and for US tax law, see Chapter 7, n 67.

236 For specific timing of deductions in the Israel, see, e.g. s 18, ITO; for specific timing of deductions in the UK tax system and in the US tax system, see Chapter 7, nn 13 and 68.

237 Exceptions to this "silence" may be found in the provisions contained in ss 8B and 49 of the ITO. Those provisions, which were mentioned in paras 4.5.1.1.4 and 4.5.1.1.5, provide that the recognition of the income from advances that are payable in connection to income from rent and insurance premiums "will be advanced" to the date on which the advances are received, and in parallel, the timing of the recognition of expenses. Section 49 directs that in respect of a transaction for which an insurance premium is received in advance, and which is liable to tax on the date of its receipt, the timing of the recognition of the liability for which the taxpayer has become liable in connection with that income will similarly be advanced. Section 8B directs that in respect of rent that is received as an advance, and which is chargeable to tax on the date of receipt, anticipated expenses relating to that advance will be deducted in the year in which they were expended and not in the year in which the advance was received. However, this provision continues by

providing that if it will not be possible to deduct those expenses in the future (in the absence of income that has already been taxed in the year in which it was received), the deduction of these expenses will then be advanced to the year in which the advance is received.

238 See, e.g. ITA (J) 30/84 *A Tragger Rental Apartments, East Netanya v Jerusalem Assessing Officer* 16 PDA 35; and ITA (H) 13/93 *Hermann Yitzchak v Haifa Assessing Officer* Taxes (April 1994), E-152.

239 See, e.g. *Nakid Ltd*, Chapter 4, n 319; CA 26/59 *Israeli Anilin Industries Company Ltd v Assessing Officer TA5* 14 PD 304: *Isranil*, Chapter 4, n 324; CA 600/75 *Tel Ronnen*, Chapter 4, n 324; and CA 159/79 *KBI Town Builders Group Ltd v AOLE* 35(3) PD 572.

240 *Southern Railway of Peru*, Chapter 4, n 51.

241 *Nakid*, Chapter 4, n 319.

242 CA 533/60 *Arkia Israeli Airlines Ltd v Assessing Officer TA1* 15 PD 1533.

243 *Tel Ronnen*, Chapter 4, n 324.

244 The *first Amisragas* case, Chapter 5, n 138.

245 CA 3468/93 *Reuven Deal and Furniture Mobile Ltd v Jerusalem Assessing Officer* Taxes (June 1996), E-58.

246 ITA (H) 157/89 *Damdo Ltd v Haifa Assessing Officer* Taxes (April 1991), E-68.

247 *Aharon*, Chapter 6, n 271.

248 And so the Supreme Court, in allowing the deduction of the provision for tax purposes, subject to the fulfillment of the three conditions mentioned, stated in *Tel Ronnen* (Chapter 4, n 324, p 91) thus: "If the company had stated that it could consider its profits [as existing] even without taking into account the legatees' claim [ie the amount of the potential liability in respect of which the provision had been claimed – M.S.] we would have considered this as fool-hardy and irresponsible, and I do not believe that the Treasury is interested in encouraging such conduct."

249 The *second Amisragas* case, Chapter 5, n 139.

250 *Pazgas*, Chapter 5, n 140.

251 The *Amisragas-Pazgas* case, Chapter 4, n 334; for the facts of this case and the above-mentioned cases, see para 5.4.1.

252 In the same vein, see ITA (H) 399/02 *Elisha Ltd v Haifa Assessing Officer* Taxes (August 2006), E-123.

253 See, e.g. A. Rosenberg, Chapter 4, n 343; Raphael and Ephrati, Chapter 4, n 343, at p 466; A. Raphael, *Income Tax – vol 1* (Shocken Publishing, Jerusalem and Tel Aviv, 1994), at p 614; and Namdar, Chapter 4, n 298, at p 2010.

254 Ibid; it should be noted that those comments were written before the *Amisragas-Pazgas* and *Elisha* cases.

255 Although as we mentioned in para 7.2.1, there are a number of exceptions to this rule, in which provisions for deductions have not been allowed, it appears that these exceptions either match the perceptions of GAAP in that they relate to liabilities whose very existence is uncertain (as distinct from doubt relating to their amount) or they originate in former case law that preceded the period in which the differences between GAAP and UK tax accounting were already narrowing.

256 See in para 7.3.2.1.3.

257 See ibid and especially the *GD* case.

258 See para 7.3.2.1.2.

259 Jensen, Chapter 4, n 229, at pp 462–7; Jensen, Chapter 2, n 22, at p 233; and see, generally Comment, "Accrual and Unusual Punishment – the Reasonable Accuracy Requirement of the All Events Test", 25 UCLA L Rev 70 (1977).

260 As mentioned in para 4.4.2.3.

261 Treas Reg §1.461–1(a)(2).
262 See, e.g. *Challenge Publications*, Chapter 7, n 156, stating that "Matching of income and expenses is not an additional requirement of 'the all events test'."
263 As defined in para 7.1.1.
264 In para 2.4.1 we saw that GAAP imputes importance to the time factor generally in relation to determining the amount of the provision, but not the very need to make it.
265 i.e. the *Pazgas* case (Chapter 5, n 140), the *second Amisragas* case (Chapter 5, n 139), the *Amisragas-Pazgas* case (Chapter 4, n 334) and the *Elisha* case (Chapter 7, n 252).
266 Although, in the UK, in relation to provisions, examples have been found adopting the Full and Immediate Deduction Approach as well as the Partial Deduction Approach, see para 7.2.1.2.
267 As presented in para 7.5.3.
268 See para 7.3.2.2.
269 See on the subject of the timing of the recognition of advances as income for tax purposes, para 6.4.
270 See paras 4.6.2, 5.5.1 and 6.5.1.
271 Ibid.
272 See para 2.3.
273 See para 2.4.
274 Ibid.
275 See para 5.2.1.
276 See para 7.2.1.
277 See paras 7.2 and 7.4.
278 As mentioned in paras 7.3.2.1.3 and 7.3.2.2.1
279 *Herbert Smith*, Chapter 4, n 72.
280 *Pazgas*, Chapter 5, n 140.
281 *Burnham*, Chapter 7, n 179.
282 *Crescent Wharf*, Chapter 7, n 133.
283 *Hughes*, Chapter 4, n 254, at pp 604–5.
284 *Gold Coast*, Chapter 7, n 160.
285 See, e.g. para 7.3.2.1.3.
286 See para 7.3.2.1.2.
287 Ibid.
288 Klein, Chapter 3, n 23, at pp 1686–7, and see references to Klein's view also in paras 4.1.2, 5.3.3 and 6.3.4.
289 See para 4.6.1.
290 Ibid.
291 Ibid.
292 Ibid.
293 See at the outset of Chapter 7.
294 See para 7.3.2.1.2.
295 Ibid.
296 See, e.g. *Mooney Aircraft*, Chapter 7, n 186.
297 See, e.g. the *GD* case, in para 7.3.2.1.3.
298 Ibid; it seems that the source of the Absolute Certainty Degree requirement and the High Certainty Degree requirement is, primarily, considerations of convenience of IRS. For such considerations, see, e.g. Gunn's view in para 7.3.4.
299 For these methods, see paras 4.2 and 4.6.3.2.
300 See, e.g. the *Burnham* case, Chapter 7, n 179; the *Ford Motor* case, Chapter 7, n 189; and the *Mooney Aircraft* case, Chapter 7, n 186.
301 These will be discussed in Chapter 8.

302 See our discussion in para 7.5.1.
303 See, e.g. para 17.2, first passage, and Chapter 7, nn 12 and 13.
304 Although we have seen in paras 4.5.1.2.4 and 4.5.1.2.5, in Israel the Advance Approach is currently applied by legislative directives to only two types of transactions (rent and insurance premiums). In those directives, the possibility has been granted of "advancing" the deduction of liabilities to the year in which the advances were received. However, over and above those specific transactions, no special reference exists on the question of the timing of the deduction of liabilities in cases where advances or deposits are received as against the timing of the deduction of liabilities in transactions that do not involve deposits or advances.
305 See in the same spirit, Butler's view, in para 7.3.4.
306 As stated in paras 2.4.2 and 2.4.3.
307 For cases where the certainty requirement will be waived in relation to transactions for which deposits or advances are received, see "the CVT model" in para 8.1.

8 Alternative models

1 See Chapter 1.
2 See para 4.6.3.
3 See para 4.6.2.
4 See para 4.6.1.
5 See in this connection paras 4.6.2.2 and 7.5.2.
6 See paras 4.6.3 and 7.5.3.
7 See also in regard to those attempts our criticism in paras 4.6, 5.5, 6.5 and 7.5.
8 With regard to the question of whether the "speedy collection interest" justifies deviating from GAAP, see our references in paras 4.6.3.1, 6.5.2 and 7.5.2.
9 See, e.g. Halperin's view in para 3.2.
10 Johnson, Chapter 3, n 27, at pp 391–2, suggests a similar model. However, one of the major differences between the CVT model and Johnson's suggestion is related to the certainty requirement. Johnson is of the opinion that future liabilities should be deducted at their present value, subject to the certainty requirement. As mentioned in para 8.1.4, in order to find the "value" of the transaction (in which a deposit or advance is received) on the date on which either is received, one must take into account on that date the full amount of the taxpayer's liabilities while absolutely waiving the requirement of certainty.
11 In a case where the repayment date of the deposit or the performance date of the other commitments is not fixed in time but can, on the face of it, be assessed on the basis of past experience and expected changes that may come about in the future.
12 The "market interest" rate for purposes of determining the present value of a deposit may be fixed according to what is customary in the market for debit loans having a similar repayment date and risk.
13 As stated at the beginning of this chapter and explained in para 8.1.4, according to the CVT model, the income from the base transaction will be recognized for tax purposes on the earlier date earned according to GAAP and the date it is actually received (hereinafter, in this chapter: **"the earliest date of recognition of income"**). For calculating the "value" of the base transaction, liabilities undertaken in order to produce this income (from the base transaction) would be matched at the same date of recognition of income from the base transaction and therefore would be recognized for tax purposes on the earlier date of their recognition according to GAAP and the date of recognizing income for tax as defined above (hereinafter, in this chapter: **"the earliest date of recognition of liability"**).

14 i.e. income that would be recognized for calculating the value of the base transaction on "the earliest date of recognition of income" as defined in Chapter 8, n 13.

15 i.e. liabilities that would be recognized for calculating the value of the base transaction on "the earliest date of recognition of liability" as defined in Chapter 8, n 13.

16 Ibid.

17 As defined in Chapter 8, n 13.

18 As defined in Chapter 8, n 14.

19 For convenience, we will assume that the repayment amount of the deposit is made on one date. Where a deposit is repaid on a number of dates throughout the "deposit life", then, in determining the present value of the deposit, these repayments must be brought into account at their present value. Where the repayment amount is paid in a number of installments, the amount of the deposit obtained (CF) will be split according to the rate of the amounts repaid, and the deposit formula will be adopted with regard to each and every portion of that sum, while adjusting the figure with regard to each portion, and totalling the aggregate result of all of the present values. The same also applies to a single advance that is earned on number of future dates.

20 As defined in Chapter 8, n 13.

21 The solution proposed regarding the amount of the deduction of the future liabilities resembles in substance that laid down in the *Ford Motor* case, Chapter 7, n 189, which is described in para 7.3.2.2.3.

22 i.e. liabilities that fulfill the substantive conditions prescribed by the specific tax system for the deduction an expense in calculating taxable income. For such substantive criteria, see, e.g. in the UK, Chapter 7, n 12, and in Israel, Chapter 7, n 235.

23 See para 7.5.2.

24 As to the manner of measuring the liabilities under GAAP, see para 2.4.4.

25 In contrast, in a case of a deposit, on the face of it, it is possible to split the economic value inherent in the deposit from the economic value inherent in the base transaction (as defined in paras 3.2 and 6.5.2). In such a case, the CVT model applies only to the economic value of the deposit, and the liabilities relating to the base transaction will be recognized (according to the matching principle) only on the dates on which the income from those services or goods are recognized, and in any event, these are not to be brought into account in measuring the value of the deposit transaction on the date on which it was received.

26 For cases in which equipment is loaned to the customers within the scope of a deposit agreement for the security of which, *inter alia*, a deposit is given, see, e.g. in the US., the *City-Gas* and *IPL* cases (referred to in para 5.3.1), and in Israel, the *Pazgas* and the *Second Amisragas* cases (referred to in para 5.4.1).

27 This cost is expressed in the formula – $[CO^*(d^*x/12)]$. This study does not deal with the question of depreciation. For the purpose of calculating the benefit inherent in the deposit, we will assume that the depreciation rate of the equipment lent indeed reflects the drop in the economic value of that equipment between the date on which it is provided to the customer and the date of the return thereof to the taxpayer, against return of the deposit.

28 Assuming that the equipment was to have been delivered to the customer against that deposit.

29 With regard to the timing of the recognition of financing income or financing expenses, see, e.g. para 2.3.2 and Chapter 2, n 45.

30 See para 7.1.

31 As defined in para 2.4.1.

32 As defined in para 2.4.2.
33 See our criticism in para 7.5.1.
34 As to the definition of this term, see Chapter 1 and the first passage of Chapter 8.
35 Ibid.
36 As to this doctrine and approach, see para 4.1.
37 Ibid.
38 Nevertheless, it might be argued that one should compare the alternative in such case not in terms of credit interest, but rather in terms of IRR (Internal Return Rate).
39 For more on this subject, see para 8.2.4.
40 On this subject, see para 8.2.5.
41 As to the differences between the ability to use the funds and the taxation imposed on the uses itself, see para 8.2.4.
42 In a case where the repayment date of the deposit or the earning of the advance is not specified in time, then, on the face of it, it is possible to assess it on the basis of experience of the past and expected changes in the future.
43 For our purposes, the definition of the "market interest" would be the prevailing rate of interest on loans determined by the demand and supply of credit, and based on the duration (the longer the duration, the higher the rate) of the loan and the type of security offered (the higher the quality of security, the lower the rate).
44 For definition of the term "market rate", see ibid. For our purposes, the rate of the average "market rate" can be defined on a yearly basis by regulations or other means.
45 For this statement, see also para 8.2.5.
46 Ibid.
47 See the beginning of this para 8.2.
48 i.e. the average interest rate that the taxpayer would have had to pay in a given year to an outside party if, in lieu of the sources that were available to it from deposits or advances, it would have been required to raise a loan for the same term that corresponds to the period between the date of receipt and the repayment date or the expected dates of being earned.
49 As mentioned, in most cases there is no instruction to repay monies in relation to an advance and, therefore, $k = 0$.
50 Adding the principal plus the difference in the interest rate on the one hand and eliminating the digit 1 leads to the result that the amount of the benefit will only extend to the difference of the interest, eliminating the principal.
51 See, e.g. Halperin's view, para 3.2.
52 One protection is afforded by means of allowing financing expenses on loans that were taken by the taxpayer for the purpose of financing that "customer credit".
53 See also para 8.3.2.
54 See para 2.3.2 and Chapter 2, n 45.
55 We should mention that in the US federal tax system, IRC§483 provides that, as a rule, a sale transaction on deferred installments (where the deferral exceeds six months) will be classified for tax purposes as a transaction including consideration for the items sold, which partly consists of a financing transaction. The division between the principal of the transaction and the financing portion will be made having regard to the present value formula. The chapter that deals with Capital Gains Tax, IRC§1274, provides that on a sale on credit of assets liable to capital gains tax, the capital gain will be fixed on the present value of the expected future payments, while the balance of the consideration inherent in those payments will be classified as financing income.

56 See para 4.6.3.1.
57 See para 4.6.1.
58 From this standpoint, the difference between the CVT model and the SFC model with respect to the timing of the recognition of income and liabilities reflects the conceptual difference between the two different approaches that we will address further on in para 8.3.3.
59 As mentioned in para 5.5.1.
60 See para 5.5.2.
61 Ibid, and see para 3.1.1.
62 Ibid. Thus, e.g. the "control and use test" of the deposit monies or the "principal objective test" or "the subjective intention test" lead to the recipient of a deposit also being taxed, although he has "not become enriched" from it.
63 See para 5.5.2. According to the various tests that have been laid down by case law, these reasons might determine the fate of the deposit as a "loan" or as "income".
64 Ibid. This determination should be qualified by the "interest test", which has also been proposed as an ancillary test within the framework of the Income Approach. It should, however, be emphasized that while the interest test serves as an ancillary test for determining whether the full amount of the deposit should be considered as income, in our case the question of interest is not applied as an ancillary test to classify the amount received as a whole, but to test the value of the component inherent in the amount received.
65 Ibid.
66 Ibid.
67 As mentioned in para 6.5.1.
68 See para 6.5.2.
69 Ibid.
70 Ibid.
71 Ibid.
72 Ibid.
73 Ibid.
74 Ibid.
75 See para 7.5.2.
76 See para 7.5.3.
77 See para 7.3.2.2.1.
78 See para 7.3.2.2.2.
79 See para 7.3.2.2.3.
80 Regarding the fact that the taxpayer itself in the *Ford Motor* case (Chapter 7, n 189) in its financial statements presented the amount of the future liability in its value in real terms and the impact of this fact on the ruling of the court, see ibid.
81 See, e.g. our discussion of the UK tax system in paras 4.6, 5.5, 6.5 and 7.5.
82 See, e.g. our criticism of the US tax system in paras 4.6, 5.5, 6.5 and 7.5.
83 As to the Proportionality Principle and the violation thereof by the different solutions that have been offered by the tax systems reviewed, see paras 4.6.1, 4.6.4, 5.5.2, 6.5.2 and 7.5.3.
84 As to our criticism of these practices, see our discussion in para 4.6.3.2.
85 See at the beginning of this Chapter 8.
86 See our discussion in para 4.6.3.1.
87 See the beginning of para 8.2 in contrast to the beginning of para 8.1.
88 As to the meaning of these definitions, see para 8.2.7.
89 See, e.g. Klein, in para 7.3.4.
90 See, e.g. the consequences of the lack of desire to make use of evaluations or assessments in US case law regarding the timing of the deduction of liabilities

as an expense, in para 7.3.2.1, mainly in the distinction drawn between cash payment liabilities and a liability to make a sale or provide services.

91 This difficulty could possibly be resolved by means of making statutory determinations relating to the alternative interest. The subject of the complexity of the solutions in tax law is perhaps worthy of study in itself, within the framework of a more general issue in law: "Truth or Stability – which is better".

92 For example, in the case of the payer of the deposit "forgetting" (see also for this purpose, e.g. in the UK – in the cases of *Tattersall* and *Anise* in para 5.2.1, and the reference to this possibility in Israel in the *Amisragas-Pazgas* case, in para 5.4.1).

93 For example, in the case of the bankruptcy of the recipient of the advance; for reference to this possibility on the subject of the timing of the recognition of liabilities, see the *Hughes* and *GD* cases in para 7.3.2.1.3.

94 Ibid.

95 Similar arguments were raised, e.g. in the *Hughes* case, Chapter 4, n 254, and the *Gold Coast* case, Chapter 7, n 160.

96 See our discussion in para 8.2.5.

97 See Klein, Chapter 7, n 211.

98 For the tax values of "efficiency" and "simplicity", see para 3.1.5.

99 See para 4.6.3.1.

100 See para 4.6.4.

101 Ibid, "the less harmful means" test as defined in para 4.6.1.

102 Compare with paras 4.3, 5.2, 6.2 and 7.2.

103 See paras 5.3.1 and 5.5.2.

104 Such as the "complete dominion test" in para 5.3.1, or "prospectus test" in para 5.4.1.

105 Such as the "control and use test", in paras 5.3.1 and 5.5.2.

106 In Israel, the Income Approach is currently applied in respect of deposits received by gas companies, whereas this approach has not been applied with regard to the remaining transactions for which deposits are received. See paras 5.4.1 and 5.5.2.

107 In Israel, the Advance Approach is currently applied by legislation to only two types of transactions, and in case law it is currently applied to advances in respect of stock supplied by gas companies, whereas this approach has not been applied with regard to the remaining transactions for which advances are received. See paras 4.5.1.2.4, 4.5.1.2.5 and para 6.4.1.

108 In Israel, the Accounting Certainty Degree as a prerequisite for recognition of liabilities for tax purposes is currently applied. See para 7.4.1.

109 See, e.g. para 7.3.2.1.2.

110 See the first passage of Chapter 3 and Chapter 3, nn 4–6.

111 See para 3.1.2.

9 Conclusions

1 Although, as seen in para 6.3.3, pursuant to administrative directives, it is possible for there to be a limited spread (until the end of the fiscal year following that in which the advances were received).

2 On Albert Einstein's "Theory of Special Relativity", see, e.g. Clifford M. Will, "Clock Synchronization and Isotropy of the One-Way Speed of Light", Physics Review D45,403–411(1992) (http://en.wikipedia.org/wiki/Timedilation; and http://en.wikipedia.org/wiki/Theory_of_Relativity).

3 Like the speed of light in a vacuum "C" (i.e. the distance of 299,792,458 meters per second).

4 See paras 5.5.1, 6.5.1 and 7.5.1.

5 See paras 5.5.2, 6.5.2 and 8.5.2.

Bibliography

Generally Accepted Accounting Principles

International GAAP

IASB Framework, Articles of the Regulation (EC) No 1606/2002 of the European Parliament and the Council of 19 July 2002 on the application of international accounting standards and the Fourth Council Directive 78/660/EEC of 25 July 1978 and the Seventh Council Directive 83/349/EEC of June 1983 on accounting.

International Accounting Standard No 1, "Presentation of Financial Statements" ("IAS#1").

International Accounting Standard No 11, "Construction Contracts" (IAS#11).

International Accounting Standard No 16, "Property, Plant and Equipment" (IAS#16).

International Accounting Standard No 18, "Revenue" (IAS#18).

International Accounting Standard No 32, "Financial Instruments: Disclosure and Presentation" (IAS#32).

International Accounting Standard No 36, "Impairment of Assets" ("IAS#36").

International Accounting Standard No 37, "Provisions, contingent liabilities and contingent assets" (IAS#37).

International Accounting Standard No 38, "Intangible Assets" (IAS#38).

International Accounting Standard No 39, "Financial Instruments: Recognition and Measurement" (IAS#39).

International Accounting Standard No 40, "Investment Property" (IAS#40).

International Financial Reporting Standards No 1, "First-time Adoption of International Reporting Standards" (IFRS#1).

International Financial Reporting Standards No 3, "Business Combinations" (IFRS#3).

International Financial Reporting Standards No 5, "Non-current Assets Held for Sale and Discontinued Operations" (IFRS#5).

UK GAAP

Financial Reporting Standards No 2, "Accounting for subsidiary undertakings" (FRS#2).

Financial Reporting Standards No 3, "Reporting financial performance" (FRS#3).

Financial Reporting Standards No 5, "Reporting the substance of transactions" (FRS#5).

Financial Reporting Standards No 10, "Goodwill and intangible assets" (FRS#10).

Financial Reporting Standards No 12, "Provisions, contingent liabilities and contingent assets" (FRS#12).

Financial Reporting Standards No 13, "Derivatives and other financial instruments: disclosures" (FRS#13).

Financial Reporting Standards No 18, "Accounting policies" (FRS#18).

Financial Reporting Standards No 25, "Financial instruments: Disclosure and Presentation" (FRS#25).

Financial Reporting Standards No 26, "Financial instruments: Measurement" (FRS#26).

Statement of Standard Accounting Practice No 1, "Presentation of Financial Statements" (Superseded by FRS 9) (SSAP#1).

Statement of Standard Accounting Practice No 2, "Disclosure of accounting policies" (Superseded by FRS 18) (SSAP#2).

Statement of Standard Accounting Practice No 9, "Stock and long terms contracts" (SSAP#9).

Statement of Standard Accounting Practice No 18, "Accounting for subsidiary undertakings" (Superseded by FRS 12) (SSAP#18).

Statement of Standard Accounting Practice No 21, "Accounting for leases and hire purchase contracts" (SSAP#21).

US GAAP

Accounting Principles Board (APB) Opinions No 4, "Accounting for 'Investment Credit' (Amending No 2)" ("APB#4").

Accounting Principles Board (APB) Opinions No 6, "Status of Accounting Research Bulletins" (APB#6).

Accounting Principles Board (APB) Opinions No 9, "Reporting the Results of Operations" (APB#9).

Accounting Principles Board (APB) Opinion No 12, "Omnibus Opinion-1967" (APB#12).

Accounting Principles Board (APB) Opinion No 13, "Amending APB No 9, Application to Commercial Banks" (APB#13).

Accounting Principles Board (APB) Opinion No 14, "Accounting for Convertible Debt and Debt Issued with Stock Purchase Warrants" (ABP #14).

Accounting Principles Board (APB) Opinion No 16, "Business Combinations" (APB #16).

Accounting Principles Board (APB) Opinion No 17, "Intangible Assets" (APB #17).

Accounting Principles Board (APB) Opinions No 21, "Interest on Receivables and Payables" (APB#21).

Accounting Research Bulletins No 43, "Restatement and Revision of Accounting Research Bulletins" (ARB, 1953) ("ARB#43").

Accounting Series Release No 150, "Statement of Policy on the Establishment and Improvement of Accounting Principles and Standards" (ASR, 1973) ("ASR#150").

Emerging Issues Task Force (EITF) 00–21, "Revenue Arrangements with Multiple Deliverables" ("EITF 00–21").

Staff Accounting Bulletin No 101, "Revenue Recognition-Questions arising from time to time and their answers" (SAB#101).

Statement of Financial Accounting Concept No 1, "Objectives of Financial Reporting by Business Enterprises" (Issued 11/78) ("SFAC #1").

Statement of Financial Accounting Concept No 4, "Objective of Financial Reporting by Nonbusiness Organizations" (Issued 12/80); (SFAC#4).

Statement of Financial Accounting Concept No 5, "Recognition and Measurement in Financial Statements of Business Enterprises" (Issued 12/84) (SFAC#5).

Statement of Financial Accounting Concept No 6, "Elements of Financial Statements, a Replacement of FASB Concepts Statement No 3 (incorporating an amendment of FASB Concepts No 2)" (Issued 12/85) (SFAC#6).

Statement of Financial Accounting Standards No 14, "Financial Reporting for Segments of a Business Enterprise" (Issued 12/76) (SFAS#14).

Statement of Financial Accounting Standards No 48, "Revenue Recognition with Right of Return Exists" (Issued 6/81) (SFAS#48).

Statement of Financial Accounting Standards No 60, "Accounting and Reporting by Insurance Enterprises" (Issued 6/82) (SFAS#60).

Statement of Financial Accounting Standards No 74, "Accounting for Special Termination Benefits Paid to Employees" (Issued 8/83) (SFAS#74).

Statement of Financial Accounting Standards No 87, "Employers' Accounting for Pensions" (Issued 12/85) (SFAS#87).

Statement of Financial Accounting Standards No 90, "Regulated Enterprises – Accounting for Abandonment's and Disallowances of Plant costs (an amendment of SFAS No 71)" (Issued 12/86) (SFAS#90).

Statement of Financial Accounting Standards No 91, "Accounting for Nonrefundable Fees and Costs Associated with originating for Acquiring Loans and Initial Direct Costs of Leases" (Issued 12/86) (SFAS #91).

Statement of Financial Accounting Standards No 106, "Employers' Accounting for Postretirement Benefits other than Pensions" (Issued 12/90) (SFAS#106).

Statement of Financial Accounting Standards No 107, "Disclosure about Fair Value of Financial Instruments" (Issued 12/91) (SFAS#107).

Statement of Financial Accounting Standards No 109, "Accounting for Income Tax" (Issued 2/92) (SFAS#109).

Statement of Financial Accounting Standards No 114, "Accounting by Creditors for Impairment of a Loan – an amendment of FASB Statements No's 5 and 15" (Issued 5/93) (SFAS#114).

Statement of Financial Accounting Standards No 121, "Accounting for Impairment of Long-Live Assets and for a Long-Live Assets to be Disposed" (Issued 3/95) (SFAS #121).

Statement of Financial Accounting Standards No 123, "Accounting for Stock Based Compensation" (Issued 12/04); (SFAS #123).

Israeli GAAP

The Institute of Certified Public Accountants in Israel Opinion No 29, "The IFRS Accounting Standards" (Issued 7/2006).

UK commentaries

Chiltern's Yellow Tax Guide Archive/2003–2004, Part I Income tax, Corporation Tax, Capital Gains Tax/Commentary on Statutes/Income and Corporation Taxes Act 1988/Part IV Provisions relating to the Schedule D Charges/74 "General rules as to deductions not allowable" (B3. 1202).

CIOT, The Chartered Institute of Taxation, Application of International Accounting Standards to consolidated tax base by Technical Department, "Submission by the CIOT to the European Commission" (6 May 2003) (http://www.tax.org.uk/showarticle.pl/?id=1776).

De Jasay, Anthony, *Social Contract, Free Ride: A Study of the Public Goods Problem* (Oxford: Clarendon Press, 1989).

Macdonald, Graeme and Martin, David, "Tax and Accounting: A Response to the 2003 Consultation Document on Corporation Tax Reform", Tax Law Review Committee, The Institute for Fiscal Studies (February 2004) TLRC Discussion Paper No 4 (http://www.ifs.org.uk/comms/ dp4.pdf).

Macdonald, Graeme and Martin, David, "Aligning Tax and Accounting Profits – The Need to Review Current Legislation", Tax Law Review Committee, The Institute for Fiscal Studies (November 2004), TLRC Discussion Paper No 5 (http://www.ifs.org.uk/comms/dp5.pdf).

Narain, Lakshmi, "The Use of Accounts for Tax-Back to basis-Account for Tax", Tax Journal (17 March 2003).

Simon's Direct Tax Service Budget Bulletin/Extract from the Financial Statement/ Economic and Fiscal Strategy Report/5 Building a Fairer Society/"Modernising the tax system".

Simon's Direct Tax Service/Binder 2 General Principles Procedures Schedules A, B and C/Part A1 General principles/Division A1.3 The construction and application of tax legislation/A1.304 "Ascertaining the intention generally".

Simon's Direct Tax Service/Binder 2 General Principles Procedures, Schedules A, B and C/Part A1 General Principles/Division A1.3 The construction and application of tax legislation/A1.315 "Artificial documents and transactions".

Simon's Direct Tax Service/ Binder 7 Inheritance tax/Part 14/ Transfers on Death/Division 14.1 Charge on Death/14.146 "Liability to make future payments".

Simon's Direct Tax Service/Binder 7 Inheritance Tax/Part 18/Valuation/Division 18.2 Principles of Valuation/18.277 "Liabilities".

Simon's Tax Intelligence/ 2006/ Issue 12, 30, March 2006/ "Extract from the Financial Statement".

Simon's Tax Planning/Part D Companies/Chapter 19 Incorporation/"1 Introduction".

Smith, Adam, *An Inquiry into the Nature and Causes of the Wealth of Nations*, 825 (R.H. Campbell and A.S. Skinner, eds, Liberty Classics, 1981) (1776) (Book V, Ch II, Part II).

Specialist Tax Regulatory Materials, Issued by Inland Revenue, "International Accounting Standards – The UK Implications (Finance Act 2004 Update)", Inland Revenue (Issued 15 September 2004).

Specialist Tax Regulatory Materials, Issued by Inland Revenue, "International

Accounting Standards – The UK Tax Implications" (Issued 1 September 2005).

Stobart, A., "Tax Deductibility of Provisions", Tax Journal (11 March 2003).

Taxation Magazine/2005 Volume 155/Issue 4021, 18 August 2005/Editorial/ "Post-marital tax".

Tolley's Corporation Tax 2005–06/64 Trading Income/ "Contingent and future liabilities," 64.28.

Tolley's Income Tax 2005–06/82 Trading Income/ "Contingent and future liabilities," 82.45.

Tolley's Tax Guide 2005–06/20 How are Business Profits Calculated?/General Rules for Computing Trading Profits (TA 1988, s 74; FA 2004 ss 50, 51; FA 2005, ss 80, 84 and Sch 4; ITTOIA 2005, ss 29, 33, 34)/ "Provisions for Future Liabilities", 20.11.

Tolley's Tax Planning/15 Electronic Commerce/"UK tax developments".

Yellow Tax Handbook 2005–2006/Part II/Inland Revenue Interpretations/ "RI 30".

Yellow Tax Handbook: 2005–2006/Part II/Inland Revenue Interpretations/"RI 231" (June 2001).

Yellow Tax Handbook 2005–2006/Part II/Press Release etc/12 April 1995 ICAEW "Relationship between accountancy practice and tax computation in the light of Gallagher v Jones and Johnson v Britannia Airways Ltd Guidance note" (TAX 10/95)/"Provisions".

US commentaries

AICPA (American Institute of Certified Public Accountants), the Code of Professional Ethics (http://www.aicpa.org/about/code/.html).

AICPA, *Contemporary Accounting: A Refresher Course for Public Accountants* (Arthur Leland, ed., 1945).

AICPA, "Conformity of Tax and Financial Accounting," 132 JA 75 (1971).

AICPA, "Official Releases: Statement of financial Accounting Standards No 98 – Accounting for Leases", 8–88 JA 151 (August 1988).

AICPA, "Official Releases: Statement No 10 of the Governmental Accounting Standards Board – Accounting and Financial Reporting for Risk Financing and Related Insurance", 4–90 JA 114 (April 1990).

AICPA "Official Releases: Ethics Notice . . . Statements of Position 98–7 and 98–9", 3–99 JA 90 (March 1999).

AICPA, "Official Releases: FASB No 144 . . . SOP 01–6 . . . Auditing Interpretation", 3–02 JA 81 (March 2002).

Aidinoff and Lopata, "Section 461 and Accrual-Method Taxpayers: The Treatment of Liabilities Arising from an Obligation to be Performed in the Future", 33 Tax L Rev 789 (1980).

Alaghband, H., "Comment: Abolition of the Completed Contract Method under Fire: A Study in Legislative Compromise", 32 Am U L Rev 1009 (1983).

Aland, Robert H., "Prepaid Income and Estimated Future Expenses: Is a Legislative Solution Needed?", 54 ABA J 84 (1968).

Allegra, Francis M., "Section 482: Manning the Contours of the Abuse of Discretion Standard of Judicial Review", 13 Va Tax Rev 423 (1994).

Andrews, William D., *Basic Federal Income Taxation* (Aspen Law and Business, 5th ed. 1999).

Andrews, William D., "Tax Neutrality between Equity Capital and Debt", 30 Wayne L Rev 1057 (1984).

Behren, Robert A., "Prepaid Income Accounting Concepts and the Tax Law", 15 Tax L Rev 343 (1960).

Behren, Robert A., "Schlude Holds Prepaid Income Taxable on 'Receipt' Rationale is Uncertain", 18 J Tax'n 194 (1963).

Bernstein, Leopold A., *Accounting for Extraordinary Gains and Losses* (New York, Roland Press, 1967).

Berry, Tim, "Q&A: Cash basis vs. accrual accounting" (http://www.allbusiness.com/business-planning-structures/business-plans/4353766-1.html).

Bice Scott, H., "Rationality Analysis in Constitutional Law", 65 Minn L Rev 1 (1980).

Bittker, B. and Lokken, L., *Federal Taxation of Income Estates and Gifts* (vol 2, Boston: Warren, Gorham and Lamont, 1989).

Bittker, Boris I., "A Comprehensive Tax Base as a Goal of Income Tax Reform", 80 Harv L Rev 925 (1967).

Bittker, Boris I., "Equity, Efficiency, and Income Tax Theory: Do Misallocations Drive out Inequities?" 16 San Dieg L Rev 735 (1979).

Bonhalm, M. et al, *International GAAP 2005* (Croyden, Surrey, UK, Ernst & Young: LexisNexis Publishing House, 2004).

Burke, Martin J. and Friel, Michael K., "Tax Free Security: Reflections on Indianapolis Power and Light", 12 Rev of Tax'n of Individuals 157 (1989).

Bushman, Melissa, "Cash Basis versus Accrual Basis Accounting" (http://www.associatedcontent.com/user/38548/melissa_bushman.html).

Butler, Gordon T., "Economic Benefit: Formulating a Workable Theory of Income Recognition", 27 Seton Hall L Rev 70 (1996).

Butler, Gordon T., "Section 461(h): Tax Fairness and Deduction of Future Liabilities", 26 U Mem L Rev 97 (1995).

Casey, J.T. and Scholz, J.T., "Beyond Deterrence: Behavioral Decision Theory and Tax Compliance", 25 Law and Soc'y Rev 821 (1991).

Casey, J.T. and Scholz, J.T., "Boundary of Vague Risk Information on Taxpayer Decision", 50 Organizational Behavior and Human Decision Processes 360 (1991).

Cliff, Walter C. and Levine, Philip J., "Interest and Accrual and the Time Value of Money", 34 Am U L Rev 107 (1984).

Coplan, Karl S., "Protecting the Public Fisc: Fighting Accrual Abuse with Section 446 Discretion", 83 Col L Rev 378 (1983).

De Caprilles, Miguel A., "Modern Financial Accounting" (Pt 1), 37 NYUL Rev 1001 (1962).

Dodge, Joseph M., *The Logic of Tax: federal income tax theory and policy* (St Paul, Minn: West Pub, 1989).

Dodge, Joseph M., "Theories of Tax Justice: Ruminations on the Benefit, Partnership, and Ability-to-Pay Principles", 58 Tax L Rev 399 (2005).

Dubetz, Michael, "Case Comment: United States v General Dynamics: The Deduction of Estimated Liabilities by Accrual Method Taxpayers: The All Events Test and Economic Performance", 49 Ohio St L J 1439 (1989).

Dubroff, Harold, "The Claim of Rights Doctrine", 40 Tax L Rev 729 (1985).

Dubroff, Harold, Chail, M. Connie and Norris, Michael, "The Relationships of Clear Reflection of Income to Generally Accepted Accounting Principles", 47 Alb L Rev 354 (1983).

Edelman, Chester M., "Is Income Tax Accounting 'Good' Accounting Practice?" 24 Taxes 112 (1946).

Edmiston, Kelly D., Shannon, Mudd and Neven, Valev, "Tax structures and FDI: The deterrent effects of complexity and uncertainty", Fiscal Studies, 24(3), 341–359 (2003).

Eid, A., "Tax – Free Security: Federal Income Taxation of Customer Deposits After Commissioner v Indianapolis Power and Light Co 110 SCt 589 (1990)", 66 Wash L Rev 267 (1991).

Emery, William M., "Time for Accrual of Income and Expenses", 17 Ins on Feb Tax'n 183 (1959).

Fiflis, Ted J., Kripke, Homer and Foster, Paul M., *Accounting for Business Lawyers: Teaching Materials* (St. Paul, Minn, USA, West Group, 3rd edn, 1984).

Geier, Deborah A., "The Myth of Matching Principle as a Tax Value", 15 Am J Tax Pol'y 17 (1998).

Generally Comment, "Accrual and Unusual Punishment – The Reasonable Accuracy Requirement of the All Events Test", 25 UCLA L Rev 70 (1977).

Ghosh, D. and Crain, T.L., "Structure of Uncertainty and Decision Making: An Experimental Investigation", 24 Decision Sciences 789 (1993).

Graetz, Michael J., "The David R. Tillinghast Lecture: Taxing International Income: Inadequate Principles, Outdated Concepts, and Unsatisfactory Policies", 54 Tax L Rev 261 (2001).

Grates, M.J and Schenk, D.H., *Federal Income Taxation: Principles and Policies* (Westbury, NY: Foundation Press, 3rd edn, 1995).

Gunn, Alan, "Matching of Costs and Revenues as a Goal of Tax Accounting", 4 Va Tax Rev 1 (Summer 1984).

Haig, Robert M., *The Concept of Income – Economic and Legal Aspects, The Federal Income Tax* (New York: Columbia University Press, 1921).

Halperin, Daniel I., "Interest in Disguise: Taxing the Time Value of Money", 95 Yale LJ 506 (1986).

Halperin, Daniel I., "Will Integration Increase Efficiency? The Old and New View of Dividend Policy", 47 Tax L Rev 645 (1992).

Hariton, David P., "The Compaq Case, Notice 985, and Tax Shelters: The Theory Is All Wrong", 2002 TNT 19–30 (28 January 2002).

Heffner, James H., "Claim-of-Right and Other Tax Doctrines Are Distorting Proper Accounting", 5 J Tax'n 20 (5 January 1956).

Hilsenrath, J.E., "On the Books, More Fact and Less Fiction", NY Times, 16 February 1997, § 3, 1.

J.M.B., "Note & Comment RCA Corp v US: The Taxation of Income from Future Services", 1 Va Tax Rev 189 (1981).

Jensen, Eric M., "The Deductions of Future Liabilities by Accrual-Basis Taxpayers: Premature Accruals, the All Events Test, and Economic Performance", 37 U Fla L Rev 443 (1985).

Jensen, Erik M., "The Supreme Court and the Timing of Deductions for Accrual Basis Taxpayers", 22 Ga L Rev 229 (1988).

Johnson, Calvin H., "The Illegitimate 'Earned' Requirement in Tax and Non Tax Accounting", 50 Tax L Rev 373 (1995).

Kahn, Douglas A., "Comments on "Tax Neutrality between Equity Capital and Debt", 30 Wayne L Rev 1081 (1984).

Kane, M., "Compaq and IES: Putting the Tax Back into After-Tax Income", 2002 TNT 43–25 (5 March 2002).

Kaplow, L. and Shavel, S., "Fairness versus Welfare", 114 Harv L Rev 961 (2001).

Kaplow, L., "A Note on Horizontal Equity", 1 Fla Tax Rev 191 (1992).

Kaplow, L., "Horizontal Equity: Measures in Search of a Principle", 4 Nat'l Tax J 139 (1989).

Kaywood, Sam K., Jr, "Comment: The Deficit Reduction Act of 1984: Reform for Deferred Payment Accounting", 35 Emory LJ 507 (1986).

Keller, Thomas F. and Zeff, Stephen A., *Financial Accounting Theory II* (New York, USA, McGraw-Hill Book Company, 1969).

Kieso, Donald E. and Weygandt, Jerry J., *Intermediate Accounting* (New York, John Wiley & Sons, 4th edn, 1983).

Kiesling, Herbert J., *Taxation and Public Goods*: A Welfare-economic Critique of Tax Policy Analysis (University of Michigan Press, 1992).

Klein, W.A. and Stark, K.J., "Compaq Computer Corporation v Commissioner – Where is The Tax Arbitrage?" 2002 TNT 48–50 (12 March 2002).

Klein, William A., "The UCLA Tax Policy Conference: Tailor to the Emperor with No Clothes: The Supreme Court Tax Rules For Deposits and Advanced Payments", 41 UCLA L Rev 1685 (1994).

Kleinrock's Tax Expert Analysis and Explanation, From January 2002 through 2009 (Rockville, MD, Kleinrock Publishing, 2001) (http://www.lexis.com/research/retrieve?m=12004a25270587265163ed931d15510&src=248035.3006719&_cat=3006719&tcfrmsrc=1&_tcid=248035&_fmtstr=TOC&tcat=initial&svc=toc&_stateList=svc&nchp=dGLzVtz-zSkAl&_md5=3885619bdbf20cec7d99d3234bdc5d46.

Kohl, Glen A., "The Identification Theory of Basis", 40 Tax L Rev 623 (1985).

Kwon, Young K., "Accrual versus cash-basis accounting methods: An agency-theoretic comparison", 8 Journal of Accounting and Public Policy 4, 267 (winter 1989).

Kramer, Johannes R., "Taxation of Advance Receipts for Future Services", 1961 Duke LJ 230 (1961).

Land, Stephen B., "Defeating Deferral: A Proposal for Retrospective Taxation", 52 Tax L Rev 45 (1996).

Lasser, J.K. and Peloubet, Maurice E., "Tax Accounting versus Commercial Accounting", 4 Tax L Rev 343 (1949).

Lipton, Richard M., "We Have Met the Enemy and He is Us: More Thoughts on Hyper Lexis", 47 Tax L Rev 1 (1993).

Lister, C.E., "The Use and Abuse of Pragmatism: The Judicial Doctrine of Claim of Right", 21 Tax L Rev 263 (1996).

Livingston, Michael A., "Reinventing Tax Scholarship: Lawyers, Economists, and the Role of the Legal Academy", 83 Cornell L Rev 365 (1998).

Lizzeri, Alessandro and Persico, Nicola, "The Provision of Public Goods under Alternative Electoral Incentives", American Economic Rev 91 (March 2001).

Malman, Laurie L., "Treatment of Prepaid Income – Clear Reflection of Income or Muddied Waters", 37 Tax L Rev 103 (1981).

May, George O., "Accounting and the Accountant in the Administration of Income Taxation", 47 Colum L Rev 377 (1947).

McCullers, Levis D. and Schroeder, Richard G., *Accounting Theory Text and Reading* (St. Paul, MN, USA, Wiley, John & Sons, Inc., 2nd edn, 1982).

McDaniel, P.R. and Repetti, J.R., "Horizontal and Vertical Equity: The Musgrave/ Kaplow Exchange", 1 Fla Tax Rev 607 (1993).

McLure, Charles E., Jr, "Taxation of Electronic Commerce: Economic Objectives, Technological Constraints, and Tax Laws", 52 Tax L Rev 269 (1997).

Musgrave, R., "Horizontal Equity, Once More", 43 Nat'l Tax J 113 (1990).

Musgrave, R., *The Theory of Public Finance* (New York: McGraw-Hill Book Co, 1959).

Musgrave, R., "Horizontal Equity: A Further Note", 1 Fla Tax Rev 354 (1993).

Myers, John H., "The Critical Event and Recognition of Net Profit", The Accounting Review 34 (October 1959), 528.

Nagel, Robert F., *"Rationalism in Constitutional Law"*, 4 Constitutional Commentary (1987).

Nolan, John S., "The Merit in Conformity of Tax to Financial Accounting", 50 Taxes 761 (1972).

Olson, Mancur, *The Logic of Collective Action: Public Goods and the Theory of Groups* (Cambridge, Mass.: Harvard University Press, 1965).

Paton, W.A. and Littleton, A.C., *An Introduction to Corporate Accounting Standards* (Ann Arbor, MI, USA, American Accounting Association, 1940).

Paton, William A., *Essentials of Accounting* (New York, USA, Macmillan Co., 1949).

Popkin, William D., "The Taxation of Borrowing", 56 Ind LJ 43 (1980).

Powell, Weldon, "Extraordinary Items", The Journal of Accountancy (January 1966).

Press, Eric G. and Weintrop, Joseph B., "Accounting-Based Constraints in Public and Private Debt Agreements", 12 J Acct and Econ 65 (1990).

Raby, William L. and Richter, Robert F., "Conformity of Tax and Financial Accounting", 139 JA 42 (March 1975).

Raby, William L., "Meaning of 'Accrued' – Accounting Concepts versus Tax Concepts", 92 TNT 223–97 (18 November 1992).

Ralph, Jacobs S., "Changing Attitudes toward Accrual Concepts", 16 Inst On Feb Tax'n 579 (1958).

Rice, R., "Judicial Techniques in Combating Tax Avoidance", 51 Mich L Rev 1021 (1953).

Root, Jennifer C., "The Commissioner's Clear Reflection of Income Power under 446(b) and the Abuse of Discretion Standard of Review: Where Has the Rule of Law Gone, and Can We Get It Back?" 15 Tax J 69 (2000).

Rothaus, Murray H., "A Critical Analysis of the Tax Treatment of Prepaid Income", 17 Md L Rev 121 (1957).

Sappideen, R., "Imputation of the Corporate and Personal Income Tax: Is It Chasing One's Tail?" 15 Am J Tax Pol'y 167 (1998).

Scarborough, Robert, "Payments in Advance of Performance", 69 Taxes 799 (1989).

Schenk, Deborah H., "A Positive Account of the Realization Rule", 57 Tax L Rev 355 (2004).

Schler, Michael L., "Sales of Assets after Tax Reform: Section 1060, Section 338(h)(10) and more", 43 Tax L Rev 605 (1988).

Schoenblum, J., "Tax Fairness or Unfairness Consideration of Philosophical Bases for Unequal Taxation of Individuals", 12 Am J Tax Pol'y 221 (1995).

Schuldiner, Reed, "A General Approach to the Taxation of Financial Instruments", 71 Tax L Rev 243 (1992).

Schwartz, Glenn P., "How Many Trades Must a Trader Make to be in the Trading Business?" 22 Va Tax Rev 395 (Winter 2003).

Schwartzstein, Linda A., "Smoke and Mirrors: Tax Legislation Uncertainty and Entrepreneurship", 6 Cornel JL and Pub Pol'y 61 (1996).

Shapiro, Donald, "Tax Accounting for Prepaid Income and Reserves for Future Expenses, in 2 Compendium of Papers on Broadening the Tax Base Submitted to Comm. on Ways and Means", 86th Cong, 1st Sess (Comm Print 1959), 1133.

Shaviro, D.N. and Weisbach, D.A., "The Fifth Circuit Gets It Wrong in Compaq v Commissioner?" 2002 TNT 19–31 (29 January 2002).

Shaviro, D.N., "Economic Substance, Corporate Tax Shelters, and the Compaq Case", 2000 TNT 132–80 (10 July 2000).

Sheppard, L.A., "Should Riskless Profit Equal Economic Substance?" 2002 TNT 11–2 (14 January 2002).

Sheppard, Lee A., "Equipment Leasing Shelters for Corporate Customers", 95 TNT 52–6 (16 March 1995).

Silk, J., "Advanced Payments – Prepaid Income: Recent Developments; an Old Problem Put to Rest", 30 NYU Inst 1651 (1972).

Simons, Henry C., *Personal Income Taxation: The Definition of Income as a Problem of Fiscal Policy* (Chicago: University of Chicago Press, 1938).

Sims, Theodore S., "Environmental 'Remediation' Expenses and a Natural Interpretation of the Capitalization Requirement", 47 Nat'l Tax J 703 (1994).

Smith, Christina I., "Challenging the Treasury: United Dominion Industries, Inc v Unites States", 17 Akron Tax J 61 (2002).

Smith, Jay M. and Skousen, K. Fred, *Intermediate Accounting Comprehensive Volume*, 11 Edition (Southwestern Publishing: Cincinnati, OH, USA, 1992).

Stanger, Vander Kam and Polifka, "Prepaid Income and Estimated Expense: Financial Accounting versus Tax Accounting Dichotomy", 33 Tax L Rev 403 (1980).

Stewart, Dave N. and Woods, Glen R., "Analysis of the Trend toward Deferring Recognition of Prepaid Income", 59 Taxes 400 (1981).

Stiglitz, J.E., *Economics of the Public Sector* (New York: 3rd edn, W. W. Norton, 2000).

Stout, Lynn A., "The Unimportance of Being Efficient: An Economic Analysis of Stock Market Pricing and Securities Regulation", 87 Mich L Rev 613 (1988).

Stuart, L., "The Taxation of Economic Reality: The Role of Anti Abuse Rules in Tax Administration", 431 Pli/Tax 1215 (1998).

Van Home, James C., *Financial Management and Policy* (Prentice Hall, NJ, USA, 5th edn, 1980).

Warskett, George, Winer, Stanley, and Hettich, Walter, "The Complexity of Tax Structure in Competitive Political Systems" 5th vol, Num 2, International Tax and Public Finance, 123 (Springer, Netherlands, May 1998).

Weary, Daniel C., "IRS Creation of Hybrid Methods: Prepayments and the Cash Method; Prepayments and the Accrual Method", 35 Inst On Feb Tax'n 59 (1977).

Weisbach, D.A., "Ten Truths about Tax Shelters", 55 Tax L Rev 201 (2002).

Yin, G.K., "Getting Serious About Corporate Tax Shelters: Taking A Lesson from History", 54 SMU L Rev 209 (2001).

Zolt, E.M., "The Uneasy Case for Uniform Taxation", 16 Va Tax Rev 39 (1996).

Israeli commentaries

"The Report of the Public Committee for Reform in Income Tax" ("Ben Bassat Committee") (Ronnen Ltd, Tel Aviv, Is, 2000).

Azbetzki, A., *Financial Accounting – Vol. 1* (Boursi Legal Publishers, Tel Aviv, Is, 2001).

Barak, A., *Interpretation in Law Vol. 3, Constitutional Interpretation* (Nevo Publishing, Tel Aviv, Is, 1994).

Barkai, Y., *Accounting and Monetary Reporting – Vol. 1* (Bar-Or Publishing House, Ramat Hsharon, Is, 2003).

Barkai, Y., *Accounting and Monetary Reporting – Vol. 2* (Bar-Or Publishing House, Ramat Hsharon, Is, 2003).

Edrey, Y. and Dotan, A., "Taxation of Rental in Advance in Income Tax", Legal Research D (1986), 79.

Edrey, Y., "A General Tax Base for Israel", 12 Mishpatim (1982) 431.

Gliksberg, D., *The Boundaries of Tax Planning* (Jerusalem: Hebrew University of Jerusalem, Is, 1990).

Granot, O., "Purposeful Interpretation in Tax Law: from Declaration of Principles into Practical Practice", Taxes (April 2004), A-79.

Gross, J., *The New Israeli Tax Law* (3rd edn, Tel Aviv University, Is, Tagidim Ltd, 2003).

Klimovski, A., "Accounting Rules and Legal Principles in Income Tax Laws", Tax Quarterly (December 1965), 424.

Lovenberg, H.S., "Accounting Principles and Income Tax Laws in Case law", 18 The Accountant 125 (1968).

Margaliot, Y., "Examination of the Recommendations of Ben Bassat Committee in the Light of Tax Policy", Taxes (June 2000), A-56.

Namdar, A., *Tax Law (the Substantial Law)* (Hoshen Le'Mishpat, Tel Aviv, Is, 1985).

Nov, A., "The Tax System and the Encouragement of Investments", Taxes (February 2005), A-1.

Raphael, A., *Income Tax – Vol. 1* (Shocken Publishing, Jerusalem and Tel Aviv, Is, 1994).

Raphael, A. and Mehulall, Y., *Income Tax Laws, Vol. 1* (5th edn, Shocken Publishing, Jerusalem and Tel Aviv, Is, 1995).

Raphael, A. and Ephrati, D., *Income Tax Laws, Vol. 1* (Shocken Publishing, Jerusalem and Tel Aviv, Is, 1984).

Raphael, A., "The Date of the Liability of Advance Payments", 21 The Accountant 25 (1971).

Rosenberg, A., "Advance Income – Why is the Tax Liability for Reporters on an Accrual basis", Taxes (September 1989), A-45.

Samet, Y., *Financial Accounting – Theory and Practice – Vol. 1* (Ahiyosef Publishers, Netanya, Is, 1990).

Shekel, M., "Reporting Methods: Accrual or Cash, Response to Circular 12/2003", 328 Yeda Le'Meida (January 2004), 23.

Shekel, M., "Classification of Deposits in the Amisragas case – Reliance on Foreign Caselaw that does not Even Exist", Taxes (April 2006), A-1.

Shenhav, A., "Tax Expenditures in the Israeli Tax system: Legal Aspects, Economic Aspects and Lines for Reform", Taxes (April 1998), A-1.

Shuv, S., *New Financial Accounting: IFRS – Vol. 1* (Globes Publishing House, Tel Aviv, Is, 2007).

Strauss, Y., "On Accounting Principles and the Income Tax Ordinance Rules", 18 The Accountant 135 (1968).

Vita, Y., "Transactions by Means of Coupons – Timing of Recognition of the Income", Taxes (May 1989), A-52.

Witkon, Y. and Neeman, Y., *Tax Laws* (4th edn, Shocken Publishing, Jerusalem and Tel Aviv, Is, 1969).

Witkon, Y., "Income Tax Cases and Accounting Principles", 15 The Accountant 5 (1965).

Zuckerman, A., "Anatomy of a Judgment: The Life and Death of Section 86 of the Ordinance", Taxes (October 2003), A-54.

Other commentaries

Clifford, M. Will, "Clock Synchronization and Isotropy of the One-way Speed of Light"," Physics Review D45 (1992) (http://en.wikipedia.org/wiki/ Theory of Relativity).

Draft United Nations Manual on Anti-Corruption Policy, "Global Program against Corruption".

Sterling, Robert R., *Conservatism: The Fundamental Principle of Valuation in Traditional Accounting* (Accounting Foundation, University of Sydney, Aus, Abacus, 2nd edn, 1967).

Index

	DATE DUE		
Aug 3/10			
Feb 9/17.			